Kids Who Murder

Kids Who Murder

Ten American Cases

ELLIE HAYES

Exposit
Jefferson, North Carolina

LIBRARY OF CONGRESS CATALOGUING-IN-PUBLICATION DATA

Names: Hayes, Ellie, 1998– author.
Title: Kids who murder : ten American cases / Ellie Hayes.
Description: Jefferson, North Carolina : Exposit, 2023 | Includes bibliographical references and index.
Identifiers: LCCN 2022058676 | ISBN 9781476681191 (paperback : acid free paper) ∞
ISBN 9781476644967 (ebook)
Subjects: LCSH: Juvenile homicide—United States—Case studies.
Classification: LCC HV9067.H6 H39 2023 | DDC 364.152/3083—dc23/eng/20221209
LC record available at https://lccn.loc.gov/2022058676

BRITISH LIBRARY CATALOGUING DATA ARE AVAILABLE

ISBN (print) 978-1-4766-8119-1
ISBN (ebook) 978-1-4766-4496-7

© 2023 Ellie Hayes. All rights reserved

No part of this book may be reproduced or transmitted in any form or by any means, electronic or mechanical, including photocopying or recording, or by any information storage and retrieval system, without permission in writing from the publisher.

Front cover image: DGIM studio/Zurijeta/Shutterstock

Printed in the United States of America

Exposit is an imprint of McFarland & Company, Inc., Publishers

Exposit
Box 611, Jefferson, North Carolina 28640
www.expositbooks.com

Contents

Introduction	1
Eric Smith (1993)	5
Holly Harvey and Sandy Ketchum (2004)	40
Derek and Alex King (2001)	56
Josh Phillips (1998)	85
Alyssa Bustamante (2009)	108
Cody Posey (2004)	144
Jasmiyah and Tasmiyah Whitehead (2010)	166
Daniel Petric (2007)	183
Cristian Fernandez (2011)	204
Melinda Loveless, Laurie Tackett, Hope Rippey and Toni Lawrence (1992)	228
Chapter Notes	273
Bibliography	287
Index	297

Introduction

Children. They are the embodiment of purity and innocence. That's why every time we turn on the news and hear about a child committing a horrific act of violence it never fails to provoke a public outcry. Children are thought to be naive about the world around them, incapable of doing wrong, so they are the last demographic that we expect to hear about being involved in atrocious crimes. Yet it happens. Despite the number of juveniles (individuals under the age of 18) who kill being extremely small, juvenile homicide has been a hot-button issue for the past five decades. Studies show that the rate of juvenile arrests for murder has been fluctuating over the last couple of decades. The U.S. has seen two drastic upswings in juvenile murders. The first one happened between 1960 and 1975,[1] and the second wave, of what experts called "superpredators,"[2] came between 1984 and 1993.[3]

According to the Office of Juvenile Justice and Delinquency Prevention, the murder arrest rate reached its peak in 1994. However, between 2003 and 2006, the estimated number of juvenile murder offenders jumped by 32 percent and has been on the decline ever since. As of 2017, the approximate number of juvenile arrests for murder and nonnegligent manslaughter was only 910, which is 27 percent lower than the juvenile murder arrest tally in 2008. Overall, members of law enforcement made an estimated 807,700 juvenile-related arrests in 2017, which fell by 59 percent since 2008.[4] The past three decades have borne witness to the many legal challenges that juvenile offenders, particularly homicide offenders, coming in and out of the court system face. Americans were at a loss for what to do when youth crime and violence swept the nation. The situation was out of control. U.S. legislation made it easier for juveniles to be tried as adults, which meant that they would be subjected to harsher punishments, including the death penalty and mandatory life in prison without parole.[5] Both have since been abolished for juveniles as there has been a recent push for leniency for juveniles in the legal system. But our treatment of juvenile homicide perpetrators—and the question of what to do with them—remains a controversial topic in the U.S.

This only begs the question: what propels a child, or adolescent, to commit murder? First, we must attempt to tackle one of the most blood-curdling controversies of all: are killers born or made?

In one 2008 survey that studied the lifetime and past-year exposure to violence for children age 17 and younger, the U.S. Department of Justice revealed some shocking statistics: more than 60 percent of children living in the U.S. reported that they had been exposed to violence in their daily lives either directly or indirectly. This exposure could include witnessing an act of violence or learning that a violent act had been committed against a family member, neighbor or friend. Even threats against their school and online harassment count as exposures to violence. In just the past year alone, 46.3 percent of minors had admitted to being assaulted at least once, and one in 10 had been injured from an assault. One in 10 admitted they had suffered from child maltreatment (ranging from emotional and physical abuse to neglect and family abduction), and one in 16 had fallen victim to sexual assault. Furthermore, 24.6 percent of children reported being victims of theft, robbery, and vandalism.[6]

That is a startlingly large proportion, but to what degree does exposure to violence impact the mental state of juveniles?

Thankfully, most kids who are exposed to cruel behavior at school or home are not motivated to kill. So what pushes a child to the edge? It's a matter that still confounds psychologists, and although there is no clear-cut answer, attempts at explanations can be offered. Typically, juveniles who commit murder tend to emerge from poor socio-economic backgrounds and have toxic home lives. The early years of one's life are crucial, because that is when one learns and develops the most vital human emotions: love, empathy, and compassion. Subjecting a child to neglect and abuse can inhibit their ability to develop these emotions, thus causing them to act out defiantly and have difficulty forming healthy and intimate relationships with others. Instead of love, they may be consumed with feelings of hatred and anger at the world. Without receiving the affection and care they need, they eventually begin reacting to their environment, and sometimes lives are taken. The motive may vary, from jealousy, to revenge, to asserting control and dominance.

As children grow, their brains are extremely vulnerable to stressful situations, such as abuse and neglect. This type of stress has been shown to permanently alter the brain and produce some negative outcomes later in life, including an increased risk of developing mental illness.[7] The teenage years are an especially sensitive time, as the adolescent brain experiences the most change it ever will for the rest of one's life, which may explain why mental disorders begin to emerge during adolescence.[8]

Research has shown that adults' and adolescents' brains function differently. Adults tend to think with their prefrontal cortex, which is the area of the brain that is responsible for managing complex processes, such as planning, decision-making, logic and reasoning. The prefrontal cortex also helps adults pause to consider the long-term consequences of their actions. Adolescents process information with the amygdala—the emotional part of the brain that is responsible for immediate reactions like fear and aggression. The amygdala develops first, while the prefrontal cortex isn't finished developing until around the age of 25 or so.[9] This is why teenagers are less likely to think before they act and more likely to react impulsively, engage in risky and dangerous behavior, and misread or misinterpret social cues as well as emotions.[10] Unlike adults, teenagers are guided by their emotions, not logic. The prefrontal cortex can also be stunted by childhood trauma.[11]

Scientists have studied the brains of those who have committed murder, compared their findings to "normal"' brains, and found astonishing differences. For example, compared to non-homicidal youth, adolescent homicide offenders have reduced total grey matter volumes as well as reduced white matter volumes specifically concentrated in the temporal lobes. The temporal poles are strongly implicated in social emotional processing, including detecting deception and moral decision-making.[12] Not surprisingly, this area of the brain is also at risk of being damaged from child maltreatment.[13]

Surely, brain abnormalities can play a role in youth violence, and the genes we inherit from our parents can be the root cause of such abnormalities. But there is no distinct gene that predisposes one to violence alone. The ongoing nature versus nurture debate involves whether human behavior is determined by one's environment or genes. Scientists would agree that it is not simply one or the other; rather, we are all a product of both nature and nurture. Genes serve as a blueprint for who we may become, but that can be significantly influenced by environmental factors.[14]

Peering into the mind of a killer can certainly give us insight as to what makes them tick. Who, or what, do we blame? Parents? Schools? Bullies? Video games? Violent movies? An unfortunate case of bad genetic makeup? Whatever the case may be, one thing is certain: we have learned that the kind of environment in which children grow up certainly shapes who they become and that trauma can affect the anatomy of the brain tremendously. According to a publication of the Office of Juvenile Justice and Delinquency Prevention, which takes a deep look into family life and juvenile delinquency, "Children who are rejected by their parents, grow up in homes with considerable conflict, and are inadequately supervised are at greatest risk of becoming delinquents."[15] In this book we will take a look at ten murder cases in modern American criminal history and pick at the brains of the children who perpetrated them. Hopefully, by the end of this book, we may unveil as close to an answer as we may ever achieve to the question: why do kids murder?

Eric Smith
(1993)

Savona. It is a small community located some 70 miles southeast of Rochester, New York, shadowed by thick-wooded hills. This pastoral village, formerly known as "Mud Creek" and named after the seaport and commune in Italy, held only 970 residents in 1993. Nestled in the lush hills of this rural community were only a hardware store, a couple of motels, a single grocery store called King's Market, and, of course, the most popular gathering spot for locals—the Savona Diner. From an onlooker's perspective, the lack of excitement and attractions was enough to not draw many tourists. But the village possessed a secret charm only experienced by those living in it. Inhabitants had no apprehensions about leaving their doors unlocked and allowing their children to roam the streets free of parental supervision. Everyone knew and trusted one another, and most importantly, it was safe! Locals had heard all kinds of horror stories about the violent crimes that occurred in nearby big cities, but things like that just didn't happen here. Savona residents wouldn't trade the security they felt in their "boring" small town for the recognition and appeal that the hustle and bustle of big New York cities had to offer.

But the squeaky-clean reputation that this close-knit community prided itself on would take a serious blow one overcast August morning in 1993, when a tragedy struck Savona without any forewarning. It caused an uproar of panic to sweep through the rural area, threatening its welfare and tranquility. Citizens were now locking their doors and keeping their children off the streets. Over and over they asked themselves, "How could this happen?" This was the kind of misfortune one would hear from, say, Rochester, Buffalo, or Niagara Falls ... but not Savona.

And when the shockingly young ages of the individuals involved were revealed to the public, it quickly ignited a fiery outrage that garnered national media attention and spread internationally. Obscured in the eastern part of the Town of Bath, Savona, once a safe and quiet village that most people probably hadn't heard of, was now receiving unwanted media attention from all over the world.

"It was a totally random event," remarked Lt. Mark Fischer, a criminal investigator for the New York State Police. "It could have been any child. You can't help but think what that poor little guy was thinking of during his last few moments on earth."[1]

Growing up in this picturesque village was Derrick Joseph Robie, an endearing child with a mop of blond hair, pinchable cheeks, and a radiant grin that made it nearly impossible for adults not to dote on him. Only four years old, Derrick had an insatiable curiosity about the world. A notably friendly child, he habitually sat on the corner of his street with his bicycle and waved hello at passing cars.[2] He knew how to make peanut butter cookies and meatloaf all on his own, and he had a penchant for t-ball and fishing. He helped unscrew lug nuts from the car wheel and stocked hickory nuts in his coat pocket. Every night he read his baby brother the famous Dr. Seuss book *Green Eggs and Ham* before bed. During the first sliver of sunlight in the aftermath of a rainy day, young Derrick would dig for worms in the backyard and line them up on the porch, each representing every member of his family: mom and dad, baby brother, and, of course, himself. He would then give each one a kiss.[3]

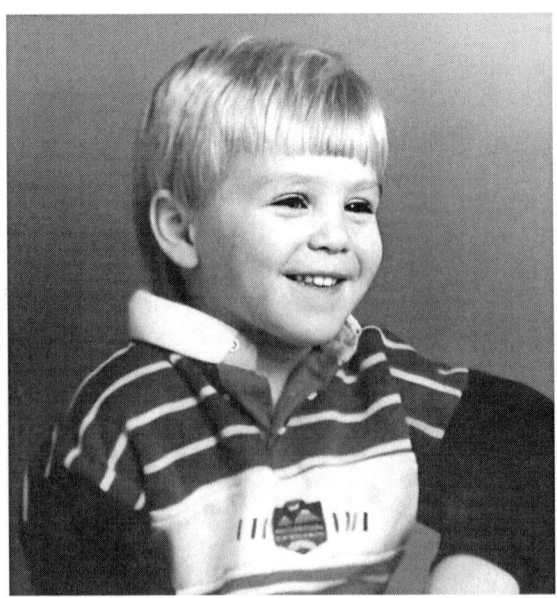

Derrick Robie, four, was found brutally murdered in a wooded area by the village park (courtesy Doreen Robie).

"As much of a boy as he was," his father, Dale Robie, would later recall, "he was very gentle with things."[4]

The summer of 1993 was an eventful

one for Derrick. Even though he was already a pretty active youngster, his parents decided to ensure that their little boy was kept especially busy during those sultry months by enrolling him in a recreation program held in a local village park at the end of McCoy Street, a road lined with maple trees and 15 houses. The Robies resided on this seemingly idyllic road. At the corner of the street sat a town hall; just across from it stood a church, which was attached to the Robies' stone home. All the way down the dead-end street was an elementary school, which was just on the other side of the recreational park. It was perfect for Derrick, as it was only a block away from the Robie home and he could walk himself there.

Rainfall was threatening to strike Savona on the morning of August 2, 1993. The sky was a slate gray, the weather was murky, and the leaves hung languidly from the trees. In spite of the particularly leaden day outside, Derrick was fully dressed and eager to leave for yet another exciting day of checkers and kickball at the park. His mother was busy and she wasn't quite ready to leave the house yet; she was tending to his younger brother, Dalton, who was being especially fussy that morning. Derrick grew increasingly more impatient and implored his mother to allow him to walk alone.

"It's okay, Mom, I'll go by myself!" he had assured her.[5]

Initially, Doreen felt some apprehension about this. Usually, she would walk her son out to the end of the driveway and watch his every step to the park. But after giving it some more thought, her worries eased. Every day there was always a throng of youths flocking to the park at the end of the road. There would be no streets for him to cross. What could possibly go wrong?

As soon as she gave in, Doreen gave her son a peck on the lips. "I love you," she told him.

Derrick reiterated the sentiment, and, in the blink of an eye, he bolted out the door and was ebulliently hopping down the sidewalk of his home with his canvas lunch bag thumping against his side. Just a few minutes into Derrick's embarking on this one-block journey to the park, the recreation counselor, Bill Horn, was driving down McCoy Street when he spotted the lone boy walking along and waved to him. He would be one of the last people to have ever seen the bright and radiant boy alive.

Five minutes later, storm clouds broke and Doreen felt a sudden spark of worry flare within her. Perhaps it was just paranoia, or maybe her motherly instinct was telling her that something terrible had happened. Little did she know, at that moment, her life would be changed forever.

A Missing Boy

Forty-five minutes after Derrick's departure, a thunderstorm burst over Savona, rendering the recreation program canceled. Doreen went to the park to pick up her son at 11:00 a.m., only to learn something that would trigger an alarm in any parent's head: Derrick wasn't at the park. In fact, he had never shown up at all. The panicking mother promptly notified police and an investigation into the preschooler's whereabouts was launched right away.

In less than an hour, Savona locals were pouring onto the streets in search of the preschooler. Kids on bicycles were combing through the neighborhoods. Firefighters were stomping up and down the streets, shouting Derrick's name through a bullhorn. Residents were going door to door asking if anyone had seen the missing child. By 3 p.m., state troopers were zealously scoping out the area in their cruisers and flying over the georgic village in helicopters. The Robies clung to the hope that, somehow, Derrick would be found alive and well.

But that fiery determination and hope would be extinguished four hours into the relentless search when a couple made a heartbreaking discovery. In a small patch of woods, a local hangout that kids called "The Fort," about midway between the Robie home and the park where he was headed, was the mutilated body of Derrick Robie.[6]

His body, which had been fully undressed, had ostensibly been posed. Derrick's left running shoe had been placed beside his right hand, while his right running shoe was found resting by his left hand. There was a gaping wound in the boy's tiny head, and two rocks sat nearby with notable traces of blood. Whoever the cruel killer was had also callously rummaged through the boy's lunch bag, squashed his banana, and poured red Kool-Aid into Derrick's head wound. From the looks of it, the child's death wasn't one that was quick and painless; whoever had killed him had made a point of desecrating him.

Later, the autopsy report would reveal severe head injuries including skull fractures, tearing and bleeding of tissues in the chest, a perforation of the intestinal wall, and petechial hemorrhages (tiny pinpoint marks indicative of asphyxia) on the neck, face, and eyes. Derrick's cause of death was determined to be blunt force trauma to the head combined with asphyxia.[7]

Hunt for the Killer

With the discovery of Derrick's body, law enforcement now had a new mission: to find the monster who committed this heinous murder. A vast majority of the small town's residents suspected it was all done by an outsider, possibly an adult pedophile.[8] Parents were now so paranoid that they made their kids wear whistles around their necks when they went to play outside in case a stranger tried to approach them. After all, what kind of sick person would lure a young child into a wooded area and batter him to death? Even the police were convinced that an adult male was the culprit and began reviewing parolees within the area. Over the course of the next week, investigators interviewed a startling total of 500 witnesses, including the 68 kids signed up for the program. Many were interviewed more than once. But it seemed like police were chasing a ghost in the woods. Nobody had seen the little boy before his final moments left on earth; at least, nobody who did was coming forward.

One of the witnesses they interviewed was just a child himself. On the morning of August 5, four days into the exhaustive investigation, a 13-year-old boy with coppery hair, a mask of freckles, and aviator glasses walked into the police command post. He introduced himself as Eric Smith and thought he could be of aid in solving the crime. First, he spoke with Trooper Alan Morse and asked him some questions regarding the status of the investigation. After their brief exchange, Trooper Morse stepped out and met with Investigator John Hibsch, telling him that the kid was asking "some real strange questions," and asked if he could go talk to him. John, who was just finishing up with a task, agreed to do so. Entering the library, he spotted the adolescent boy seated on a bench. John approached him, formally introduced himself, and asked Eric how he could be of help.

That's when Eric began firing off his questions. He was curious to know about the progress of the investigation and if they knew who killed the little boy yet. Investigator John Hibsch responded with mostly vague answers, knowing he couldn't disclose much information to the public as the investigation was still ongoing. As the two spoke, Eric's demeanor kept shifting between focused and nervous. At some point during their conversation, Eric suddenly reached over to the shelf on his left and pulled out a book titled *The Blooding*, written by author Joseph Wambaugh, based on the true story of the discovery of DNA identification through the police's relentless hunt for a serial killer who disturbed a quiet English village.

"Do you know anything about DNA?" Eric inquired.

"Yes," Officer John responded, and asked Eric what he knew about DNA. Eric told him that he had read the book and enjoyed it. Then he wanted to know if they had collected any DNA from the crime scene.

"We have a lot," he answered. "The results will be back within a couple of days."[9]

The investigator proceeded to interrogate Eric about his whereabouts several hours before and after the homicide. Eric revealed that he attended the same recreation program as the four-year-old and had been in and out of the park quite a few times that morning but failed to see him. Hibsch had no reason to suspect he was lying; after all, he was just a kid himself and was a long way from matching the criminal profile of an adult predator that the police were already seeking.

As a matter of routine, Investigator John Hibsch began questioning individuals that Eric said he was with on the day of Derrick's death. But only some of his actions could be verified by witnesses; most of Eric's story didn't quite line up. So on the afternoon of that same day, at around 5:00 p.m., Investigator Hibsch, along with Trooper Alan Morse and Officer John Mitchel, paid Eric a visit at his home. After Hibsch went to the front door and knocked, he was greeted by Eric's adoptive father, Ted Smith, and later by his mother, Tammy Smith. The investigator asked for permission to speak with Eric again. He explained that he just wanted to clear up some minor discrepancies between his account and those of other witnesses they interviewed.

After his parents granted their permission, the officers left the front porch with Eric and plopped themselves down on the picnic table on the front lawn, which stretched twenty feet away from the house. Investigator Hibsch wanted to clarify some things about Eric's travels on the morning of August 3. Eric revealed that he was riding his bike around town and had been in and out of the village park where the recreation program took place. After he got into some trouble, a recreation counselor told him to leave.

So he did just that, Eric told him. He left the park and began pedaling down McCoy Street. Only this time, in a strange turn of events,

Eric's story suddenly changed. "This is when I saw the boy," he told John Hibsch.[10]

The three policemen sitting around Eric couldn't believe their ears when they heard him suddenly reveal that he had, in fact, spotted the lone Derrick walking to the village park that morning, when before Eric denied ever seeing him. Investigator Hibsch queried where specifically Eric had spotted him. He happily answered his question, stating it was near the bottom of the hill, across the street, where logs were being cut up. Eric was pedaling on the east side of the road, while Derrick was strolling on the opposite side.

Investigator Hibsch was speechless. Before that, he had no reason to suspect this kid wasn't telling everything he knew. But now, they were getting somewhere. Now, they were taking a very keen interest in Eric.

"This revelation was highly important, as up to this point in our couple hundred interviews, no one had seen Derrick this far up the road," he later said.[11]

Could this young teenager have witnessed something traumatic? Might there have been some sort of obstruction in his recollection from that morning, or did someone threaten him to keep quiet?

Officer Hibsch began to probe further. At times, Eric was talkative, cooperative, and upbeat, seemingly relishing the attention. Other times, he was withdrawn and upset. Hibsch asked the teen what the little boy had been wearing. Eric was able to perfectly describe the outfit Derrick was garbed in that day, also including the fact that Derrick was carrying a lunch bag in his right hand. When Hibsch asked him if he could also describe the lunch bag, Eric said it was "cool." He told him that it was made out of a pair of jeans and had a cloud imprint on it, like the kind you would see on a cereal box, he said. This, in particular, piqued investigators' interest, because not only was Eric revealing new information police hadn't heard before, but also because Eric was able to see all that detail when they were on opposite sides of the road from each other.

Eric, too, must have noticed the increased interest the officers were taking in him because, out of nowhere, without even hinting at an accusation that he was responsible for Derrick's murder, Eric uttered in a raised, indignant voice, "You think I killed him, don't you?" He then began to cry.

And just like that, Eric put himself right at the top of the suspect list.

The investigator tried his best to calm Eric down, assuring him that he wasn't accusing him of anything, only that he had just revealed numerous facts that the officers didn't know before. Hibsch then thought it was best to divert from the topic for a bit and asked Eric if they could take a look at his bike. Eric was more than happy to oblige and got up to retrieve it. Once he was no longer within earshot, Hibsch turned to the other two officers and asked if they had any thoughts. Both of them agreed that he should continue to push harder for more information.

Upon Eric's return, Hibsch inspected his red BMX bicycle and thanked him. Afterward, they resumed the interrogation, slowly easing back into questions about Eric's exact whereabouts when he saw Derrick. When Eric burst into tears once again, Hibsch decided to change the subject and take a different route. He asked Eric if he was wearing his eyeglasses, which he had broken several weeks before and were held together by tape now, when he saw Derrick walking. Eric said he was not. The investigator proceeded to instruct Eric to remove his glasses and try to read the large house numbers across the street. But he couldn't. Hibsch even had to point them out for Eric, but the teen was still unable to locate them. Then he asked Eric to read aloud his vehicle's license plate numbers, which were less than 15 feet away. His poor vision still betrayed him.

That's when police became even more dubious about Eric's statement. How, Hibsch questioned, could Eric have observed such accurate and close details about Derrick from across the street, from his outfit right down to his lunch bag, if he couldn't even read the numbers off of his license plate?

The more he pressed Eric on the matter, the more distressed the youth became. He could feel the pressure building up and surrounding him as the walls started to close in on him now. Lowering his head, Eric clenched his fists and asked once again, his voice cracking, "You think I killed him, don't you?" Tears streamed down his face as he angrily slapped the picnic table over and over again.[12]

Once more, Hibsch tried to soothe Eric back into a composed state. During this, Ted Smith stepped out of the house to see what was going on. Hibsch spoke to him in private, informing him that his adoptive son just revealed some crucial information that was unknown to the investigation, and he believed there was more that Eric wasn't telling for some inexplicable reason. They decided to take a brief break from the interrogation, and Investigator Hibsch asked Ted if he could get Eric something to drink. Ted agreed, left, and returned shortly after with a very large glass of red Kool-Aid.

Ted asked Eric if he was okay as he placed the glass on the picnic table in front of him. The boy responded yes.

As Ted headed back into the family home, Eric watched him closely, simultaneously seemingly fixated on the red Kool-Aid sitting in front of him. In less than a moment, he picked up the Kool-Aid and threw it on the ground. He started crying that he hated the drink.

Numerous vital and disturbing details about the crime scene were never disseminated to the public during the voracious hunt for the killer, including the fact that the victim had red Kool-Aid doused all over his deceased little body.

"At that exact point," John Hibsch said, "I became convinced Eric was responsible for the killing of Derrick Robie."[13]

Officer Hibsch tried even harder to extract more details from Eric, but to no avail. Now that the boy was aware police were on to him, he remained tight-lipped. He must have realized he'd probably said too much, and any more information he gave would be used against him. Officer Hibsch pushed for Eric to admit if he had seen anything else, but Eric was still emotional and defensive. "I'm not the type of person that would kill, hurt, or sexually molest anyone," he told the officers in a hoarse voice.[14]

Feeling aggravated with the interrogation between him and Eric going around in endless circles, Hibsch got up from the table with the others, leaving the boy behind as he went to speak to the family. He expressed to them that he would like a more statesman-like investigator to continue with the interview, someone with a little more experience in the field. He was met with strong objections, and Eric's great-grandfather, a retired sheriff's deputy, demanded that the officers shut down the interview and leave.

Approximately an hour later, several state police investigators returned to the Smith home and had a pleasant conversation with Eric's great-grandfather. To dispel his worries, they assured him that they weren't accusing Eric of being involved; they were simply trying to gain more information from him, since he, as far as they knew, was the last person to have spotted the youngster before his tragic murder. Eventually, his family relented when investigators suggested that Eric accompany them to McCoy Street the following day, where they would do a re-enactment of Eric's trip on his bicycle and his observations of Derrick on that fateful day.

The next morning, on August 9, Eric and his great-grandfather accompanied police to McCoy Street to do the re-enactment, which was videotaped. The now-calm Eric, with his bicycle, was told to show investigators where he was when he supposedly saw Derrick. On the opposite side of the street, an officer portrayed the little slain boy while carrying an unknown object in his hand that was meant to represent the canvas lunch bag Derrick was holding. To nobody's surprise, Eric was unable to identify what the object was and also failed to describe others' movements. It quickly became evident that there was no way Eric could have discerned such meticulous details about Derrick's clothing and lunch bag from that distance. The officers began to feel skeptical about Eric's declarations.

Eric was brought to the command post and, in the presence of his great-grandfather, was grilled for an onerous two hours about the morning of Derrick Robie's murder. Eric would dodge any questions concerning whether he had really seen the little kid or not. The inquiry was seemingly going around in endless circles once again. The more police struggled to get answers from the 13-year-old, the more he closed up, and by the end of the interview, police were still uncertain as to whether he had really seen Derrick. People make false confessions all the time, and maybe this kid was just seeking attention. Investigators began to fear that they were wasting their time chasing a false lead and sent him home for the day.

∼

More than 700 people arrived at Derrick's wake to pay their respects. One by one, they walked by the open white casket and murmured a quick prayer for the little boy within, dressed in his baseball uniform with a catcher's mitt tucked snugly beside him. A teddy bear rested on a nearby table. On August 6, in the pouring rain, Derrick was buried.

"The real question is, where was God?" said Pastor Strong, going on to say that the answer was "God was with Derrick," that "his heart broke and then a part of him died when Derrick died."[15]

Two days after the burial, and one day after the re-enactment of the scene, family members sat Eric down and implored him to spill everything he knew about the little boy's tragic murder. They felt he knew something and was hiding it.

Finally, Eric made a shocking confession: he was the one responsible for brutally murdering Derrick Robie.

Eric's Confession

On the same day of his confession, his great-grandfather arranged a meeting with district attorney John C. Tunney at the Steuben County Office Building in Bath and told him about the redheaded teen's admission of guilt. He pleaded that they solve the matter "as peaceful and quiet as we can," meaning he didn't want the state police to get involved and Eric to be apprehended and go before a jury. Tunney convinced him that the police would have to take the boy's statement and called Captain Walt DeLap from the New York State Police to come to his office immediately. Meanwhile, Eric's great-grandfather phoned his family and told them to come to the district attorney's office right away and to bring Eric with them.

It took at least two hours for the Smith family to arrive. They were met by District Attorney Tunney and Captain Walt DeLap, who would be conducting the interview. It was decided that only Eric's adoptive father and great-grandfather would be present while Eric spoke to Captain DeLap in the district attorney's office.

Captain DeLap sat directly across from Eric and peered into his eyes as he carefully explained his Miranda rights to him, breaking things down in simpler terms to ensure that Eric didn't misunderstand or misinterpret anything.

"You have the right to remain silent," the captain explained to Eric. "That means you don't have to talk to me." He looked up at Eric, his adoptive father, and great-grandfather, and he clarified with them that they understood the first warning. Each of them nodded their heads.

"Furthermore, that is only the first part of that," he continued. "If you give up the right to remain silent, anything you say, good or bad, can be used in a court of law or used anywhere against you. If it goes against you, so be it." The trio indicated once again that they comprehended the warning.

Capt. DeLap read off his final right to a lawyer and further elaborated, "That means you have a right to a lawyer right now. We can stop right now and you can go buy a lawyer, have yourself a lawyer. If you can't afford one, or your mom or dad can't afford one because they don't work or are out of work, whatever the case may be, one will be appointed to represent you before any questions."

The adolescent could only think of one question. "What's an attorney?"

"An attorney is a lawyer," the captain replied. Hie eyes darted between Eric and his family, asking one last time if they understood the rights he just read before them. They all nodded in response to his query and agreed that Eric would waive his Miranda rights and talk to Captain DeLap.[16]

Over the course of the next three hours, Eric took them all through the gut-wrenching details of how he had lured little Derrick away from the sidewalk and ultimately to his death. After getting kicked out of the recreation program for the day, Eric was riding his bicycle on McCoy Street, just killing time, until he spotted the lone little boy heading toward the direction of the village park. Eric called out, "Hey, kid," prompting Derrick to turn around. Eric coldly stated that it was at this point that he knew he wanted to take the preschooler somewhere secluded and kill him.

Eric quickly came up with a ruse that he thought might tempt him off the sidewalk. He said he knew of a shortcut to the recreation program, but Derrick wasn't easily swayed by this ploy. As friendly as he was, he was also obstinate.

"No, I'm not supposed to go off the sidewalk. My mommy told me that," Derrick had said.[17]

"It's okay, I'm right here," Eric assured him over and over. It had taken the teen four or five tries to successfully coax the preschooler into following him. He then got off his BMX bicycle and led Derrick through a bush-lined wooded area behind a vacant lot, just adjacent to the park. They were away from the road, out of the view of anyone who could witness Eric's sinister plan to inflict cruelty unfold. As the boys reached an overgrown hedgerow, Eric quietly set down his bicycle and allowed the young boy to walk ahead of him. He came up behind him, and in less than a second, his right arm looped over and seized Derrick's little neck in a chokehold.

It quickly dawned on Derrick what was happening to him. He let go of his lunch bag, letting it drop to the ground, and began flailing his arms and legs in an attempt to escape Eric's firm grasp. But the four-year-old didn't stand a chance against the older boy's much bigger and stronger stature. As Eric began to release his hold to readjust his grip on Derrick's neck so he would be strangling him with his hands, Derrick started to puff and pant, struggling for a breath of air. Eric quickly reaffirmed his tight hold around Derrick's neck, this time exerting more strength.

In approximately 30 seconds, Eric alleged, the youngster quieted down and not a peep left his mouth. Eric then "figured he was dead" and laid his body down on the ground. But Eric thought wrong. Soon, Derrick began gasping for air again. He was still alive, clinging to the frail thread of life. In a panic, Eric quickly grabbed Derrick's lunch bag and emptied it of its contents. In an attempt to silence the young boy, he stuffed a paper napkin into his tiny mouth. But when he also tried to pack his sandwich bag in there, he was met with aggression: Derrick chomped down on his assailant's finger. Eric immediately retracted his hand. Derrick may have been on the ground, overpowered, but he wasn't going down without a fight.

Eric scanned his surroundings, searching for anything within arm's reach he could use to kill the little kid. He picked up a small stone, knelt over Derrick, and battered him three times over the head with it. He tossed the stone aside and hoisted a 26-pound rock in the air and brought it down, smashing Derrick's head three times. He lifted another large rock and this time hurled it twice into his chest and once into his midsection. Afterward, he took the boy's Kool-Aid and poured it all over his face and head wounds. Then he flipped over his body, tugged his pants down, and sodomized him with a stick. (It is believed that at this point Derrick was already dead.)

The freckled teen rolled Derrick's presumably lifeless body onto his back once again, then began dragging him some several feet to a rock pile. He then mounted his bike and left the scene, only to return five minutes later to ensure Derrick was dead.

"I was worried if he wasn't there, he might say something," Eric told Captain DeLap. "However, I figured if he's dead, and I believed he was, I won't have to worry about anything."[18]

When Eric ascertained that the child's body was right where he'd left it, and that he hadn't miraculously survived the unbelievably vile acts and gone running to tell an adult, he departed once again.

Once Captain DeLap finished typing out Eric's oral confession, he had him do a re-enactment of the murder. Eric, who was previously described as having a very "flat" and "matter-of-fact" demeanor as he gave his own account of what happened on August 3, had now become animated as he demonstrated the killing through actions. After a slight change was made to the statement per Eric's suggestion, everyone in the room signed the statement.

Eric was subsequently escorted to court in the Town of Bath where he was indicted for a single count of murder in the second degree, under a law that was passed by the legislature allowing juveniles as young as 13 to be tried as adults. Then, he was admitted to the Monroe County Children's Center in Rochester.

The Life of Eric Smith

Eric M. Smith came into this world on January 22, 1980, in Savona, New York. The middle child of three, he primarily grew up with his mother, Tammy Smith, and adoptive father, Theodore "Ted" Smith—whom he believed to be his biological father for most of his childhood. He had an older sister named Stacy and a younger sister by one year, Holly.

In many respects, Eric was just like any other typical American boy. He played with G.I. Joes and Matchbox cars, and he liked to doodle in his free time. He especially enjoyed watching TV, listened to Garth Brooks tapes, had a penchant for ghoulish Stephen King novels and participated as a drummer in the school band. A boy with an upbeat temperament, he found joy in cracking jokes and making people around him laugh—even if it was at his own expense. He enjoyed doing favors for his neighbors, such as taking out their garbage and shoveling their driveways. Throughout the majority of his childhood, Eric spent a lot of time with his grandparents, Red and Edie Wilson, to whom he was very attached.

"He'd always come in and give us hugs and kisses," his grandfather later said. "He liked being a clown."[19]

Eric was especially close to his younger sister. The kids lived in a strict household and were seldom allowed to visit other kids' homes or even ride their bikes together around the block. Tammy was a big worrier, especially when it came to her children playing near water after having lost two of her siblings in drowning incidents during her childhood. However, this didn't preclude Holly and Eric from finding other creative ways to have fun, just as many children with big imaginations do. One activity they particularly liked was the popular "pretend-play" game. Memories of building forts out of old bedsheets and taking on the roles of "cops and robbers," "school," and "doctor and patient" loomed large in Holly's mind.

"He was a great listener," Holly recalled of her older brother, adding that he "held in many things."[20] At ages 12 and 13, the siblings were finally permitted to ride their bikes across the bridge that took them to the other side of town, where they attended the summer recreation program.

As much of a loving older brother and grandson as he was, Eric was beset with many issues from an early age which persisted throughout his childhood and adolescent years. Since he was a toddler, the young boy was prone to temper tantrums which occasionally resulted in him banging his head on the floor. He also suffered from developmental delays such as walking, speaking, and learning as well as physical deformities. The cause of this was later revealed to be Tammy Smith's usage of a prescription drug used to control epilepsy while she was pregnant with her son.

Eric had very little luck when it came to making friends his own age. Starting around the second grade, he found himself falling victim to the vicious world of schoolyard bullying. His red hair, big-framed glasses, and malformed ears made him an easy target for other kids, who found his physical appearance rather peculiar. He was subjected to frequent name-calling—"freak" and "weirdo" seemed to be popular ones used by his peers. It didn't help Eric that he was struggling academically as well. The bullying only became worse when he had to repeat the fourth grade after failing it, placing him in the same grade as Holly, who was one year younger. The other kids began picking on him for being "stupid" and "dumb."

His jokester personality didn't do much to earn their respect, either—instead, he was told he should paint his face like a clown because he already looked and behaved like one. Perhaps the worst part of Eric's day was when he was on the school bus. His peers would "accidentally" bump into him or trip him as he was boarding the bus. Others would flick his ears. For the most part, Eric tried to be a good sport and simply laugh it off. Sometimes, as a defense mechanism, the boy tried to beat his bullies to their own punch by making jokes at his own expense. It was the only way he could feel like he was being laughed *with* as opposed to being laughed *at* for a change. But there were many times when Eric found it difficult to merely laugh off the bullying. The constant gibes and name-calling would still get to him, although he would never let his tormentors see just how badly it was affecting his self-esteem. More often than not, Eric would come home from the school bus in tears. Other times, he would be angry. As soon as he'd get home, he would get his frustration out the only way he knew—hitting, slamming, or screaming in his room, especially into his pillow. Sometimes, he would seek out petty revenge by shoving apples and bananas into the car exhaust pipes of people who were mean to him.

Although there wasn't much his mother could do to stop the

bullying Eric was enduring at school, she never failed to lend a sympathetic ear to her son. She tried her best to calm him down and urged him to ignore what the other kids were saying.

"Do your best not to let it get to you," she would reiterate.[21]

Ted initially offered Eric sympathy and advice on how to deal with school bullies, essentially advocating that he "toughen up" and encouraging him to not let his bullies win. Eventually, however, he got fed up after many times of Eric coming home from school either crying or venting about the harassment he had to deal with every day. He started demanding that Eric "stop being a damn whiner" and told him to "suck it up" and "grow a backbone."

"For quite a few years I had a little hot temper myself," Ted would later testify in court. He admitted to saying and doing harsh things to his kids, which included telling them he was "sick and tired of their crap" and "kicking their butt up over their shoulders."[22]

"I'm gonna kick your ass over the moon," he would sometimes yell at his kids. "You won't be able to sit down!"[23]

A robust man towering just over six feet, Ted exuded intimidation to all who knew him and wasn't generally well-liked in the community. Although he did at times resort to corporal punishment, such as spanking by hand or belt, his stentorian voice was enough to keep the kids' behavior under control. His goal as a father was to teach them as many life skills as possible and toughen them up for the real world. He took them fishing and showed them how to properly use a fishing rod and bait a hook. Once they had mastered those techniques, they frequented rivers and streams and caught many crayfish. Having been a cook at a few different restaurants, he used his passion for cooking to teach them various skills in the kitchen. He also taught them the basic mechanics of vehicles whenever he happened to be working on one.

On a surface level, Ted and Eric seemed to have a normal father-son relationship. They had their moments when they butted heads, especially when it came to meeting Eric's emotional needs. Ted Smith thought his tough love approach was doing his kids a favor in preparing them for the real world, although he was especially hard on Eric growing up because he was a boy. Ted was raised to believe that being callous and macho were essential qualities that made one a "real man." Wearing your heart on your sleeve, in his eyes, was a sign of weakness.

But for a sensitive child like Eric, who cried easily and was already going through hell at school, being subjected to his father's verbal abuse and having his feelings constantly trivialized was doing the opposite for his tremendously low self-confidence. Savona villagers who were familiar with the Smiths characterized Ted as a domineering and aggressive man who was ashamed of his adoptive son, whom he perceived as both an academic and athletic failure. A couple of residents claimed to have personally witnessed the six-footer aggressively kicking Eric, who just barely stood over five feet tall, on one occasion.[24]

Of all of the family members living in the Smith home, Eric was said to be the most caring one. He especially got upset if anyone hurt his mother, sometimes to the point of tears.

During times of heated arguments between Eric's parents, sometimes Ted would call out, "Tammy, you bitch. I'm out of here."

Eric would cry and beg, "Dad, don't get mad. Stop, come on, please."[25]

As Eric aged, all of the pent-up anger accumulated inside of him after years of being harassed by his peers at school was starting to get out of control. The temper tantrums were increasing in frequency as he never learned how to find an outlet to unleash his repressed feelings in a healthy manner. In one such incident, Eric was so upset that he approached Ted with shaking and trembling fists and confided that he really wanted to hurt something and needed help with releasing his anger.

Ted advised him, "When I got angry when I was your age, I grabbed a bag in our barn and I just started beating on it until I was too tired to do anything else."[26]

Before Ted could say anything more, he heard the door behind him click shut, and just like that, Eric was gone. He returned shortly thereafter, his demeanor calmer than before, the skin on his hands and knuckles partially flayed and bleeding. Eric revealed he had punched a tree a couple of times.

Eric eventually took up baseball at the same time his sister began playing softball. He didn't end up having a feel for it and ultimately dropped off the team. However, he finally did find an active hobby that he liked and stuck with for a good while: the school's wrestling team. It was during this time that Eric's bond with his adoptive father strengthened as Ted became more involved in his adopted son's life. Together, the pair practiced various wrestling moves and techniques. Eric was also taught self-defense tactics if anyone were to ever attack him. While there was a point in Eric's life when the youth had thoughts of quitting the wrestling team, he stuck it out—perhaps in fear of disappointing his father and ruining the strong relationship they had formed.

When he was around eight, Eric's life would take a dramatic turn when he accidentally discovered a family secret that was intentionally hidden from him. While his older sister Stacy was at the optometrist with Ted, she learned that she and Eric actually shared the same biological father, who wasn't Ted, but a man named Randy. Stacy knew and spent quite some time with her real father growing up and was raised to believe that Eric and Holly were her half-siblings. Although Stacy herself didn't inform Eric of this new information she learned, it didn't matter. Word spread quickly at school, and Eric learned the news from an older kid in his sister's grade. Confused and upset, he came home crying and demanded that his parents tell him the truth about his parentage.

Tammy and Ted sat him down and confirmed everything Eric had heard at school. They apologized that Eric had to find out the way he did. They had intended to tell him later in life when he would be able to understand the situation better. They still waited a couple more years when Eric was older and more mature before revealing the truth or what was believed to be the truth; they explained that at the time they got together, Tammy was pregnant with Eric. Ted wanted to adopt Eric and raise him as his own son, and Randy had no scruples about signing away his rights as his father. When Eric was born, Ted signed Eric's birth certificate claiming to be his father.

What was left of Eric's low self-esteem was destroyed by this revelation. He felt betrayed. To think that all of his life he was practically living a lie concealed by the very people he was supposed to trust the most, and that his own biological father was aware that Eric was his son yet wanted nothing to do with him, only reaffirmed the constant sense of worthlessness he felt.

"What's wrong with me?" the tormented Eric often questioned. "Why doesn't he want me? Why doesn't he love me?"[27]

Even after Eric found out the truth about his father, Randy continued to pick up Stacy to spend time with her. But never Eric.

But "the grass is always greener on the other side," as the old saying goes. In Eric and Holly's eyes, Stacy was the typical older sister who got everything she wanted. However, that wasn't necessarily the case; Stacy was surviving a battle of her own.

"We weren't allowed to do much," Stacy recounted of her childhood. She remembered her friends in high school no longer inviting her to outings because they knew she wouldn't be permitted to go. When she wasn't completing household chores, which typically took hours at most, she was cooped up in her bedroom. "It was a very secluded home life." She described her upbringing as "strict" mostly on account of her authoritarian stepfather. Her mother, she'd say, was "a victim of co-dependent behavior and narcissistic manipulation."[28]

Stacy, who would later describe her home life as "hell," found she had more freedom to do what she wanted when she was at her father's. However, most of the time when Randy picked her up, he wouldn't spend much-needed quality father-daughter time with her; instead, he dropped her off at her grandparents' house. As the oldest stepchild, Stacy didn't have a good relationship with anyone in the Smith home, not even Eric. The two regularly got into fights as siblings often do, but she would also state that Eric was the most caring member of the family.

"Eric would tell me that I looked good and always tried to make me happy when I was sad," she said. But she never returned that same kindness to him, something she would later regret in life. "Something inside me couldn't give the caring back."[29]

With the lack of feeling any sort of love from her caregivers at home and being told that her voice didn't matter all throughout her childhood, her mind and soul became isolated and separated from every member of her family.

"I had fifteen years to build up the tolerance to the abuse," she said. "Thankfully, I was gifted with strength and faith."[30]

After those 15 years, however, Stacy was no longer mentally able to live under the same roof with her family after something disturbing happened that would be traumatic for anyone, especially a vulnerable teenage girl like Stacy. Ted Smith had molested her twice, when she was 11 and 14, causing her to spiral into a deep depression during which she tried to overdose on Tylenol. She knew she had to move out, otherwise she would die in that house. So she packed her bags and moved in with her father permanently. Eric was well aware of the molestation that had occurred against his older sister, something psychiatrists would later suggest affected his emotional state too.

Eric Smith was a definite loner, though not by choice. By the time he reached his teenage years, he had no friends and was often seen riding around town by himself on his BMX bike for hours on end. On top of being ridiculed at school on a daily basis for his academic struggles and comical looks, having his feelings trivialized at home, and then the shocking revelation that his biological father did not want any involvement in his life whatsoever, the fury, hurt, and loneliness he harbored for years was engulfing him. By 1993, 13-year-old Eric was a ticking time bomb that nobody saw coming.

Trial

Eric Smith's trial commenced on August 2, 1994, exactly a year after the slaying of Derrick Robie. Reporters, family members from both sides, and townspeople of Savona all flocked to the courthouse to catch a glimpse of the baby-faced killer being escorted into the walnut-paneled courtroom by the brawny deputy. Now age 14, Eric had grown a couple inches and put on some weight since his arrest last summer.

He settled himself at the defense table as his attorney, Kevin Bradley, contended in his opening statement that Eric was driven by an "unprovoked urge" to cause harm upon Derrick that spiraled out of control, which resulted in the fatal bludgeoning that the adolescent boy was incapable of stopping.

"The things Eric Smith did to Derrick Robie are going to be horrible," warned the defense attorney in an attempt to prepare the jury for the pending gut-wrenching testimony presented by the prosecution. "When you hear them you are going to be sick." But he implored the members of the jury to take this as a sign of how deeply emotionally disturbed the 13-year-old was.[31]

District Attorney John C. Tunney stepped in and delivered his own powerful opening statement. He walked the jurors through the awful details of how Eric heartlessly lured the youngster away from the sidewalk and into the rear of an empty parking lot under the pretense of showing him a shortcut to the day camp. As the prosecutor described how Eric had strangled and bludgeoned his victim to death with a heavy rock, which weighed nearly as much as the victim, to the members of the jury, the cherub-faced adolescent didn't display a hint of emotion or remorse in the courtroom. Nor did he crack when the prosecutor revealed how he continued to desecrate Derrick's body even after he was presumably dead.

Eric maintained his impassive and unfeeling demeanor as Prosecutor John Tunney faced him and pleaded with the jury to treat every piece of testimony and evidence that the defense would throw their way carefully in an attempt to shift away the blame of Eric's cold-blooded actions with a grain of salt. "As you listen, ask yourself if it's his mom's fault. His dad's fault? Is it his doctor's fault? Maybe even Stephen King's fault?"[32]

While the district attorney wasn't disagreeing that Eric likely did have some emotional deficits, as evidenced from his young age and the brutal nature of his crime, he argued that "a person who has a fascination or desire to hurt others doesn't mean that person is not responsible for his acts."[33]

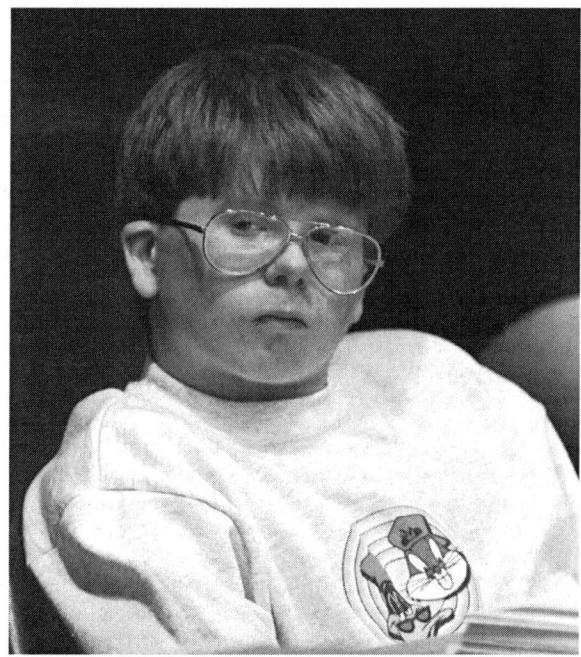

Eric Smith was 13 years old when he was arrested and charged in connection with Derrick Robie's death. His lawyers claimed he suffered from intermittent explosive disorder (AP Photo/John Hickey).

At any rate, the defense attorney was determined to prove that Eric was not criminally liable for what he did as he was seized with an impotent anger attributed to a behavioral disorder and developmental abnormalities. If found not guilty by reason of insanity, Eric would be avoiding a sentence of nine years to life in prison—the then-maximum term for juveniles as young as 13 being tried as adults under state law—and instead be admitted to a psychiatric hospital.

In his opening statement, defense attorney Kevin Bradley claimed that Eric was suffering from a major mental disturbance that had clouded his judgment at the time of the murder and his actions were beyond his power and control.

And what exactly was this mysterious mental disease Kevin Bradley was pushing that allegedly gripped his client at the time of the murder? Dr. Stephen Herman, a child psychiatrist hired by the defense, took the stand and testified on Eric's behalf. After spending quite a lot of time mentally examining him, Dr. Stephen Herman diagnosed the redheaded teen with *intermittent explosive disorder.*

The psychiatrist characterized this disorder as "literally deadly rage and anger. After the episodic rage, the child may appear to be normal."[34] Sufferers of intermittent explosive disorder (IED) experience periods of violent impulses which can occur very abruptly with little to no forewarning and may last for 30 minutes or less. Once the individual explodes into rage, they have very little power to contain it.

This so-called impulse that drove Eric to commit acts of violence had a name of its own. Dr. Herman wasn't able to extract very many answers and details out of his patient in regard to the actual killing; Eric claimed not to remember why he did it and how he was feeling at the time. But when he had inquired about the driving force behind his attack on little Derrick that fateful August morning, Eric blamed it on "the mad switch."

"It was the mad switch," Dr. Herman quoted from Eric. "I got mad. I got angry. I wanted to get it out."[35]

According to the Yale psychiatrist, Eric confided in him that he just "became angry" when he spotted the child walking alone on the sidewalk and immediately felt the urge to hurt him. Once his hands were around his neck, the older boy found it impossible to let go. However, murdering Derrick wasn't even on his mind. He simply wanted to get his anger out.

And why did Eric select the four-year-old as his victim of towering rage? The answer he provided was one that was probably an obvious one, but still nevertheless sent chills down the spines of all who sat within the paneled walls of the courtroom: "He's smaller and practically helpless."[36]

Once "the mad switch" was flipped on, Eric was subsequently powerless to stop the horror that transpired. Dr. Herman believed that Eric's mental disorder definitely had an impact on his anger outburst, and he lacked any sort of insight as to what the consequences of his actions would entail. "Eric was in an altered state of mind," the psychiatrist said, adding that he didn't get the sense that Eric "was fully aware enough or could stop himself at the time."[37] Therefore, he did not believe Eric was capable of understanding or appreciating the nature and consequences of his actions.

The psychiatrist also described an interaction Eric had just minutes before he killed Derrick that may have been the source of his rage that morning. Eric had been bumping his bicycle into the picnic table where some insurance agents were having a meeting. The two were exchanging witty banter back and forth about who could run the fastest when the seemingly playful conversation took a dark turn. The agent told Eric, "I bet I can beat your head in," followed by "I bet you I have a gun in my glove compartment and I can shoot you."[38]

Eric then left. According to Dr. Herman, this brief exchange may have been the tipping point for his mounting anger. When he encountered Derrick not too longer after, the little boy stood no chance. Eric was already seeing red.

Dr. Herman unveiled glimpses of glaringly obvious signs of a troubled mind dating all the way back to his early childhood. Since he was a toddler, Eric "suffered from pathological rage attacks as evidenced by abnormal temper tantrums, breath-holding spells, and head-banging."[39] He ascertained that Eric was unable to control his rage due to developmental abnormalities brought on by Tammy Smith's usage of a risky anti-epileptic drug called trimethadione during her pregnancy.

"Even now, I have absolutely no belief that the medication caused Eric to be violent," he insisted, though he stated that it was his belief it had led to his developmental delays, such as learning, speech, and walking, in addition to his low-set ears, upturned eyebrows, and vision problems. All of these factors combined undoubtedly impaired his self-esteem, proclaimed the Yale University psychiatrist.[40]

Eric's rage disorder was only exacerbated by schoolyard taunts directed at his physical appearance and learning difficulties, in addition to a turbulent home life where violence and verbal abuse were commonplace, mainly perpetrated by Eric's own adoptive father. Dr. Stephen Herman described the disciplinary acts Eric and his two sisters endured as "extreme" and "terrifying" for a child like Eric who already suffered from a mental problem to begin with. The child psychiatrist, who interviewed both of Eric's parents, wrote in his report that Ted "probably hit Eric much more than he admits."[41]

He also suspected that his young client was sexually abused, despite Eric denying it. "The nature of what he did to Derrick Robie makes me wonder whether something happened to Eric he hasn't told anyone," he said, perhaps referring to the post-mortem sexual assault with the stick. Although Ted had admitted to molesting Stacy on at least two separate occasions, he denied having ever been sexually inappropriate with his adoptive son.[42]

The child psychiatrist also stated that Eric had a sadistic streak and cited a few incidents relating to Eric's history of cruelty toward small animals and people, such as shooting at birds with a BB gun, gutting animals, and throwing rocks at frogs. Dr. Stephen Herman described an incident dating back to 1989 when Eric allegedly strangled his neighbor's Siamese cat to death with a garden hose because it was "bothersome."[43] A couple of years later, when a schoolmate of Eric's was killed in a car accident, he phoned the student's family on more than one occasion and asked to speak with the deceased teen—a clear indication that Eric took delight in harming others. Aside from his rage disorder, the freckle-faced adolescent was dealing with a plethora of other mental issues, according to Dr. Herman's preliminary report, which included depression and nicotine addiction from smoking cigarettes since the age of nine.

"He grew up a lonely child who was easily hurt," read Dr. Stephen Herman from his report back in May 1994. "He cried frequently. As he grew, he was not able to modulate his anger."[44]

In rebuttal, Prosecutor John Tunney called upon several lay witnesses of his own that contradicted certain facts of Eric's supposed history of sadism which undermined Dr. Stephen Herman's testimony. In relation to the neighbor's cat, the owner testified that Eric had only placed an automotive clamp around its neck (which was removed) and the feline had actually passed away much later from leukemia. One by one, the prosecutor dismantled the foundation of the psychiatrist's opinion and diagnosis, shining a light on the apparent cracks in some of the key factors that the defense's case heavily relied on. After an intense cross-examination, John Tunney got Dr. Herman to concede two things. The first was that the young defendant attacked Derrick because he saw an opportunity to do so clandestinely but would have been able to control his anger and actions had others been around. The second was that in order to be sadistic, which he had characterized Eric as being multiple times throughout the trial and defined to mean "intentionally cruel," the person must be consciously aware to derive pleasure from their sadistic actions.

After getting the psychiatrist to acknowledge that Eric Smith was a liar and likely did lie to him, John C. Tunney had successfully discredited the most essential witness that served as the backbone for the defense.

When Dr. Kathleen Quinn, a child and adolescent psychiatrist from Cleveland, approached the stand to deliver her challenging testimony, her expert opinion on Eric's mental state butted heads with the defense's. While she agreed that the youth was indeed beset with developmental abnormalities brought on by Tammy Smith's use of trimethadione while she was pregnant with Eric, she rejected Dr. Herman's diagnosis that Eric suffered from intermittent explosive disorder.

She fiercely disagreed that he suffered from a "major mental illness" or defect. Instead, she claimed that the teenager suffered from a mild case of attention deficit hyperactivity disorder (ADHD) which isn't correlated with violence. She described the adolescent as a boy who is "comfortable and excited by aggression."[45]

It was not intermittent explosive disorder that propelled such a senseless act of violence for Eric, Dr. Kathleen Quinn suggested; rather, it was envy—and Derrick was the trigger.

"He symbolizes someone who appears well-cared for, successful and athletic—all things Eric was not," she explained.[46]

When she asked Eric what caused him to kill Derrick, he offered very little explanation.

"My life was junk," Eric had told her. "My sister treated me like trash. Kids treated me like trash."[47]

Dr. Quinn believed that years of abuse and feelings of inadequacy bubbled to the surface of his mind and took over his body when he saw Derrick. Discounting everything that Dr. Herman had said, she maintained that Eric Smith didn't just "snap." He knew exactly what he was doing before, during, and after the murder and he knew it was wrong. In fact, Eric told her that he had deliberately hidden his bicycle before the murder because he knew he couldn't choke Derrick and hold his bike at the same time, suggesting that Eric took calculated, premeditated steps. After the murder, Eric said he rode his bike, played Nintendo, and "slept like a baby."[48]

"Only a very small number of children, five percent, have a psychotic illness. More likely you'll find social and personal behavior problems," she said. "It's possible to do something terrible without having had a major mental illness."[49]

In fact, specialists from both sides subjected Eric to extensive medical testing where they examined hormone levels and brain function. Neither of them found any abnormalities that could offer an explanation for Eric's violent behavior.

After a draining two weeks of testimony, the heart-wrenching trial was coming to an end. It was time for prosecutors to step in with their final closing arguments. If convicted of second-degree murder, Eric faced a maximum sentence of nine years to life in prison. If, however, he was found guilty but of a lesser charge, he would be sent straight to a psychiatric institution.

Prosecutor John C. Tunney was eager to sway the jury from the sympathy that the defense was trying to invoke among the jury the past couple of weeks. His biggest concern was that the jury would be misled by Eric's young age and baby face.

"If the defendant was 35 years old, you would be impatient to get into the jury room."[50] He argued that Eric consciously chose to coax the youngster to death. The prosecutor once again painted a macabre canvas of Derrick's various injuries and presented jurors with vivid details of his final moments while the adolescent sat stolidly throughout the two-and-a-half hour session. Only occasionally did he lift his downcast gaze to peer at the courtroom camera through his wire-rimmed glasses.

While the prosecution didn't disagree that the freckle-faced killer was indeed not normal, it did not, by any means, certify that he was unaware of his actions. Tunney fervently believed that the defense failed to prove that Eric suffered from a mental disorder that prompted uncontrollable rage. "Was there some anger there? There probably was … was he angry that in his mind he wasn't attractive or that he wasn't popular? Was there some level of anger that he believed he had not been dealt a perfect hand in life? Absolutely, I wouldn't doubt that for one second."

He further contended that the court failed to hear any reasonable excuse for Eric's emotional state. "There is absolutely no evidence of rage. Eric Smith made choices about his conduct."[51]

Turning to face the 12 jurors seated in the jury box, the six men and six women who held the young defendant's fate in their hands, he stated, "He intended to take control and be the victimizer instead of the victim."[52]

Defense attorney Kevin Bradley was not backing down on his original strategy that was entirely built on the insanity defense. He reiterated that Eric suffered from intermittent explosive disorder which is characterized by periodic episodes of uncontrollable anger.

"Is Eric Smith a normal boy?"[53] he asked while pacing in front of the 12 jurors, pointing out that even the prosecutor himself agreed that the young defendant was not normal.

"It's pretty startling—Eric Smith suffers from a very serious mental disease." Kevin Bradley picked up the 26-pound rock recovered from the crime scene, the same rock the teenage defendant used to brutalize his young victim. "To pick this up and throw this down on a little boy's head ... does that suggest calm, deliberate action, a plan?" he addressed the court, cradling the large rock in his hands for all to see. "The fact that he seemed normal afterwards shows that he's not normal."[54]

He labeled his young client as a "sick boy in need of treatment" and cautioned the 12 men and women of the jury that if Eric doesn't receive the psychiatric help he desperately needs now, he may remain a threat to society if he walks out of prison in his 20s.[55]

Members of the jury began their deliberation. Now it was up to them to decide whether Eric Smith was criminally responsible for the brutal slaying of Derrick Robie. The men and women carefully went over every shred of evidence as presented by the defense and prosecution. They considered Kevin Bradley's argument that for a 13-year-old boy to inflict such cruelty on a four-year-old for no apparent reason must indicate that a deep emotional disturbance must be going on inside the youth's brain that prevented him from being able to control his acts—and if he didn't urgently receive psychiatric treatment, he might emerge upon the streets untreated in his 20s. The ladies and gentlemen of the jury also ruminated over John C. Tunney's line of reasoning that there was no evidence in the young defendant's history to suggest he suffered from a mental illness or defect that prevented him from knowing the moral differences between right and wrong. Now it was a toss-up between the two lawyers' arguments: *was* Eric Smith aware of the enormity of his actions and was he able to control them?

After 11 hours of deliberation, the jurors reached a decision.

Conviction and Sentencing

There was a notably thick whirlwind of emotions and tension in the courtroom atmosphere on the night of August 17, 1994, as townsfolk, reporters, and loved ones from both the defendant's side and the victim's side waited to hear the verdict. Just before 10 p.m., the jury announced their decision: the defendant, Eric Smith, was guilty of second-degree murder.

As soon as the guilty verdict was read aloud, Eric sucked in a breath and shot a nervous glance at his family—the most emotion he ever displayed in the courtroom. His mother choked out a sob and his grandmother, consumed with the shock of the conviction, fainted and was promptly rushed to a local hospital. Meanwhile, perched on the other side of the spectator area, the Robies felt a flood of relief. Doreen dropped her head into her hand, silently thanking God.

"The verdict is not going to bring Derrick back," Dale Robie said just minutes after leaving the courtroom; however, he was grateful "that the system is starting to be responsive to these kids' actions," referring to the rise of violence among juveniles in America.[56]

But the year-long ordeal wasn't completely over for the Robies. Now, Eric was facing a maximum prison sentence of nine years to life. His sentencing date would occur two months after the guilty verdict was read. On Monday, November 7, 1994, the copper-haired boy appeared in court one final time to officially hear just how long he would spend behind bars. Eric had been the focus for the past year but now Derrick's parents seized the opportunity to read a statement in court pleading for their son's killer to receive the maximum sentence. They wanted to tell everyone in the courtroom what a great kid Derrick was.

Dale fought to stifle his sobs as he read from a heart-wrenching statement he and his wife Doreen had prepared. He went over a list of all of his son's accomplishments and hobbies in his young but no less fulfilling life, such as his penchant for sports like baseball and fishing and his impressive ability to make peanut butter cookies and meatloaf all on his own. Then they recited a list of things their little boy would never be able to experience because of Eric cutting his life short.

"When Derrick came into this world, I cried, and when Derrick left this world, I cried," said the victim's father, his voice quivering. "I have felt the whole realm of loving and losing."[57]

He told the court that he prayed Eric would never have the opportunity to take another child's life.

Adhering to the heartbroken father's plea, it wasn't at all difficult for Judge Donald Purple to finally deliver the sentence to the young defendant: nine years to life in prison. Eric lowered his gaze, keeping the same flat, unreadable expression he had maintained throughout his trial. The teenage boy was to spend the first portion of his sentence in a state juvenile detention center before being transferred to an adult prison once he turned 18, where he would be spending the remainder of his incarceration. He might be eligible for parole in eight years to the day of his sentencing.

"We got what we came here for," said Dale Robie minutes after leaving the courtroom for the last time.[58] This painful chapter in their lives was somewhat coming to a close, and while the grief this whole experience caused had put a permanent hole in their hearts, they felt a sense of relief that justice was finally served.

Doreen, who stated that she had no feelings for Eric whatsoever, was also satisfied with the sentence, saying that it will "send a message to some of these kids who have no concept of what life is worth that they won't be getting away with these crimes." She hoped it would deter said kids by reminding them that consequences exist and they would be serving time for their actions.[59]

As the trial and sentencing finally came to a close, the redheaded boy with the wire-rimmed aviators remained just as much an enigma as at the beginning of his arrest. The most daunting question was still left unanswered: *why?*

Afterword

Derrick Robie continues to occupy the minds of not only those who loved and cared for him but also local residents of Savona who never met him. Just a few months before the trial, the small community came together and cleared all the pines at the base of the hill where Derrick's body was found. To keep Derrick's name and memory alive in the community, they turned it into a t-ball diamond and planted a crabapple tree. A flagpole and a 42-inch bronze statue of Derrick swinging his baseball bat stand upright on a hill overlooking the new park.

"As horrid and as negative as this has been, you just look for something to try to turn positive," said Doreen. "I hope people can look at the statue and just remember what childhood was supposed to be about, because we've lost it somewhere … with all these teenagers that have gone totally haywire. I feel kind of naive because I thought I tried to keep him from everything."[60]

What happened to their son on McCoy Street, the street he grew up on and died next to, will forever haunt the Robies. This was no longer a street that was safe and comfortable enough to raise their remaining child. They packed their belongings and moved almost a mile out of town, hoping to somewhat start their lives anew and return to normalcy. But photographs of their son with his ever-radiant smile and twinkling blue eyes were hung all across the walls of their new dining room, serving as daily reminders of what were once carefree, more

Derrick Robie's statue in the field where he was murdered. The field has been transformed into a T-ball diamond (courtesy Doreen Robie).

secure times. Other keepsakes had been plastered alongside the pictures, including a letter of condolence from former president Bill Clinton and a poem written by neighbor Mary Davidson, whose backyard became the murder site of Derrick Robie.

It continued to haunt her. "You try to keep the memories down, but it takes a lot of energy. Every time I look in my backyard, I see the spot where a 4-year-old was murdered."[61]

Eric Smith was incarcerated at Brookwood Secure Center, where he underwent intensive therapy for three years before being transferred to a prison for young adults. He was relocated three different times before permanently settling in Gowanda Correctional Facility, a medium-security prison located in Erie County, New York. In 2004, after a decade of living within walls and steel bars surrounded by razor-wire fences, the now-grown child killer was up for parole for the second time. He had already been denied parole once before, in 2002. It was now time for him to build his own case and convince the parole board that he had been rehabilitated and deserved a second chance at life on the outside.

"It upsets me that we have to beg for them to keep this killer behind bars," said Doreen. She, along with her husband, had sent a letter to the parole board pleading against the release of their beloved son's murderer. They also included a home video depicting the short life of Derrick Robie. "My biggest worry is that I still have a 12 year old. There's certainly enough things to worry about with an adolescent, other than the fact that there could be a killer running loose. I don't like to say that very often, because I don't want to scare Dalton. But that's the way I look at it."[62]

While the Robies fought hard to campaign his release, Eric, then aged 24, broke his 10 years of silence and publicly apologized to his victim's family on the show *48 Hours*.

"I know my actions have caused a terrible loss in the Robie family, and for that I'm truly sorry. I've tried to think as much as possible about what Derrick will never be able to experience: his 16th birthday, Christmas, anytime, owning his own house, graduating, going to college, getting married, his first child. If I could go back in time, I would switch places with Derrick and endure all the pain I've caused him. If it meant that he would go on living, I'd switch places, but I can't."[63]

And for the first time ever, maybe after spending nearly half his life behind razor wire and having enough time to reflect on his monstrous actions, Eric was now able—or willing—to offer an explanation for why he did it. "After quite a few years of verbal abuse and having been told I'm nothing, I shut down my feelings so I wouldn't feel the emotional pain which made me feel vulnerable and weak. But the damage was done. I began to believe I was nothing and a nobody. And my outlook on life was dark. I felt that when I was going to school I was going to hell. Because that's what it was for me, it was hell. However minor or major the abuse is, it all adds up 'til it gets to the point where the individual cannot take it anymore. After a while they may cope in a horrific way. Take their emotional anger and rage out on someone who had done nothing to bring on such violence, like Derrick. Not because they're evil, or Satanic little kids. It's because they want the abuse to stop and it's the only way they know how to."[64]

Eric insisted that he would no longer be a danger on the streets and, in fact, would be an "asset" to society. He expressed the desire to become a counselor for bullied children and hoped one day he could be a forensic psychologist and study and research kids who kill. He read out loud from a poem he wrote, stating his fear that he will one day pass without leaving behind a positive name for himself.

Despite what seemed to be a clear implication that Eric was abused, which was a question that was repeatedly raised in court, Eric himself had denied it to Dr. Stephen Herman and to the parole board. Eric admitted to a board member that choking his young victim had given him a good feeling at the time. When asked why that was, he gave the following chilling response: "because instead of me being hurt, I was hurting somebody else."[65]

After much deliberation as to whether Eric deserved to be a free man, the parole board ultimately denied his release to paroled supervision, much to the Robies' relief.

Every two years, Eric relentlessly tried to apply for parole and was met with rejection each time. The Robies and townspeople of Savona always fought the tiring battle once again to make sure that Eric remained behind bars. It seemed worth it to them, though, with the lingering fear that Eric would one day be granted parole and would walk the streets again.

The Robies wanted to ensure that other families that are going through the same situation are spared from such an anguishing experience. Along with other families of murder victims, they advocated for the passage of Penny's Law in Penny Brown's name. Brown was a beloved New York mother, wife, and midwife nurse who was brutally raped and slaughtered by 15-year-old Edward Kindt on Mother's Day of 1999 while she was out for a jog on a recreational trail. Her teenage killer had only received nine years to life behind bars, the same prison term Eric Smith was given. The purpose behind Penny's Law was to essentially enforce tougher laws by lengthening prison sentences for juvenile killers and increasing the amount of time between parole hearings. This way, families who are also suffering from the loss of a loved one at the hands of a child or teenager have more time to heal before facing parole hearings.

"Supporting Penny's Law was a proud moment," said Dale Robie. "It gave us a little meaning, more meaning … he was here for a short time. But now look at the impact his five years have had."[66]

Indeed, all of that hard work paid off when Penny's Law became a reality in New York on July 22, 2003, after Governor George Pataki signed a compromised version of the bill into law. Now, juveniles convicted of second-degree murder, who would have previously received nine years to life, would be handed 15–25 years to life in prison. It was a victorious moment for everyone who was involved in the campaign, but, of course, it couldn't have been successful without efforts of State Senator Patricia McGee and Assemblywoman Catharine Young, who drafted the New York State Assembly Bill #A1628 that was named for Penny Brown.

"Rape is rape. Murder is murder. A sexual predator is a sexual predator. Youth is no excuse," Assemblywoman Catharine Young powerfully stated on the day of the bill's passing.[67]

It seemed like a never-ending war that Derrick's family is fighting, a war they could not escape or put an end to. But then came the day that the Robies had dreaded for the last two decades.

At Eric's eleventh parole hearing on October 5, 2021, Eric presented himself as a rehabilitated man with accumulated insight into his 13-year-old brain. He discussed the self-reflection and emotional progress he had achieved over the past 28 years of his incarceration.[68]

"I've thought about the fact that Derrick is never gonna graduate high school and go to college and be a man, get married, have kids, be successful, and I took that away from him," he told the commissioners. "It's not easy to deal with every day but it's hard."[69]

He also finally answered some looming questions that had remained largely unanswered for decades, such as why he inserted the stick into Derrick's rectum.

"I was frantic and scared, terrified at what I had just finished doing, and the only thing I could think of was if he gets up he's gonna tell on me and I'm gonna be in trouble for hurting him, and the only thing I could think of was to try to stop his heart," he told the parole board. First, he explained, he attempted to penetrate his eye with the stick in hopes of piercing his brain and killing him. When that attempt had failed, he then tried to jab the stick through his chest in order to stop his heart. When that proved to be unsuccessful, he then inserted the stick in Derrick's rectum, thinking he might be able to pierce his heart through that route.[70]

After killing Derrick, he went back to the recreation center for a bit, then rode his bike around town while "freaking out" in his head. "From the time it happened until the time I confessed a week later, it's the only thing I could think about."[71]

"I ask that you take into consideration that the 13-year-old kid that took Derrick's life, and had so many things going on internally with him at that time, is not the man sitting in front of you talking," promised Eric. "I assure you that if you were to give me the chance I would not only prove that I'm not a threat, I would definitely be an asset to society."[72]

Two days later, he was granted parole at the age of 41.

While Eric remains a notorious child murderer in America, there is a small percentage of the population that disagrees with the "harsh" sentence that was imposed on him while he was a juvenile. This delves into the ongoing debate regarding the issue of strict prison sentences given to juvenile killers who may suffer from mental health issues and are in need of serious psychiatric help. In spite of the jury's conviction and resolution of the case, the question remains: did they make the right judgment?

John C. Tunney stood by the argument he built for the prosecution's case against Eric in 1994. He firmly rejected that Eric suffered from IED, but didn't necessarily disagree that the youth possibly suffered from a mental illness of some sort. He pointed out two vital key components in the criminal law context that would constitute a proper insanity defense. One, did he suffer from a mental disease or defect? If so, as a result of said mental disease or defect, was he unable to appreciate the nature and consequences of his acts or know what he did was wrong?

"In other words, it's not enough to have a mental disease or disorder," he said. "If you do, it has to affect you in a very specific way for it to constitute a defense."[73]

But how do we know that Eric was aware of the enormity of his actions?

"Derrick had been dead for a week. Eric knew very clearly that the police were looking for the person who did it. If he didn't know what he'd done was wrong, he would have raised his hand and said 'over here. I did it. I did it.'" But instead, he said, Eric having initially lied to the police about having seen the preschooler that fateful morning was a clear indication that he surely grasped an understanding of the consequences of his actions—something that an individual with no concept of what's right and wrong would have. "He was not delusional. He did not believe that he was picking daisies or chasing the snakes out of Ireland," maintained the prosecutor, while additionally pointing out that intermittent explosive disorder isn't classified as a delusional disorder.[74]

John wasn't quite convinced that Eric is less of a threat than he was when he was just a 13-year-old kid. "I simply don't see our prison system as having a significant rehabilitative effect," said the prosecutor. His current stance is that dangerous offenders like Eric Smith "need to be warehoused so as to protect the rest of us, to punish the offender and to deter others who might be tempted to victimize. As to how much punishment is enough, there's no real answer. Our system of punishment rarely delivers a punishment that is proportional to the harm caused. In other words, it's largely arbitrary."[75]

Two and a half decades later, Savona locals continue to feel the stain that the slaying of Derrick Robie has left on the cloth of this once tight-knit and safe community. On the surface, things have returned to normal since the tragedy that struck the small village; townsfolk still shuffle in and out of King's Market with their arms full of grocery bags. They continue to dine out at Mom's Savona Diner, which still sits on 82 Main Street. Kids still run around loose on McCoy Street. But residents will never forget what happened in the summer of 1993. Many have conflicting emotions themselves. In a way, they think the town suffered a double tragedy—they didn't lose just one boy. They lost two—the other one being Eric Smith himself.[76] Those who knew Eric either personally or in passing have also been affected by his actions and wonder to what extent he is a victim. The killing of a child never fails to spark outrage, but perhaps one of the most soul-stirring aspects that emerged from this was that the murderer was not an adult child predator like everyone originally suspected, but, rather, one of their own: a bespectacled, 80-pound teenage boy.

Was Eric Smith the cold-hearted monster that the media portrayed him to be? Or was he also just a victim of his own circumstances and upbringing and who was in need of critical help? Whatever the case might be, one thing was for certain—a piece of the town's innocence was taken away on the morning of August 2, 1993, never to be restored.

Holly Harvey and Sandy Ketchum
(2004)

On August 2, 2004, a very distraught neighbor called 911 with some jarring news. She informed the dispatcher that she had just peeped through the door of her neighbors' house and found that they had been savagely killed. Fayette County sheriffs took this report very seriously and immediately made their way to the address where this alleged murder had taken place. They pulled up in front of the white-brick ranch-style home in Fayetteville, Georgia, and forced their way inside. What they walked into was sufficient to shake even the most experienced officers to their core.

"I've never seen a crime this serious in the twenty-eight years that I've been a sheriff, of this magnitude, on kinfolks," commented Fayette County sheriff Randall Johnson, one of the first arrivals at the scene.[1]

As soon as they walked through the front door, which led directly into the kitchen, it was like they had just stepped into a battlefield. The blood spatter that covered all four walls and the floor emanated a very metallic, pungent smell, indicating that it was fresh. Over by the sink, the telephone cord had been pulled. They first came across the dead body of 74-year-old Carl Collier lying face down on the kitchen floor in a pool of his own blood. He had more than 15 stab wounds riddling his chest and back. The officers advanced through the house, watching for more clues and evidence. They followed the blood trail to the basement, where they found the body of Carl's 73-year-old wife, Sarah Collier, lying face up at the base of the stairs. She, too, had been viciously stabbed in the chest and back more than a dozen times.[2]

The keys to Carl's dark blue 2002 Chevrolet Silverado pickup truck had been stolen and the truck itself was gone too. While the beginning of the investigation progressed, another phone call came through. It was a teenage girl who identified herself as Sara Polk living in Griffin, Georgia. In complete hysterics, she claimed that her friends had just come over to her house and confessed to murdering the Colliers. They had just left in a blue pickup truck and she had no idea where they were headed.

If they were to go on Sara Polk's report, they now knew who was responsible for these brutal murders. It was just a matter of finding them, which was going to be difficult. They didn't know where they could have fled to afterward. For all they knew, the alleged culprits might have fled the state.

Immediately, hunting down these killers was bumped all the way up on their list of priorities, and they wasted no time in securing two warrants for the arrests of 15-year-old Holly Harvey and 16-year-old Sandy Ketchum, while trying to figure out why two teenage girls would murder an innocent couple.

Background

Carl Collier previously worked at Delta Air Lines and his wife, Sarah, was a retired bank teller.[3] Carl and Sarah Collier were described as pious and hard-working people who were very active in the Baptist church. Upon discovering that they could not bear biological children of their own, they decided to adopt. First, they adopted Kevin, who was born on Christmas Day in 1965 and taken into the home of Carl and Sarah three months later. Baby Carla was born on June 30, 1967, and adopted a few months later as well.[4] Kevin developed into a diligent young man who patterned his footsteps after his father's and made a career as an avionics mechanic at Delta Air Lines.

Carla did not similarly meet the Colliers' expectations, for she went down a much more misguided path in life that was a frequent cause for concern for the Colliers. She aged into a rebellious adolescent girl who frequently fought her parents over her choice of friends and turned to a world filled with drugs and alcohol, which led to jail time. When she was 17, she ran away from home. She began working as a stripper in her early 20s and met an ex-con named Gene Harvey, with whom she would have her first child at the age of 21.[5] In March 1989, she gave birth to her daughter, whom she named Holly.

If anyone thought for a moment that Carla would put her partying days and reckless lifestyle behind her and step up to her responsibility as a parent, they were sadly mistaken. Carla was described as a very negligent mother who would frequently leave Holly unattended at an early age or drop her off at random people's homes when she needed to catch a break. Her relationship with Gene was volatile on its own, and eventually it fell apart. Throughout the 1990s, Carla hopped from relationship to relationship, and Holly didn't have contact with her biological father after Carla and Gene broke up.

In 2002, when Holly was around the age of 13, she and her mother got into an argument over Holly refusing to do something Carla wanted her to do. It escalated into a physical altercation which ended in Carla choking her daughter. The Department of Children and Families got involved, removing Holly from the home and placing her with her grandparents, Sarah and Carl Collier. But for reasons unknown, Holly ended up moving back in with her mother.

It was in middle school when she first made the acquaintance of a girl named Sandra Ketchum.

Sandra, called "Sandy" by all those who knew her, was born on April 19, 1988. When she was just 15 months old, her mother, Sandra Maddox, abandoned her, so she was placed in the custody of her father, Tim Ketchum. Throughout her life she had three stepmothers, one of whom allegedly physically abused her. Her new stepmom, Beth, came into her life when Sandy was just 12. When Sandy entered middle school in 2002, her entire personality took a 180-degree turn. She began dressing more masculine and wore baggy pants that hung low on her hips. She was resistant to authority and hung around a group of social outcasts.

It was through these outsiders that she met Holly Harvey, and the two instantly clicked. The girls started off as friends, but soon, that relationship evolved into something more. Eventually, the pair were inseparable—a dangerous fact that everyone would come to learn.

One time when Holly spent the night at Sandy's house, the couple spent a lengthy amount of time in the backyard shed. That's when it hit Tim: they were lovers. From then on, the girls were forbidden from sleeping in the same room whenever Holly would spend the night, as Tim and Beth did not want the two being sexually intimate in the household.

Georgia is one of many states making up what is often dubbed the Bible Belt, and its clear evangelical influence has a very powerful hold over the community and politics. Over 80 percent believe that religion is important and 21 percent affiliate themselves with Baptist beliefs.[6] Social conservatism is especially representative of Fayetteville County, where a great deal of community bonding is centered on church activities.

In such a God-fearing state, intolerance towards homosexuals is rampant, and girls like Sandy Ketchum were no exception to persecution. In school she was subjected to homophobic slurs on a near-daily basis and was told that what she was doing was a sin. Having never had a stable motherly figure in her life and suffering from abuse committed by one of her stepmoms, she sought out female companionship elsewhere and found solace in her relationship with Holly. To Sandy, Holly was her rock, and she would do anything if it meant not losing her.

But concerns from both sides of their families began to surface when the two were continuously breaking rules and resisting their parents' attempt to control them.

"She used to sneak out of the house when her mother was at work," said Carla's ex-boyfriend, Scott Moore. "I had to go up and down the street to chase her down." Many times he found her with Sandy.[7]

Tim and Beth Ketchum were noticing strange things on their end as well. More than once, gas from their truck would mysteriously be reduced when they had just replenished it. At first, they suspected that the neighborhood kids were stealing the truck at night, but they came to find out that it was Sandy and Holly. More than once they would take the Ketchums' truck and go joyriding around Fayetteville at night.

Things took a turn in the spring of 2004, when Carla was imprisoned for a drug conviction and driving under the influence, leaving Holly all alone. Holly's father was unable to care for the young teen, having been involved in a car accident that left him paralyzed and wheelchair-bound. Holly's grandparents were more than happy to open their doors to her, hoping that maybe having a positive and stable influence in her life might set her on the right path.

Things didn't pan out as the elderly couple had hoped, for Holly proved to be even more of a handful than they'd anticipated. Holly took after her mother and, she too, developed into a defiant teenager with a taste for drugs. Carl and Sarah tried to provide Holly with the love and compassion she had lacked her entire life, only to be repeatedly disrespected by the young, troubled girl. They laid down some ground rules that are typically expected of teenagers, such as no smoking or drinking or staying out late, quite simple rules that Holly refused to abide by. But they weren't going to let up so easily.

While the Colliers were desperately trying to subdue Holly's rebellious ways by forcing her to dress nicely and attend church, there was one ongoing issue that would be the subject of many domestic disputes, causing a rift between Holly and her grandparents. That was her romantic relationship with Sandy, which they strongly disapproved of. Not only was being gay an abomination according to their religious beliefs, but they were convinced that Sandy was a bad influence due to her criminal record. The Colliers' biggest fear was that Holly would go down the same path in life that Carla had. While both of the Colliers took up the challenging task of raising Holly, Carl was the more laid back of the two, although he did issue discipline when needed by taking Holly's phone away and grounding her when she was being out of control. But nothing would stop Holly from doing whatever her heart desired. Sarah, who primarily raised Carla and was generally sterner when it came to raising girls, was typically the one to take charge when Holly was acting up and seemed to be the most troubled about her lesbian love affair. She frequently aired all of her dirty laundry to her church friends regarding the problems she was experiencing with her granddaughter at home. She openly condemned her homosexual relationship, imploring others to help "pray the gay away."

But no amount of prayer and public shaming was going to change the intense feelings of love that Holly had for her girlfriend. She had texted her, "I'm glad I found you. God sent you to me. I don't care what it says about gay people in the Bible."[8]

In May 2004, both the Ketchums and the Colliers put their foot down and said enough is enough. They forbade Sandy and Holly from ever seeing each other. But being separated from her one true love was doing even more harm to Sandy's mental health. With no one to talk to and nowhere to go, she turned to self-harm as a coping mechanism for all of the pent-up anxiety, pain and heartbreak she was experiencing. She rubbed erasers against her skin, causing burns and skin abrasions, and she used knives and razors to cut herself. In total she had more than 100 self-inflicted scars marring her body, which she covered with long-sleeved shirts and pants.

Holly, too, was aching to reunite with her lover. She constantly begged her grandparents to let her see Sandy, but they stood their ground. In a letter to Sandy, she wrote, "I try so hard to really let you know how much I love you. What would I do if our love had no meaning? I want you to have faith that this will soon be over but it's a price to pay though. And I asked myself if life is worth loving."[9]

On June 10, Sandy went just outside the house to play basketball. Beth kept tabs on her stepdaughter, ensuring that she was still well within earshot in case she tried to run off without her knowledge. But about 45 minutes later, Beth could no longer hear the repetitive sound of the ball dribbling against the pavement, so she went outside to check on her.

Sandy was gone.

Beth immediately told Tim about Sandy's disappearance as soon as he came home from work, and together they tried to file a missing persons report. They were told by police that they could not take action yet as the teenage girl had not been missing for a full 24 hours. The panic-stricken stepmom scoured the streets searching for Sandy; meanwhile, Tim was worried that his daughter had committed suicide.

But it appeared as though Sandy wasn't the only one who seemingly fell off the face of the earth. Holly was nowhere to be found. People could only speculate that the two were together. Missing persons fliers were plastered all around the city, and volunteers within the community banded together to help look for the girls. Everyone prayed day and night for Sandy and Holly's safe return. Days had gone by and there was still no word from either of them. Then, on the fourth day, authorities spotted two individuals matching Holly and Sandy's description sitting in an abandoned car together 20 miles away in Griffin, Georgia. And, indeed, it was none other than the teenage girls that people had been desperately searching for the past few days.

A couple of weeks later, the pair ran away together again. Carl was officially at the end of his rope and reported Holly to the authorities. A stipulation of their probation forbade the girls from having any form of contact with each other whatsoever. As soon as Holly walked out of the courthouse, she lit up a cigarette and stubbed it out on her grandfather's blue pickup truck. Just as he was about ready to pick her up and carry her back into the courtroom, Sarah had a sudden softening of the heart and told her husband to leave it be; Holly had already been through enough today, she said.

From there, Holly's growing sense of entitlement only got worse. During dinner that weekend, she blew up when her grandparents refused to let her drive their pickup truck to the beach despite the fact that she didn't have a driver's license. Even Holly's mother was disappointed when she heard her daughter had been placed on probation and sent her a letter from prison, hoping to pass down some motherly wisdom so that Holly would learn from her own mistakes and not end up in Carla's position one day.

"It ain't no joke," Carla Harvey chided in the letter. "If you care about your freedom at all you'd better fly right and straighten up." She also sympathized with Holly's living situation and apologized for being the reason she was placed in it. "I can't stand the thought of you being there and what you have to go through," she wrote. "I want you to have faith that this will all be over soon. And believe that we are gonna be together and happy real soon."[10]

Sandy was having a difficult time adjusting as well; one day, Beth had tentatively given Sandy permission to hang out with some neighborhood kids. A few hours later, there was a knock on the door. It was Sandy. When Beth opened the door for her, the teenage girl immediately collapsed and began vomiting. She had overdosed on 16 oxytocin (Pitocin). After she recovered, she began to see a counselor. Throughout these sessions, the counselor told Beth and Tim that part of Sandy's problem was that she never developed a connection with her mother and recommended that she be able to reunite with her so they could spend quality time with each other. At the urging of both Sandy and her counselor, Tim relented and allowed his daughter to live with her mother temporarily. He warned Sandra Maddox that Sandy was to stay away from Holly, but it was a warning that went in one ear and out the other. Her mother frequently let Sandy drive without a license and even took her to see Holly multiple times.

Carl and Sarah's efforts to keep the lovers apart proved to be futile. They continued to see each other in secret; nothing, and nobody, was going to stand between the forbidden love these two adolescent girls shared for each other without paying the ultimate price for it.

The Slayings

The day before the double murder, Sandy had sneaked into Holly's basement bedroom and stayed there overnight. They spent the morning of that fateful day lounging in Holly's room, listening to music. At some point, they considered hitting up a local drug dealer for weed and cocaine.

But to do that, they needed a car. That's when Sandy suggested they steal Carl Collier's truck.

"We'll have to kill them to do that," Holly replied.[11]

It may have come off as a sick, twisted joke at first, but a light bulb lit up above both their heads simultaneously. Suddenly, the girls found themselves toying with ideas for how to kill Holly's grandparents.

Maybe we can bludgeon them with a lamp? Sandy suggested.

No, they both agreed, the grandparents' chances of survival would be too high. They needed to concoct a more lethal plan. That's when Sandy suggested that they stab them to death. Holly agreed that that was the best idea, and she gleefully hurried to the kitchen and returned with the biggest knife she could find. Holly began practicing how they were going to murder the elderly couple by stabbing Holly's mattress and pictures of puppies plastered on her bedroom wall to test the sharpness and durability of the blade.[12]

On her arm with ink, Holly broke the murder plot down into four simple steps: *Kill, keys, money, jewelry.*

As long as they stuck to the plan, then everything would work out accordingly, and they would have the freedom to be together without the nosy intervention of Holly's grandparents.

The pair quickly came up with a ruse to lure the grandparents into the basement. Holly lit a joint while Sandy, also armed with a knife, hid behind the bed. Then they waited. The skunk-like smell soon wafted through the vents and made its way to the Colliers. In no time, they heard their thumping footsteps descending the stairs. The girls braced themselves and Holly clutched the knife harder. Carl and Sarah knocked on the basement door and innocuously asked if they could retrieve a suitcase from the cupboard.

Then the violent confrontation ensued.

As soon as they entered the bedroom, Holly squeezed her eyes shut and plunged the knife right into her grandmother's back. Carl reacted immediately by pinning her down on the bed in an attempt to protect his wife.

"You're on drugs, you don't know what you're doing!"[13] cried Carl, hoping he could talk sense into Holly and calm her down.

Sandy remained stationary beside the bed.

"Why aren't you helping me?!" Holly called out, and, as if on cue, Sandy sprang to her feet and joined in the attack.[14]

Holly drove the blade into her grandfather's chest. The much older man, though in his 70s, was able to muster enough strength to run upstairs. Holly hesitated, unsure of what to do next, but her girlfriend ordered her to go after him. They couldn't just let him get away, otherwise their whole plan would be foiled. So she promptly leapt off the bed and gave chase while Sandy stayed behind and continued stabbing Sarah until the job was finished.

Carl made a beeline for the telephone on the wall and picked it up, his fingers itching to dial those three vital digits that could ultimately save his and his wife's lives. But Holly was faster. Racing after him with the knife, she promptly ripped the phone cord out of the wall, rendering him helpless. But Carl wasn't going to go down without a fight. He managed to grab hold of the knife, and the duo briefly wrestled over it. In the end, Holly's reflexes proved too quick as she won the intense struggle and began stabbing him. When Sandy was done with Sarah, she joined her lover upstairs, where she dodged a coffee mug hurled by Carl while he attempted to fend off his granddaughter.

Sandy stood and watched as Holly dealt the final jab to her grandfather's neck, which shot out blood that Holly could only describe as "like somebody just poured a big old bucket of hot water on me."[15] This fatal blow would send Carl to the floor. He never got back on his feet. It was over now, and both girls were blood-soaked from head to toe. But they did it. They accomplished the first thing from their to-do list. Next, they rummaged through the house for money and jewelry, but only managed to find the latter. They tossed that in a bag, along with other essentials—clothes and such—before stealing Sarah's cell phone and the keys to Carl's pickup truck on the way out.

Womanhunt

While in the car, the girls phoned several of their friends and told them to tune in to the 10 o'clock news. Among the friends they called was Sara Polk. They paid her a visit at her home in Griffin, Georgia, about twenty miles away from the Colliers' home that had now become the scene of a crime. When Sara opened the passenger side door, she was stunned when she saw the girls drenched in blood. Holly was as cool as a cucumber; but when her eyes drifted over to her friend Sandy, who was behind the wheel, she wasn't sharing that same carefree attitude. She was as white as a ghost and avoiding eye contact.

At first, Holly explained to Sara that they had been jumped but refused to tell her why. In the meantime, Sara retrieved some towels for the girls to clean up. While Holly was wiping off the blood, something caught Sara's eye. It was the inked to-do list scrawled across her arm. That's what prompted her to press Holly for the truth, so she cracked. Ominously, she held up the knife by her head, looked at it, and said, "We killed my grandparents."[16]

Shaken up, she immediately ordered them to leave. And so they did. She subsequently informed her parents about the murders and then she phoned the police.

While the police were conducting their investigation and trying to locate the girls, they were already at a beach on Tybee Island, approximately 234 miles away from Fayetteville. There, they met two boys who had just moved into a new house with their parents several hours earlier. One of the girls told the older brother that their grandmother just recently passed away and now they had no money. They asked him if he could pawn her grandmother's jewelry for cash, but he refused. They then asked if they could spend the night at his house—they had nowhere to go, nowhere to sleep. His mother gave them permission, having no clue that she was inviting two fresh murderers into her new home.

Overnight, U.S. Marshals were able to trace the girls' location on Tybee Island through Sarah Collier's cell phone that Holly still had with her. By 7:30 in the morning, there were approximately 20 officers scoping out Tybee Island in search of Holly and Sandy. They found the blue truck abandoned by the shoreline, but there was no sign of the girls anywhere. They began searching the backyards of beach houses when a teenage boy emerged from one of the homes to observe all of the commotion going on outside his balcony. He curiously asked the SWAT officers what was going on and they informed him that they were looking for the girls. The boy told them they were inside his house and his family had taken them in the night before.

Immediately, they forced their way into the home and marched to the second floor. They burst into one of the rooms, where they found Sandy and Holly embracing one another. Sandy still had one of the knives used to kill the Colliers peeping out of her back pocket. The girls were promptly handcuffed and the family watched in complete shock as they were led out of the house and ushered into police cruisers.

After she was booked at the police station, Holly asked a chilling question: "Are they really dead?"

"Who?" replied Tybee police officer Frederick L. Anderson III.

"Did they die all the way?"[17]

Lt. Col. Bruce Jordan of the Fayette County Sheriff's Department, who described Holly as "manipulative" and "stone-cold," claimed that Holly had laughed at the more than 25 police officers who had shown up at Tybee Beach during her apprehension.

"She was callous and cocky. She is the coldest and most heartless individual I've ever interviewed. It almost made her giddy to know we had brought that many people to arrest her," he said.[18]

Unlike Holly, who was not cooperative during the interrogation whatsoever, Sandy actually displayed remorse for her actions and tried to provide answers as truthfully as she could. When Jordan had asked why she was so compelled to kill Holly's grandparents, she replied, "We just wanted to leave to be together forever. Those people didn't deserve to die."[19]

Jordan later offered his opinion to reporters who wanted to know why two seemingly sweet and innocent adolescent girls would commit such a heinous crime against the Colliers, who were pillars of the community and very well known in the Baptist church. He told them that he thought Sandy was strictly in it for the love.

"I believe the evidence at trial will be that the motive was to gain freedom and be able to stay together forever," he asserted.[20]

During the investigation, police recovered two bloody knives (not including the one in Sandy's pocket) that they believed were used in the attack against Sarah and Carl wrapped in a towel as well as their bloodied clothes left behind in the truck. Through several interviews with neighbors, friends and family of the Colliers, and friends of Sandy and Holly, investigators learned that the girls had been planning the double murder for quite some time, and it was not as spontaneous as they were led to believe. Friends that Sandy had met during her previous time spent in juvenile detention claimed that she had called them looking to get her hands on a gun, which they planned to use on the Colliers, and Sandy had expressed fear that she was going to go to jail for murder.

And just five days before police would walk into the horrendous crime scene that would leave detectives scarred for life, Carl had confided to his son, Kevin, that Holly had threatened to kill them. Kevin advised them to call 911 for any little thing.

"I wish we'd taken that a little more seriously," he later said.[21]

Jordan also came across a poem Holly had written where she described her depression and how she cried herself to sleep. But there was one line that had sent shivers down his spine. It read: *All I want to do is kill.*

Court Proceedings

On the day of their arrest, both girls showed up to court wearing bulletproof vests and sniffled as they were read their set of charges: two counts of felony murder and two counts of malice murder. They would both be tried as adults and faced a maximum of life in prison without the possibility of parole unless a plea bargain was settled. They were to be held in separate juvenile detention facilities for the time being, and Sandy was placed on suicide watch after expressing the urge to kill herself.

Judy Chidester, Holly's court-appointed lawyer, said that her teenage client's world "has been turned upside down. She still appears to be in shock. She's acting like a scared 15-year-old which is exactly what she is."[22]

Two weeks later, a hand-shackled Sandy entered the courtroom for yet another hearing, her eyes red and puffy from crying. Holly also showed up for the hearing. They were both now facing a fresh charge on top of the other charges against them: armed robbery.

Sandy's attorney, Lloyd Walker, tried to pin some of the blame on the legal system for practically allowing Sandy to get to where she was today, explaining that his client had been in and out of juvenile detention and failed drug tests with only so much as a slap on the wrist as punishment. He also threw Sandy's mother, Sandra Maddox, under the bus for failing her daughter by not heeding probation orders and allowing Sandy and Holly to continue seeing each other in private.

"The evidence shows that a lot of people have failed Sandy," he said. "Up until now, everybody, including the state, has failed this child."[23]

While seeking a grant for bond, Tim and Beth Ketchum both testified on Sandy's behalf that their daughter was a "victim of society" and they would be equipped to surveil her 24 hours a day should she be released on bond.

Holly attended the court hearing to be read her charge of armed robbery. She kept her head down on the table the entire time, only occasionally looking up to converse with her lawyer. While requesting bond for her client, Judy Chidester admitted that there would simply be nowhere for Holly to stay, as her mother was in prison, her father was a quadriplegic, and nobody else would be willing to open their doors for such a dangerous and murderous teenager.

Without explanation, Fayette County Superior Court Judge Paschal English denied bond for both girls in his ruling. One family member shouted, "I love, you Sandy!"[24] as the girls exited the court once

Sandy Ketchum, 16 (left), and Holly Harvey, 15, pictured together in an undated photograph. They plotted the murders of the Colliers so they could have the freedom to be together (AP Photo).

the hearing wrapped up. Afterward, Judy told reporters that Holly was upset that nobody bothered to testify on her behalf and vouch for her bond in court.

Sentencing

On April 14, 2005, Holly pleaded guilty to two counts of malice murder after learning that Sandy, her co-defendant, planned to testify against her during the trial. As part of her plea deal, she had to stand before Judge English's hard stare and endure intense grilling for 30 minutes to help him comprehend why she would commit these grisly slayings. She described that it was Sandy's idea to steal the grandfather's truck, but Holly first made the flippant remark to kill them in order to achieve that.

"But I didn't mean nothing by that," she swore.[25]

She detailed how she had gone upstairs to grab the biggest knife she could find and practiced stabbing the mattress.

Judge English cut her off right there. "Why did you do that?"

"To see if the knife was sharp enough," she said.

"Sharp enough for what?"

"I guess..." she trailed off.

"Don't guess, tell me," he snapped. "You know. You did it."

"To see if it was sharp enough to stab them wherever the knife went," she answered.[26]

After telling him about how she had sprinted after her grandfather upstairs mid-attack and pulled the phone cord from the wall before he could call for help, she said, "He grabbed the knife and I thought he was going to stab me."[27]

She described the brutal stabbing that would finally send her grandfather crumbling to the floor. Before he would deliver her sentence, Judge English gazed at her in shock and disgust, only one question coming to mind: "Why?"

"For Sandy," she said. "So that we could be together."[28]

"I would have had no problem, had the law allowed us to do so, to have tried you for the death penalty in this case. However, that cannot be done because of your age," Judge English chillingly told Holly before her sentencing, his harsh words coated with hate.[29]

After he sentenced her to two consecutive life terms with the possibility of parole after serving 20 years, he asked her if that was a good deal. Holly said no. When asked what she thought she should have gotten instead, she answered, "I think I should be dead."

"We both agree on that," he muttered.[30]

Sandy's sentencing hearing was a speedier process. Because she had cooperated with police and agreed to testify against Holly in the event of a trial, she did not have to go into the grim details of the crime for Judge English and received a much lighter sentence in return: one life sentence and the possibility of parole after 14 years.

Outside the courtroom, Tim Ketchum apologized on his daughter's behalf. "I can't explain it. I'm not that type of person," he said. "I didn't raise her to be that type of person. I want to say to the community I'm very sorry this happened."[31]

Carla Harvey, who had since been released from prison, was present during the hearing. Dressed in a two-piece suit, she told reporters during a press conference that she took zero responsibility for what happened to her parents. She admitted that raising a child as a single mother was the most difficult task in her entire life and she had done the best she could, but "her actions were her doing and I can't hold myself responsible for that," she said. "You raise your children up, but they get to a point where they make their own decisions."[32]

Even though she was not proud of her daughter's heinous actions in the slightest, she stated that she would continue to be there for her and provide emotional support during her prison sentence as it was her duty as a mother.

Kevin Collier also commented during the press conference that his adoptive parents loved Holly unconditionally. "They would do anything for her," he said. "They would watch her whenever she needed to be watched. They would take her anywhere she needed to go."

Although he was incredibly hurt by what Holly did, taking away the most important people in his life who adopted him and raised him to be the incredible and successful man he was today, he said he also loved her unconditionally but it would take time for him to forgive her. "This is one part of the closure that I need and the family needs. Time will heal certain things. There's nothing we can do to bring my parents back, but time will heal the tensions and the feelings that I have for Holly."[33]

Afterword

Two years after their sentencing, both Holly Harvey and Sandy Ketchum's names would be published in the paper again, this time bringing in a more positive light.

Garbed in full cap and gown, 18-year-old Sandy was handed her GED after graduating from high school within the confines of razor wire, tall fences and prison bars at the Metro State Prison in south Atlanta while her father and stepmother proudly looked on.

Tim showed nothing but unwavering support for his daughter since her incarceration and puts effort into visiting her in prison every other weekend. He spoke of an entirely different version of events than what actually happened on that sultry August day—a story of self-defense.

"They [the grandparents] were beating the crap out of her [Holly]," he maintained. "The argument that started it was Holly wanting to go off to the beach with Sandy, and Sandy got caught in the middle of it."

Tim said he didn't doubt his daughter's version. "She's my best friend, my blood."[34]

Holly was serving time in Arrendale State Prison, about 70 miles northeast of Atlanta. Unlike her ex-partner, she did not seek a GED but, according to the attorney who represented her a few years earlier, she had adjusted to prison life with ease.

"She's doing pretty well," she commented on Holly's progress. "Because of her young age when she went to prison, there were adult women who watched out for her and protected her from unpleasant people that you can find in prison." She further stated that the former lovers no longer had contact.[35]

District attorney Scott Ballard also chimed in with his opinion that the death penalty would have been justified for the girls just for the sheer barbarity of their actions, if state law hadn't prevented minors from being sent to death row. He protested against their ever being released. "I don't ever want 'em out," he said. "I wouldn't want to take the chance, any chance, that they might do it to anyone else."[36]

The murders of Carl and Sarah Collier were a gruesome and appalling crime that shook the faith-bound community of Fayetteville, which once took pride in its safe and sound city and left the Colliers' loved ones scarred and fellow locals grieving the loss of two people who undeservedly had their lives taken away with so much dishonor. However, despite this, Carl and Sarah Collier left a godly impact behind that would touch many others within the Baptist church.

"Many times they could have thrown up their hands and said, 'I quit,'" said their pastor, the Reverend Glenn Stringham. "They chose, basically, to give their life to their granddaughter because of their love for her."[37]

The community regularly gathered to pray and remember the patience, selflessness, and sacrifices of the ever-loving Colliers as motivating forces to heal, restore and strengthen faith, all while doing their best to model the virtuous examples that Sarah and Carl epitomized throughout their lives.

Derek and Alex King
(2001)

In the brisk early morning hours of November 26, 2001, dispatchers received a call from a concerned resident from Cantonment, Florida, a small community in the suburbs about 10 miles north of Pensacola. The caller reported that the house behind him was in flames. Within a matter of minutes, fire crews from Escambia County were racing down the 1100 block of Muscogee Road, their blaring alarms disturbing every neighbor from their slumber. They stopped before one small, wood-framed home. These types of houses are highly flammable, making it seem like an open-and-shut case to first responders at first glance. Only half of it was engulfed in the blazing fire. The flames were immediately extinguished, damaging only one bedroom.[1] Firefighters subsequently began the process of searching for any survivors and investigating the scene to determine the source of the fire per standard protocol. And what they discovered was jarring.

Firefighters detected suspicious spill patterns on the floor, which indicated that this was no accidental fire. Whoever was responsible had deliberately set the house ablaze and used an accelerant to fuel the flames.

They continued their search around the small home for survivors, moving on to the opposite side that remained unscathed by the fire. When they entered the living room, they made an even more disturbing discovery: what they found was a man who appeared to be in his early 40s seemingly asleep in his chair, his feet propped up on the love seat, hands resting across his stomach and a cup of coffee wedged between his leg and the chair. Firefighters initially assumed that he had succumbed to the toxic fumes and died that way.

But a closer look painted a much, much more sinister story. They noticed that the man had sustained very serious head wounds, including a cracked-open skull and a bashed-in face. They also noticed blood spatter on the walls around him. A deputy on the scene could not tell if he had taken repeated blows to the head or if the fire could have "caused his head to pop like an eggshell."[2] They would need to call on the expertise of a team of homicide investigators for a second opinion. They arrived shortly before dawn. Among them was Detective John Sanderson. A quick look at the deceased man's body told him that, without a doubt, this man had died of blunt force trauma to the head.

And just like that, the small, single-story home at 1104 Muscogee Road became a crime scene.

Investigation

Detectives soon learned from curious neighbors who flocked to the property to see what the commotion was about that the dead man was 40-year-old Terry King and that he had only moved into the residence the past summer. He kept to himself a lot, so neighbors didn't really know anything else about him, except one crucial detail that would spark the investigators' interest. They learned, through neighbors, that Terry King did not live alone. He lived with his two sons, Derek and Alex, ages 13 and 12.

But strangely, his kids were nowhere to be found. Might they be staying with some friends or relatives for the night? Or perhaps ... could they have been abducted by the intruder who killed their father and set the house ablaze? Whatever the case, authorities could not rule out the possibility that the boys could be in serious danger, so they made it their next priority to locate the missing boys.

A quick background check later in the day turned up something interesting. Just ten days before, on Friday, November 16, Terry had reported his two sons missing after they failed to come home from Ransom Middle, where they attended school. Police also learned that Terry had taken it upon himself to call the *Pensacola News Journal* to vent his frustration with the Escambia County Sheriff's Department's lack of effort to find his children. He told them he did not believe that they ran away as they didn't seem to have taken anything of value with them, but he believed they had been kidnapped. By whom? Terry didn't say.[3]

However, police also learned that Terry's children were returned to him after a week of being missing, as neighbors reported seeing the boys with their father outside in the yard just hours before he died. With this newfound knowledge they had about Alex and Derek being reported as missing by their father just days before in a possible kidnapping case, and now being nowhere to be found once again, they could not rule out the possibility that they might very well be in danger. Finding them safe was paramount.[4]

Very early on in the investigation, a suspicious character arrived at the scene of the crime and spoke with police. He introduced himself as Rick Chavis, a family friend of the Kings. He claimed he had heard about the fire at 1104 Muscogee Road on his police scanner and, recognizing that it was his good friend Terry's house, immediately rushed over to make sure everything was okay. Right away, this waved a red flag for one important reason: the police scanner never revealed the precise address of the house fire. So if Rick Chavis heard about the report from the police scanner, how did he know this was Terry King's residence?

Wanting to know more about Rick Chavis, the police ran a quick background check later that morning, which revealed some rather alarming information. They discovered that back in 1984, he was convicted of sexually assaulting two 13-year-old boys, for which he served six months in jail. His five-year probation was revoked, and he was placed behind bars again two years later for burglary and petty theft, serving three years.[5]

With very good reason, Detective John Sanderson began to suspect that Rick Chavis might have more knowledge in connection with Terry King's murder than he was letting on and questioned what his involvement was in the case. At 11 a.m. that same day, with Rick's permission, police took a look around his mobile home in Brentwood. The 40-year-old convicted child molester had surveillance cameras installed around the outside of his house, along with a high privacy fence bordering his yard equipped with an electric fence on top of it and a "WARNING NO TRESPASSING" sign plastered on his gate. They did not find Alex and Derek as they had hoped, but they did collect some rather strange evidence: a broken, red aluminum baseball bat in the backyard; a strip of gauze with what appeared to be blood; a marijuana pipe; boys' clothes; a computer system and software; and, perhaps most disturbing of all, a photograph of Alex King plastered on the wall above Chavis's bed.[6]

And the search through the King home turned up even more

disturbing evidence. Investigators came across what appeared to be a journal belonging to Alex, the younger of the two brothers. It revealed some disturbing notes about his love for Chavis that would make their stomachs churn.

> *My life used to be cloudy before I made friends with Rick. I had a whole lifetime ahead of me and I didn't know what to do with it. I had no goals. I was confused. What to be? Teacher? Governor? President? What? I thought that was what life was about. But I was wrong. Rick let me see what I didn't understand. Life isn't about having a job. Life isn't about importance. Fame. My ultimate goal in life now is what his is. It is about sharing your life with someone elses [sic]. Before I met Rick I was straight but now I am gay.*[7]

Clearly, there was something sickening going on. Police were certain that Chavis must have had an inappropriate relationship with Terry's sons and must be somehow involved in his twisted murder. They had a large puzzle with several missing pieces that only the King brothers held. And if they didn't find the King brothers, they might never know the truth about what happened in the early morning hours of November 26, 2001.

All of that would change the following day.

～

On November 27, the sheriff's office received a surprise. Whether that was a pleasant surprise or not was unclear at the time. It was Rick Chavis, but he wasn't alone.

He was in the company of Derek and Alex King.

The boys claimed that they spent the last two days in the woods before they called Rick Chavis for help. Rick, of course, brought them to the Escambia County Sheriff's Office immediately. The brothers were done with hiding; they were ready to tell the truth.

So Detective John Sanderson took them in for questioning but decided to interview them separately for the purpose of determining whether their stories aligned precisely. Under Florida law, juveniles are allowed to be questioned by police without a parent or guardian present.

While initially the detective felt sorry for the boys who had just lost their father in such a tragic manner, his empathy withered away when they began to explain what happened. The truth was colder than the police initially suspected.

The detective decided to start with Derek, the elder of the two.

When he inquired about the events on the night Terry was found dead by firefighters, Derek confessed to having killed him, but it wasn't in cold blood, he said. His father had grabbed his brother Alex by the wrist and thrown him to the floor. Derek, acting on his protective instinct as the older brother, picked up an aluminum baseball bat and bludgeoned Terry to death. It was all in self-defense, he claimed.

But his version of events wasn't exactly adding up with the story that the crime scene told. Derek wasn't easily going to fool Detective John Sanderson, who had a great deal of experience dealing with homicides. Sanderson remembered the crime scene vividly, from the blood spatter tarnishing the walls to Terry King's body resting snug in his chair. He was most likely sleeping when the murder happened. There was no possible way that Terry posed a threat to his sons in that moment.

When Detective John Sanderson passively mentioned that crime scenes told stories and that he was able to determine his father's cause of death and what he was doing as he died, Derek shifted his account of what happened dramatically. Feeling backed into a corner, he suddenly admitted to killing his father in cold blood while he was sound asleep in his chair.

"I went in there, I hit him once, and I heard him moan," Derek explained. "And then I was afraid that he might wake up and see us so I just kept hitting him. Hit him somewhere around ten times."[8]

Derek admitted that Alex was standing right next to him the entire time, watching each and every hit inflicted by the older brother. Afterward, he claimed he had lit the frayed end of a rug so as to conceal the crime he committed, which escalated into the house fire that firefighters would soon be hosing down. Interestingly, Derek never admitted to using an accelerant and denied having wet the rug before igniting it, despite the distinct pour patterns observed by firefighters.

But what would drive two young boys barely in their teens to brutally murder their father, a seemingly hard-working man who tended to keep to himself and tried his best to provide for his family?

According to the older brother, they didn't want to face punishment for running away a couple of days earlier. While he denied that their father was ever physically abusive besides some pushing and shoving, he claimed he could be abusive in other ways.

"Did he threaten you in any way?" asked the detective.

"No, sir. Not, like, verbally," he responded.

"Okay, what do you mean?"

"Like he was ... he was staring me down some,"[9] answered Derek, who said he felt that the stares were a form of mental abuse. He told Detective John Sanderson that sometimes, as punishment, Terry would force the brothers to sit in a room where he would stare them down menacingly.

After the interview wrapped up, Detective John Sanderson moved on to the younger brother, hoping to extract more information about what happened. As predicted, when he inquired about the events that had unfolded that fateful night, Alex began reiterating the exact same story of self-defense as his brother. But when Alex started feeling pressured to tell the truth, he immediately backpedaled, and, just like Derek, the truth began pouring out. He was now admitting that Derek bludgeoned his sleeping father to death while he stood and watched the whole time. But even though Derek was the one to take the bat to his father's head, it was Alex who came up with the idea, he confessed. He was even the one to suggest that they use a hammer, but both settled for the bat, agreeing that it was the better choice.

The 12-year-old, who only weighed 75 pounds and barely stood five feet tall, described the whole ordeal in macabre detail.

"The noise he made, the first impact was a groan, and he squeezed his eyes shut. You could tell that he was in pain. The second time he made contact, which was the third time he swung, I think it knocked him out," he said. "But the fourth time he swung, the third time he made contact, the blood came from his forehead so I knew he was out. By the time he got done he was still trying to breathe."

He revealed that he was afraid that his father would spank them as punishment for running away. In the past, he claimed, Terry had spanked him with a belt. He also talked about the alleged mental abuse he suffered at the hands of Terry.

"It had been going on for a real long time," he told the officer. "I got informed by someone that he was doing this and so—"

Detective John Sanderson cut him off right there. "Who informed you of that?"

"Um, I don't really want to say...."

"Well, no, you need to tell us who informed you of it. It was Rick, wasn't it?" he pressed with a hint of suspicion in his tone.

"Yeah," the 12-year-old admitted.

"Rick said that he was mentally abusing you?"

Alex described their relationship as "good friends" and confirmed that Rick indeed told the boys that their father's staring-down actions were a form of mental abuse.

"Until you told him, did Rick know anything about what happened that night? Did he know beforehand it was going to happen? Did he know right after?"

"He knew, I don't think he knew anything beforehand. He said that he felt it might come down to this, but we didn't tell him about it beforehand," said Alex.[10]

Investigators still believed that there was more going on than what the boys admitted, and they couldn't shake the feeling that Rick Chavis had a role in it, either directly or indirectly. Still, the King brothers confessed to premeditated murder with their own mouths, and their accounts were consistent with the detectives' findings at the scene of murder, so they had sufficient grounds to arrest both Alex and Derek. The following day, the boys were both charged with an open count of murder and sent to the county's juvenile detention facility.

Rick Chavis was accused of murder, child molestation, and tampering with evidence, among other crimes (AP Photo/Phil Coale).

Even though the police had already found the culprits for Terry King's brutal murder, they were not in any way done with their investigation. They brought Rick Chavis in for further questioning, during which he would basically admit to having more involvement in the case than he was originally letting on.

The first two times they questioned him, he denied having any knowledge of the boys' whereabouts until the day after the killing. But officers obtained phone records from an EZ Serve, a convenience store located only half a mile away from the King residence. It clearly indicated that only two minutes after the report of the house fire was called in, there had been a call made from the pay phone at the EZ Serve to Chavis's home.

Chavis could no longer deny the evidence that was right before him. He finally disclosed that, yes, the boys did call him right after committing the murder, and shortly after, he picked them up and brought them back to his place, where he kept them for two nights and even washed their blood-stained clothes before escorting them to the police station. He also admitted to police that during the week that Derek and Alex were missing, they weren't actually hiding out in the woods like they had claimed; they were with him. When Terry King came to his mobile home to search for his sons, Chavis hid them in the back bedroom and pretended to help his friend look for the boys.

But the one thing he had always adamantly denied was having participated in the murder of Terry King or having any prior knowledge that it was going to happen. However, none of that mattered, because Chavis had just unknowingly confessed to two crimes that warranted jail time. On December 11, two weeks after Terry's murder, the 40-year-old ex-con was called to court to testify for a closed-door grand jury proceeding. Right after, he was arrested and arraigned on two charges: accessory after the fact for taking the boys into hiding after they had just committed a serious crime and tampering with evidence for washing their clothing. He was thrown into the Escambia County jail and held on a $50,000 bond.

The very same day, the King brothers appeared in court to face their charges. They were indicted on first-degree murder and arson charges by a grand jury; they would be tried as adults. On this day, they officially became the youngest murder suspects in the state of Florida. Since in the eyes of the law they were deemed adults, they had to be transferred to an adult county jail—the same jail that Chavis was currently confined in—while they awaited trial. The next day, on December 12, Alex and Derek both pleaded not guilty.[11]

The case grabbed headlines all around the country and even around the world. Surely, a story about two teenage boys bludgeoning their father to death, setting their house on fire and fleeing the scene was enough to pique the nation's interest, especially when it involved a creepy child molester looming somewhere in the picture. In a subsequent bond hearing, the media had the opportunity to finally see Alex and Derek in the flesh. Even with the knowledge of the horrendous, evil crime they had confessed to committing, their boyish looks and angelic smiles were enough to capture the hearts and sympathy of curious onlookers. Alex, standing at 4'7", could barely see over the rail of the jury box. Derek, who had a few inches on him, was more charming and outgoing. He waved and smiled at everyone.

People were in denial that these two innocent-looking boys could have committed such a gruesome and shocking murder on their own. Naturally, they were searching for someone else to point the finger at. And Chavis the child molester made himself an easy target for blame.

Everyone wanted to know more. Who were the members of the King family? And what exactly was Rick Chavis's relationship to them?

Backstory

Terry King met Janet French in 1985. He fell in love with and eventually moved in with her. Three years later, on May 4, 1988, Janet gave birth to their first child, Derek. Then, on July 12, just a little over a year after Derek came into this world, Janet gave birth to their second son. They named him Alex. Terry and Janet continued to live together for many more years, but the couple never married. Terry, who worked a series of menial jobs such as a printer and a caregiver for an elderly man, was also a stay-at-home father. He struggled to support his family on minimum wage work while Janet contributed to paying the bills with whatever money she made from her job as a nightclub dancer. But there was a problem: the couple had a serious spending issue and didn't know how to prioritize their spending, often blowing their paychecks on their social life and Terry's car hobby. Linda Walker, the King boys' maternal grandmother, and her husband would frequently lend the family money to help with groceries and utilities.

In 1991, Janet became pregnant again. But not by Terry. Instead, she was impregnated by another, unknown man, and she gave birth to a set of twin boys. Terry agreed to help raise these newborns as his own, and their struggle to provide and care for the kids only became more onerous. Terry continued to work long, grueling hours while Janet was forced to be a stay-at-home mother. More than once, Terry, Janet, and the kids moved in with Linda, but things would never work out, and they would move back into their own place.

The household was in a chronic state of disorder and chaos, as Janet rarely issued discipline for the children and Terry was seldom at home to do it himself. The kids were neglected and were rarely bathed. Janet had a habit of staying up late into the early morning hours and sleeping in during the day, thus never being able to wake up on time to take her kids to school. She solved this issue by letting her kids stay up until five in the morning sometimes and taking them to school later on in the day. Every single day, Derek was late to kindergarten. Not surprisingly, he was far behind the other children in his class.

In the middle of Derek's kindergarten year, when he was just five years old, he moved in with his grandparents. This move sparked immediate positive results. Linda enrolled Derek in a new school, where he thrived. His attendance improved, and he finally learned how to skip, hop and talk. His grandparents took him camping, boating and fishing. This angered Terry, who only saw his son occasionally. He accused Linda of teaching his son how to be a "redneck." Just before Derek started the first grade, Terry took Derek back into his care.

The horrible living conditions at the family home had not improved. Eventually, looking after four rowdy boys all under the age of six running around and tearing the house apart every day became too much for Janet to bear. In 1994, the mother just left, abandoning all of her children. She seldom visited afterward, leaving all of the parental responsibilities on Terry's shoulders.[12]

Despite their one-year age difference, Derek and Alex had quite a few distinct differences. Derek was a few inches taller and had a mop of dark brown hair paired with blue eyes and an impish smile. Although a bright and outgoing kid, he suffered from ADHD, so he was more hyperactive and tended to get in trouble often. Alex, on the other hand, was a much smaller boy with blond hair framing his more angular face. Unlike his older brother, he was shyer and more reserved, preferring to spend his time buried in books, even at an early age.

Now that Terry was burdened with four children to care for on his own, he had to set things straight around the house by escalating his no-nonsense attitude. He tried to be a strict father, forcing the kids to look him in the eye whenever he spoke to them and snapping his fingers in their faces whenever they glanced away and murmured something snarky. He worked a string of minimum wage jobs and seemed to be holding down the fort well on his own at first. But soon, the single father was struggling to make ends meet. He became swamped with too many problems. He suffered from a sleep disorder called narcolepsy, had a few traffic accidents, and was caught writing bad checks to acquire food for his family.

With too much on his plate to handle as a single parent, he knew he needed to get his life in order. He placed the four boys in a group home, the Heritage Home in Pace, Florida, described as a "Christian-oriented" facility for children. The kids stayed there for several months. It closed down in 1994. Derek, Alex and the twins were transferred to separate foster families. The twins were eventually adopted. But Alex was now split from his blood brother, and, for the first time in his life, he was completely alone. The six-year-old failed to acclimate to his new environment and was constantly crying, so he was returned to Terry's care.

After Alex moved back in with his dad, the family became much more reclusive. Extended relatives rarely, if ever, heard from them, which they attributed to Terry's severe trust issues that stemmed from Janet and other life experiences with people that left him emotionally scarred. Meanwhile, Derek was eventually taken into private foster care by Pace High School principal Frank Lay and his family in Pace, Florida. Alex and Derek were now living completely separate lives and would not have any contact for the next several years.

Overall, Alex was quite happy to be living with his father again. As he aged, he remained the same clever child and eager bookworm he was always known to be. He was still quiet and reclusive, much like his father, but was well-behaved kid nonetheless and regularly attended the Pentecostal church with relatives. Terry ultimately pulled Alex from school at an early age and would sometimes bring his son along to work with him. He usually sat in the lunch room reading Harry Potter books, playing on his Game Boy, coloring or napping.[13]

And this is where Rick Chavis entered the picture.

Rick Chavis, sometimes called "Ricky," was an old friend of Terry's whom he met several years prior when they lived in the same trailer park. It is unknown if Terry was aware of Chavis's prior convictions before he entrusted him with regularly babysitting his seven-year-old son while he was busy with work and such, but Rick became an important figure in Alex's young life nevertheless, filling the role of a so-called "family friend."

According to Alex's written statement to police, it was shortly after his 12th birthday that Rick began taking a disturbing interest in the child and started to sexually abuse him.[14] Of course, having been groomed for such a long time, Alex's innocent mind did not interpret this sexual relationship as inappropriate. Rick had manipulated him so well that he successfully convinced the pre-teen that he was homosexual and they were in love with each other.

About 17 miles away in Pace, Derek wasn't having the smoothest transition of his own, either. Although he was living in a 2,500-square-foot house surrounded by plenty of toys, a swimming pool, and access to a PlayStation, it wasn't enough to keep him from stirring up trouble wherever he went. From the start, Derek demonstrated some serious behavioral problems, both at school and at home, that would be attributed to his ADHD. Within the first two weeks of first grade, he was sent home for being too disruptive in class.

Although he was described as a sweet, outgoing and loving child who was popular at school, played in a youth basketball league and was active at Olive Baptist Church where his foster dad was a deacon, his rebellion only worsened once he hit his teenage years. His impulsivity and defiant behavior were at their maximum. He lied frequently and stole from and manipulated everyone around him. He developed a fascination with starting small fires and also turned to drugs, even sniffing lighter fluid. He began acting out in violent ways, like slashing his mattress with a razor when he got upset.

The 13-year-old's aggression became too out of control for the Lays to handle, and they reached their breaking point. They worried that he might pose a threat to other children. To straighten out his behavior, they threatened to send him to military school. But there was one little problem—they didn't have legal custody of Derek. So they phoned Derek's biological parents and asked for permission to send their son to military school.

But Terry refused. So, on October 1, 2001, they sent Derek to live with his father in a small shack in Cantonment, Florida, a poor suburb of Pensacola.

When Terry came to pick up his son, Frank Lay issued one warning about Derek: "You're not ready for this."[15]

But this warning didn't deter Terry, who was more than happy to have his son back. Finally, after several years of no contact, the Kings were reunited as a family.

∽

One may have hoped that Terry, Alex, and Derek would have their happily ever after. Perhaps it would involve plenty of father-and-son bonding over fishing, wrestling and even Terry teaching his kids how to drive a car one day.

But in two months, Terry's battered corpse would be discovered in his blazing home and his two sons would be charged with his murder. What might have happened between the time Derek first moved in and the early morning hours of November 26 that ultimately led to this utter tragedy?

Terry was thrilled at this fresh start to raise his children, but things quickly began going awry. Derek was said to have had a difficult time adapting to his new home, specifically conforming to his father's strict rules. Terry had enrolled the boys in Ransom Middle School and instructed them to come straight home after each school day and lock the door. The home lacked a television, phone, or stereo, since loud noises and music seemed to trigger Derek's aggression, so the boys couldn't even entertain themselves while they were cooped up inside, isolated from the rest of the world. The loneliness was slowly gnawing away at them.[16]

The only social life they seemed to have outside of school was when Chavis would pick them up after school and bring them to his place. Chavis's fenced compound was designed to mimic every kid's dream house after a dreary day at school, exactly as one would expect from a pedophile. Unlike their father's home, it was not at all lacking in entertainment for the King brothers to indulge in. Chavis's dwelling was loaded with video games, computers, even television. It was also revealed that Chavis would supply the kids with marijuana. Chavis practically let the kids do whatever they wanted, whenever they wanted. So, safely speaking, Alex and Derek were never bored during their time with Chavis.

For the first month and a half after Derek moved in, the brothers spent most of their days hanging out with Chavis. And it is believed that during this period, Chavis began wielding his adult influence over their naive, malleable minds. The kids often complained about their father's torturous "stare-downs" which Chavis convinced them was mental abuse. He told the boys that if they ever wanted to run away, they would always have a place to stay with him. His unhealthy obsession with Alex festered and the molestation continued. It was very apparent that the much older male was trying to pit father against sons.

In early November, it seemed as though Terry began catching on to his longtime friend's mind games because he started creating more distance between Chavis and his sons. But it was too late to undo all of the manipulation. Chavis had already succeeded in getting into the brothers' heads, because on Friday, November 16, 2001, the brothers ran away. Terry had last seen them when he dropped them off at school, but they never returned home at the end of the day. He promptly called police to report his sons missing and began plastering missing persons fliers all around town. For reasons that are unknown, he paid Ransom Middle School a visit and had Rick Chavis's name removed from the list of individuals permitted to pick up his children. Chavis's name was the only one even on the list. It was obvious, now, that Terry suspected something was off and no longer wanted his long-time trusted friend having contact with his children.

During the eight days that Terry was relentlessly searching for his sons, they were, not surprisingly, hiding in Rick's house. Rick continued to manipulate the boys. He again told Alex he was gay and only he could understand him. He allowed the boys to skip school, smoke marijuana and stay up late. He offered to have sex with Derek and allowed him to smoke cigarettes. Derek witnessed Rick kissing Alex a lot while the boy sat on his lap.[17] When Terry went looking for his sons in Rick's mobile home, Chavis hid the boys in the back bedroom and pretended to help Terry search for them.

On November 24, Chavis drove Derek all the way to Pace so he could visit a girl that lived just down the street from his old foster home. The girl's parents knew he had run away and immediately called Frank Lay. When the Lays arrived, Derek froze in shock. Then he began pleading.

"I can't go back to my dad's house!" he begged.[18]

He then tried to run, but Frank Lay caught up with him. Derek continued to beg, saying that his father was a control freak. Frank asked him why he was having such a hard time adjusting to his new home life if he got along with Alex.

"Alex hates my dad. He hates him. He said he'd like to see him dead."[19]

And, in a final desperate plea, he said, "You can't send us back because my brother is going to kill him. We already have a plan."[20]

Regardless, Derek's claims didn't cause much alarm, and he was promptly returned to his father by the police. Somewhere along the line, Chavis started getting nervous about Derek opening his mouth, so on November 25, he rang up his old friend and told him he had found Alex. Both of the brothers claimed they had been hiding out in the woods.

After both of the brothers were returned to their father's care, the trio spent the rest of the evening and night taking down all of the missing persons fliers posted around town.

Within a few hours, Terry King would be found slumped in his recliner, his brains and blood sprayed all over the walls.

Court Proceedings

Even behind bars, Chavis still tried to control the young boys like puppets on a string. He was caught making repeated attempts to reach out to the Alex and Derek inside the jail in a series of creative ways. The first time he was caught by guards carving the words "Alex don't trust..." in the cement in the jail's recreation area. The second time he left another message on the wall of a holding room at the courthouse. In it, he warned the brothers not to trust anyone or change their statements. Guards also came across a note in the trash can of Alex and Derek's shared jail cell, where the boys played games and watched TV.

The note read: "*I L U forever. Be strong and patient. I'm still with you. Watch who you talk to. I will always be there for you, nothing changed, everything is still the same, even in court.*"[21]

Chavis, of course, denied being the author of these perverse messages.

As if by magic, the powerful hold he once possessed over Derek and Alex seemed to vanish. Now, the boys turned their backs on him and would pull a stunt that would change the entire game. Rumors circulated that the brothers now claimed that Rick, and Rick alone, was responsible for the murder of Terry King. So in April 2002, when a grand jury reviewed Rick Chavis's charges, the prosecutor summoned the King brothers to court to verify these rumors.

It was true, they testified.

Now, Rick Chavis was being indicted for kidnapping, child molestation, and murder on top of the other charges that were stacked against him. Most of the population following the case were relieved to finally hear the truth of it all, as nobody wanted to believe that two endearing teenage boys would be capable of such a monstrous act. It was much easier on the conscience to pin the blame on the convicted child molester. The authorities and prosecutors, however, did not share this same glee. Neither of them believed Rick was solely responsible for

Terry King's murder. Now, three individuals were going to be tried for the same murder.

Nobody could predict what the outcome would be. All they could do was wait and see.

⁓

It was decided that Rick Chavis would have his trial first. Prosecutor David Rimmer only had a few months to strategize his case after the unpredictable change of story from the King brothers. Chavis was guilty of many vile crimes, Rimmer thought to himself, but he wasn't a murderer. Yet here he was, prosecuting a potentially innocent man (of homicide, at least) when he was almost positive that the true culprits were Alex and Derek. So, with only four months to prepare, he finally concocted a plan.

The trial of Rick Chavis commenced in August 2002. The prosecution argued that although Rick Chavis was not the one who actually took the bat to Terry King's head and battered him to death, he was, however, responsible for planting the seed in Derek and Alex's minds.

This is what is known as the "principal theory." In Florida, an individual is guilty of being a principal to a crime if he helped another "co-conspirator" carry it out, directly or indirectly. He does not actually have to be present while the crime is being committed in order to be held equally as liable as the person who actually committed the crimes he has been accused of. To prove that someone is a principal, the state would have to prove two crucial elements:

    1. He had a conscious intent that the criminal act be done and
    2. He did some act or said some word which was intended to incite, cause, encourage, assist, or advise the other person or persons to actually commit the crime.[22]

To further validate the theory that the older man was very much involved, the state called upon the King brothers to testify with immunity about the early morning hours when their father was killed. Nothing they were to say could be used against them. Unfortunately, this move proved to be a mistake, as it precisely deviated from the point David Rimmer was trying to make. The prosecutor wanted to prove that Rick was a principal to murder by persuading the younger boys to kill their father. But when Alex and Derek took the stand, they maintained that Rick committed the murder himself. This made their testimony flawed and unreliable, and it became all too easy for the prosecution's assertions to be discredited.

"Now, did you develop a relationship with Ricky Chavis?" the prosecutor asked Alex on the stand.

"Yes, sir."

"Did you, at some point, believe that you were in love with Ricky Chavis?"

"Yes, sir."[23]

Prosecutor David Rimmer approached him and produced a note with the initials "AK" and "RC." Alex confirmed that this was his handwriting and the initials stood for his and Rick's names. The state produced another note in which Alex had written "I love you Rick" in block letters. Another letter handwritten by Alex was shown to him, and Alex was asked to read it aloud for the court.

"Alex Steven King loves Ricky Marvin Chavis so, so much, always and forever," Alex read.

Rimmer presented several more similar love notes along with a letter written for his father, Terry King, and had Alex verify that he had written each of them. Rimmer confronted Alex with one such letter where Alex stated that before he met Rick he was heterosexual.

"At the time you wrote this note, did you think you were gay?" asked Rimmer.

"Yes, sir," replied Alex.

"Why did you think you were gay?"

"Because Rick told me that."

"Alex, did you have a sexual relationship with Ricky Chavis?"

"Yes."[24]

The 13-year-old charged with first-degree murder kept his eyes down the entire time, speaking just barely above a whisper as he answered the prosecutor's questions.

"I was in love with Rick. He let me play video games and stuff. It was fun living at his house," he said.[25]

During the direct examination, Alex claimed that they called Chavis on November 25, 2001, to pick them up after his father had grabbed his wrist and thrown him across the room. Rick arrived in no time and instructed them to hide out in the trunk of his car and wait while he went in to talk to Terry. They had no knowledge of what was going on until minutes later, when he re-emerged and broke the tragic news to the brothers.

"He said there had been a fight, said there had been an accident,"

Alex testified during questioning by Prosecutor David Rimmer. "He said that my dad was dead and then he said he had done it for us and he said that my dad would have killed us before he let us live with him."[26]

Derek King pretty much corroborated the new story Alex described on the stand. Unlike his younger brother, who kept his eyes down the entire time and answered questions quietly, Derek spoke with clarity, looking the attorneys right in the eyes. He told the jury that after the murder, Ricky had instructed the boys to cover for him and take the blame for what happened.

"What did he say about you and Alex taking the blame?" asked David Rimmer.

"He said that we had to take the blame for him because he promised his mom right before she died that he would never get locked up again."[27]

The state played the taped recording of the Kings' confessions they made on the day that Chavis had escorted them to the police station for the jury in the hopes that they would ignore their new story and pick this up as an example of the clear influence Chavis had over the young boys.[28] Overall, Rimmer was satisfied with how the testimonies from Alex and Derek went. During the trial, Rick Chavis seemed amused by everything going on. He would often rock back and forth in his chair with a smirk on his face, seemingly relishing the spotlight.

But there were several inconsistencies between the brothers' testimonies. For one, it still didn't make a lot of sense how Terry was found resting peacefully in his recliner when a supposedly nasty fight had ensued between him and Chavis. The defense would cast a lot of doubt on the teenage boys' credibility as seen throughout the cross-examination.

Chavis's defense attorney, Michael Rollo, inquired about Alex's shoes, which tested positive for paint thinner, a known fire accelerant. The boy attributed it to earlier housework. When he asked Derek why he had changed his story so many times, the 14-year-old told him, "I didn't want to spend the rest of my life in prison for somebody else's act."[29]

Furthermore, as pointed out by the defense, Alex testified that Chavis told him he had used a baseball bat after he had emerged from the house. But Derek testified that Chavis didn't make any mention of what weapon, if any, was used against his father.

Rollo also dug into Derek's troubled past to demonstrate that the youth was not the innocent he may have appeared to be on the outside.

There were signs of early disturbances even before he moved back in with his father that indicated he was on the path to a life of crime, starting from his history of lying and stealing to starting fires when he lived with his old foster family in Pace and even assaulting a prison guard.

"We don't like to say that children with cherubim faces can be cold, calculating, homicidal psychopaths," said Rollo.[30]

But the case would take yet another unpredictable turn that would change everything. As soon as the state rested its case, Judge Frank Bell decided that Rick Chavis could no longer be tried for being a principal to murder but rather as the one who actually committed the murder. Just like that, the entire argument Rimmer had spent months carefully devising fell to pieces. He was now at a loss for what to do or say to persuade the jury to convict the defendant. At this point in the trial, his hands were tied.

During his closing arguments, he simply told the ladies and gentlemen of the jury, "I'm going to let you decide. I don't have a dog in this fight."[31]

Once they did, the judge decided to seal the verdict and not disclose the jury's decision until after Alex and Derek finished their trial.

Innocent or Guilty?

In the early morning hours of November 26, 2001, someone took a bat to Terry King's head multiple times. The million-dollar question was *who*.

The trial of Derek and Alex, now 14 and 13, set out to settle the case and determine the question once and for all on September 3, 2002.

Previously, Rimmer had called on the boys to testify that Ricky Chavis was the one who killed their father and coaxed the boys into taking the fall for his own heinous actions. Now, Rimmer was prosecuting Alex and Derek for the exact same murder. It was an unusual circumstance that the court had rarely seen before, and it was going to be tricky for Rimmer to sway the jury's minds from their biases formed by the previous trial. His second theory was that the King brothers were guilty of murdering Terry King, and one of the brothers had convinced the other to do the evil deed.

He focused on the boys' original confessions to police, highlighting the inconsistencies. First, they both claimed to have killed their father in self-defense, but after some pressing, they both backtracked and told a completely different version of events that corroborated the other's story. Given the fact that they were interrogated separately by investigators, this was very telling. The first story was a lie invented by Chavis. The second story, argued Rimmer, was the truth.

With that, the prosecutor had to implicitly convince the jury that the Kings' testimonies from Chavis's trial were completely false. Consider it perjury, if you will.[32]

The defense team, consisting of Sharon Potter and James Stokes, called Rimmer's new theory into question. They noted some discrepancies in Alex and Derek's original confessions, including the origins of the fire. For example, Derek had told police he started it by setting one of the rugs on fire. He adamantly denied ever using any sort of accelerant, contrary to the spill patterns found in the house by fire personnel and police. Why, James Stokes wondered, would the boys confess to murder and arson but deny using an accelerant?

Second, they pointed out how the brothers used very "mature" vocabulary uncommon for boys of their age. Clearly, they were regurgitating the same fabricated narrative like a loop recording that was drilled into their heads by Ricky Chavis. Prosecutor Rimmer found this implication preposterous. Anyone who had ever had a single conversation with Ricky Chavis could tell that he was not the brightest bulb in the chandelier. He wasn't nearly as eloquent as the kids.

On the second day of the trial, the defense had Alex take the stand after previously deciding that only one of the brothers should testify in their defense.

The soft-spoken 13-year-old repeated the same story to the jury as before: while they waited in the car, Chavis entered their home and killed their father. But he never informed them that their father was dead until they got back to his place.

"He pulled me aside into his bedroom and told me there was a fight between him and my dad," he testified. "He was saying how bad it was, saying it was terrible. And he was saying that if we took the blame we could get off on self-defense because we were juveniles."

Defense attorney Stokes asked, "And did you rehearse what you were to say to the police?"

"Yes, sir," the young boy affirmed. "We were talking about it constantly—well, basically constantly, during the time we spent at his house."[33]

After three days of testimony, it was now the jury's turn to sort it all out for themselves. But before that, Rimmer urged the jury to not allow their ultimate decision to be influenced by the boys' young ages and innocent faces. He also read a letter that Alex had written for his father, in which he accused Terry of mental abuse and referred to their home as a prison.

During deliberation, the jurors struggled to reach a conclusion after hearing so many different explanations and conflicting accounts from both sides. The boys went from claiming self-defense to taking full responsibility for murdering their father in cold blood, then made another leap by pointing their fingers at a convicted child molester who got into the boys' heads and manipulated them into taking the fall for him. In truth, the 12 men and women had no idea who to believe. They spent hours picking apart Derek and Alex's confessions to police, inspecting them sentence by sentence and word by word.

Initially, they unanimously concurred that their confession did sound somewhat strained, almost as if they were merely repeating the words of some older influential person. But there were some parts of their confession that seemed too elaborate, too circumstantial, to be the result of the overactive imagination of children or coercion, such as when they described in vivid detail the sounds the elder King emitted as he took the repeated blows to his skull. In Alex's own words, he said the bludgeoning sounded like "wood cracking or hitting concrete."[34]

Therefore, the boys must have been present at the time it was happening.

The jurors concluded that, although the boys didn't single-handedly kill their father, they watched it all unfold before their very eyes while Mr. Chavis wielded the bat himself.

∼

On September 6, the courtroom was packed. The young boys looked dapper with their slicked-back hair and dress shirts paired with ties. Their trial ended with the court clerk announcing a guilty verdict for second-degree murder. Someone in the crowded room began sobbing. It was their mother, Janet French. Alex remained stoic. Derek was the only one who displayed a hint of emotion. His head dropped, and he promptly wiped away a tear and slumped into his chair.

They were now facing a prison term of 22 years to life and an additional 30 for arson.

Meanwhile, Ricky's verdict, which had been undisclosed

throughout the duration of the trial, was now for the first time revealed to the public. He was declared not guilty of murdering Terry King.[35]

This caused mass confusion in the courtroom. Ricky was found innocent in his own trial; however, the jury for the Kings' trial reached an entirely different conclusion. From beginning to end, the legal proceedings had been a circus, spreading nothing but chaos and disorder. To further add to the pile of plot twists, which the court had seen time and time again with this case, Circuit Judge Frank Bell would pull a move that no judge had ever done before in Florida history. He threw out the jury's conviction of Alex and Derek and then criticized the prosecutors for the way they organized the case by arranging two separate trials with contradictory arguments and theories for essentially the exact same slaying. He referred to it as "unusual and bizarre."[36]

He told the attorneys on both sides that they needed to resolve the case in mediation or he would have no choice but to order a new trial for the brothers.

On November 7, two months after the boys' convictions were discarded, everyone gathered in the courtroom again to mediate and reach a final compromise. The prosecutor proposed a plea deal for Alex and Derek to plead guilty to reduced charges of third-degree murder and arson in exchange for a lighter prison sentence. At the end of the day, the boys both submitted written confessions to murdering their sleeping father with an aluminum baseball bat. Their confessions were nearly identical to their initial statements to police.

"I murdered my dad with an aluminum baseball bat," Derek's statement said. "I set the house on fire from my dad's bedroom."[37] The reason for the killing, according to the boys' confessions, was so that they could live with Ricky Chavis, who gave them more freedom.

After the boys torched their home, they ran to the EZ Serve just on the corner of Muscogee Road and immediately phoned Ricky Chavis. Mike Chavis, Ricky's brother who had lived with him for years, said that when Ricky picked up the phone, he looked shocked. Just then, the police scanner in the living room announced a fire on Muscogee Road. Everything began to click, and in less than a second, Ricky was out of the house.

According to Derek King's signed confession, the older man picked them up and drove them to a desolate field just over the Alabama line, where he had them remove their blood-stained clothes and hide out in the dark.

In 30 minutes, Ricky returned to their mobile home with two

mostly-naked boys holding their clothes. Mike would later testify that Alex looked too shocked to say anything, whereas Derek's demeanor seemed normal, unfazed. The older King explained everything that had happened. Then they washed their clothes, took a shower, smoked marijuana, and went to bed. The boys slept with Rick in his bed.

The next day, Rick Chavis coached the boys on what to tell police.

"He told us to say we killed our dad because our dad abused us," said Derek in his confession. "That was not true."[38]

He made them rehearse a story of self-defense over and over until they got every line, every minuscule detail, perfect.

Then he dropped them off at the police station.

Alex King received a seven-year sentence. His older brother received one extra year of time served.

Under the plea agreement, the boys would both be serving their time in a state juvenile facility where they would receive counseling, schooling, and vocational education.[39]

But what was to become of Ricky Chavis, now that he had been acquitted?

Even though he had managed to weasel his way out of the most severe of charges stacked against him, he wasn't quite off the hook yet. He still faced charges of false imprisonment, accessory after the fact, and committing lewd and lascivious acts on the youngest King. As per the plea agreement, the brothers had also consented to testifying against their old, trusted family friend during his trial.

In February 2003, the jury acquitted Ricky Chavis of molesting Alex King. How, with the surfeit of evidence, including Alex's handwritten love notes and Ricky's history of molesting children, could this have happened?

The jury felt that the boys had altered, tweaked, and dramatically changed their story so many times that it erased any credibility they may have had. But on the brighter side, Chavis was declared guilty of his other charges in his participation after the murder and was sentenced to 35 years in prison. Some may have considered this justice well served.

After the Trial

Janet French was left heartbroken by the outcome of her sons' trial. She believed her sons were too young, too naive, to fully grasp the gravity of the situation and the deal they had agreed to. She had requested that the boys be psychologically examined, which the judge refused.

"My children are smart and intelligent, but they don't know about life. They have no wisdom. They can't make this judgment for themselves," she said outside of the courtroom.[40]

Even the jury that convicted Alex and Derek of second-degree murder felt particularly conflicted over the case. A rally was held outside of the Pensacola courthouse to protest the Kings' sentences. Among the protesters was Lynne Schwarz, one of the jury members who decided on the boys' fate and was now protesting the verdict.

She maintained that she still fervently believed in their innocence. Other jurors never actually believed that the guilty verdict would lead to some serious jail time for the boys.

"We always thought that there was going to be some kind of rehabilitation, that the boys were going to be taken somewhere where they could have a new life and be productive citizens," she said during the morning's rally.[41]

Dennis Corder was also critical of the manner in which juveniles accused of committing serious offenses were handled in Florida's criminal justice system.

"The juvenile system can only hold someone until he is eighteen, but to put someone in prison for the rest of their life is over the top," he said. "If this were a U.S. citizen accused in a foreign country and they were exposed to that, we'd say what an incredibly unfair justice system they have."[42]

In contrast to the public outrage, during an interview with CNN anchor Paula Zahn, all of the Kings' attorneys expressed satisfaction with the case's ending.

"Well, we're very happy with what happened today. We think the outcome is fair. We think that it's something that all parties can live with," said Dennis Corder, one of the brothers' attorneys. "And we think that for someone who a month ago was facing first-degree murder and a mandatory life sentence to be sentenced to a situation where by the time he's able to drink his first beer he's going to be out of prison is an amazingly fortunate consequence."[43]

When Zahn had asked Prosecutor David Rimmer if he was confident that the adolescent brothers fully understood what was agreed upon during the plea deal, he responded, "There's nothing, no information that I have that indicates they did not understand what they were doing. And they did because they even admitted when they killed their dad they set the house on fire to destroy the evidence. And they took measures to avoid being caught."

He further stated, "So they understood the crime, they understood the consequences and therefore I have no reason to believe they didn't understand what they were doing yesterday."

Paula Zahn directed her last question to Sharon Potter, the other attorney of the brothers. "Given the very complicated circumstances surrounding the murder, who do you think is to blame for the murder of Terry King?"

She hesitated. "I don't think that's a fair question for me to answer."

"Is there a better way to phrase that?" Zahn pushed.

"I think what I can tell you is I believe Terry King would be alive were it not for Ricky Chavis."[44]

Parricide

What makes people hold such a soft spot for the King brothers? What made them want to fight for their innocence? Was it their youth? Their baby faces and juvenile antics? Was it the fact that there was a child molester hiding somewhere in the shadows, inculcating their every move? Are the King brothers really cold-blooded murderers or helpless, brainwashed victims?

While most people would agree that Derek and Alex King are very much guilty of murder, as per their confessions, the real brain teaser in all of this is how culpable these two children of 12 and 13 could really be. Did Ricky Chavis have a strong hold over their young, impressionable minds? Were they capable of contemplating the consequences of their actions at such young ages? Do any of these circumstantial factors excuse or diminish responsibility for their role in their father's death?

Parricide is the act of killing one's parent or another close relative, typically a father. Although only accounting for 2 percent of all homicides, parricide is the one type of crime that never fails to invoke enormous societal backlash.[45] Yet there are very few studies that deeply examine parricide, so why it happens continues to baffle many people. Some studies of parricide have been able to piece together a victim and offender profile. This information is important because it provides the criminal justice system with a better understanding of who may be at greater risk of committing such a vile offense and makes early detection and treatment more possible.

Most incidents of parricide involve one single victim and are perpetrated by one single offender. Victims of parricide tend to be the fathers of the perpetrators, and the perpetrators are more likely to be white, middle-class males in both matricide (killing of mother) and patricide (killing of father) cases. The weapon of choice also varies depending on the gender of the offender and the victim. Firearms are more likely to be used against fathers, whereas mothers are more likely to be killed with a blunt instrument or a sharp object.[46] The majority of parricide cases take place in the victim's home and are not premeditated. They typically occur on a whim following a heated argument or altercation. For this reason, it is much more difficult to spot early warning signs so that preventative measures can be taken in time. However, family dysfunction and tension exist between the parent and child leading up the murder.

What drives someone to kill their own parents? According to prior research, unlike adult perpetrators of parricide, who usually suffer from a severe mental disorder, long-term abuse (sexual, emotional, or physical) is the number one motivator for youth, followed by serious mental illness (least common) and being "dangerously antisocial." Dangerously antisocial children will usually murder their parents for selfish reasons, such as monetary gain.[47] Repeated public humiliation by the parent is also said to be another motivator for parricide.

Children who are subjected to severe abuse at home tend to fear retaliation from their parents, which explains why they are less likely to disclose the abuse to other adults who may be able to intervene. Some may have a misplaced sense of loyalty or devotion to their abusive parents. Other children may have attempted to reach out for help from an adult outsider, but their abuse claims were not taken seriously or believed. Sometimes, an adult is skeptical of an abusive situation if the abused child in question appears to come from a well-adjusted home and the abusive parent successfully pulls off the facade of a loving caregiver. This skepticism fosters a feeling of being trapped with no way out for the abuse victim. And that is when his mind wanders to more sinister solutions as a way to escape his predicament.

We may never fully comprehend what was going through the Kings' minds on that fateful day. But there is one truth in this matter: while people were so absorbed in all of the debates and protests about the boys not getting justice, we lost sight of the most tragic aspect of all: the victim's life was callously stolen from him.

"Terry's been forgotten in all this," said Wilbur King, Terry's father. "My son is gone and while people say his boys didn't get justice, it's my son who did not get justice. They aren't trying to find the killer of my son anymore. They are trying to let those two boys off scot-free."[48]

Since the case's closure, the charred remains of what once was a quiet little home that Terry King worked hard for and raised his boys in were bulldozed, not leaving behind a single trace of the evil that occurred there.

Life After Prison

Alex King was released from prison in October 2008. His older brother walked out a free man just one year after.

The infamous King brothers were no longer the same little kids with angelic faces that seized the hearts and sympathy of the nation. More than a year and a half after their release, they both revealed glimpses of their life during incarceration in an interview with *Dateline*'s Keith Morrison. There was one lapse of judgment during his prison term that brought the younger King brother to his senses and prompted him to do some grown-up thinking for the first time in his life. With only three more years to go in his sentence, Alex and another inmate attempted to escape from the juvenile detention facility where they were serving time. They were charged, but a judge had mercy on Alex and decided to give him a second chance.[49]

Alex realized just how lucky he was. After that incident, he began to re-evaluate his life and consider how all of his actions have consequences that can mess not only with his future but other people's futures as well.

"It really hit me that my actions don't affect me alone. They affect other people. And I really felt things for the first time," he said.[50]

Afterward, he made it his mission to turn his life around. He raised his grades, read more books, and earned his high school diploma. When he emerged from prison doors, he went to live with a woman named Kathryn Medico, who had been in touch with Alex since 2002 and had become a surrogate mother of sorts for him. She opened her doors for him in her Jacksonville home and fully accepted him as a member of the family.

Alex claimed to not remember much about life prior to juvie, and the media circus that surrounded the sensational trials were all but a blur. He still cannot figure out what drove him to the crime.

"I don't really know. Maybe it was stress, you know. Maybe it was Ricky Chavis' influence. Maybe it was, I don't know, something else."[51]

From what little he remembered of Terry King, he recalled him being an overworked, endlessly tired father trying to make ends meet who spent his off days sleeping. Since Alex wasn't in school and wasn't allowed to mingle with other children his age, his only real "friend" was Rick Chavis.

But now, Alex doesn't like to dwell on the past. When he came out of prison an entirely changed person, he made it his goal to focus on the future and never look back. "I don't even associate myself with the person who went through all of that."[52]

And the other King?

When Derek re-entered the outside world, he found himself disoriented by an ever-changing society that was so unlike what he remembered at 13. He had no clue what Facebook was. Going from a highly-structured environment with strict rules and discipline for eight years to having almost total freedom and flexibility, with nobody telling him what to do and when to do it, was enough to incapacitate him. Making simple decisions, such as choosing toothpaste brands, caused much frustration. It was going to take a long time for him to be able to adapt to post-prison life, but he was determined to build a future for himself, one that included settling down with a family.

His ultimate dream was to get married one day, but his idea of what constituted a healthy family dynamic was completely skewed due to the less-than-ideal examples he grew up with: shuffling from negligent parents to foster care, then being abandoned by his foster parents whose patience with the rowdy teen had worn thin and who sent him to live with his estranged biological father who isolated him from friends. He knew nothing but a dysfunctional family.[53]

Derek was taken in by Dan Dailey, a child advocate who lives off-grid on a tiny ranch situated in the Chihuahuan desert on the west side of Texas. Dailey has called this place Estrella Vista. He first took notice of the boys while their trials were making headlines. Immediately, he sent $100 to their attorney and mailed the imprisoned brothers some books. He had kept in touch with Derek since then, exchanging letters back and forth up until his release.[54] He had become a sort of father figure for Derek. The elder King brother stayed with Dailey for about six months and left. Being so isolated from society made him lonely.

"I had great parents. They never hurt me in any way," Dailey explained. "The thought of any parent abusing or abandoning their child just seemed outrageous to me. I came to the conclusion that these kids needed a good parent."[55]

He firmly held the stance that juvenile parricides are almost always a knee-jerk reaction to mistreatment by the parent. Kids can only handle so much stress until they eventually snap and lash out. Dailey also criticized the way that the justice system handles juvenile offenders in their care who have already been growing up in abhorrent conditions. He claimed that it deprives them even more of the love and freedom they lacked in their childhood.

"I mean, they've lived their whole life in prison. That's like living on a worse desert than I live in. That's worse than death."[56]

Dan Dailey had worked at a business consulting company in Minneapolis but he became weary of life's mundane cycle. He decided on a whim to find an 60-acre piece of land in the middle of the Texas desert and start a sanctuary for parricides who have nowhere to go after juvie or prison. He started an advocacy organization called the Redemption Project which aims to hire attorneys for parricides and help them integrate back into society after prison.

Alex King's transition from prison life to the real world was anything but smooth. In 2011, he was arrested for violating his probation after causing an automobile accident and fleeing the scene on foot. He was also having a hard time maintaining a stable job, for his criminal record came to haunt him everywhere he applied. Eventually, he settled into the remote land that is Estrella Vista, knowing that Dailey always offered a cushion for him to fall back on in times of despair, as he had done for Derek.

Although Derek was set on his future, he also acknowledged that his past is something that will always stay with him.

"I made adult choices when I was a kid, and I paid adult consequences," he said. "I take responsibility for killing him. I will pay for it for the rest of my life."[57]

Josh Phillips
(1998)

On November 3, 1998, at approximately 6:30 in the evening, an extremely fear-stricken mother phoned the Jacksonville Sheriff's Office (JSO) with an emergency. She identified herself as Sheila Clifton and wanted to report her eight-year-old daughter, Madelyn Rae Clifton, missing. According to Sheila, her daughter had been at a neighbor's house watching the other neighborhood kids hitting golf balls at around 5:00 p.m. According to FBI records, about 15 minutes later, the little girl had gone back home to retrieve some golf balls of her own. At 5:30, she returned to the outdoors to continue playing. When Sheila Clifton called her two daughters, Maddie and older sister Jessica, to come home for dinner, only the elder returned. Jessie told her mother she had not been playing with her younger sister and had no idea where she might be.

JSO sheriffs arrived at tranquil Fleetwood Road where the Cliftons' residence was located. They did a quick canvass of the neighborhood where Maddie was last seen playing and began questioning witnesses. The Cliftons, with the help of their neighbors, frantically searched the streets into the evening and night with flashlights. But there was not a single clue as to where the eight-year-old girl vanished. And as the hours of relentless searching dragged on without any results, the little ball of dread sitting in the stomachs of Maddie's parents inflated. In their minds, they kept replaying the last moment they saw their daughter leaving the house to go outside and play. Might it have been the last time they would ever see her again?[58]

"It was like she shut the door and just, poof, vanished off the face of the earth," said Steve Clifton, Maddie's father, who worked as a foreman at a local metal shop.[59]

Maddie's parents went knocking on every door in the neighborhood to inquire if anyone had seen their little girl. But nobody had. Sheila stood in her front yard and screamed her daughter's name with desperation. And by the end of the night, they still hadn't found a sign of Maddie.[60]

By now it was obvious that Maddie was in danger. Little girls don't just disappear into thin air. Search efforts to locate the missing girl continued the next day, but this time, the number of volunteers aiding in the search grew larger and stronger, somewhere over 400. Participants in the search began distributing missing person fliers with the youngster's school photo featured on the front, with details about her physical appearance to make it easier for someone to identify her.[61]

They knew to keep their eyes peeled for a little girl with chin-length brown hair and brown eyes that stood only 4'4" tall and weighed approximately 44 pounds. She was garbed in a red YMCA basketball shirt with her name proudly imprinted on the back shoulders and a big number 5 just below it.

They plastered these fliers all over town, including at a local Jaguars-Bengals game, and stood on the side of St. Augustine Road nearby where Maddie was last seen playing, showing her picture to each and every car that drove by, hoping—praying—that someone would recognize her and have knowledge as to what might have happened to her.[62]

While the community was gathering together to find the eight-year-old by doing thorough sweeps of the neighborhood and passing out fliers, the police were busy investigating possible suspects related to her disappearance. The first person of interest was a neighbor with a bit of a shady past. The man had been apprehended twice within the past 15 to 20 years after being accused of sex crimes, although the charges in both cases had been dismissed.[63]

FBI records indicated that during a consent search of his home, they discovered rather incriminating items such as an ax, rope, tape, camouflage clothing, a shovel with fresh dirt on it, and "various types of pornography." The police had him put under 24-hour surveillance. Even more suspiciously, when the neighbor agreed to take a polygraph test in an effort to clear his name, he failed it. However, he was able to provide an alibi, and the police concluded that the items they found at his residence, however incriminating they might appear, were not evidence of guilt.

The police were also investigating three other potential suspects in this missing person case. During a neighborhood canvass on the second day of Maddie's disappearance, the JSO learned some news that would pique their interest. About six weeks prior, a witness observed a suspicious blue 1981 Dodge van bearing a Georgia plate loitering in the very neighborhood that Maddie went missing from. Its occupants were described as two white males with very "dirty and unkempt" appearances. Police were able to trace the owner of the car and discovered that he had a criminal history.

Three days later and still no luck. By now, there were more than 1000 volunteers all across northeast Florida assisting in the search for Maddie.[64] A reward of $50,000 for the safe return of the child was announced, which would later be doubled.[65] Madelyn's parents appeared at a press conference, sobbing as they pleaded for their daughter's safe return. Finally, the JSO requested the help of the FBI as they continued to look into the leads that were piling up. The day before the FBI officially joined the case, the JSO received an anonymous tip that an individual driving a 1993 blue Chevrolet Lumina also bearing a Georgia license plate had tried to abduct a young girl in Kingsland, Georgia, on November 1, just two days prior to Maddie's disappearance, so they began the process of attempting to locate the vehicle. Then, on November 7, a sergeant of the JSO also received an email from a Georgia police department revealing that they had received an email from an unnamed individual stating that their roommate, a recent parolee, was involved in the possible kidnapping of Maddie Clifton.

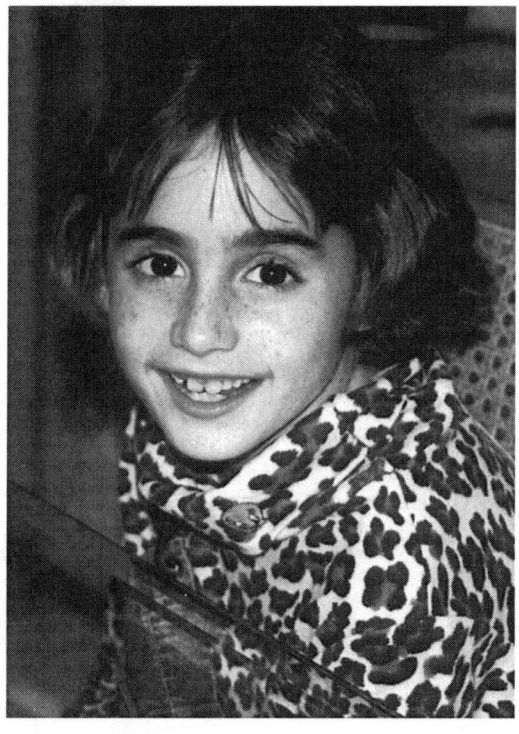

Maddie Clifton, eight, mysteriously disappeared after some outside playtime, prompting a week-long search in which the FBI was involved (courtesy Jessica Clifton).

Also on November 7, the show *America's Most Wanted* (*AMW*) had broadcast Maddie's story on national television. The next day, a potential witness contacted the Mobile office of the FBI. FBI records indicate that she was an employee of Headstart Hair Care of Mobile, Alabama, and claimed that a very young child who bore a striking resemblance to the picture of Madelyn Clifton, and was featured on *AMW*, had walked into her salon accompanied by a white woman for a haircut the week the girl disappeared. Although she could not verify it, she strongly believed the child's name was also Madelyn. She stated that she had no idea if the child was in a vehicle or where she and the woman went after leaving the hair salon.

What investigators didn't know at the time was that they were looking in all the wrong places, because after an anguishing week of searching, the investigation into eight-year-old Maddie Clifton's disappearance would come to a grinding halt. The truth would finally be revealed, and nobody could believe their ears when they heard what happened and who was responsible.

A Mother's Discovery

It was 7:30 a.m. on November 10, 1993. Melissa Phillips, who lived just across the street from the Cliftons, went into her 14-year-old son Josh's bedroom to do some cleaning while he was on his way to school. Immediately upon entering his bedroom, she noted a very strange, almost putrid, odor permeating the room. She also noticed her son's waterbed frame appeared to be leaking, which she assumed to be the possible cause of the foul smell. To further examine the source of the strange leak, she pulled apart the baseboard to have a look under his bed. And what she came across was enough to send a thousand electric jolts of sheer terror through her body.

It was a human foot.

Without looking any further, she immediately bolted out of her son's bedroom and ran across the street to find the nearest police officer staged in the neighborhood to report her shocking discovery. Her brain pulsated with anxiety. She felt her dreams for her family's future falling apart all around her. She silently prayed that this was not the missing girl who lived just across the street. But, in her heart, she knew it was. Starting today, her life would be turned upside down forever.

She guided the officers to her son's bedroom but could not muster the will to re-enter his room after what she had just seen. She felt entirely shaken and nauseous. She simply pointed to the waterbed to indicate where the police needed to look.[66] Right away, they saw Maddie's tiny feet hanging out from underneath the mattress. They inspected further. There, wedged between the waterbed frame and bed liner, was none other than the decaying body of a little girl, curled up in a fetal position and naked from the waist down.[67] It was pretty obvious that this was the same young girl for whom community had been frantically and restlessly searching for the last week. And from the looks of her battered corpse, she did not go out in a swift and relatively painless manner. This child had quite clearly suffered tremendously in her dying moments.

The two officers searched the room and took photos. From afar, it would look like any typical teenage boy's bedroom, but there were some seemingly innocuous items that, up close, would send chills up their spines. Tape had been used to keep the bed frame in place so as to conceal Maddie's body. On the nightstand at his bedside, he kept a copy of Maddie's missing person flier right next to recently-burned incense and air fresheners which he presumably used to mask the terrible odor of the eight-year-old's decomposing body. They also found a photograph of Jessica Clifton, his victim's older sister, that he had stolen from the Clifton home. They recovered the Leatherman knife Josh had used to stab Maddie, in addition to the baseball bat he used to batter her, which he had stashed behind his dresser. Investigators also found books on devil worship in his bedroom, and an inspection of his computer would show that he took delight in watching violent pornography.[68] He had watched such videos half an hour before the murder and continued to watch them even after the murder. Later, when they would remove her body, they noticed her hand still grasping the frame, just how she had died.[69]

Their findings could not have been more incriminating. There was no doubt that Josh was responsible for killing Maddie Clifton.

Across the street, the Clifton family noticed police putting up crime scene tape around their neighbors' home. They didn't want to believe that this was in any way connected to little Maddie's disappearance. But their worst fear was confirmed when shortly afterwards detectives knocked on their door. They sat down with Steve and Sheila Clifton and broke the tragic news.

"Where was she?" was the first question Steve could ask.

"Right across the street," replied an officer.

Jessie Clifton came downstairs and saw her family huddled in a circle in tears. As soon as they saw her, they pulled her close and informed her that her little sister was no longer with them.

She almost didn't believe it.

She bolted out of the garage door and shouted Maddie's name over and over again. She collapsed onto the concrete, screaming and crying out for her little sister. But Maddie wasn't ever coming back, no matter how many times she called for her. She knew she was gone. She knew, starting today, her family's lives would never be the same.[70]

Meanwhile, the police had raced toward the school 14-year-old Joshua Phillips was attending and brought him down to the police station for questioning. There, he was met by his parents, who sat by his side in the interrogation room. How was he going to explain a rotting corpse stuffed under his mattress? The teen might have realized that there really was no way out of this because, in no time, he was pouring out the details of what happened.

He knew Maddie, he told JSO detectives. They lived diagonally across the street from each other. Despite the six-year age difference, they were playmates. On the day of her disappearance, he said, the eight-year-old had stopped by his house asking to play baseball with him. Initially, he objected, informing the youngster that he had plenty of chores to get done and he was not allowed to go outside while his parents were not home. But she persisted, so he finally agreed, telling her they could only play for a few minutes as his father would be home any time now. He knew his father, Steve Phillips, would get angry if he caught him playing with Maddie, as he had told him in the past that he was too old to be playing with her.

They went into his backyard with their bats and baseballs and started hitting them back and forth. At one point, she threw the ball in his direction, and he walloped it with the quick swing of his bat. The ball went flying through the air and struck her in the head with force, opening up a large gash. Immediately, the child dropped to the ground and started wailing in pain. The older child had panicked. Knowing his father would arrive at any minute and he risked getting into deep trouble if his father found out he had stepped out of the house for a bit of playtime. The only solution he could think of was to kill her and hide the body.[71]

So he picked the little girl up in his arms and carried her inside and into his bedroom, where he set her down. But she was still fussing over her injuries. In an attempt to silence her, he grabbed his baseball bat and bashed her in the head a couple of times before stuffing her under the base of his bed. Thinking she was now dead, he went to wash up. When he returned to his bedroom, he heard the muffled moans of his eight-year-old playmate, meaning that she had somehow survived the unbelievable torture that was just inflicted on her. He reasoned that he had to finish the job; there was no going back now. He lifted the mattress, dragged her out, and stabbed her multiple times in the chest and neck. He pushed her back under the mattress once again. She was still alive, clutching the frame of the bed. And that's how she died.

Then there was the question of whether he had sexually assaulted her, due to the fact that, when police found her, the little girl was stripped entirely of her clothes save for her t-shirt and white socks. He denied ever touching her in that manner, insisting that her clothes had slipped off as he dragged her into his room.[72]

After his terrifying confession, 14-year-old Joshua Phillips was arrested and taken into custody. Meanwhile, Jacksonville sheriff Nat Glover was burdened with the task of holding the press conference that would announce the end of the investigation as Maddie's body had unfortunately been located. Onlookers, neighbors, and loved ones watching the press conference from a tiny television propped up on a vehicle gasped and covered their mouths in shock. Some looked down. Others held their chests. Members of the community embraced each other for solace and comfort. One person actually collapsed, prompting the arrival of a medic.

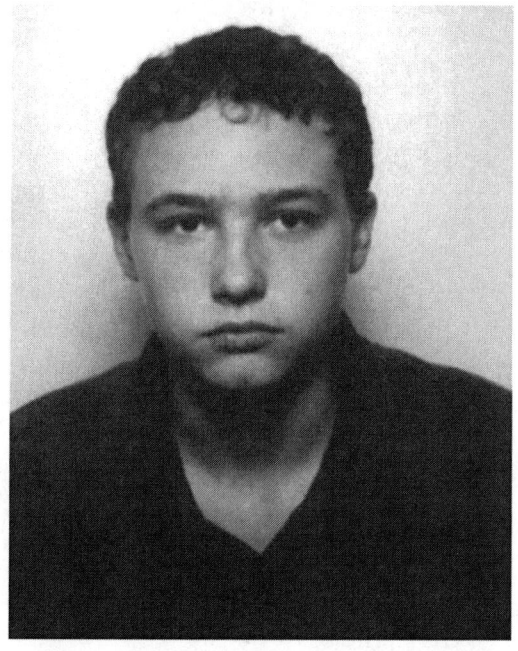

Joshua Phillips, 14, was charged with Maddie's murder after Maddie's body was discovered under his bed by his own mother.

The sudden murder of Maddie Clifton was not

just a tragic loss to her family. It was one that was deeply felt by the entire community, even those who never knew the Cliftons but were nevertheless determined to find Maddie alive. Everyone was suffering.

One volunteer, Kenneth Hensley, passed out purple ribbons upon the tragic news that Maddie's body was found in a neighbor's home, while others removed all the missing person fliers plastered around town at the request of the family and stored them in cardboard boxes topped with bouquets of flowers which were promptly carried over to the Clifton home. At the end of Christopher Road in Lakewood, where Maddie's $100,000 reward poster was taped to a van's window, a temporary shrine appeared. People adorned it with flowers, teddy bears, and ribbons.

In the distance, onlookers gazed in sheer horror at the Phillipses' two-story home which was now a crime scene. Millions of questions raced through their minds. How was it that after all these days of searching, combing through neighborhoods, passing out missing person fliers and interrogating possible child predators, Maddie Clifton was stashed away under another child's mattress just across the street from where she lived? A child that she knew and played with, no less. A child that picked up a flashlight and participated in the search right alongside other volunteers.

Whatever answers the public were desperately trying to seek could not be given now. Four days after her body was found, Maddie Clifton's funeral would be held. In front of the San Jose Catholic Church, well-wishers formed a beautiful memorial embellished with teddy bears, candles, posters, and brightly-colored flowers before the funeral. Afterward, San Jose Boulevard was lined with hundreds of people—men, women, and children—all holding hands while Maddie's funeral procession passed by. Big towering signs bore the words "GOD BLESS YOU MADDIE" and "GOODBYE MADDIE." Two pastors wrapped a purple shroud around one of the pillars that stood outside of Lakewood United Methodist Church along San Jose Boulevard. The vehicles traveled down the funeral route to Maddie's final resting place at Oaklawn Cemetery.[73]

Legal Proceedings

The day after Joshua's confession, he was brought to the Duval County Courthouse and arraigned on first-degree murder charges.[74]

Five days later, state attorney Harry Shorstein revealed at a press conference that the 14-year-old would be tried as an adult for his egregious crime. The police continued their investigation of the murder.[75]

An autopsy was conducted on Maddie's body, and the results would confirm some aspects of Josh's own account of how Maddie sustained her injuries. Thankfully, there was no evidence of sexual assault, but she had suffered terrible blunt force trauma from the head-bashing and had also been stabbed twice in the neck and nine times in the body. The autopsy also verified that, sadly, Maddie was still alive when she was shoved underneath her killer's waterbed mattress.[76] Also, at the request of state attorney Harry Shorstein, the Florida Department of Law Enforcement sent a letter enclosed with some evidence to the FBI laboratory for the trace evidence unit to examine. They wanted to determine the type of body hair found on Maddie's abdomen, specifically, if it was a pubic hair. They had provided 13 samples of hair from Joshua's pubic region accompanied by a piece of hair collected from Maddie's abdomen.

On March 5, 1999, the trace evidence unit mailed back their results. Their findings were that the brown Caucasian hair was "microscopically dissimilar" to the pubic hair samples belonging to Joshua. They also advised that a suitable known public standard should consist of at least 25 randomly-selected hairs from different areas of the pubic region, as opposed to the insufficient 13 samples detectives provided.

In April of that year, Judge Charles Arnold moved Josh's trial to Polk County in the central Florida town of Bartow 200 miles away because the media coverage was too great and the emotional grief was too severe in Jacksonville for the selection of an impartial jury.[77]

The trial, beginning in July 1999, was a short one, lasting only two days. Floridians tuned in while it was broadcast live on Court TV. Despite the overwhelming evidence against Josh, including his own confession, he had pleaded not guilty to the first-degree charge he was facing in court. Since he was under the age of 16, he was not eligible for the death penalty according to Florida state law, but he did face a potential life without parole sentence.

The trial was so short because Joshua's attorney, Richard Nichols, did not bother to present any witnesses or evidence on his behalf. His entire defense relied solely on his opening and closing statements, which was a rather unusual, risky strategy that would invoke much criticism from the prosecution and public and frustration from Joshua's family.[78] He even blocked Josh from taking the stand to tell his side of the story. The defense attorney exhorted the 12 members of the jury to convict his young client of manslaughter as there was a lack of evidence that this murder was premeditated.

"We're not here to act out of some form of vengeance," he said. "We're not here to act as a bunch of well-dressed vigilantes."[79]

He referenced the autopsy report indicating the brutal beating and stabbings Maddie had suffered before she drew her last breaths. "The evidence shows us there was an accident that deteriorated into panic and then murder," argued the defense.[80]

Both state attorney Harry Shorstein and his chief assistant, Jay Plotkin, didn't buy into Joshua's confession that this was a mere accident that escalated into murder because there was a lack of physical evidence to corroborate his claims. The autopsy did not reveal any injury on or around the eye where Josh claimed the ball had hit her. There was neither dirt nor sand on her body from when he had supposedly dragged her into the house, nor was there any blood in the yard or in the house from Maddie's bloody wound, which strongly suggested that she had never gotten injured in the first place.

The prosecution argued that this was a sexually-motivated crime, pointing toward her missing pants and underwear, which Josh had previously explained came off as he was dragging her. He also mentioned that Josh had previously spoken to the eight-year-old girl and her older sister about sex.[81]

There were some interesting pieces of evidence that, for unknown reasons, were ruled inadmissible in court and therefore not presented in the trial. These were pieces of evidence that might have served as additional pieces to the puzzle of Maddie's murder and indicators of Josh Phillips' true motive.

According to the prosecutor, the 14-year-old defendant was viewing violent pornography on his home computer only half an hour prior to the murder. To add to this, defense attorney Richard Nichols had hired a neurologist who had discovered brain abnormalities in Josh, including bilateral frontal lobe lesions which may cause impaired judgment and panic. Shorstein believed that the violent pornography might have triggered his sudden onslaught of violence, and that, combined with his brain lesions, was a recipe for disaster.[82]

Furthermore, the defense also hired a psychologist to determine if Josh had any emotional disturbances that could explain what led him to rationalize that killing a little girl over an accident was the best solution to his problem.

But the psychologist could not identify any underlying mental illness. Josh stated he never suffered from anxiety or depression, and, in fact, he loved his parents dearly. He was deeply afraid of his father, who was known to have a terrible anger problem.

Tom Bowery, the psychologist, said that there were two circumstances that made Josh terribly frightened of his father, and those were "whenever he was afraid that he had done something wrong or whenever his father was angry at anyone."[83]

Josh had confided, "If I did something wrong, he always had kind of a short temper, and sometimes I never knew what he'd do." In his free time, which the youth certainly had no shortage of behind bars, he buried himself in books to take his mind off the violent murder he committed. "That's one of the reasons I like to read because if I'm reading I can't think about anything else."[84]

There was nothing in Josh's background to indicate that he had a propensity for violence or suffered from any mental health issues. Overall, he seemed like an average kid with a pretty sane mind. "This is not what I would've seen as the typical kind of sociopathic, wanting to kill, wanting to maim, deriving-pleasure-from-the-pain-of-others kind of kid," said Dr. Tom Bowery.[85]

During the trial, piles of evidence were stacked against the defendant. These items ranged from the two murder weapons—the baseball bat and the Leatherman tool used to brutalize his young victim—and his blood-stained tennis shoes, all the way down to the most damaging piece of evidence—his confession. Harry Shorstein presented numerous witnesses, including investigators who worked on the case. Richard Nichols, on the other hand, introduced a grand total of zero, which would draw much backlash. Why would a defense lawyer not want to call any witnesses that could help his case?

His intent was to make a lasting impression on the 12 members of the jury. It was clear, however, that this strategy would not work well for his client. From the beginning, 14-year-old Joshua Phillips never stood a chance.

"Joshua Phillips is not a monster but because of an act that began as an accident and deteriorated through panic that bordered on madness," his attorney said in his closing argument.[86]

His plan to make a lasting impression on the jury wouldn't exactly work in his favor, for it took the jury two hours of deliberation to reach their verdict. They returned to the courtroom and read their unanimous verdict: guilty of first-degree murder.

Josh returned to the courtroom on August 20 to hear his fate. But before he would learn how many years he would spend behind prison bars, he would hear a word from his victim's family. Before they could even express the unimaginable pain they had suffered from their loss, all at the hands of their neighbor, Josh's family had the opportunity to speak. They started by expressing their sorrow to the Cliftons for their loss. Then the Cliftons had to sit and listen to the Phillipses as they talked about what a wonderful boy Joshua was, how generous and caring he was.

"I have thought of your daughter very often," said Dan Phillips, the older half-brother of Joshua. "Then, I think of my little brother; when I look at him, I still see a baby."[87]

He assured the Cliftons that while Josh might not be showing all that much emotion in the courtroom, he did indeed shed tears for the little girl he killed while tucked away from the public eye. "I know in my heart my brother is remorseful for what has happened, but he's still a boy." This statement pulled some strings on young Joshua's heart; his lips trembled while his brother stood up for him.[88]

It was then Melissa Phillips' turn to speak. In spite of her frightful discovery underneath her son's mattress, and listening with her own ears to the macabre details of how he killed a child barely over half his age, she still supported him throughout the whole ordeal. She strongly believed that the brain lesions really did propel his violence toward Maddie.

"I cannot undo what is done and there is not a day that passes that I don't think about Maddie and her family that loves her," said the killer's mother. "I'm sorry for their grief, but I cannot repair the heartbreak any more than I can repair our own."[89]

Josh's other brother, Ben Phillips, also managed to get a word in, pointing out to the court that Maddie's uncle was once convicted of a crime and was given a second chance to start his life over as a free man. When it was Steve Phillips' time to have his say, he pointed the finger at JSO investigators and accused them of lying on the stand, a crime known as perjury that carries a punishment of up to five years in jail in Florida, but failed to mention what exactly they were untruthful about. He also lashed out at state attorney Harry Shorstein and his chief assistant, Jay Plotkin.

"For the state to prosecute a 14-year-old for first-degree murder is ludicrous and obscene," he criticized. "Mr. Shorstein and Mr. Plotkin should be ashamed of themselves in this manner. Their actions were carefully plotted for the press and to further their own political gain."[90]

Finally, Madelyn's loved ones came forward to speak about the harrowing loss that had left their hearts shattered and scarred their lives permanently.

"I will never see Maddie again," said the grieving mother. "I will never see Maddie fulfill her dreams."[91]

Twelve-year-old Jessica Clifton also spoke about how much she had suffered after losing her little sister. She was still in disbelief that someone Maddie considered a friend would consciously choose to end her life.

"I don't know why God wanted Maddie to leave so early in her life, but we all have to learn to accept that," she said. The young girl missed her younger sibling but always felt her spiritual presence in a room, looking after her. Maddie's father also testified that he was not able to see his daughter's body before her burial as the funeral director strongly advised against seeing her in such a mangled state.[92]

After her loved ones spoke, it was time to wrap up the hearing.

"This hearing brings a sad end to one of the most tragic proceedings of one of the most heinous crimes in our city's history," said Shorstein. "Everyone has suffered, everyone has lost. Only the system of justice has prevailed." Despite Steve Phillips' opinion, the prosecutor said that Josh's heinous actions justified being tried as an adult.[93]

Before sentencing the young boy, Judge Arnold had something to say to Joshua Phillips. "I do not perceive you to be a child. Your monstrous act in causing the death of Maddie Clifton made you an adult," he told him. "I'm certain that on Judgment Day, you, Joshua Earl Phillips, will be given a far harsher sentence than I can impose." Then, quoting Jesus Christ from Luke 17, he went on to say, "It would be better if a millstone were hung around your neck and that you were thrown into the sea than to cause harm to a child."[94]

With that, in spite of his young age, supposed brain lesions, and horrible upbringing, the judge imposed a merciless sentence of life in prison without the possibility of parole. He was ordered to be transferred to Marion County Correctional Facility near Ocala, Florida, to serve out his sentence, where the now-15-year-old would officially become inmate J11775.[95]

As soon as the Phillips family left the courtroom, journalists and photographers swarmed around them, besieging them with questions.

Steve shouted at them to get out of his way, shoving a Tampa videographer to the side. Meanwhile, the Cliftons said they simply wanted to move on with their lives, although the knowledge of Maddie's killer being locked up for the rest of his life provided very little relief for their heartbreak and anguish; it still wouldn't bring their little girl back.

"I think Maddie is watching over all of us," said Maddie's mother. They would never forget what a pleasure the lively eight-year-old was to be around.[96]

Appeals and Resentencing

On February 6, 2002, just three years after Josh Phillips began his sentence of life in prison, a state appeals court upheld his sentence after the chief prosecutor reaffirmed the ruling by stating that life in prison was not "cruel or unusual punishment" when taking into account the brutal torture that was inflicted on the eight-year-old victim before her death.

In the court's ruling, Judge Casanueva stated that "Joshua Phillips' sentence for this crime cannot be said to be unusual punishment." State attorney Harry Shorstein commented on the tragedy of sentencing Josh to life in prison, but noted that it was equally, if not more, tragic that a beautiful young girl had to die such a brutal, needless death at the hands of this adolescent. Assistant state attorney Angela Corey revealed that Josh Phillips' attorney could appeal his case to the Florida supreme court on account of the juvenile receiving incompetent representation during his trial.[97]

What the public feared is exactly what ended up happening almost three years later.

On December 16, 2004, a new trial for Josh Phillips, who was now 20 years old, was being sought. His new attorney, John Bonaccorsy, argued to the judge that his previous lawyer, Richard Nichols, now deceased, did a poor job of defending his client and building a case for him. Not only did he fail to introduce witnesses on behalf of the adolescent, but he also refused to allow young Josh to testify on his own behalf. Furthermore, he contended, his previous attorney never raised questions as to whether or not Josh was even competent to stand trial. He argued that 14-year-olds generally do not share the same mental capacity and maturity as an adult.

Sitting in the courtroom, arguing for the killer, was Melissa Phillips, who was also pushing for the reversal of her son's life sentence.

"Something terrible happened, and we have to deal with that and he has to take responsibility," she said, admitting that her son was guilty as charged for the crime he was convicted of. But there was one significant factor that people were overlooking—his young age at the time he committed the offense. This, she believed, should have been the judge's main guide as he considered his sentence. She hoped that one day he would be given another chance to walk out of prison a free man and start his life over.[98]

In 2008, both Harry Shorstein, who personally prosecuted Josh Phillips, and Sheriff Nat Glover, who took part in the investigation of Maddie Clifton's murder, would come forward and concede that perhaps life in prison without parole was a tough sentence to impose on a teenage boy. Shorstein said he wished he could have offered a plea deal of second-degree murder because Josh seemed like a normal albeit timid kid who liked computers.

Sheriff Nat Glover said, "I never got the feeling that it was a malicious, mean-spirited, calculated murder. It was kind of an impulsive act that, given a different set of circumstances, would never have happened."[99]

But the real turnaround for the case was when the U.S. Supreme Court pronounced that mandatory life sentences without parole for juvenile offenders were unconstitutional in 2012. This made the United States the last country in the world to abolish life sentences for offenders under the age of 18.

How did the U.S. Supreme Court come to this conclusion, exactly, and what took them so long? During *Roper v. Simmons*, 543 U.S. 551 (2005), the Supreme Court abolished death sentences for underage offenders, citing their poor capacity to make proper and responsible decisions as would be expected from an adult. This lack of capacity, combined with their vulnerability to succumb to outside influences and peer pressure, acted as mitigating factors regarding their culpability. Furthermore, their substantially larger reception to rehabilitation compared to their adult counterparts should render them qualified for entirely different standards when it comes to their sentencing. Therefore, considering all of these components, the U.S. Supreme Court would declare that imposing the death penalty on underage offenders was "cruel and unusual" punishment. Prior to the *Roper* ruling, 22 inmates were executed for crimes they had committed as juveniles since 1976 alone. In the aftermath of the *Roper* ruling, 72 juveniles from 12 states had their death sentences commuted. Eighteen states banned the death penalty for minors and 12 states banned the death penalty for all offenders, regardless of age and circumstances.

Removing the death penalty as an appropriate punishment for juveniles left life without parole as the maximum sentence a juvenile could receive for their crimes. But five years later, in *Graham v. Florida*, 130 S. CT. 2011, the Supreme Court ruled it unconstitutional to impose a life without parole sentence on any juvenile offender who was not convicted of homicide. The court described life without parole as "an especially harsh punishment for a juvenile ... a 16-year-old and a 75-year-old each sentenced to life without parole receive the same punishment in name only." For that reason alone, the consequence of life without parole should be strictly reserved for juveniles who committed homicide, the most severe of offenses.

Following *Roper* and *Graham*'s rulings on the abolishment of the death penalty for juveniles and the limited use of life without parole sentences, roughly 2500 juveniles were serving life sentences for crimes related to murder. Then, in 2012, the court declared in *Miller v. Alabama* and *Jackson v. Hobbs* that mandatory life sentences without any possibility of parole were unconstitutional because they breached the Eighth Amendment of the United States Constitution, which clearly forbids the federal government from imposing cruel and unusual punishment. Justice Elena Kagan described adolescence as marked by "transient rashness, proclivity for risk, and inability to assess consequences." The U.S. Supreme Court highlighted that judges would be required to consider the unique circumstances of each and every juvenile defendant who walks into their courtroom while deciding on an appropriate sentence for them.[100]

This new ruling would serve as the gateway for Josh's new attorneys to file a request for a resentencing hearing. In 2016, they successfully appealed his case, and he was granted a new sentencing hearing because the mandatory life sentence he was currently serving was ruled unconstitutional by the Supreme Court. The new hearing was scheduled for 2017. Over the course of the year, his attorneys dedicated themselves to preparing for this hearing.

The hearing day would arrive on Monday, August 7, 2017, at the Duval County Courthouse before Judge Waddell Wallace. Josh Phillips was now in his early 30s, having spent more than half his life in prison. During the four-day hearing, the court would hear once again the emotionally raw testimony from the Clifton family, who would reiterate the pain and suffering they had gone through at the hands of Josh Phillips. They implored the judge to keep him behind bars for the rest of his life.

During his opening statement, state prosecutor Bernie de la Riondia characterized the 33-year-old as diabolical. He described him as a teen who was obsessed with Maddie's older sister, Jessica, reminding the court of the photograph he kept of her in his bedroom. He also reminded the court of his disgusting habit of watching pornography featuring cheerleader brutality on his computer.

He pushed for a life sentence with a review in 25 years, because it should not be ignored how heinous the crime was and Josh's callous actions in the aftermath of the murder—participating in the search for the dead girl while at night he slept on the mattress she was stuffed under and even keeping a missing persons flier of his victim in his bedroom. Not once did he come forward and confess to authorities that he knew where Maddie was. Not once did he ever show remorse. Instead, he burned some incense and taped his bed frame to conceal the ugly secret hidden in his room.

Should he get released, who is to say he won't reoffend based on his history?

Josh's attorneys, however, recommended that the judge base his decision on the rehabilitated man Josh had become during his imprisonment, not the 14-year-old boy he was in 1998. They requested a 40-year sentence with credit for time served. He would be 55 by the time of his release, should the judge heed this request.

Defense attorney Tom Fallis called for witnesses to speak on behalf of Josh Phillips, testifying to his emotional growth, his remorse for his actions, and his outstanding behavior in prison. First to testify was clinical psychologist Stephen Bloomfield, who had evaluated the defendant earlier in the year. Josh had opened up to him regarding his less-than-ideal childhood, which included a mother with depression, an abusive father with a hot temper, and some sexual abuse.

Although he called Josh's past actions "horrendous" and "tragic," he did not believe that the murder was in any way premeditated. "It seems to me it fits into a pattern of an immature thought process, not a psychosis."[101]

The psychologist also pointed to many accomplishments of Josh's that only proved his complete turnaround in prison. Josh, described as an intelligent man with an above-average IQ, had acquired his GED while serving time and now taught GED math and science to other inmates. In May 2007, he earned a legal assistant/paralegal diploma from Blackstone Career Institute, a distance learning program based in Allentown, Pennsylvania. Now working as a law clerk, he advised fellow inmates and employed his skills and qualifications to assist them with their appeals.

"This tells me he is being rehabilitated, if not totally rehabilitated ... that he's not engaged in anti-social behavior," said Dr. Bloomfield. He admitted that he was just as baffled as to how Josh was able to behave so normally and sleep in the same bed with Maddie's body for seven days straight while everyone was looking for her, calling it "bizarre." He stated that the 14-year-old was scared and confused.[102]

He also testified about how the human brain changes over time and how young people simply do not have fully-developed brains that allow for proper decision-making and judgment.

The following day, defense attorney Tom Fallis called to the stand six more witnesses who were also in favor of Josh's potential release into society someday in the future. The first to testify was a department of corrections officer by the name of Todd Mitchell, who kept tabs on Joshua during his incarceration. He went over Josh's disciplinary history during his imprisonment, citing four minor reports on file, albeit none past 2005. Former *Florida Times-Union* reporter Paul Pinkham also took the stand to attest that Josh did appear remorseful during an interview he did back in 2008 and even teared up. Dr. Laura Bedard, the former prison warden who worked with the defendant in an inmate rehabilitation program, and the Reverend Robert Huguenin, an Anglican priest who looked after Josh, both testified on their faith that he truly was a changed man and a model inmate.[103]

The final witness that the defense called to testify on behalf of Joshua Phillips would come as a surprise to many. It was the very man who had a hand in ensuring that the 15-year-old would spend the rest of his life within prison walls without a chance of ever walking the streets again: Harry Shorstein. In light of all the scientific studies that revealed evidence for the under-developed adolescent brain, he voiced his regret for seeking the harshest sentence that was available for Josh at the time he was prosecuted. Had he known then what he knew now, he would not have sought a conviction for murder in the first degree.

But perhaps the most crucial person to take the stand to convince the court of the rehabilitated man the defendant had become was the defendant himself. Slouching into the chair and positioning himself before the stand, he began reading from his letter of apology addressed to the Clifton family.

"I don't pretend to know or understand your pain or to grasp the void I created in your lives," he read. "I can say this: I do understand pain. I have become quite intimate with suffering. Growing up in prison, I have seen many dark things and I've been through dark places. Many times throughout this journey, I became dreadfully close to ending my life just to escape it all."[104]

He spoke of the whirlwind of emotions he had endured during this dark period of his life, from guilt and shame to fear and despair. But, he said, he was able to stay strong and continue pushing forward, not wanting to put his mother through any more trauma.

"There were times that I was angry at her because I couldn't end my pain because of her love. Yet now, I'm eternally grateful to her. I'm grateful to her because as I've grown up, I've learned the value of life. I've learned to see the beauty and joy in a world full of strife, and experienced the truth of unconditional love. I wish to God that I could've known this or understood it when I was 14," he said. "I did something horrible. I'm so sorry. I'm so sorry for what happened."

Concluding his four-minute apology, he told the Clifton family, "My next breath is always devoted to wishing peace and healing upon you all. My hopes, fears, and wishes probably mean nothing to you, but they're there all the same. May you know peace, may you be free from suffering, and may you feel the love that is the sustenance of life itself. May God bless you and heal your wounds as much as possible."[105]

With that, the defense rested its case. Now, it was time for the prosecutor to call forth Maddie's family to recall their pain that resulted from Josh's actions nearly two decades ago.

"The defendant now wants a second chance to live a second life. What does Maddie get to appeal her death to?" said Sheila. "Should he ever be released from prison, I pray that I will no longer be on this earth."[106]

Maddie's father, Steve Clifton, was also against the appeal for Josh's sentence. He, too, believed that Josh should spend the remainder of his life in prison. Even though his incarceration would not bring his beloved daughter back from the grave in which Josh had put her, there should still be some sort of retribution for the damage he caused.

He talked about how his girls were being raised in a Christian household where daily prayer took place. But what he, along with everyone else, was unaware of was that the devil himself, the chief spirit of evil, resided just across the street from them. "That same devil picked up his flashlight and proceeded to look for her, knowing good and well where she was the whole time."[107]

Jessie Clifton spoke about her anguish in her victim impact statement. She told the judge there had been days when she needed someone to talk to, someone who truly understood her, only for it to sink in, once again, that the one person she could open her heart and soul to was no longer there. "There are days when I go to the cemetery and I sit down in the grass because I don't have anybody else to talk to, so I talk to her and the ground."[108]

A former JSO evidence technician who had also worked the case and photographed Josh's bedroom, which had become a crime scene upon the discovery of the eight-year-old's mangled corpse, testified that it was one of the worst murder scenes he had seen in his 16-year career. Interestingly, Joe Plotkin, the state attorney chief's assistant who worked alongside Harry Shorstein during Josh's trial in 1999, testified for the state to oppose Joshua ever re-entering society.

Wrapping up the four-day hearing, for a little over 30 minutes Judge Wallace spoke about the influx of changes sparked by scientific discoveries and how they have impacted the justice system when it comes to sentencing youths in America. With Melissa clasping her hands hopefully, and the Clifton family silently praying that Maddie's killer would stay locked up for the remainder of his life, the judge issued a re-sentence of life in prison.

Despite the witnesses who had worked with Josh over the course of his imprisonment testifying on their confidence of his rehabilitation, Judge Wallace was not quite convinced that Josh wouldn't still pose a threat to others if he were to ever walk the streets again. He couldn't get past the sheer callousness of the murder and his detached demeanor afterward. The crime was too extreme and brutal to elicit mercy from him, even though, in his words, it "saddened" him to sentence Josh to life.

In his 31-page sentencing order, Judge Wallace laid out his reasoning. "The actions of the defendant in this case reflect characteristics not generally found in criminal behavior typical of juveniles. His actions were motivated by deviant, prurient intentions. He targeted a helpless victim and carefully planned his actions toward her. His actions in inflicting injuries causing death, particularly in silencing Maddie Clifton by repeated stabbings after he had dismissed her as dead, as well as his cold and callous demeanor in hiding her decomposed body, represent a level of depravity that cannot be explained or attributed to immaturity, impetuosity or recklessness or headless risk-taking."

He finished by saying, "The crime committed by the defendant is indeed the uncommon case that qualifies for a life sentence."[109]

Afterword

Was Joshua Phillips' sentence—life in prison—appropriate and fair? In fact, is it *ever* justifiable to send a child to prison for the rest of his or her life?

When Shorstein took office in 1991, he was concerned about the high rate of juvenile crime in Duval County, Florida. To tackle this problem, he launched the Juvenile Justice Program, which aimed to reduce juvenile crime rates. He took an authoritarian approach by aggressively prosecuting and warehousing repeat and violent juvenile offenders in local jails, hoping to deter juvenile crime. But simply incarcerating juveniles wasn't enough, so he introduced rehabilitative programs promoting life skills, schooling and anger-control training. Last, and probably the most important element of the program, was to take preventative measures by instituting early-intervention programs for at-risk youth showing early signs of delinquency.

Shorstein's efforts to keep juvenile crime at bay proved to be a success—between 1993 and 1995, the University of Florida concluded that the at-risk programs and incarceration of juvenile offenders drastically decreased juvenile crime in Jacksonville by 45 percent, saving the public approximately $6 million yearly.[110]

"Over the years, there has been a tremendous amount of science dealing with the adolescent brain. The right frontal lobe of your brain really controls your impulses." That part of the brain, he says, is not fully developed until an individual is around 25. He asserted that this fact doesn't excuse the behavior for the juvenile offender; however, it should be taken into consideration. "The more the science evolves, you become more aware that children are different and that should be taken into consideration. A 14-year-old murderer is not the same as a 25-year-old murderer."[111]

Shorstein had a change of heart not only on harsh sentencing for juveniles but also on the death penalty. "I was a very, very tough prosecutor. I think I had more death penalties than any state attorney in the state. I've changed my position on that," he said. "I'm against the death penalty except for the extreme cases, but I wasn't that way thirty-four years ago. It just doesn't work. It doesn't make a lot of sense."[112]

During the trial, it was insinuated that Joshua's consumption of violent pornography before Maddie's murder may have been the driving force behind his senseless crime. While there's no way to tell if it was, it makes one wonder: how much influence does exposure to pornography, particularly violent pornography, have on one's mind?

While there are fewer studies that concentrate on the effects that violent pornography has on its consumers, there are quite a few that zero in on the impact that exposure to pornography may have. Pornography that features violence and even nonviolence overwhelmingly portrays males as dominant and females as submissive. Pornography tends to promote abusive language and behavior toward women, which increases concerns that this will only normalize such sexually aggressive behavior toward women and girls. Research has shown that boys on average were exposed to pornography at a younger age than girls and were more likely to view more extreme pornographic images, such as depictions of rape and child pornography. Girls were less likely to view pornography and were usually involuntarily exposed to pornography.[113] Even more concerning is that children and adolescents who viewed violent pornography were six times more likely to report sexually aggressive behavior compared to those who did not view violent pornography.[114]

There's evidence that there may be neurological repercussions to porn consumption. The brain chemical dopamine is released when we view porn. Much like drug addiction works, repeated exposure to pornography causes one to build tolerance and become desensitized to the sexual content. This damages the dopamine reward system, as users seek out harder sexual themes to achieve that same dopamine rush.[115]

The topic of whether pornography does more harm than good remains controversial. Defenders of pornography will point to contrary research suggesting that pornography actually serves as a healthy outlet for those who are predisposed to sexually aggressive behavior and in turn reduces the risk of perpetration of sexual violence.[116] Sex crimes have decreased over the decades despite the fact that pornographic production now makes it more accessible, further giving proponents of pornography more evidence.[117]

Thanks to the Internet, pornography is now more accessible than ever. Today, the average age that individuals stumble upon pornography is around 11 years old.[118] With evidence on how pornography rewires the human brain, there is increased concern about how it warps the young minds of child consumers when they are being fed unhealthy perceptions about sex, women and girls before they reach adolescence.

Unlike many other kids who have killed, there was no singular element in Joshua Phillips' background that stood out to possibly rationalize the absolute cruelty that he, just a kid himself, could bestow upon another child. The outcome of Josh's trial has prompted many questions that remain widely disputed and unresolved. Do we need to seriously rethink the way we treat juveniles in the court system based on the scientific evidence of the adolescent brain? And do kids who kill deserve leniency and a second chance?

Alyssa Bustamante
(2009)

It was October 2009. Temperatures had dipped from a hot 80 degrees Fahrenheit to more brisk conditions. Residents of Jefferson City, Missouri, had long ago ditched the T-shirts, shorts, and umbrellas that they had been sporting through the humid, rainy summer months in favor of sweaters and scarves to better bear the cold. The decline of warmth in the city's atmosphere hadn't dampened the spirits of the state's capital like chilly weather tends to do—at least, not yet. There was a reason for that: Halloween was just around the corner. Party warehouses were brimming with costumes, make-up, and other freaky accessories; nearly every other residential home that lined the streets was embellished with awe-inspiring decorations. Passersby couldn't help but slow their cars every now and then to admire the ornamented homes. Even the ones that didn't go all out at least had a couple of frightening jack-o'-lanterns sitting on their porches. Halloween isn't just a time of spooky fun; it is a way for many people to channel their inner creativity in a morbid way that is socially acceptable.

About 10 miles away from the capital, a little girl was growing up in St. Martins. Elizabeth Kay Olten was the youngest of five siblings. She was born December 15, 1999, in Jefferson City, Missouri, to Patricia "Patty" Preiss and Dale Olten, Sr. She had many hobbies that were typical of a girl within her age range, such as listening to music, particularly Hannah Montana and Taylor Swift, playing with her friends, and baking cookies. Described as a huge lover of animals, especially horses, she derived amusement from dressing up her pets in her free time. Elizabeth was close to and spent much quality time with her mother, Patty; one of their favorite activities to do together was solving puzzles.[1] In the fall of 2009, she entered the fourth grade at Pioneer Trails Elementary

School and made an exciting start to the term by deciding to participate in the school play. The brown-haired, brown-eyed beauty spent much of her after-school time rehearsing her lines and practicing her singing.

October 21, 2009, was another one of those days for the nine-year-old. That evening, between practicing her lines, singing her songs, and hassling her older brother, Anthony, there was a sudden knock at the front door. Upon opening the door, she saw the person standing on the front porch was no stranger to the family—it was the six-year-old girl who lived just down the street on the 600 block of Route D. Elizabeth lived only a quarter mile away on the 200 block of D, near the intersection of Highway 50. It was not uncommon for the two girls to be seen frolicking about the rural neighborhood together or entertaining themselves with their dolls. Elizabeth and her siblings often went over to their trusted neighbors' house to play with all the kids who lived there.

Emma, the six-year-old, had stopped by their house for one reason: could Elizabeth come out to play?

At first, Patty said no. It was already 5:15 and she was just about to prepare dinner. But the girls clearly weren't going to take no for an answer. Their eyes flickered with excitement as they eagerly bounced up and down on their feet, begging over and over for Elizabeth's mother to give permission. Of course, like many parents, Patty couldn't resist their incessant hopping and pleading; she didn't want to deny her daughter a fun afternoon of playtime, so she gave in, but on one condition: she had to be back in exactly one hour for dinner. Elizabeth threw on a pink sweater over her pink, butterfly-themed shirt and wrapped a two-tone pink scarf around her neck. In less than a minute, Elizabeth was seen skipping off with her playmate, their high-pitched giggles growing more distant the further they drew away.[2]

As 6:15 rolled around, Patty was expecting her daughter to walk through the door at any minute. But when she didn't, Patty was immediately struck with panic. She tried to stay calm as she picked up the phone and dialed the number to Emma's home. Her grandmother and legal guardian, Karen Brooke, picked up the phone. Patty wanted to know where Elizabeth was and received some jarring news: Elizabeth was never at her house. In fact, she had not seen the little girl at all that day. Patty gave it some more time, but, by 6:56, Elizabeth was still a no-show. Patty couldn't wait any longer and called the police to report her daughter missing. In no more than 15 minutes, the Cole County Sheriff's Department was on the scene. The first thing the sheriff's deputies decided to do was go to the last known place where Elizabeth was headed: her neighbor and playmate's house. Emma was home, but everyone denied having seen Elizabeth that day. By then it was clear: there was a missing child and she needed to be located as soon as possible.

The fire department and local law enforcement agencies were called to join the search for the missing nine-year-old, conducting what is known as a "grid search" in the area around Elizabeth's and her playmate's houses.

There are five common search patterns investigators implement when looking for physical evidence. Search patterns are thorough and systematic, not haphazard or meandering, and it's crucial for police to stick to the routine step-by-step method and pay close attention to detail. In this way, investigators avoid chaos and overlooking evidence; protect evidence from contamination; and maintain professionalism. Usually, one person is assigned to be in charge of a search. The scene type needs to be analyzed in order to determine how to search. There are different search methods designed specifically for different types of environments and crime scenes. Some examples of scene types can include buildings (prisons, schools, offices, homes), vehicles (cars, trailers, buses), open areas (parks, lawns, streets, yards), and persons (victims or suspects). The most difficult environments to investigate are outdoor crime scenes, as evidence in the outdoors tends to be destroyed or contaminated by the frequent exposure to elements like heat, wind, rain and animal activity.

The purpose of the search also needs to be established in order for investigators to know what type of evidence to search for. Again, this depends largely on the crime that has been committed. In the event of a burglary, for example, crime scene investigators would keep an eye out for shoe prints, broken glass, fingerprints and signs of forced entry. For a homicide crime scene, CSIs will search for fingerprints, bullets, shell casings and trace evidence such as hair, blood and saliva.[3]

The investigators will then establish how to conduct the search based on the scene and type of crime. The five search methods are as follows:

> 1. **The grid method.** One of the most common search patterns used by investigators, it is best employed in large areas such as woods or fields. Searchers may start from the west side of the scene and march alongside each other at arm's length toward the opposite

end of the scene. Then, they will turn at a 45-degree angle and repeat the same process, except they are now moving along the opposite direction toward where they started. They will then perform the same search starting from the north end of the field, striding across the scene in consecutive laps until they've completed their search. Although it is time consuming, it is the most thorough and effective tactic to use to look for evidence.

    2. **The wheel method.** Otherwise known as the "pie method," this search pattern is another good way to search for evidence in large and open areas. Several investigators are needed for this one. Typically, searchers will gather in the center point of an imaginary circle and move outward in a straight direction, dividing the scene into several sections resembling pie slices. This method, however, can be a bit precarious, as investigators risk sabotaging evidence if they are not extremely cautious of where they are stepping as they congregate in the starting point of the search area.

    3. **The zone method.** This involves splitting the scene into four squares or quadrants. One or more investigators will then be assigned to search each section before swapping quadrants and recovering the area to ensure that no evidence was missed somehow. Usually, these square sections are divided into smaller squares.

    4. **The spiral method.** Investigators will position themselves in the center of the scene and gradually spiral outward until they reach the perimeter of the scene. Conversely, they may also choose to start from an outer point and work their way inward until they reach the core of the scene.

    5. **The strip or line method.** This search pattern proves productive when scouring for evidence in the outdoors. It is similar to the grid method, except investigators only move along a path starting from one end of the search area to the other side in one direction, before turning around and completing a second lap back to where they started. The line method is often treated as an alternative to the grid method when there are multiple obstacles in the scene such as trees, rocks, etc.[4]

    As the hours ticked by, Patty grew more anxious. She made repeated phone calls to Elizabeth's cell phone that the girl carried on her wherever she went, desperate with each ring that she would finally pick up, but, every single time, Patty was directed to her voicemail. Sheriff's deputies tried to comfort Patty by telling her there were no signs of foul play so far, but that did very little to ease her worst fear. Although her daughter was a tomboy, she was deathly afraid of the dark and would never dare wander outside alone by herself or set foot in the woods. She was an extremely shy girl, not one to talk to strangers, much less get into their cars. If confronted, she would have screamed and run away.[5] So how could a nine-year-old girl just ... vanish into thin air?

There were at least 50 sheriffs assisting in the search, some by foot and others driving their four-wheelers. They combed through ditches and fields, shining their flashlights over every inch of the ground surface they covered. They assigned a search team to the Extreme Body and Paint shop. Over 100 volunteers aided in the search, traipsing through the rural area around the missing girl's home. As the rain poured down, Lowe's Home Improvement donated rain gear for searchers. Before 10 p.m. hit, a helicopter hovered near the St. Martins city limits with infrared sensors, which can detect various aspects of the environment such as motion and the heat of an object. But even this tactic was hindered due to fall foliage. It was around this time that investigators came up with the idea of contacting Elizabeth's phone carrier, AT&T, and requesting an emergency ping.[6]

It didn't take long for them to receive their first two pings from the missing girl's cell phone. Elizabeth's phone transmitted one final ping before the battery seemingly went dead. But it didn't matter, because AT&T was able to triangulate the missing girl's approximate cell phone location deep in the dense wooded area that ran several hundred yards in diameter behind Elizabeth's home.[7] Why her phone would be in the woods was a mystery to everyone. Elizabeth was afraid of the woods, and she would most certainly never walk through it as a shortcut back from Emma's home. The younger girl lived only four houses away. Elizabeth only walked along Route D, the longer but safer route.

Now, police knew where to focus their search. Assuming Elizabeth wasn't separated from her phone, they could find her. There was only one problem: search efforts were being curtailed by the soaking rain, uneven stretch of land and high brush.

"If you go to Iowa and look at a flat piece of farmland that's 140 acres," you go, "well, it's not that big. You translate that to Missouri and you use the same thing, you walk a long time to cover that same amount of land," said Cole County sheriff Greg White. "It's muddy out there now. It's difficult terrain, it's difficult weather."[8]

Deputies knew they were going to need backup. Although they hadn't issued an Amber alert yet as they didn't think there was any evidence of child abduction or foul play, Elizabeth was nevertheless listed as an "endangered missing person." They issued missing person reports and alerted neighboring police agencies as well as fire departments about Elizabeth's disappearance. They continued to relentlessly search until the early morning hours. By 2:30 a.m., all search crews, save for one, decided to wrap it up and resume early the next morning.

Day Two

The following day, it was still pouring. The Cole County Sheriff's Department enlisted the help of the Missouri State Highway Patrol, Regional West Fire Protection District, Cole County Fire Protection District, and Cole County Mobile Emergency Operations Center. Even the FBI joined the investigation. Together, they worked to locate this missing girl. They summoned K-9 units as well as diver teams to search nearby lagoons, creeks, and the muddy brown ponds among the farm fields. They called for the aid of a helicopter again, but the thermal radar was again hampered by the soaking weather. News about the missing nine-year-old girl broke fast, drawing 300 volunteers within the community to participate in the search, people who weren't even affiliated with Elizabeth's family. Many of them were parents themselves, and they knew that if one of their own children disappeared, they would want others to help as well.[9]

A long line of emergency vehicles from multiple local agencies was parked along the highway, stretching past all the houses. Investigators went knocking on every neighbor's door, questioning their whereabouts on the day of Elizabeth's disappearance and asking if they had seen anything suspicious. Missouri State Highway Patrol sergeant David Rice didn't think the nine-year-old could have gone too far, but he also accepted the likelihood that she could have been abducted by a child molester and whisked away in a car. It was a prospect that made his stomach turn, one that nobody wanted to think about. Just as they would in most early investigations of missing child cases, they reached out to any registered sex offenders in the area and interrogated them about their whereabouts on the day Elizabeth went missing.

Investigators knew that someone must have heard or seen something. The only person who could provide any clues as to where Elizabeth was headed would be her six-year-old neighbor and friend, the last confirmed person to have seen Elizabeth. When the FBI spoke with Emma, she didn't reveal much, only stating that she played with Elizabeth for an hour and then she headed back home. But agents pushed for more details from the six-year-old, and eventually, they got more. One detail stuck out. Emma disclosed that her older friend had fallen into a thorn bush and gotten stuck among the sharp, wooden projections.

"Alyssa, come help me!" she allegedly cried out, referring to Emma's older half-sister.[10]

Alyssa. This wouldn't be the first time investigators heard that name.

∼

Search crews continued canvassing the woods behind her playmate's house. At roughly 12:30 in the afternoon, local volunteers stumbled upon "disturbed dirt" in the woods roughly where Elizabeth's phone transmitted its final pings. To be more specific, the "disturbed dirt" resembled that of a small grave, perhaps large enough to hold someone of Elizabeth's size. Of course, everyone felt a sense of profound dread in the pit of their stomachs, especially when a cadaver dog responded positive for human remains. Was this it? Was this hole going to mark the end of their search? Sergeant David Rice instructed his unit to process the scene; they also sent a cadaver dog to Emma's house where Elizabeth was last seen playing before she disappeared. There, they received further dreadful results: the cadaver dog also hit positive for human remains in the trunk of the vehicle that was parked in the garage there. But that was a dead end, because when they opened it, there was nothing unusual that would indicate Elizabeth had been inside.[11]

Now, new circumstances were coming to light. Investigators believed that the family might have more knowledge about the little girl's strange disappearance than they were letting on. They further interviewed the owner of the home, Karen Brooke, and requested consent to search the inside of her home. They also wanted to speak with her 15-year-old granddaughter, Alyssa Bustamante, who was supposed to be in school during that time but was reported to be absent after having skipped to go to her 16-year-old boyfriend's house.

Alyssa ended up returning to school by the end of the day. Karen and her granddaughter Emma were brought to the Jefferson City

Resident Agency to be questioned while two investigators drove to Jefferson City High School shortly before 4 p.m. They explained to school personnel that they needed to speak with one of their students and shortly thereafter met with Alyssa. The agents introduced themselves to Alyssa and told her that FBI agents needed to speak with her. Alyssa left her high school with the police. They assured her that the interview wouldn't take too much time; they just wanted to know if she had any information regarding her missing neighbor.

While they were driving to the Cole County Sheriff Command Center, a change of plans occurred when an FBI agent gave instructions to instead bring Alyssa to the local FBI office. The driver immediately turned his car around and brought her over. Alyssa was introduced to FBI agent Shawn McDermott upon arrival. There was nothing amiss about her demeanor, and she calmly answered any questions he had for her. She told him that she was aware Elizabeth had vanished the day prior and authorities were still trying to locate her, but she stated that she didn't have any information about what might have happened to her. At this time, Alyssa was not considered a suspect in the case. Other than her eccentric style, she looked to be your average teenage girl, and how likely was it that a 15-year-old girl would be responsible for the disappearance of a much younger child? Not very.

After the interview, Shawn McDermott and one other FBI agent brought Alyssa back to her residence, not to drop her off safely, but to lead her to that suspicious hole in the woods which police had closed off as a crime scene. Sergeant David Rice was already waiting there, prepared to ask Alyssa if she happened to know anything about the hole. She admitted to him that, yes, she had brought her shovel over last Sunday and was responsible for digging that hole.

Rice was in shock. "Why did you dig the hole?"

"I just like digging holes," Alyssa casually responded. She explained that she liked to bury animal carcasses that she found in the thick forest.[12]

Eyebrows were raised and awkward glances were exchanged among the investigators. They silently agreed that it was certainly bizarre behavior to take into consideration. There aren't too many 15-year-olds who like to dig holes for the purpose of burying dead animals as a pastime. It almost made them feel uneasy. But they did not manage to unearth Elizabeth's body even though the cadaver dog hit positive for human remains. Once again, it felt like they had hit another dead end, but search crews felt immense relief. That meant they could continue their search, that there was still hope they could find the little girl alive and well.

David Rice was still shaken over his encounter with Alyssa. Did he have any evidence that the hole was anything more than the result of a harmless morbid hobby, as the teenage girl claimed? No. But he could not quell the gut feeling that there was something seriously suspicious about that hole. It was about the perfect size for a small child.

It had now officially been a full 24 hours since Elizabeth was reported missing and search efforts commenced. So far, they had come up with nothing. They still failed to locate her cell phone or any witnesses who had any information on her whereabouts. It was almost impossible to decide whether it was a good thing or a bad thing that Elizabeth hadn't been found yet. It might have meant she was still out there, but it could also have indicated that something more sinister happened. At this point in the case, authorities had not recovered any evidence that indicated foul play, so it did not meet the standards of an Amber alert despite it having been an entire day since the little girl inexplicably vanished. This was extremely frustrating for Elizabeth's family, who were dissatisfied with the slow pace of the search and how it was being conducted. It was glaringly obvious that Elizabeth was an endangered missing child. She wasn't one to wander off, run away and hide, or interact with strangers.

"I just don't understand," expressed Elizabeth's aunt, Vicki Olten, through sobs at a press conference on Thursday. "Her mom's a wreck."[13] She was grateful for the number of locals who went out of their way to help, some driving from great distances just to provide their support. But more could be done, Vicki argued. She contended that the volunteers should be provided with more adequate training so they could stay out even longer and that there should be a change to the Amber alert's system so that missing cases like her niece's could be distributed quicker and earlier. It was her belief that Elizabeth was grabbed by someone.

AMBER is a backronym for America's Missing: Broadcast Emergency Response. It was named after Amber Hagerman, a nine-year-old Texas girl who was kidnapped in broad daylight while riding her bike in 1996. One witness had seen a man snatch her from her bicycle as she kicked and screamed, shove her into his truck, and drive off. Her body was found in a creek four days later, just a few miles away from the Hagerman home. Her throat had been slit and she was completely nude.

Amber's heartbreaking murder, unfortunately, was never solved, but it inspired her parents to become avid child advocates, which led to the well-known Amber alert system starting nine months after her passing. The purpose of the system is to broadcast the news of a child's abduction almost immediately after it occurs to enhance the chances of locating the child. As of 2019, the FBI estimated that the use of Amber alerts assisted in the safe return of more than 900 missing children over the past two decades.[14]

However, the U.S. Department of Justice issued strict guidance containing certain criteria that must be met in order for a missing child case to reach Amber alert level to avoid potential false alarms.

1. Law enforcement must confirm that an abduction has occurred.
2. The child must be at risk of serious bodily injury or death.
3. There must be sufficient descriptive information of the child, the abduction, the suspect and the suspect's vehicle.
4. The child must be 17 years of age or younger.[15]

Elizabeth's father, Dale Olten, Sr., had found out that his daughter was missing while watching the news on the tiny television in his prison cell. He was currently serving four years in prison for drug possession after being sentenced in April of that year. Vicki knew how much Dale cherished his daughter. He was not considered a suspect in her disappearance, a point that was verified by Cole County sheriff Greg White.

"She's the apple of his eye," said Vicki. "It was just so hard for me to hear him crying on the phone and tell me, 'Please find my baby.'"[16]

Elizabeth's loved ones weren't the only ones getting frustrated with the search; so were many of the hundreds of volunteers police had begun turning away starting Thursday afternoon, sparking rumors that a body had been found. Greg White promptly spent the next few hours dispelling these rumors that were starting to quickly circulate among the volunteers within the community.

Investigators believed that they were doing everything they could to find Elizabeth during this exhaustive search. The Missouri Highway Patrol conducted a roadblock on Road D where Elizabeth was last seen between 5:30 p.m. and 7 p.m.

"The same cars usually travel an area at the same time every day, so we hope that somebody might have seen something that we didn't find out about earlier," said Colonel Jim Keathley, the highway patrol superintendent. They stopped every passerby to hand out a missing person flier and ask if they had witnessed or heard anything suspicious in the area on Wednesday evening, but nobody came forward with valuable information.[17]

The FBI finally acquired consent to search the entire Bustamante home. The Bustamantes weren't the only ones in the neighborhood who had their home searched; police didn't want to rule anyone out as a possible suspect. The search team was comprised of several FBI agents who split up to comb through different areas of the home. FBI agent Patricia Gentry was assigned to 15-year-old Alyssa Bustamante's bedroom. As soon as she twisted the doorknob and opened the door, just about every hair on the back of her neck bristled from the disturbing imagery she saw within. Every wall was covered with macabre writings handwritten in pen and, chillingly, in blood. On one side of the bedroom, inscribed in blood, were the words *It was written in blood, it was written in blood!* Also adorning her bedroom were cards and letters from her father, Caesar Bustamante, who was currently serving time in prison for assault.

Gentry noticed what appeared to be some more writings scrawled in one corner of the room. She walked a little closer to get a better look when it became obvious that this was, in fact, a handwritten poem authored by Alyssa, voicing her inner struggles with self-harm.

> *I cut to focus,*
> *when my brain is racing,*
> *I cut to make physical,*
> *what I feel inside*
> *I cut to see blood,*
> *because I like it*
> *I don't like to cut,*
> *but I can't give it up*[18]

Agent Patricia Gentry backed away and slowly eased her body around, taking in her disturbing surroundings once more, from the bloody writings on the walls to the hand-drawn sketch and poem, before she began rummaging through the teenager's belongings to find something that could be incriminating. She collected a pair of blue jeans, a pillowcase and fitted sheet, a pair of white socks and tennis shoes, muddy pants, a ratchet with "residue," and a baggie with seeds and another containing pills.

She then noted what appeared to be a diary. Of course, owning a diary is nothing out of the ordinary for someone Alyssa's age, but considering the sickening words covering every wall in her bedroom, it was certainly worth nosing into.

She cracked open the diary and observed the passages inside. She didn't think it could get any more disturbing than what she had just seen, but she was wrong. In one entry, Alyssa described her desire to set an entire house on fire and watch all of its occupants burn to death. She continued to flip through the delicate pages until she reached the very last entry, dated October 21, 2009, the very same day Elizabeth went missing. This obviously piqued her interest, but there was one problem: whatever Alyssa had written on that day had been scribbled out with blue pen, making it indecipherable to the prying eyes of the agent. For some reason, she chose to leave only the very last sentence unscathed. It read: "Kay, I gotta go to church now ... lol."

Interesting, Agent Gentry thought, as she seized the diary and added it to her collection of evidence. If her partners could manage to decipher the writing beneath the scratched-out ink, they might find something that would implicate her. Gentry also seized two shovels found at the side of the house.

A Confession Is Made

October 23 and two days after nine-year-old Elizabeth Olten's mysterious disappearance. Investigators had spoken with and searched the homes of numerous persons of interest, including local registered sex offenders, but all of those leads only provided routes to dead ends. They still had to go through the evidence they seized from those homes, but they felt just as stumped as they had been on day one. They did, however, have their eye on someone, and that was 15-year-old Alyssa Bustamante. They thought her behavior was strange and wanted to conduct a more in-depth and personal interview to clarify her version of events on the day her younger sister's little friend went missing. Alyssa, accompanied by her grandmother and legal guardian Karen Brooke, was brought to the Jefferson City Resident Agency of the FBI once again for another "talk." This time, she would be speaking with Sergeant David Rice of the MSHP.

Sergeant Rice was certain that this interview would move toward a full-blown interrogation. He, along with other investigators, felt confident that Alyssa was somehow involved in Elizabeth's disappearance. It was just a matter of finding the right method to get her to cough up the information she was potentially withholding. But right before it was set to begin, an agent wanted to give the sergeant something that might be helpful during the interview. It was the diary that had been recovered from Alyssa's bedroom just the day before. They only managed to uncover two words by the use of backlighting, but those two words were enough to reveal something potentially incriminating: *slit* and *throat*.

Alyssa and her grandmother settled into the interrogation room with Sergeant Rice and a juvenile officer. He wanted to start things slowly, with baby steps. He asked her one question and waited. Alyssa would take some time to ponder before answering. Sergeant Rice would pause before asking another question. He would allow these prolonged silences to fill the room for 45 seconds, sometimes even a minute, at a time. It was making the teenager visibly uncomfortable, all the way from her trembling head to her shifty blue eyes.

"Silence is very effective during an interview or an interrogation because people feel very uncomfortable in silence," he stated. Recalling the juvenile's demeanor during that tense time, he noted, "You can see the stress affecting Alyssa."

Suddenly, Sergeant Rice pulled out her diary and gave it to Alyssa. There was a notable change in her behavior as soon as she was confronted with her old journal in which so many of her darkest thoughts had been documented. Alyssa must have felt like she had been stripped naked in front of a large crowd.

"We have your diary," he said. "We read your diary, even the last entry which was scribbled out."[19]

Then, he waited. The tension in the small interrogation room increased. Suddenly, the jumbled words of a half-confession began tumbling from Alyssa's mouth. She said that what happened was an accident. She had been walking with the child in the woods when she suddenly tripped, fell, and hit her head, dying as a result. But Sergeant Rice wasn't going to buy her made-up story of a fatal accident, not with the words "slit" and "throat" at the forefront of his mind. He warned Alyssa that once they retrieved Elizabeth's body, an autopsy would be conducted that would reveal every injury she sustained and her cause of death.

Giving her one last chance to spit out the truth of what really happened on October 21, he asked her bluntly, "Was her throat cut?"

Another moment of silence.

"Yes," she admitted.[20]

Alyssa's grandmother burst into tears. She didn't suspect or want to believe that Alyssa was somehow involved in her neighbor's disappearance, but hearing her own granddaughter admit out loud that she was responsible for brutally killing a little girl, her own little sister's friend, was too agonizing a reality to bear.

Karen stood up from her chair and walked out of the interrogation room. This wasn't the granddaughter that she knew. She'd worked hard to provide her with a stable and loving home when her own parents couldn't, and, in the end, she felt like she had failed her.

Knowing that she had been caught, and that she was at the point of no return, Alyssa began opening up to Sergeant Rice about the harrowing truth of what really happened on the fateful evening of October 21. He was shocked when Alyssa revealed that she had orchestrated the entire thing in advance.

Elizabeth Olten, nine, never came home after an evening of playtime with her neighbor. Her body was found buried in the woods not too far from her home (courtesy Patricia Preiss).

To prove she wasn't lying, she led him through the wooded area to the precise spot where Elizabeth's corpse had been buried the entire time, retracing her footsteps over the ridges, through the valleys and hedges of the uneven terrain that made it difficult for search crews to comb through the area during the past few days. It was quite clear that no nine-year-old would have simply wandered off in this area; one would have to *really* want to be back here to find this place. And, finally, several hundred yards away from all the houses, was Elizabeth's grave.

Now they had written evidence, a confession and a body, which was more than the reasonable grounds needed to arrest the adolescent for murder. She was brought to a juvenile detention facility, where she was to remain until it would be decided how exactly Alyssa would be dealt with by the law. The tricky question was, should Alyssa face consequences as a juvenile, since she was under the age of 18, or was her crime so depraved that it would warrant trying her as an adult?

The crime scene was processed and photographed before Elizabeth's muddy remains were exhumed from the dirt grave. Along with her body, authorities recovered Elizabeth's cell phone, which was collected as evidence.

The next day, investigators returned to Alyssa Bustamante's home as soon as their request for another search warrant was approved. This time, they set out to locate a large, black-handled kitchen knife. They discovered it sitting in the upper tray of the dishwasher and promptly photographed it. The knife appeared to have been recently washed, as the blade was somewhat wet and warm when they retrieved it for evidence.

Don Lock, a forensic consultant who specializes in handwriting analysis, was able to use a blue light to read the rest of Alyssa's diary entry on the day that she killed Elizabeth, which she'd attempted to obliterate.[21] The entry was one that would make investigators sick to their stomachs.

One might wonder what exactly would drive this 15-year-old high school girl to commit the senseless murder of a much younger child. The only motive Alyssa would ever divulge to Sergeant Rice was "I just wanted to know what it felt like."[22]

∽

Just before three o'clock on that gloomy afternoon, Cole County sheriff Greg White, along with Highway Patrol superintendent Jim Keathley, finally broke the news regarding the heart-breaking discovery at a press conference. A small crowd assembled at the St. Martins VFW emitted audible gasps. They quietly hung on every word the sheriff revealed, although he didn't go into specifics; he only explained that written and physical evidence had led authorities to their suspect, an unnamed juvenile who was described as an "acquaintance" of the victim. Even though they found Elizabeth's body and knew who was responsible for her death now, Sheriff Greg White asserted that the investigation was far from over.[23]

Later that evening, a relative of the Olten family, Liza Adrian, stood in front of the VFW hall during a press conference and expressed the family's immense grief and sadness over the news and their eternal gratitude for everyone who had gotten involved to relentlessly search for Elizabeth.

The press conference continued the next day, as there was still some leftover frustration regarding questions for which the public desperately sought answers. There was a child-killing predator in their community—why couldn't they know who it was and what happened? But, once again, Cole County sheriff Greg White, this time with juvenile director Michael Couty, faced the crowd of reporters at the VFW hall in St. Martins to try to answer some of the community's inquiries. Sheriff White continued to release only vague details around the subject matter, declining to provide the time of Elizabeth's death or how she was murdered, or even so much as the juvenile suspect's gender. He once again confirmed that the victim and suspect indeed knew each other but clarified that they were not related.

"I know it would be cathartic for the public to know exactly what happened," White acknowledged, but he added that they needed to maintain a prosecutable case and feared that sharing all of the ghastly details while the investigation was still ongoing might "contaminate" the jury pool. The only information he was willing to share with the reporters was that the event happened shortly before or at the beginning of the missing person report and they had discovered the location of the body between 2:30 and 2:40 p.m. on Friday in the middle of the woods where searchers had been more than once.[24]

But why hadn't anybody seen anything?

"The body was very well concealed," he noted.[25]

He declined to release any more information about the juvenile. Juvenile director Michael Couty told reporters that the 15-year-old suspect was being detained in juvenile custody and that they would be filing for a certification hearing the following week.

During the hearing, which the public would be prohibited from attending as it would be held in juvenile court, Cole County Prosecutor Mark Richardson and juvenile officials planned to present the judge with evidence from the case. Then it would be up to the judge to decide whether the teen should remain in the juvenile court system or face adult charges. Michael Couty stressed that the objective of the hearing wasn't to prove that the suspect was indeed guilty in the case but rather to "determine if we have the means of taking care of that individual within our setting, or if there is another setting that we can refer that juvenile to." Prior to going before a judge, they would have to complete a full background check and psychological assessment on the minor.[26]

Missouri state law states that if a petition alleges that a juvenile has committed murder in the first degree, then a court hearing will be held to determine, at their own discretion, whether to dismiss the juvenile petition and transfer the minor to the adult criminal system, where they will be prosecuted under general law. If the judge resolves that the minor is certified to stand trial as an adult, then the case will be held in open court, meaning all of the details and evidence will be publicized. The juvenile will also lose his or her rights to protected anonymity, meaning their identity, too, will be exposed to the public. But even so, since the suspect in this case was under the age of 16 at the time the violent offense was committed, they would not be eligible for the death penalty under state law. Should they be tried as an adult, the maximum sentence they would receive is a life sentence without parole.

Juvenile director Couty further explained that there are other sentencing options for convicted juveniles. They may be kept in the local juvenile facility such as the Division of Youth Services, where numerous programs are held that are designed to take proper care of youthful offenders through treatment programs. These programs offer group and individual counseling which emphasizes development of communication skills and problem solving, recognition of negative emotions and improvement of poor decision making, and, lastly, restoring justice and empathy. Educational programs are also offered to youth, such as academic training and vocational preparation. In Missouri specifically, a juvenile offender may be eligible for placement in what is called a "dual jurisdiction" program, which essentially imposes a combination of a juvenile and an adult sentence. Therefore, the child could be committed to the Division of Youth Services and, simultaneously, the Department of Corrections. To be considered for this program, the individual must be under the age of 17 and must have been convicted or have pled guilty to felony charges. Once the juvenile reaches the age of 17, a mandatory hearing will be held to determine the next steps. They may be transferred to the Department of Corrections, placed on probation, or remain in custody of the DYS. However, the youth offender may not remain at the DYS past their 21st birthday and could be transferred to adult prison thereafter.[27]

~

The day everyone in Jefferson City was waiting for came on November 18, just over three weeks after Elizabeth's Olten tragic slaying. On that morning, Alyssa Bustamante was indicted on one first-degree murder charge and an armed criminal action charge as an adult at the certification hearing for which the Cole County juvenile officer had filed a petition, requesting that the juvenile court allow the state to prosecute Alyssa in circuit court.

Count I of the indictment read that Alyssa "knowingly caused the death of Elizabeth Kay Olten by strangling her, cutting her throat, and stabbing her." Count II of the indictment read that on October 21, 2009, "Alyssa Bustamante committed the murder charged in Count I by, with and through, the knowing use, assistance, and aid of a dangerous instrument, a knife." Since first-degree murder was deemed a class A felony, she could face a life sentence without the possibility of parole. Armed criminal action, her second charge, was an unclassified felony, warranting a minimum of three years of prison time.[28]

Cole County Circuit Judge Jon Beetem granted this request after pondering Missouri's 10 criteria to charge a juvenile as an adult and considering the suggestions of juvenile court authorities. He ruled that the crime she committed was so serious and heinous that he thought the state lacked the well-equipped juvenile facilities and services needed to properly care for such a young and violent individual.

Of course, the state did have secure youth detention facilities, with locked gates and fences, but only for boys. Juvenile court rarely encounters a young female accused of such a gruesome crime.

"Our girls tend to be more violent toward themselves," stated Bill Herbele, deputy director of the Division of Youth Services. Of course, a glimpse into Alyssa's background would prove that she, too, had a history of mental health issues and self-harm. She was currently being treated for depression with Prozac and had been since her last suicide attempt.[29]

Herbele stated that they would certainly make appropriate accommodations for the teen if the judge decided to commit her to the DYS for treatment, which was still in the cards for her should she be found guilty.

The prosecutor of the case, Mark Richardson, thought that Cole County sheriff Greg White being adamant about Alyssa being charged with first-degree murder only indicated his belief that the murder was premeditated and not a spur-of-the-moment decision; it was not a simple opportunity that Alyssa seized as she saw the chance. This was planned.

Alyssa's attorney disagreed with the judge's decision to try her as an adult, believing that the adolescent was in dire need of mental health rehabilitation in a safe and secure setting and that she would not survive in an adult prison. The day after the certification hearing, the teen girl's public defender, Jan King, filed a motion stating that Alyssa was exhibiting symptoms of severe depression and anxiety. Not only had she attempted to self-harm by cutting herself with her own fingernails, but she had also been placed under suicide watch while being held in juvenile custody. Jan King insisted that his young client would need immediate psychological treatment to "assess her current mental state and to prevent the possibility that she may harm herself."[30]

Cole County Circuit Judge Patricia Joyce heeded the lawyer's request and had Alyssa admitted to a psychiatric hospital for up to 96 hours, where she was to undergo a psychological evaluation and receive immediate treatment.

It seemed that no one truly knew the right thing to do in this case. After all, what *do* we do with a 15-year-old girl who so callously stabbed and slit the throat of a nine-year-old?

Suspicions about the involvement of Alyssa Bustamante's mysterious boyfriend, whom she skipped school to spend time with the day following Elizabeth's death, began to arise. He was interrogated by the FBI as well as the Missouri State Highway Patrol a total of eight times after the murder. He repeatedly denied having any knowledge about Elizabeth's disappearance, explaining to police that Alyssa never told him anything except that her nine-year-old neighbor was missing and the police had searched her house. He also disclosed to police that he found what appeared to be a box cutter or a black knife in her backpack, but they were much smaller than the actual murder weapon. When the FBI informed him of Elizabeth's murder, naming Alyssa as the culprit, he vomited.

Although he had failed a polygraph examination, police didn't feel they had enough evidence to charge him in connection to Elizabeth Olten's murder. They were confident that Alyssa acted alone.[31]

With the killer's identity finally unveiled to the public, the case began to reach national headlines. Residents of St. Martins and Jefferson City were rather pleased after hearing the news that Alyssa would be tried as an adult. The last thing anybody wanted was to hear the same old story of a violent offender receiving a slap on the wrist after committing an egregious crime simply due to their age. No, youth was no excuse, and such offenses warranted the perpetrator being punished to the full extent of the law. Many people expressed their glee at the outcome of the certification, regarding this as just another step closer to justice for Elizabeth Olten.

Alyssa Bustamante

Alyssa Dailene Bustamante was born on January 28, 1994, in California to Michelle and Caesar Bustamante. At the time Alyssa was born, her mother was only 15 years old. Both parents were heavy drug users whose lives revolved around alcohol, marijuana, and even meth—Alyssa was already off to a rather unlucky start in life. The couple frequently relocated around the state of California and then moved to mid–Missouri in 1996, where they continued to move often. Caesar would later testify in court that he and Michelle were "cousins by marriage" and that mental illness ran in the family. He admitted that he had a history of self-harm by cutting and had attempted suicide before, behavior that would also catch up with his first offspring later on in her life.

Michelle would have three more children: Joseph, Nathaniel, and, lastly, Emma. Due to Michelle and Caesar's frequent run-ins with the law and their substance abuse, Alyssa was forced to take on the role of caregiver for her younger siblings. That job was only made more difficult once Caesar was incarcerated for three counts of felony assault; he served his sentences concurrently in the Missouri Eastern Correctional Facility. At home, Alyssa witnessed domestic violence between her parents and heavy drug use. Michelle also had her fair share of run-ins with the law, racking up three misdemeanor charges, including marijuana possession and driving under the influence. She struggled to pay the rent, and her drug abuse was still out of control.[32]

That's why, in 2002, when Alyssa was just eight years old, her grandparents decided to remove Alyssa and her siblings from their turbulent household and they were granted legal custody. They moved from California to St. Martins, Missouri, hoping to provide a more stable and happier home life and childhood for the kids. In later court testimony, Karen Brooke, Alyssa's grandmother, noted that Alyssa had a particularly difficult time adjusting to her new, healthy living conditions as she was used to parenting her younger siblings, but over time, Alyssa acclimated to her new environment.[33]

Despite Alyssa's setbacks in her early childhood, she was, at least on the outside, a happy and friendly young girl. She regularly attended the Church of Jesus Christ of Latter-Day Saints, where she participated in a number of youth activities in which she made several friends.[34] She demonstrated her inner creativity through her poetry writing and eccentric style; in a school full of Abercrombie & Fitch, a particularly popular clothing brand that targeted adolescents in the late 2000s, Alyssa definitely stood out with her heavily-lined blue eyes, dark and alternative apparel (particularly those featuring Jack Skellington from *The Nightmare Before Christmas*), rubber wristbands, and straight brown hair that swooped across her forehead in one dramatic fringe, partially obscuring her face. The fashion sense in question is quite often affiliated with what is known as "emo subculture."

But Alyssa's outward appearance as an average teenage girl was a façade; buried deep inside her psyche was brewing turmoil and self-hatred. At the tender age of 13 she was already battling mental health issues, but, instead of getting help, she dealt with it in self-destructive ways. She found particular solace in mutilating her wrists and arms with sharp razor blades and knives, the pain and oozing blood serving as a release from her emotional anguish.

Non-suicidal self-injury (NSSI) is when someone harms or mutilates themselves without the intention of dying. It is more often than not used as a coping mechanism for stress and a release for pain, and it may also be used as a form of self-punishment. Sometimes it is used to alleviate everyday tension and anger and serves as an escape from perpetual feelings of numbness. The most common form of NSSI is cutting one's own skin with razor blades or a piece of sharp glass, but it can also manifest itself in other equally destructive ways, including, but not limited to, head-banging and hitting; burning oneself; scratching or picking at scabs to prevent wounds from properly healing; inserting objects into body openings; and pulling out hair and eyelashes.[35]

How common is NSSI? According to studies, 4 percent of adults engage in some form of self-injury, compared to 15 percent of adolescents. But that number jumps to a staggering rate of 17 percent to 35 percent among college students.[36] People who engage in self-harm often begin in early adolescence, and it's more prevalent in females. People who suffer from depression and anxiety are more prone to NSSI, but there are other predictors that may increase one's risk of self-harm, including the loss of a loved one, a family history of mental illness and self-harm, substance abuse, bullying, abuse and neglect. Other related mental disorders where high NSSI rates are reported include bipolar disorder, borderline personality disorder and post-traumatic stress disorder.

According to court testimony, self-harm marks were finally brought to her school nurse's attention in August 2007. She observed 25 cuts covering Alyssa's left arm and more than 125 marring her right wrist and forearm. Shortly after, Alyssa began receiving mental health treatment at Pathways Mental Health Center. She had gone through a number of therapists since then, none of whom were able to help her. One of her therapists, Ron Wilson, who was a children's services supervisor at the mental health center, would also testify that seeing so many therapists in such a short period of time is detrimental to sufficient treatment. Not once did he suspect that Alyssa could pose a danger to others. From his time analyzing Alyssa, the only threat she seemed to pose was to herself.

Alyssa's downward spiral into poor mental health would take a terrifying turn when Karen found her granddaughter unconscious from an attempted suicide over Labor Day weekend in 2007. Alyssa, then 13, had attempted to overdose on Tylenol. Quickly, an ambulance was called, and Alyssa spent the subsequent two weeks hospitalized at the Missouri Psychiatric Center, where she was psychologically assessed. She was transferred to a more intensive program for her treatment and was then prescribed Prozac.

She entered Jefferson High School the year after her suicide attempt. She took her education seriously, rarely, if ever, skipping class and earning A's and B's. By all appearances, Alyssa, aside from having an edge to her quirky personality coupled with a dark sense of humor, was a pretty normal teenage girl.[37]

But since her 2007 suicide attempt, friends who knew Alyssa before would note a drastic change in Alyssa's personality. Instead of getting better, she plunged deeper into the depths of her depression, her propensity to self-harm only evolving in even more pernicious ways. Her self-mutilations manifested all over her body in the form of bite marks, burns, and a carving of the word "hate" into her arm. She made no attempt to hide her cuts and often brushed off her friends' concerns. They knew about her troubled past; they knew she was struggling mentally and being medicated for her depression. However, Alyssa still wore a smile on her face every day.

In the middle to late 2000s, the popularity of social media was at an all-time high, attracting young audiences who were given opportunities to express their identities in an entirely new way, completely different from the pre-social media world. Alyssa Bustamante was no exception, participating in several platforms such as MySpace, Facebook and Twitter. Selfies recovered from her online profiles would depict a seemingly normal, somewhat quirky teenager who sometimes posed with stuffed animals, flashing a demure smile on camera. In other selfies, she would paint her face in scary makeup and make silly faces. Many photos that would later resurface showed her surrounded by friends from youth camp, an average girl with an active social life. If one was to judge from the point of view of an outsider who knew nothing of Alyssa Bustamante, they would never suspect the everyday self-loathing she carried with her.

But Alyssa's massive social media presence would also shed a light on a much darker side of her personality, portraying a grimmer portrait of the seemingly normal teenager.

On her YouTube channel, where she listed "killing people" and "cutting" as her hobbies, she uploaded a video where she shocked herself on an electric fence and encouraged her two younger brothers to do the same. Again, from an outsider's perspective, it may have looked like kids being kids. But watching the video again after Alyssa confessed to murdering a child would make anyone's skin crawl.

Twitter seemed to be her main platform, serving as a safety valve to channel her innermost morbid thoughts and pent-up rage, which friends would only glimpse. In her Twitter bio she wrote about her love for music and friends and her distaste for authority. In the month before Elizabeth was killed, Alyssa would fire off the following tweets that were blatant cries for help: "the world goes by my cage and never sees me" and "this is all i want in life; a reason for all this pain."

Over the couple of years since Alyssa's suicide attempt, Alyssa's grandmother desperately sought multiple therapists for Alyssa as her mental health continued to decline, but nobody seemed to be able to help her. Then, in early October of 2009, Alyssa's daily dose of Prozac was increased to 40mg, the highest level of the medication she had ever been prescribed.

Immediately, Karen Brooke noticed a change in her granddaughter's demeanor. She seemed more withdrawn and sullen. She wasn't returning home from the school bus, nor was she joining family dinners as she normally did. While Karen was alarmed, she tried to keep in mind that Alyssa's doctor did advise her that it could take at least a month for the dosage to balance itself out, and changes in behavior were to be expected. But before a full month had elapsed, Alyssa snapped and somebody died.

Alyssa vented in her diary about not being able to use her cell phone due to her charger breaking. Not having her friends to talk to during her low moods was taking a toll on her mental health.

"If I don't talk about it, I bottle it up, and when I explode, someone's going to die," she chillingly wrote in her diary one week before Elizabeth's murder.[38]

There was no school on Friday the 16th, and 15-year-old Alyssa Bustamante came up with a plan for how she would spend her day off. She fetched a shovel from the barn and traipsed through the dense woods behind her house. She dug one shallow grave, then moved to another area and dug a second one, this one much larger than the first. Now all she had to do was sit back and wait for the perfect opportunity to bring her darkest fantasy to life.

Five days later, she thought of the perfect victim.

On October 21, she sent her younger sister, Emma, to the Olten home to retrieve her nine-year-old neighbor for some "playtime." When the unaware Emma returned with Elizabeth, Alyssa immediately instructed Emma to go back inside. Then, she took Elizabeth by the hand and led her into the woods. Guiding her through the trees and shrubbery, carefully stepping over fallen branches and other obstacles in the way, Alyssa felt the scared Elizabeth grip her hand tightly.

"I've got something that I really need to show you," Alyssa told her with an excited edge in her voice. "It's just a little further up here."[39]

After about 15 minutes, Alyssa came to a halt before the shallow grave she had dug. She turned, coming face to face with the much smaller child. Without a second thought, she began living out her darkest fantasy. She wrapped her hands around Elizabeth's throat and began strangling her. She took out a large knife she had been carrying with her and thrust it through the little girl's chest six or seven times. In her final evil act, she brought the sharp blade to Elizabeth's neck and slit her throat. She buried her in the hole, covered it with leaves, and went back home.

Her veins pumping with adrenaline, she immediately took to her diary to log the event. It read: "I just fucking killed someone. I strangled them and slit their throat and stabbed them now they're dead. I don't know how to feel atm. It was ahmazing. As soon as you get over the 'ohmygawd I can't do this' feeling, it's pretty enjoyable. I'm kinda nervous and shaky though right now. Kay, I gotta go to church now … lol."⁴⁰

She then closed her diary, swapped her muddy clothes for more modest attire, and attended a youth dance at her church, her spirits more uplifted and carefree than usual while a massive search was being launched for Elizabeth.

Legal Proceedings

Despite the overwhelming evidence against Alyssa, and despite the fact that she admitted that she was responsible for the horrific slaying of her neighbor and led authorities to her body in the woods, she entered a not guilty plea for first-degree murder and armed criminal action on December 8, 2009.⁴¹ A trial start date was set for May 16, 2011, but soon after, issues arose in the case that seriously hampered the process. They started when the defense counsel filed a motion to disregard Alyssa's confession because many of the questions she was asked during her interrogation with Sergeant David Rice were not legally permitted under Missouri law since she was a minor. The judge agreed with the defense's argument, ruling that the juvenile officer who was in the interrogation room with Sergeant Rice had "used deceptive tactics" while he inappropriately inserted himself into the questioning. This ruling eradicated one of the most important pieces of evidence in the case—Alyssa's voluntary confession.⁴²

Then came another setback. The U.S. Supreme Court was on the verge of ruling life sentences without parole for anyone under the age of 18 to be unconstitutional. The prosecutor hastily proposed a plea bargain to the defense, stating that if Alyssa pleaded guilty to second-degree murder, she could receive a punishment of anywhere between 10 and 30 years with the possibility of parole, versus the original life without parole she might have faced. The defense team had no objections.

When Patty was informed by prosecutor Mark Richardson of the reduced charges and sentencing against her daughter's killer, she was livid. Alyssa's trial was now set to start on January 30, 2012. But on January 10, Alyssa Bustamante, just over two weeks short of her eighteenth birthday, appeared in court for a preliminary hearing. In a surprising twist of events, Alyssa pleaded guilty to the two charges against her.

During the hearing, Alyssa dropped her head, her long brown bangs shielding her eyes as Judge Pat Joyce read aloud her charges and asked her if she was aware that she was revoking her right to a trial.

"Yes," Alyssa affirmed.

She asked the adolescent to describe to the court how she killed Elizabeth.

Alyssa, raising her head to look the judge in the eye, responded, "I strangled her and stabbed her in the chest."

"Did you cut her throat too?" queried the judge.

"Yes." She also admitted she was aware of her actions at the time.[43]

Alyssa's sudden confession was a surprise to the people awaiting the beginning of a lengthy trial for her. It elicited a sharp, audible gasp from the spectators sitting in the public gallery. Among the spectators was the victim's tearful mother.

―

On February 6, Alyssa appeared in court once again to finally face the consequences of her actions, no longer pretending she was innocent and admitting she had killed Elizabeth Olten in the most brutal way imaginable. But the sentencing phase wasn't going to be smooth and easy either. Now, both the defense and prosecution were going to bring in witnesses to fiercely spar over Alyssa's deserved fate. The defense played the "mentally ill teen with horrible upbringing" card, while the prosecution wanted to prove that Alyssa was mentally sound enough to know that what she was doing was wrong and that this murder was premeditated, as the two graves dug a week prior to the killing demonstrated.

Prosecutor Mark Richardson decided to give Elizabeth's family the chance to deliver their powerful, emotional testimonies before anyone else. The first person to come to the stand was Patty Preiss, Elizabeth's mother. She recounted the last time she saw her daughter alive. She described her beloved Elizabeth as a happy and sociable girl who loved school and got along with everyone. She and the prosecutor played a slideshow that included pictures of happy moments in Elizabeth's short, nine-year life. Patty stated that, because of "that monster Alyssa," Elizabeth would never get to experience the monumental milestones of life, such as her first school dance or getting married. She implored Judge Joyce to put herself in her shoes and imagine how she would feel if her own child had her entire future ripped away from her.

"So much has been lost at the hands of this evil monster," she said. "Elizabeth was given a death sentence and we were given a life sentence."

Alyssa, sitting only a few feet away from the grieving mother, stared at her impassively.

"I hate her, I hate everything about her," she continued. But once she described Alyssa as "not even human," Judge Joyce had to bring her testimony to an end.[44]

Elizabeth's older brother also took the stand in support of his slain sister. Anthony was only 13 when Elizabeth was stolen from him. He took his responsibility as the protective older brother very seriously, and he knew that when Elizabeth was older and inevitably taking an interest in boys, he would have to chase them off. However, he testified, he never once thought that he would need to guard her from a trusted neighbor just down the street.

Elizabeth's father, though not present in the courtroom as he was still incarcerated, wrote a letter pleading for the judge to serve his daughter's murderer with the maximum punishment.

After the emotional testimonies from the victim's family, members of law enforcement who took part in the investigation were called to testify. FBI Agent Shawn McDermott recalled how supposedly normal Alyssa had appeared when he interviewed her the day after Elizabeth went missing. FBI Agent Patricia Gentry, who was assigned to search and collect evidence from Alyssa's bedroom, described the disturbing writings and photos she found plastered on the walls, as well as the violent entries she read in the teen's diary. She also participated in the process of exhuming the slain girl's body from the grave. She described the marks covering her body and the stab wounds on her chest. The defense team cross-examined the FBI agent, reading through some of the diary entries in the weeks leading up to the murder where Alyssa was clearly going through a rough mental spot. She referenced her suicidal thoughts and her self-harm with a "silver blade" multiple times throughout her journal.

Sergeant Rice also took the stand and described his interactions with Alyssa and the first hole he had stumbled upon, the very same hole Alyssa admitted to digging for pleasure. This grave, he testified, was rectangular in shape and appeared as though it was dug by hand. The hole in which Elizabeth was buried was round in shape and seemed to be more hastily dug.

After the lunch recess, it was the defense's turn to summon

witnesses. The first witness that the defense would call was licensed psychiatrist Dr. Edwin Johnstone. Although the psychiatrist had never actually evaluated Alyssa in person, he suggested a diagnosis of borderline personality disorder after thoroughly studying her diary. Borderline personality disorder (BPD) is a recognized personality disorder falling under Cluster B in the *DSM-5*. It is characterized by an extreme fear of abandonment, impulsive behaviors, mood swings, and issues of self-worth. Those living with BPD possess a markedly disturbed sense of identity, ongoing feelings of emptiness, and uncontrollable emotional outbursts. These issues lead to stormy relationships with others.

Dr. Johnstone had 16 years of experience in clinical research on antidepressants. He testified that fluoxetine may come with some serious and dangerous side effects, such as suicide, irritability, impulsiveness, insomnia and violent behavior. Among those taking this medication, adolescents and females had the most risk of suffering from these side effects. According to Alyssa's medical records, in early October 2009, she was given an increased dosage of fluoxetine, the generic name for the antidepressant Prozac that she had been treated with since her suicide attempt in 2007. The psychiatrist observed that her diary entries showed a surge in violent thoughts after she was put on a higher dose.

Prosecutor Mark Richardson was quick to challenge Dr. Johnstone's credibility as a medical witness on cross-examination, criticizing the dearth of scientific data in his cited research.

Elizabeth's corpse was brought to the Boone County Medical Examiner's office for the autopsy, which was conducted by Dr. Carl Stacy, a forensic pathologist with years of experience. He had performed more than 3000 postmortem examinations, and now Elizabeth was being added to that impressive number. It was safe to say that she was in experienced hands, and Dr. Stacy's report would help bring her justice. He inspected her body and documented every injury she had sustained, from the physical marks left by Alyssa's tight grip around her neck to the stab wounds on her chest and the laceration on her neck from where her throat was cut. He was uncertain if Elizabeth was first stabbed then strangled, or the other way around, but what was important was that Alyssa's own account of the killing was consistent with the pathologist's findings.

The defense called their second witness, Caesar Bustamante, who was still completing his 10-year prison sentence for felony assault. He spoke about his own history of mental health issues and the substance abuse that he and Michelle, Alyssa's mother, had gone through while raising their daughter.

Karen Brooke, Alyssa's grandmother, approached the stand to deliver her own emotional testimony, describing Alyssa's less-than-ideal childhood and her struggle to find Alyssa the mental help she so desperately needed.

The final witness for the defense was a neuroradiologist from Nevada by the name of Dr. William Orrison, whose testimony was pre-recorded and played for the court. In a nutshell, he stated that the human brain isn't fully developed until around age 25; until then, adolescents and young adults are susceptible to poor decision-making and impulsive behaviors. Day 1 of the sentencing phase concluded at 5:40 in the evening and would resume the very next day with more witnesses to come.

~

Day 2 of the sentencing phase was the prosecutor's and defense's final chance to sway the judge's decision by providing their last witnesses and presenting their closing arguments. It was a day of emotional turmoil for both families. In the morning, the prosecutor would summon a crucial witness in hopes of discrediting Dr. Johnstone's testimony and, in turn, knocking the defense's entire case to the ground. Approaching the stand was Dr. Anthony Rothschild, a psychiatrist and professor at the University of Massachusetts. This wouldn't be his first time testifying in a court case against the claims of Prozac being to blame for suicide or murder.

He testified that fluoxetine played no role in the death of Elizabeth, calling it "nonsense." He cited scientific studies that found no evidence to support any correlation between fluoxetine and hostility and aggression, and, in fact, suggested that Prozac decreased those sorts of emotions and behaviors in individuals with borderline personality disorder and major depression like Alyssa.

"There is no reliable evidence in the medical and scientific literature that Prozac causes people to commit murder," he said.[45]

Alyssa Neitzert, a registered nurse from the University of Missouri hospital who thoroughly examined Alyssa's self-harm marks back in 2010 while she was in jail, painted a much more frightening image of how severe this issue had become since then. The nurse had recorded more than 300 self-inflicted scars covering Alyssa's body and presented the photographs in the courtroom to prove it. She had carved the words "hate" and "pain" into her arms, along with a peace sign and two broken hearts. But cutting wasn't her only method of harming herself, as evidence showed a self-inflicted burn and bite mark and what appeared to be an attempt to pierce the inside of her lip. Alyssa Neitzert testified that she had inspected more than 50 cutters throughout her career, and this was by far the worst case of self-harm she had seen. The adolescent girl had completely mutilated herself from head to toe.

In the afternoon, two more witnesses took the stand. The first was Ron Wilson, the children's services supervisor at the Pathways Mental Health Center where Alyssa began her counseling treatment following her suicide attempt. He had started seeing her in August 2007, shortly before her suicide attempt, and had seen her on October 9, 2009, two weeks before the tragic murder. He testified that through all of the years he had met with Alyssa, she never suggested that she could pose a threat to anybody beyond herself. The last time he met with her, she was extremely depressed, but again, there was not a glimmer of an indication that she posed a danger to others.

The second person to take the stand was expert witness Dr. Rosalyn Schultz, a psychologist from St. Louis who practiced in clinical forensics. She had gone over the teen's medical records and interviewed several family members. To her, it was very clear that this was a traumatized young girl who witnessed domestic violence and substance abuse growing up, which severely impaired her mental state. Alyssa revealed to Dr. Schultz that cutting herself helped her fall asleep and she didn't feel pain when she self-harmed.

When the two spoke in December 2011, Alyssa appeared to be haunted by her atrocious actions. She claimed that she constantly suffered from nightmares and saw Elizabeth in her mind. She confided that as the murder happened it was almost like she was in a trance and watching it happen in the third person. Alyssa also revealed the reason for the two graves—the first one that investigators encountered was hard to dig through the roots, therefore she opted for another location.

Dr. Schultz described the counseling Alyssa received from Pathways as insufficient. She cited a record dating back to September 2009 where Alyssa expressed suicidal thoughts. She should have been hospitalized then and there, as she would be under direct supervision and given more adequate treatment. She could have had a chance to improve. Suicide and homicide often go hand in hand, the psychologist testified, and homicide is just projecting inner feelings of suicidal ideation.

∼

Now it was time for the closing arguments. To prove that this murder was very much premeditated, and Alyssa was aware of the gravity of her actions and the consequences they would entail, the prosecutor referred to that last journal entry where she reflected on the murder and described it as "enjoyable" and "ahmazing." He also referred to the defense wounds on young Elizabeth's hands from trying to fend off the knife attack. He alluded to the holes Alyssa dug in the woods just five days prior to the murder. He contended that all of the psychiatrists that testified in the courtroom unanimously agreed that Alyssa knew the difference between right and wrong.

When prosecutor Mark Richardson went into the uncomfortable details of Elizabeth's murder, Alyssa's grandmother became very upset and left the courtroom in tears. Alyssa, who was able to maintain a blank expression throughout the court proceedings and heart-wrenching testimonies, showed a crack in her thick armor when she finally broke down crying.[46]

With all this evidence being brought to light, Mark Richardson pleaded for Judge Joyce to give Alyssa life in prison for the murder charge, with no less than 71 years for armed criminal action. His reasoning behind the "71 years" sentence was that the average life span of a woman is 80 years, and Elizabeth's life was cut short just before she reached the age of 10, meaning that Alyssa callously, maliciously, and deliberately robbed 71 years from the youngster.

"The motive has to be the most senseless, reprehensible that could be in humankind, and that is to take a life for a thrill," said Mark Richardson.[47]

The defense did their best to sway the judge away from the prosecutor's portrayal of their young client as a "thrill killer." Her attorney, Donald Catlett, cited testimony from the mental health professionals that Alyssa was "severely emotionally disturbed" and "psychologically damaged," a teen who suffered from depression and also showed symptoms of borderline personality disorder and early signs of bipolar disorder. He reiterated the details of her history with depression and cutting and her 2007 suicide attempt. Alyssa was especially going through a rough patch in her life starting in 2009, and her treatment with Prozac didn't seem to be of any benefit to her mental health—in fact, it had the opposite effect, making her more prone to violent and unpredictable behavior. Had Alyssa been hospitalized in October after the increased dosage of her medication, the murder could have been prevented, if she was getting the help she truly needed at the time.[48]

He reminded the judge that at the end of the day, Alyssa was still only 15 years old, which left room for at least 10 more years of brain development. Even though she was being tried as an adult, the individual sitting at the defense table was still only a young person with an underdeveloped brain that could lead to poor judgment and impulse issues. That, combined with her already present mental instability and a troubled childhood, was a recipe for disaster. None of the trauma Alyssa had endured in her life was any excuse, of course, but they pleaded for leniency when the judge took all of these mitigating factors into account.

The court saw plenty of emotional outbursts from both families during the closing arguments, from Alyssa's grandparents storming out of the courtroom to Alyssa's emotional breakdown. But that wouldn't be the last of it. When Judge Joyce said she would announce her decision the next day, Elizabeth's grandmother, Sandy Corn, yelled from her wheelchair, "Alyssa should get out of jail the same day Elizabeth gets out of the grave!"[49]

Whatever the judge decided, one thing was certain: nothing was ever going to ease the pain, grief, and betrayal felt by both the victim's and killer's families.

∽

Court resumed the next morning. Judge Joyce warned the court that she would not be tolerating any outbursts, and anyone who disobeyed this rule would be immediately kicked out of the courtroom. Today, Alyssa would learn her fate. It had been a long and trying three years, but, hopefully, today would mark the end of this nightmarish chapter and provide the families with at least some closure.

Before Alyssa would hear her sentence, she was given the chance to address the very people who were impacted the most by her vile actions: the Olten family.

"If I could give my life to bring her back, I would," she told the weeping family. "I just want to say I'm sorry for what happened. I'm so sorry."[50]

Judge Joyce sentenced Alyssa to life in prison for second-degree murder with the possibility of parole and 30 years for armed criminal action. After the sentence was read, the victim's family all embraced each other in relief. Finally, they thought, the monster that took their special girl from them would be locked away for good.

Alyssa Bustamante appears in court on January 30, 2014 (AP photo).

Afterword

The story of Alyssa Bustamante, a 15-year-old killer, is one that continues to confound the justice system. It has left those close to the tragedy haunted by memories and wondering what could have motivated her to commit such a senseless crime totally unprovoked. And that's the most daunting aspect of this—there was no apparent motive, no logical explanation behind her seemingly-random burst of violence other than pure bloodlust with mysterious origins, which begs the question: could something have been done to prevent such a tragedy from occurring?

Alyssa clearly had a troubled childhood. The trauma of witnessing domestic abuse and substance addiction in the household at an early age, having both parents locked up, and being abandoned by her mother evidently played a role in shaping her psyche. But what other factors came into play?

Karen Brooke, Alyssa's only savior in life, seemed to have done all the right things. She removed Alyssa from a dysfunctional household and provided her with a healthier one. She was quick to seek psychological help for her granddaughter once she began showing signs of emotional disturbances. Her quick intervention and constant vigilance were not adequate to rescue Alyssa from venturing down such a dark and destructive path.

Should we then fault the mental health services that took Alyssa under their care for not watching for any red flags of an adolescent girl with homicidal ideation? Is Alyssa Bustamante a glaring reflection of the failure of our mental health care system? Or are there certain inevitable limitations in its ability to care for severely mentally ill children?

Do we blame selective serotonin reuptake inhibitors (SSRIs), which have gained a negative reputation for their possible correlation with violence? Alyssa Bustamante was not the first—or the last—example of a child or adolescent who has committed a violent crime shortly after being prescribed antidepressants, leading some, including researchers, to question if this really is just a dark coincidence or if antidepressants may be causing some severe negative side effects in our youth.

It is a query that is still under research, with different studies yielding different results, raising even more questions than answers. However, there are some studies that do point toward an association between SSRIs and violence.

Low levels of serotonin, a neurotransmitter that works as a chemical messenger which carries signals between nerve cells (neurons) in the brain, is thought to be linked with depression. Serotonin is typically reabsorbed by the nerve cells, which is called "reuptake." SSRIs work by blocking ("inhibiting") that reuptake of serotonin; thus, the neurotransmitter stays in the gaps between the nerves, which are called "synapses." When serotonin levels are increased in the brains of depressed individuals, it is thought to relieve their depressive symptoms.[51]

In 2007, the Centers for Disease Control and Prevention issued a warning for fluoxetine, the drug Alyssa was being treated with, and one of the most commonly-prescribed psychiatric medications.

In a 2012 study, Rich Melloni, a professor of psychology and director of the program in Behavioral Neuroscience in the Northeastern University College of Science, and his research team used healthy adolescent hamsters as models to get to the root of the problem as to why fluoxetine was causing negative side effects such as irritation, impulsivity, and aggression, particularly in youth.

During the research, he and his team discovered that the hamsters with a lower dose of the drug were significantly more prone to aggression when exposed to an intruder or the scent of an intruder and that repeated administration of fluoxetine altered the serotonin and vasopressin neural development in the hamsters. But here was the real twist in the study: there are neurological systems other than serotonin which, when impaired, may also play a role in depression but may present as symptoms of serotonin deficiency instead. Children with a dysfunctional dopamine or norepinephrine system, for example, who are mistakenly prescribed fluoxetine will obviously not reap the benefits of the drug and, in fact, may become more aggressive, as fluoxetine only works on patients with an impaired serotonin system. Perhaps, if fluoxetine were administered to hamsters with low serotonin levels, they would have had entirely different findings.[52]

Research published in the *PLoS* medical journal found that young people between the ages of 15 and 24 who are medicated with Prozac and Seroxat are substantially more likely to commit violent crimes, their risk raised by 43 percent. However, their likelihood of criminal violence was not much different from those in that age group who were not on SSRIs. Furthermore, the study also found that their propensity for violence was reduced when taking higher doses of the drugs, suggesting that the root of the issue may just be that they were being medically undertreated and it is not the drug itself causing the violence.[53]

Due to the lack of conclusive studies, it is indeed hard to say whether these concerning side effects are really a direct result of the medication itself or just original problems being exacerbated, which would require a higher dose of medication. More research is needed before we can definitively say whether there is enough cause for blame.

Patty Preiss was not at all satisfied with her daughter's killer's sentence and attempted to sue Pathways Behavioral Healthcare, where Alyssa was previously hospitalized, as well as two of its employees. She believed the convicted murderer killed her daughter while she was under their care and they should have foreseen this would happen because they were already aware of her "violent tendencies," including the video in which she urged her younger brothers to touch an electric fence and listing "killing people" and "cutting" under the hobbies section on her YouTube channel. Cole County Circuit Judge Jon Beetem dismissed that lawsuit. In July 2017, a settlement was reached which declared that Alyssa Bustamante owed her nine-year-old victim's mother $5 million—plus 9 percent interest per year until the debt is paid.[54]

There is no pain in the world that can even compare to the experience of losing a child, especially to something as heinous as murder. No amount of money will be able to fill the void. Nobody will ever be able to say with confidence what drove a 15-year-old girl to murder an innocent child, totally unprovoked. How can we identify, and prevent, another Alyssa Bustamante from going down the same path?

Cody Posey
(2004)

On July 6, 2004, ABC News anchor and reporter Sam Donaldson felt that something was awry. He had hired 34-year-old Paul Posey to take care of his New Mexico ranch, but he was not able to reach him by phone that day. Donaldson and his wife hopped in their vehicle and made the drive to Chavez Canyon. As soon as he set foot inside the home the Poseys occupied, his horrible gut feeling was verified. Beside the refrigerator, he spotted traces of congealed blood. There was a sickening, dried up, reddish swath of blood across the floor, seemingly left behind by a body that had been dragged, and the floor was littered with broken glass. But there was no sign of his dedicated employee or anyone else in his family, for that matter.

Horrified by what he bore witness to, he promptly called authorities, who arrived at the scene shortly thereafter.[1] One of the first to arrive was Sheriff Tom Sullivan. Before he had even walked through the front door, he knew this sprawling ranch was a crime scene. He spotted blood and chunks of hair with more blood on them on the front porch.

But they could not find anyone in the family either in or around the house. Something violent had clearly happened within the household, yet where the body, or bodies, were hidden was a mystery to the detectives.[2]

All they had to go on was one note left behind for police officers: "Sorry coppers I needed the kid to do the dirty work."[3]

Then they found their first clue. One of the detectives had noted some backhoe tracks. Collectively, the officers followed the tracks, which took them around some bluffs until they stumbled upon a pile of manure. But it wasn't necessarily the manure that caught the detectives' eyes. When they took a closer look at it, they noticed a plethora of blowflies buzzing around one particular area of the large pile.

Using a stick, they began the taxing process of trying to uncover whatever was immersed in the pile of animal dung. They began poking and prodding at it with the wooden stick, moving dirt and manure out of the way until they discovered their first sign. Peeking out from the manure was somebody's belt and a Levi's T-shirt. By morning, the officers unearthed three bodies that had already begun to decompose. Two were adults, one male and one female, and the other was just a child who looked no older than 13.

The only one missing from this family pile was 14-year-old Cody Posey, who was nowhere to be found.

Cody was, in fact, not too far away. And when it was announced that Cody Posey was charged with the annihilation of his own family, all those who knew him were in shock. This didn't seem like the quiet and polite teenage boy and straight-A student they knew at all.

Often, pictures can be deceiving. Behind recovered photographs of a happy, smiling, blended family was a disturbing collection of dark, hidden secrets that never left the small community who knew but kept their mouths shut and heads down. A picture is worth a thousand words, it is said, but not once did these family photos convey a teenage boy, soon to be dubbed a "cold-hearted killer," who was on the verge of snapping.

Background

Cody Posey was born on October 9, 1989, in New Mexico to Carla Brust and Delbert Paul Posey, known simply as "Paul" to most. Paul was known to be very hard on his family, especially his young son. There had been witnesses to Paul's horrific and uncalled-for abuse toward his only child as early as his diaper days.

James Forrester was a longtime family friend, one of the first to see the abuse with his own eyes. He recalled a time when he was installing a heater in the family home. Cody, just two years old, was not understanding his father's demands that he move out of the way while James worked.

"All of a sudden Paul just leaped and whipped his belt off and grabbed that kid by the arm and just went to warpin' him down across the head and ears and face and neck and back," said James. "The kid was just screaming, you know, bloody murder, big, wide cowboy belt."[4]

He continued to strike him somewhere between 50 to 75 times until his body was covered in welts. He then heedlessly tossed him onto the couch. At that point, the boy could no longer squeeze out a tear. Urine and feces were seeping out of his diaper and dribbling onto the floor.

Shortly after this incident, in 1992, Carla and Paul both filed for divorce, sparking a lengthy custody dispute that spanned eight years. The physical and verbal abuse from Paul only heightened in intensity during this time. In 1994, Carla joined the Navy, so the four-year-old Cody was sent to live with his father, who had since married Sandy Schmid.

Sandy absolutely doted on her young stepson and acted as a mother to him.

"Oh, he was a dear little boy. Everybody loved him," she recalled of Cody. "He was sweet and kind and polite. You know, he was my son."[5]

But Paul's radical behavior against his son didn't stop. He resumed his old-fashioned parenting style, taking out his anger with aggressive language and often physical discipline over the most trivial matters. Sandy recalled having to frequently rush to Cody's aid and intercept these beatings during their five-year marriage.

"He would yank him out of the bed, the bunk bed on the top, yank him off on to the floor." She also remembered Paul repeatedly bashing his son against the floor.[6]

One particular beating remained burned in her mind. She recalled returning home after a long day of work to the sight of Paul battering Cody, then seven, with a board because he had brought home bad grades.

"Paul, that's enough. That's enough!"[7] she exclaimed.

At once, Paul heeded her pleas and ceased the beating.

When Carla saw the bruises and marks left behind from the beating, she got the police involved. Cody's injuries were photographed and he was promptly brought to the hospital to be examined by a medical professional, but no charges were ever filed against Paul. Cody was returned to the care of his father.

Sandy, Cody's only protector to this point, divorced Paul in 1998. But Paul moved on from the divorce rather quickly; he was drawn to a woman named Tryone who had a daughter just one year younger than Cody, Marilea Schmeed. The couple married, forming a new blended family comprising Paul, Tryone, Cody, and Marilea.

Cody didn't stay very long with his father. In 2000, when he was 10 years old, Cody finally got what he had been yearning for the last several years. When his mother retired from the Navy, Paul signed over his parental rights to Carla, terminating the stressful eight-year-long custody battle over Cody. At last, she had gained full custody of her son, and Cody was reunited with his mom.

But their reunion would be short-lived.

A few months after Cody was safely returned to his mother, he, Carla, and her new husband, William Russell Brust, had left the state in their pickup truck for Washington, where Brust was stationed in the Navy. They got into an accident in Wyoming when Brust fell asleep at the wheel. Carla was sent flying from the backseat.[8]

At Cody's mother's funeral, Paul Posey showed up at the church with a police officer demanding that Cody be returned to his custody. Cody's cousin, Sherry Gensler, listened to the sobbing 10-year-old's heartbreaking pleas to not be returned to his old life of perpetual pain and abuse at the hands of his father. Cody did not get his wish. It was only after Carla's tragic death that the custody agreement between Paul and Carla was declared invalid, as Paul had hand printed his name instead of signing the document. The boy also pleaded with the officer, who simply gave him his card and told him to call him in the event that abuse took place. At the end of the day, Cody had no control over the situation, and he was returned to the care of Paul at his ranch.[9]

Cody's living situation with his father, stepmother, and stepsister did not improve. In fact, it worsened. The torment that Cody would suffer in the following four years would be unimaginable.

In Paul's last marriage, Cody had someone who defended him and tried to end the abuse. But this marriage was totally different. Tryone was not an ally of Cody, for she, too, would subject her stepson to extreme psychological and physical abuse alongside her husband. Very early on, family roles were assigned to the two children. Cody, of course, was the scapegoat; everything he did was either wrong or not good enough, which warranted severe punishment. Marilea was the golden child. Paul and Tryone put Marilea up to the task of keeping tabs on her older stepbrother at school and reporting on his behavior to her parents in exchange for "rewards." In fact, any time Cody made a mistake, Marilea would be rewarded for it. Naturally, this engendered in Cody some jealousy toward Marilea, with her being the favorite child and him feeling so alienated from the rest of his family, wanting nothing more than to gain their love and acceptance after losing someone so important to him.

But no matter how hard Cody worked to please his father, he was never good enough.

Cody was forced to work long hours on the sprawling ranch almost daily. If he made a mistake, or his work didn't meet his father's expectations, he would be punished with psychological and physical abuse ranging from daily kicking and punching, being whipped with a lariat, choked, and having rocks pelted at him to being struck in the back of the hand with the pointy end of the hay hook if he stumbled while trying to load bales of hay onto a hay truck.[10] Tryone actively participated in the abuse by slapping him and calling him names. She made no secret of her true feelings of contempt toward her stepson, once telling a teacher that she "hated" Cody and documenting an incident in her journal when she made Cody cry by calling him stupid.[11]

Cody was not allowed to have a social life, something which is extremely important during an adolescent's formative years. Besides the two weeks of basketball and two Knowledge Bowls in which he was permitted to participate, the only sort of socialization he had was school. Other than that, he was extremely isolated from the outside world.

Fifteen-year-old Gilbert Salcido, a close friend of Cody's who described him as the smartest kid in the class, said, "Every day he'd come to school he'd be sad."[12]

He, along with other friends, would do their best to lift Cody's mood. But as the school day ticked closer to ending, that sadness and despair would return. The day was over, and he would be sent back to a home full of constant turmoil and pain.

The boy knew from a very young age to keep his mouth shut about the abuse, fearing retribution from his father. But that didn't mean no one knew about the disturbances going on at the ranch. Many residents of the community knew that Cody was being abused but failed to call for help in fear of their identities being exposed and facing social repercussions. Cody's two attempts to run away both failed, as each time authorities simply returned him to his father.

"In the West, you just don't talk about it. I mean, you just don't, it's just not something you put around," said Slim Brittan.[13]

Slim Brittan was a cowhand who once worked for Paul. He

witnessed the cruelty that Paul unleashed on his son every single day, including the whipping of Cody with a coiled rope.

"He rides up to him, and hits him. 'Whack' with the rope, just right in the back," he said. "You're out of the drive. Whack. Right across the back."[14]

He only worked for Paul for eight months before he was let go, but in that time, he never saw his employer give affection to his son. "I never saw a hand laid on him in love."[15]

Isabel "Pilo" Vasquez, who also worked on the ranch, was another witness who later corroborated Cody's abuse claims. He spoke of an incident in which Paul Posey had threatened to cut off his son's testicles with the hay hook if he popped the clutch of the ranch pickup truck he was driving.

Alvera Lerma, whose husband worked for Cody's father on the ranch, had witnessed a lot of the horrible abuse as well. She still recalled vividly how Paul's anger often turned to violence. One time, Cody rolled up his sleeves in front of her, exposing the cigarette burn marks that covered his arms.

She told her husband something that would serve as an eerie form of foreshadowing, which would make her blood run cold in the coming months: "I feel that something's gonna happen to that family, either Cody's gonna kill Paul, or Paul's gonna kill Cody."[16]

Four months later, Paul, Tryone, and Marilea would be found dead on their own property.

The Murders

It all started on the night of July 3. Cody had been summoned by his father to the master bedroom. As he stood by the foot of the bed where his stepmother was under the covers, Tryone threw off the blanket, revealing herself to be completely nude. Paul turned on a flashlight and ordered Cody to do something completely inappropriate, dirty, and outrageous: he instructed his son to get into bed with Tryone and have sex with her.

Completely repulsed, and almost frozen in shock by this repulsive demand, the 14-year-old teenager flat-out refused. But it was not a refusal without consequence. Paul heated up a welding iron and burned Cody with it. But the boy still didn't give in to his father's sick demands. That's when Tryone grabbed his hand and forced it onto her breast.

Cody tried to pull away but she wouldn't let go. As a last-ditch effort to defend himself, he bit her. Paul burned him a second time. Cody was able to muster enough strength to run out of the room. He hid in his bedroom for the rest of the night, his mind reeling. He felt dirty all over.

The following morning, he was still in a complete daze. As he was cleaning the horse stables, his father walked in, and, dissatisfied with his work, brought up a hand and slapped him across the face.

All of the pent-up anger from the night before, and the years of mental and physical torture that his father had subjected him to, finally reached its boiling point. He thought about how much better his world would be without Paul Posey. He thought about how much better the entire world would be without his father. All at once, his emotions fogged over his better judgment, the years of patience and passivity dwindling away as feelings of rage and betrayal coursed through his veins.

He located his stepsister's saddle bag. He reached inside and grabbed a .38 special, a gun that Marilea used to shoot at snakes. He emptied it of its snakeshot ammunition and loaded it with more lethal bullets. He marched into the house, zeroed in on Tryone, who was sitting on the living room couch reading a book, and shot her once in the head. To ensure her death, he put a second bullet through her head. He targeted her first to prevent her from calling 911, since she was in the house and had closer access to the telephone.

When the noise of gunshots reverberated through the home and traveled outside, Paul immediately ran through the door. But Cody had been lying in wait behind the fridge, prepared to ambush him. His father met the same fate as Tryone when Cody aimed the gun at him and fired a shot. Marilea, who had come in through the door right behind Paul, met the same fate too.

After gunning down his whole family, he dragged their bodies outside and one by one loaded them into the bucket of the John Deere backhoe.[17] Initially, he was planning to bury them in a plot of land, but he was unable to break the ground himself, so he instead hid their bodies in the manure pile. He subsequently scrawled a quick note to police, broke the window glass to simulate a robbery, and then took off in his father's truck. He tossed the murder weapon into the river, then made a quick stop at a local store to buy himself a can of Sprite before heading to the home of his friends Gilbert and Leo Salcido, who lived just down the street.

One of the striking things about Cody that stood out to his friends the most was his upbeat demeanor. They stayed up all night shooting fireworks, watching the bright colors burst into the dark sky. They laughed, they horsed around, and they played basketball while police were digging out the bodies. Perhaps these moments were the first time in Cody's life that he truly felt free.

The Salcido brothers had no idea of the eerie story behind Cody's positive mood. "I've never seen that side of Cody, really. I've never seen him so happy."[18]

The fun and games were interrupted by a law enforcement officer knocking on their door two days later at 5 p.m., looking for Cody.

Interrogation and Arrest

Lincoln County sheriffs brought Cody to the police station, where they began what seemed like innocent questioning about the family's murders. The boy had two adults present: his friends' father, Faustino Salcido, and their uncle, Eli Salcido, a ranch hand. After a period of questioning the 14-year-old, it became clear to the uncle that this sounded an awful lot like an interrogation. Eli, growing increasingly concerned, inquired as to what they were doing, questioning a minor without the presence of a lawyer.

The sheriffs informed him that it wasn't an interrogation. Yet, they escorted Cody to a "safe house," a room for interviewing children, and two sheriff's deputies, one female and one male, began firing off their questions.

More than an hour into the interrogation, Cody finally cracked and confessed to the brutal slayings.

"Okay, now I'm sitting here and I'm watching you, Cody. And you got tears in your eyes, and I need to know why. So what did you do, Cody?" asked one of the deputies.

Cody felt like his arm was being twisted at this point. With no way out of the sheriffs' scrutinizing gaze and dubious inquiries, he came clean to everything.

"I tried getting rid of him."

"How?"

"Get him off this planet 'cause it would be better here without him."

"So what did you do, Cody?"

"I shot him."[19]

Somehow, Cody was able to keep a calm, cool, and collected demeanor as he explained how he took out each member of his family. He explained that the reason he shot his stepmother was because she would participate in the physical abuse and was often "mean" to him. As for Marilea, he was afraid she would turn him in. Therefore, she, too, had to go.

With Cody's full-blown confession, he was arrested and eventually charged with committing one of the most heinous crimes in Lincoln County history that would rock the entire community to its core.

∼

In his first court hearing before Judge James Counts on Friday, July 9, 2004, 14-year-old Cody, wearing glasses, a T-shirt, and blue jeans, stood quietly by the side of his defense attorney Gary Mitchell as he denied the charges against his client. The Twelfth Judicial district attorney Scot Key and the defense had agreed to give the state 30 days to decide whether to prosecute the youth as a juvenile or an adult. Gary stated that he himself would need much more time to investigate the background of the case, including allegations of physical and emotional abuse Cody had suffered at home, as well as to get a psychological assessment of the boy.

"I suspect there's going to be a lot of questions as to why people ignored the signs that should have told them we had a young man desperately fighting for his sanity and help," said his attorney.[20]

Despite the brutality Cody unleashed on his family, he still had accumulated quite a bit of strength in his corner. Several members of the Hondo community were present in court that day to show their moral support. These were people who truly believed, or knew for a fact, that Cody was abused by his father.

Scot Key was planning to seek a grand jury indictment against the 14-year-old to give the state six months to prepare for the trial, as opposed to the standard 30 days in children's court. Either way, the trial would still be held in children's court, but the prosecutor maintained that they would not rule out the possibility of "adult sanctions" against Cody Posey. If deemed a juvenile offender by New Mexico law, he would receive juvenile penalties, which entailed incarceration at the Children, Youth and Families Department until he turned 21. If he were to be tried as an adult, he could very well be facing a maximum of 30 years in prison and, on top of that, an additional three years for the four counts of tampering with evidence that were also against him.

"We'll look at all of the evidence before making a decision about how to go after it, and that includes mitigating and aggravating circumstances, if there are any," said Scot Key, who also stressed that there were three victims in this case, and families of the victims, to take into consideration when processing the evidence.

In the meantime, Cody would remain in custody at a juvenile detention center in Albuquerque.

Defense attorney Gary Mitchell made it clear that he was going to fight to ensure that his young client would be treated with fairness and given a lenient sentence for his actions.

"You have a young man who's shattered, who needs lots of love and attention to understand everything going on in his life," he told reporters after the court hearing.[21]

Trial

"It was a day that dawned as bright as any other on the Sam Donaldson ranch. But that was a brightness that soon was to be dimmed in horror. Because Cody Posey decided his world would be better off without his family. He made an unbelievably vicious and selfish decision that his belief was more important than the most basic universal human belief of all: that life is precious."[22]

These were the first words that crossed prosecutor Sandra Grisham's lips during her opening statement at the start of Cody Posey's trial. From the beginning, the prosecutor made her main objective very clear. Even though the trial was being held in children's court, her ultimate goal was to have Cody convicted of all three counts of first-degree murder and have him put behind bars for the rest of his life. She explained away her motive to dismantle the "battered child syndrome" angle that the defense would certainly use. She wanted to fully convince the jury that the young boy sitting approximately a dozen feet from them was a liar, a manipulator, and a cold-blooded killer who fabricated these tales of abuse as a cover-up for his calculated family annihilation.

Cody knew that Sam Donaldson would not be on the ranch on the day of the murders. Removing the snakeshot from the revolver and replacing it with .38 caliber ammunition to get the job done required serious intent and malice aforethought, she argued further. She pointed out that he had admitted to killing his stepmother first so she couldn't call 911 and shooting her twice just to ensure her death. Pulling back the hammer before firing each shot indicated that the 14-year-old boy was using a "thought process."[23]

Even more startling was that Cody admitted to ambushing his father by hiding behind the refrigerator and killing his sister so she couldn't turn him in.

She also went into detail about how Cody covered up the crime by smashing the window with an ax and leaving a note behind, actions that only a highly mature individual could even conceive of accomplishing. These were not the actions of an abused boy who just snapped. Everything Cody did that morning required malice aforethought and premeditation.

"This is not an issue about a battered woman," she said. "Battered women don't kill their husband and then turn around and kill their sister and their kids."[24]

She played back the most damning piece of evidence against Cody: the confession tape in which he calmly opens up to police about his murderous acts and describes them in detail as nonchalantly as if one were talking about the weather.

"Ladies and gentlemen, the first thing we want to know is why. Why? But there's no legal need to prove the why. The legal need is to prove how these killings occurred, where they occurred, and who committed them. Cody Posey himself answers these questions," she said.[25]

The first witness she called was Sam Donaldson, the first man to walk in on the complete and utter horror of the crime scene in its aftermath. He described the first hints of red that he caught sight of on the front porch and seeing that same reddish substance smeared across the kitchen floor when he entered the home. The direct examination lasted only 15 minutes, as Donaldson refused to answer many of the prosecutor's questions.

When Cody took the stand, she questioned him about his somewhat shady past—which included pretty typical acts most if not all teenagers engage in from time to time—in an attempt to expose him as a manipulative liar whose word could not be trusted.

"You had a lot of problems with lying, a lot of arguments over lying, didn't you?" she asked him.

"In my past I have lied, yes, ma'am," he replied demurely.

"Stolen?"

"I had stolen one time."

"Cheated?"

"I believe so. I believe it was in a card game."

"So you only cheated one time too?" she asked skeptically.

"To my recollection."

"You did illicit drugs?" she asked.

"I believe—as we covered earlier, I had experimented with marijuana."[26]

In yet another attempt to besmirch Cody's outward image of an abused victim who massacred his whole family in an act of self-defense after years of torment, she hired a psychiatrist to prove that the boy displayed "psychopathic tendencies" during the slayings and especially to stress Cody's characteristic of chronic lying.

Dr. Wade Myers was a psychiatrist whose specialty was child and adolescent psychiatry and forensic psychiatry. The University of South Florida graduate had years of experience in testifying in high-profile court cases and served as an expert witness in the trial of infamous serial killer Aileen Wuornos.

He came to a conclusion based on six hours of face-to-face interviews, a series of tests issued to Cody, a review of psychological reports and case evidence, and additional interviews with two of the teen's relatives. He surmised that the boy did not, in fact, suffer from post-traumatic stress disorder like psychiatric experts hired by the defense would have the jury believe, nor did he conclude that depression played a role in Cody's violent episode.[27]

One of the tests he had administered to the juvenile was the controversial Psychopathic Checklist, now called the Psychopathic Checklist—Revised (PCL-R), which is a diagnostic tool developed by Canadian psychologist Robert D. Hare in the 1970s to measure one's psychopathic or antisocial traits or tendencies.[28] The PCL-R was partially based on his assessments of male offenders in Vancouver but also drew on some findings from American psychiatrist Hervey M. Cleckley's book *The Mask of Insanity* published in 1941. It became a framework for the clinical description of a psychopath based on his clinical interviews with patients in a locked facility. The phrase "the mask of insanity" originated in the psychiatrist's belief that psychopaths often wear a mask of charm and normality that conceals a deep-seated mental disorder.

The PCL-R contains 20 items that are scored on a three-point scale: 0 means "does not apply," 1 means "somewhat applies," and 2 means "applies a lot." It is said that a score of 30 or above qualifies for a diagnosis of psychopathy. A person who lacks a criminal background will score around five on average. The items that offenders are rated by are a list of accumulated traits that are believed to be common among psychopaths.

Dr. Myers testified youths in particular will usually score around 3.2, and children being treated in a clinical setting for conduct disorders will score around 17 on average. Cody had a startling score of 19, indicating high psychopathic tendencies. Some of the traits he scored particularly high on were pathological lying, impulsivity, sexual promiscuity, and poor anger control.[29]

The psychiatrist was unable to determine for the court, however, whether Cody was being entirely truthful about the sexual assault inflicted on him by Tryone and Paul the day before the murders. He also testified that the boy had two girlfriends in the months before the slayings, one from Hondo and another from Capitan, a village in Lincoln County, New Mexico. Cody also disclosed to the psychiatrist that he had engaged in oral sex with three separate girls as well, something that the defense co-counsel Tim Rose would clarify later to reporters that Cody mistakenly believed to mean the same thing as French kissing.

He referred to Cody's confession tape when he used the words "get the job done" which, to Dr. Myers, indicated a chilling example of "a pretty serious degree of callousness." With regard to the crime scene, he said that it demonstrated a level of "pretty high sophistication."[30]

"Should he run away? Should he tell a teacher or tell his teachers or should he just live with it?" Dr. Myers said in response to the prosecutor's question about what Cody had been thinking about the ongoing abuse.

"And did he tell you what he decided to do?" she asked.

"Yes," he answered. "In his words, he said, 'nothing else worked, might as well just do it, so I did.'"[31]

There was an ongoing dispute as to whether Cody was mature enough to understand his Miranda rights to waive them, and Dr. Myers was there to settle it once and for all. He testified that Cody was an emotionally intelligent young boy with an IQ of 115 and scored above average on standardized tests. His ability to maintain friendships, obtain a romantic relationship, and get along with teachers and coaches indicated to the psychiatrist that the adolescent boy was "advanced beyond the average 14-year-old."[32] His testimony pandered to the state's argument that Cody's actions were the result of a mature and intelligent young boy who knew exactly what he was doing, contradicting the defense's claim that Cody was rather immature.

Under cross examination, Dr. Myers testified that he was paid $14,000 for the seven days he spent in Alamogordo. Gary Mitchell was determined to prove to the court that Dr. Myers was not a reliable witness as he conveniently ignored the various witness accounts of Cody being hit, punched, and demeaned on a regular basis by his father. In response to that, Dr. Myers admitted that Cody never disclosed this information to him, and this was his first time hearing these grim tales of abuse. Mitchell also smoothly got the psychiatrist to admit that Cody potentially suffered from depression and started treatment with Zoloft on April 20, 2004—nearly three months before the family annihilation.

Verlin Posey, Cody's uncle and Paul's brother, testified that Paul was able to rely on Cody to fulfill his duties around the ranch without guidance or supervision, which is exactly the high level of maturity that is commonly adopted by children raised on a ranch.

"He was mature enough to get up in the morning with an alarm," he said.[33]

It was with this maturity that Cody was able carry out the cold-blooded murders and cover it up afterward, insisted prosecutor Sandra Grisham. She also wanted to use Verlin's testimony as evidence that the murders were premeditated and not a spur-of-the-moment decision, although the testimony would be blocked by the judge.

"Do you know if at some point in time Paul started locking up his guns in a gun safe?" she asked.

"Yes, ma'am," he replied.

"Objection!" blurted the defense. "It's hearsay."[34]

Although the jury never got to hear it, Verlin was referring to a strange discussion in which Tryone and Paul were heading out of the house and informed Cody they would be back soon. The boy allegedly asked, "Well, how do you know I won't think you're an intruder and I won't shoot you?"[35] When he continued asking this same question, his father and stepmother, feeling intimidated by these seemingly veiled threats, began locking the gun safe.

Dr. Christine Johnson, one of the psychologists hired by the defense, conjured up a very different depiction of Cody Posey.

"I got the impression he was often walking on eggshells to stay out of trouble at home," she testified. She further diagnosed Cody with major depression and post-traumatic stress disorder, originating in witnessing the death of his mother when he was just 10 years old.[36]

Her expert opinion was backed up by yet another psychologist who testified on behalf of the defense, Dr. Susan Cave, who believed that Cody was "physically, emotionally and possibly sexually abused as a child ... his life was very strictly and rigidly controlled and limited."

"I think the physical and emotional abuse was something he endured," Dr. Cave added. "He was carrying around a tremendous family secret."[37]

But Grisham wanted to prove to the jury that there weren't any mental illnesses involved that precluded Cody being able to think clearly about the damage he was doing and the repercussions by getting Dr. Johnson to admit it.

"When he takes the snake shot out because 'I didn't think that would do the job' that is indicative of some thinking and some intent, isn't it?" she asked.

"Yes," responded Dr. Johnson.

"And when he reloaded it with .38 that he did think would do the job, that again is some indication that he is thinking, isn't it?" she pushed.

"Yes."

"And that he is intending to kill?"

"Yes," she conceded again.[38]

The defense called several witnesses to take the stand and attest to Cody's claims of being subjected to a lifetime of abuse in his father's home.

One witness was Cody's science teacher, who recounted a time when Tryone and Paul were shamelessly berating Cody for his grades during a parent-teacher conference. "They were screaming and hollering and carrying on, both of them at the same time. Cody began sobbing and I was in shock. And Paul said, 'You're gonna get it when we get home.'"[39]

Slim Brittan was another witness to take the stand and testify about the abuse he saw. Using the iron hook meant for lifting hay, he demonstrated how Paul would reach over and strike his son on the hand with it. He also described how his employer whipped Cody with the rope.

"You take one of these and if you hit someone with it across the back like that," he explained, pantomiming a whip to demonstrate, "it really hurts."[40]

Pilo Vasquez, who still worked on the ranch, also corroborated Cody's claims. He explained that he had witnessed Paul striking his son first in the stomach and then in the chest.

And to settle the ongoing back-and-forth question of incest that the defense claimed was a catalyst for the murders, both the prosecution and defense called two computer experts to the stand who would unveil the couple's salacious Internet searches.

One of them was Jack Henderson, a certified forensic computer examiner who specialized in data recovery and analysis. He noted that both Cody and Marilea's separate computers were not hooked up to the Internet. The only computer that was belonged to the home's main office. He confirmed that somebody had been viewing incest pornography sites, and whoever it was made these searches in the middle of the night when the kids would be sleeping or in the morning and afternoon during school hours.[41]

But the key question was: *who* made these cryptic computer searches?

The defense introduced another computer expert to the stand, Joseph Burchett, a graduate of the New Mexico Institute of Mining and Technology who possessed a bachelor's degree in computer science.

They had Burchett admit that he was not a full-time computer analyst and that he did not have any experience in forensic analysis. But he was allowed to testify anyway. Using EnCase forensic software, which is commonly used by law enforcement agencies, he confirmed that Marilea's computer lacked a modem and Cody's computer had had no Internet access since 1999. The only computer that did have Internet access, with which the keyboard searches were made, was indeed the one located in the ranch home's main office. Using keywords such as "incest," "swinger," "wife," "daughter" and "son," he found pornography photos and sites cached that had been viewed on the computer since 2001 as well as incest sites which had been visited since 2002. The keywords "incest" and "daughter" produced 160 cached images alone, many of which were child pornography. One such pornographic image depicted a mother and young son.

Even though incest was the primary subject of these crude searches, there were searches for rape stories and "best rape" gallery images as well.[42]

Cody was among the witnesses to testify in his own defense. Impassively, he spoke of the different forms of abuse he went through that led up to the slayings, dating back to when he was as young as seven.

"When I was a younger child and had loose teeth, I would mess with them and wiggle 'em around. My father pops me, hit me in the jaw to knock my tooth out. And he said, 'There, now you'll stop playing with it,'" he told the court.

Gary Mitchell asked how he was woken up in those days.

"I got shocked with a hot shot which is an electronic cattle prod."[43]

He spoke about how he was once dragged by a rope behind a horse for 20 feet because he had made a mistake during ranch work. He recounted the time he was forced to shoot his puppy after it had broken its foot. He revealed that he was choked until he nearly lost consciousness. Every inch of his body had been struck by his father at some point.[44]

Once he got to talking about his mother's death, the boy began displaying more emotion.

"They took me away from my mother as I was trying to help her," he said. "And they put me in the back of the ambulance. And I remember going to a hospital, sir. I asked many times if she was okay. And doctors said she would be fine. Before I went to bed that night a doctor came in and told me that she didn't make it."[45]

And all Cody ever wanted was something simple, something not too hard to ask for a teenage boy. "I wanted a family. Sir, I wanted to please everybody that I could to make a family. I wanted to be the kid that my dad said, 'You know what, look, that's my son.'"[46]

Instead, he was thrown into a family that never showed him love or affection, regularly shunned him and humiliated him every chance they got, and isolated him from the world. A family that, soon, would be ripped apart by twisted lies, disturbing secrets, and bullets, their bodies disposed of in a pile of manure as if they never mattered while the only survivor sat behind bars. But why?

"So what happened to you, Cody? What happened to you that morning?" asked Gary Mitchell.

"I just…. I lost control, sir. I didn't know what I was thinking. I didn't know what I was doing."[47]

In the state's closing arguments, trial attorney Janice Schryer called Cody's claims of child abuse a feeble attempt "to pile more and more manure on top of Paul, Tryone and Marilea."

"It's not a case about abuse," she said. "It's a case about cold-blooded, intentional murder perpetrated by Cody Posey." She further argued that Cody had loving parents who simply had high expectations for the boy who didn't enjoy ranch life and "took the opportunity to relieve himself of those expectations and that life."[48]

She painted Cody not as an abuse victim but a cold-blooded,

manipulative killer who played judge, jury, and executioner on the fateful morning of July 4, 2004.

"In the end, ladies and gentlemen, it is this: how much do we demand of a child?" Gary Mitchell addressed the jury during the closing argument. "How much do we ask him to tolerate? And do we allow them to defend themselves? Do we allow them to defend themselves from the rapes? From the beatings?"[49]

Verdict and Sentencing

When it was time for the seven women and five men of the jury to deliberate, they were at a loss for what to do. They sat through three weeks of testimony after testimony about all of the suffering, pain, and abuse that Cody was subjected to throughout his young life. They weighed the defense's argument and took the prosecution's argument into consideration. They couldn't quell the heart-wrenching effects that the testimonies had on them. So, right away, they focused on the defense's closing argument and debated the possibility of an acquittal over self-defense. Initially, the panel was divided, but it became very clear that Cody's case just did not meet the standards of self-defense, as per the carefully-written instructions given to them by the judge, who described self-defense as being in immediate danger. They had to relent when they collectively agreed that Cody, though undoubtedly a victim of horrific abuse, was not facing an imminent threat directed at his life when he acted out by gunning down his entire family.

Now it came down to determining what Cody was guilty of. This is when jurors really felt like their hands were tied. Again, the panel was divided between jurors who wanted to consider his young age and history of abuse as mitigating factors and jurors like Jonathan Bachman, the jury foreman, who thought that age was irrelevant for an act like this—in his eyes, Cody, and only Cody, was responsible for what he had done, and the blame should not be shifted to his family regardless of what they put him through. They had to reach a compromise if they wanted to avoid a hung jury.

After 12 stressful hours of debilitation, the jurors reached a decision.

The courtroom was packed on February 7, 2006. One side of the courtroom was occupied by Cody's supporters. The other side was filled with the victims' loved ones.

Judge Counts, in his strong, bellowing voice that reached the ears of every person in the courtroom, announced the jury's verdict: "In the matter of Cody Posey, a child, we find Cody Posey guilty of first-degree murder."[50]

He was found guilty of first-degree murder for the fatal shooting of his stepsister, Marilea. He was found guilty of second-degree murder for killing his stepmother, Tryone. And as for the killing of his father, Paul Posey, Cody was found guilty of voluntary manslaughter.

This verdict stirred a lot of emotion in the courtroom. Cody, who had maintained an overall impassive demeanor throughout the three-week trial, exhibited his first tug of emotion; he dropped his head to the table and sobbed while Gary Mitchell held and consoled him.[51] Ellen Brust, the mother of Cody's father, embraced Cody's cousin. Cody's maternal aunt, Corliss Clees, seemed particularly jarred by the verdict. She attended Cody's trial for two weeks straight to show her unwavering support for him. When she heard his guilty verdict, she collapsed onto the floor and wept; paramedics later arrived and carried her out of the courtroom on a stretcher.

But what's a trial without a twist at the end? Despite the fact that the jury convicted Cody of three counts of murder, it wasn't over just yet, for the members of the jury didn't have a final say in Cody's fate. Under New Mexico law, it is the judge—in this case, Judge Counts—who gets to make the final ruling in children's court. And it would be Counts who decided whether Cody Posey, now 16, would be sentenced as a juvenile or an adult. The leniency or severity of his sentence would depend entirely on the judge's decision.

Three jurors joined the crowd of Cody's supporters rallying outside of the courthouse carrying signs that read "Free Cody."[52]

The jurors were doing everything in their power to save Cody from a lengthy term in adult prison. Why, after convicting him of three very serious charges, were they now trying to soften the blow? In truth, nobody wanted to see this young child, who lived a life of hardship, go to prison for the rest of his life. Many of the jurors were simply doing their duty by carefully following the instructions handed to them by the judge. They didn't believe the verdict was truly serving justice for the youth.

Some members of the jury felt very moved by the case and "broke down" after issuing the verdict. Seven of the 12 jurors joined the petitioners and sent letters to Judge Counts imploring him to sentence Cody as a child and not an adult.

Verlin Posey told reporters that he was happy overall with the outcome of the trial, although he wished that Cody was convicted of first-degree murder in connection to his brother's death. "I didn't like it, but I can live with it," he said.[53] Verlin was one of the witnesses who testified for the state that he never suspected or detected any signs of abuse and that the father and son seemed to have a good relationship.

"Children never expect horrible things to happen. He thinks there's some sort of sense of justice in this world," Cody's defense attorney tearfully told reporters outside of the courtroom. "We put the blame on a 14-year-old for the sins and omissions of the adults. This could have been prevented if those adults who stood by came forward, yet we expect him to act with greater courage."[54]

On Thursday, February 23, just a few days after Cody heard his verdict, he walked into the courtroom one last time to once again listen as both sides would argue for and against him. The state continued to push for Judge Counts to sentence him as an adult.

"Cody Posey is a cold-hearted killer. I know that it's difficult, your honor, but I'm asking the court to protect society from him as long as you possibly can," said prosecutor Sandra Grisham.[55]

Dr. Robert Buser, Cody's psychiatrist while he was held in custody, testified that the youth's risk of re-offending upon release was very low.[56] The defense contended that Cody didn't pose a threat to society, that the murders were an isolated incident and an act of self-defense, and that Cody would respond very well to rehabilitation programs in juvenile detention.

The 14-year-old would be the last one to address the judge and hopefully make a lasting impression on his final decision-making.

"During the past two months you've heard accusations of me being a liar, a psychopath. You've heard that I'll kill again or end up back in the courtroom. I can tell you right now that I will never kill again," said Cody.[57]

After weeks of nervous waiting, Judge Counts announced his final decision.

"The court orders that the child be committed to the custody of Children Youth and Family Dept. until age 21," he said.[58]

Count Judge read from a list of sentencing criteria which guided his decision in sentencing Cody as a juvenile. One aggravating factor against Cody was that he was charged with first-degree murder, the most serious offense of all. However, one of the mitigating factors which led to this decision, the judge said, was the state's failure to prove that Cody was beyond any capacity of being rehabilitated. He also found that Cody suffered from PTSD and didn't particularly find the state's argument that Cody possessed strong psychopathic tendencies very cogent. Furthermore, he labeled the crime a "situational nature of the violence" which, in his eyes, meant a minimized risk of recidivism.

Despite the protesters outside and the online petitions fighting for Cody's freedom, the judge maintained that public opinion did not influence his decision-making.

Sandra Grisham was unhappy with the judge's ruling and immediately requested that he sentence Cody as an adult just on his first-degree murder conviction, then sentence him to five years in juvenile detention with an additional five years of probation upon his release. But the judge refused, for his ruling was final: five years maximum in juvenile detention.

The prosecutor left the courthouse without any comments that day. But Cody was in rather high spirits. Today was a victorious day for Cody, his lawyer, and his family, who all feared that he might spend the rest of his life in an adult prison. Cody's future was looking brighter.

He smiled at his supporters outside. "I'd like to say thank you to everybody," he told them before being whisked away by an Otero County sheriff's patrol car.[59]

Afterword

This wouldn't be the last we would hear of Cody Posey. On September 25, 2006, Miami attorney Jack Thompson filed a wrongful death suit, naming Cody on behalf of the surviving Posey relatives. Among those also named in the lawsuit were Rockstar Games, the creator of *Grand Theft Auto*, as well as Take-Two Interactive and Sony (the manufacturer of PlayStation). During the investigation after the triple homicide committed by Cody, police had recovered a copy of *Grand Theft Auto: Vice City*, a violent video game that was owned and frequently played by the teen. Thompson claimed that the game had "trained" him to become an "extraordinarily effective" killer.

"Posey essentially practiced how to kill on this game. If it wasn't for *Grand Theft Auto*, three people might not now be dead," Thompson argued in the lawsuit.[60]

However, on December 19, 2007, a judge would throw out the case as neither Take-Two Interaction or Sony had offices in New Mexico.

On October 9, 2010, his twenty-first birthday, Cody Posey was released from prison. While in custody, he had managed to earn his high school diploma and even completed two years' worth of college credits. He has since served as a mentor for younger juveniles. He never had any disciplinary issues.

Now a free man with a new lease on life, Cody was ready to put the dark chapters behind him and look forward to a fresh start.[61]

Jasmiyah and Tasmiyah Whitehead
(2010)

The bond between a mother and daughter is thought to be the most powerful connection that two people can share. The area of the brain that modulates emotions has been shown to be more similar between mothers and daughters than any other intergenerational pairing. One such study has found that the corticolimbic circuitry, which plays a role in processing and regulating responses to emotional stimuli, demonstrates matrilineal-specific transmission patterns. And such transmission patterns are attributed to how a mother and daughter react to one another.[1]

What can cause a bond so seemingly durable to be ruptured?

As we have learned in a previous chapter, parricides only make up 2 percent of all homicides. But even more interestingly, matricides make up only 15 percent of all parricides. And to narrow it down even further, the majority of females who kill their mothers are adults. It is rare for an adolescent to kill their mother. They account for only 20 percent of matricide cases, which comes as a shock due to how tumultuous relationships between mothers and daughters can be during these formative years. Female juvenile perpetrators of matricide tend to be between the ages 14 and 17 and typically, don't act alone. Virtually half will have an accomplice, more often than not a boyfriend or friend, and single-parent households tend to be more susceptible.

So what is the primary motivating factor for girls who kill their mothers? Female matricides typically fall under two categories.

The first and main motive is to escape an abusive situation. The majority of teen girls who kill their mothers come from dysfunctional households riddled with domestic violence, substance abuse, and neglect. Attempts to seek outside help to be removed from their toxic home life have proved unsuccessful. These are the girls who see no way out and just "snap." Rarely do they show a history of violent tendencies up until the murder.

But this is not always the case. Sometimes, it is the daughters who have become the abusers themselves. And these are the types of killers who have displayed a track record of concerning and antisocial behavior such as violence, stealing, and lying, problems that are only exacerbated once the parent steps in and tries to set firm boundaries. These girls are resistant to authority and any form of disciplinary action.[2]

These are the exact types of girls where, if you dare stand in the way of what they want, there will be hell to pay.

Background

Jarmecca Yvonne Whitehead, commonly called "Nikki" by all those who knew her, was born on August 18, 1975, within the confines of a prison to Lynda Whitehead, who was serving time for drug possession. She was primarily raised by her grandmother, Della Frazier, as her mother didn't have the means to take care of her. Nikki had developed a sort of wild side as she grew up. She got involved with a bad crowd and was a frequent drug and alcohol user. She didn't have a curfew and came and left as she pleased. Her grandmother found great difficulty in keeping her under control.

At the age of 17, Nikki unexpectedly became pregnant and, at 18, gave birth to identical twin girls on November 27, 1993, whom she poetically named Jasmiyah and Tasmiyah. Nikki, along with her daughters, lived with Della, but she soon realized that she was terribly unprepared for the responsibilities that come with raising not just one but two children, so she left her family behind and moved to Conyers, Georgia, to live with her boyfriend.[3]

Jarmecca had captured the eye of Robert Head, who worked as a truck driver, while shopping at South DeKalb Mall. He immediately followed her into Macy's to introduce himself, and he purchased an outfit for her. In spite of the age difference, Robert being three decades older, the two struck up a romantic relationship, and, eventually, Nikki would move in with him in Conyers.[4]

The twins were left in the care of their great-grandmother.

She, too, had cared for Nikki while her own mother was unable to. This situation was no different, and she vowed to be a stable influence in the girls' lives during Nikki's prolonged absences. Della worked full-time at the Coca-Cola Company, so it wasn't going to be easy, but with the help of her husband, the two raised the twin girls from infancy and kept them busy with a series of extra-curricular activities. The girls were inseparable and did everything together—ballet, music, and tennis. They were also Girl Scouts and straight-A students with dreams of enrolling in Harvard one day.

The sisters never caused any trouble, according to Della. However, friends would later say that the twins had stolen money from their great-grandmother, who eventually had to get a deadbolt for her bedroom.[5]

Jas and Tas lived with their great-grandmother until their early teen years. In 2007, Nikki yearned to become a prominent figure in her daughters' lives, perhaps at the urging of her mother, Lynda, who suffered from her own regrets about her absence from Nikki's life, and successfully gained full custody of them.

So the now 13-year-old twin sisters reluctantly stuffed all their belongings in suitcases and moved 20 miles away to Conyers, Georgia, leaving behind their lenient life in Clarkston, Georgia.

The sudden move should have played out as a happily-ever-after tale of mother and daughters reunited at last. But things didn't quite turn out as Nikki had hoped.

The young mother was having regrets of her own in terms of not being present in her children's lives, and she was desperate to make up for lost time. She was now ready to step up in her role as a mother, which she had failed to do for all these years. Nikki, who worked at a hair salon, tried to bond with her daughters by styling their hair and doing their makeup. She also enrolled them in dance and music classes to mimic the active lifestyle the girls shared back at their great-grandmother's. Nikki wanted the girls to feel comfortable, at home. She wanted her children to grow up with a mother figure and role model, something she had lacked in her own upbringing.[6]

But things in the Whitehead household turned sour fast. The twins clashed with Nikki—immensely. Once they reached high school, the girls developed a rebellious streak and defiant attitudes. Their once-impressive grades began slipping, and their interests shifted to boys, smoking marijuana, and skipping school. Nikki didn't allow her daughters to stay out late and had confiscated Tas's phone when she found out she was talking to boys as old as 17. Jas and Tas resisted their mother's attempts to control them when she tried to lay down some ground rules.

They didn't take their mother seriously and, in fact, found her hypocritical for trying to restrain them from doing the very same things she was guilty of doing—i.e., smoking marijuana and being promiscuous. They were used to living in a home where they had more freedom and were rarely, if ever, told no, so it came as a huge shock when Nikki began parenting them.

In the beginning, Della tried to insert herself into the trio's relationship when things got tense, but she backed off when that strained her relationship with Nikki. She decided to let Nikki enforce all of the discipline herself and kept her distance, watching quietly in horror as the turbulence within the Whitehead home grew to an unmanageable level. Occasionally, she had to step in when Nikki left the sisters all by themselves or left them alone at the mall, prompting the twins to call their great-grandmother, pleading for their rescue.

It wasn't long before tensions escalated to the extent that the police got involved. The first time, Nikki had phoned 911 after she discovered that Jas had snuck out of the house to meet up with her boyfriend in the middle of the night. Jas was only 13 at the time. Then, in 2008, police were summoned to the Whitehead home after yet another volatile argument had erupted.

Officer Myra Scruggs was the one who responded to the domestic call. She interviewed Jas, Tas, and their mother to try to sort out the issue at hand. It was yet another case of rule-resisting that escalated into a blow-up. The twins complained about living with their mother and insisted on moving back in with their great-grandmother.

The sisters had a sweet, innocent look to them. The girls' hair was styled to perfection and their closets brimmed with designer clothing and shoes. It was very clear that they weren't being neglected at all.

But she had an entirely different impression when she spoke with Nikki. Officer Scruggs could detect a hint of fear lurking behind her dark eyes. The young mom was quite obviously scared of her daughters, or, rather, what they were perhaps capable of.

Eventually, things smoothed over and the girls were about ready to head to bed. Officer Scruggs left the home, but something in her gut told her to stay in the vicinity; perhaps from her experience as a police officer, she had developed a strong sense of premonition when something awful was about to transpire.

Her gut instinct was proven correct. Within minutes, she heard shrill screams and shouting coming from the direction of the Whitehead home. The girls had begun beating their mom, scratching her, and dragging her across the floor.

Nikki just barely managed to escape the brutal clawing and beating; she ran out of the house, calling 911 once again. Officer Scruggs pulled up and comforted the hysterical woman who claimed her daughters had attacked her as soon as the officer left. She had the scratch marks covering her neck and chest to show for it.

Jasmiyah and Tasmiyah painted a different image of what had just gone down. They explained—calmly—that it was actually *Nikki* who began physically assaulting *them* within minutes of the office's departure. But the girls weren't behaving like victims of a violent physical attack and they didn't have any marks or scratches.

Judging by the evidence, Officer Scruggs didn't believe the sisters. She brought them into custody, where they were both charged with battery. They spent the next few years in and out of juvenile court, where mother and daughters were ordered to get family counseling. The family went through six counselors during this time.

During a court appearance, one of the many counselors who attempted to reconcile the twins and mother reported that the family "thrived on chaos."

"All members—mom, great-grandmother, and the girls—struggle to take their own responsibility for family stress. The adults in this family have failed to guide these children properly," the juvenile court counselor noted.[7]

The judge agreed that it might be best for the sisters to move back in with their great-grandmother, where there was less toxicity. Jas and Tas got their wish, and Nikki lost temporary custody of her children.

Della enrolled Jasmiyah and Tasmiyah at Tucker High, and they had minimal contact with their mother. They seldom spoke of her. Meanwhile, Nikki spoke of her daughters often. The 2008 incident stuck in the forefront of her mind. She vented about the once-happy and respectful girls that had seemingly turned their backs on her overnight.

"I got a family that does not function good," Nikki confided to one of her friends. "Sometimes I'm afraid. I don't know what my children might do to me."[8]

"Nikki, you better put a lock on your bedroom door," the friend advised.⁹

In November 2009, Nikki and her mother, Lynda Whitehead, threw a birthday bash for the twins' sweet 16. Twenty-five people showed up at an Atlanta bowling alley to celebrate, but only Tas chose to attend. Her sister decided not to come.

Lynda promptly called her missing granddaughter.

"Why aren't you here?" she demanded.

"I just don't want to come," responded the teenage girl.¹⁰

As heartbroken as the young mom was, she plastered on her best smile and celebrated Tas' birthday without the other twin.

At some point, while being separated from her daughters, Nikki began to miss having them in her care. Despite the fact that they had a tumultuous relationship, and regardless of the fact that the girls had assaulted her, they were still her children. Probably due to the unconditional love that many mothers harbor for their children, she was driven to fight for them, regardless of the danger they might pose to her well-being.

On January 5, 2013, a Rockdale juvenile court judge agreed with a counselor's sentiment that giving Della custody of the twins really just "swapped one situation for another"¹¹ and signed a court order allowing the sisters to return to the care of their mother once again. Tasmiyah and Jasmiyah became emotional after the judge's decision. They cried and begged the judge to not send them back there.

When the girls moved back in with their mother, things did not change for the better. Within days, police were called to the Whitehead home twice on domestic disturbances. The first time, Nikki claimed Tasmiyah was throwing food; the second time, an altercation occurred between Tasmiyah and her aunt during a "welcome home" party thrown for the twins.¹²

Eight days after the court order, Nikki Whitehead would be found brutally murdered inside her own home.

A Dead Mom

In the afternoon of January 13, Deputy Al Irwin from the Rockdale County Sheriff's Department was passing through the Conyers subdivision after having just served a warrant to another resident on an unrelated matter. As he was getting to the gate, a distraught teenage girl flagged him down. It was one of the Whitehead twins.

In a panic, she told him that she and her sister had just come home from school and found their mother's slain corpse in their house.

Deputy Irwin followed the young woman to her one-story home and entered. As clear as day, there were perceptible traces and droplets of blood staining the hardwood floor and tan-colored carpet that smelled of bleach. He tracked the blood spatter from the living room into the master bedroom, which led directly to the bathroom where the 34-year-old mother was slumped on her side, completely naked, in a filled, blood-soaked bathtub.[13]

He promptly called for backup, and in no time Conyers police were there to investigate. One of the first officers to arrive at the scene was Captain Jackie Dunn. He made a startling observation as soon as he stepped through the front door: the pungent scent of sweet and coppery blood permeating the house. Detective Sergeant Ken Swift was among the first to arrive. Immediately, he could determine that a vicious struggle had taken place; there were knocked over chairs and broken vases throughout the living room.[14] He followed the scarlet trail into the master bedroom, which took him to the bathroom where Nikki's battered corpse remained. She had 80 stab wounds covering her body, penetrating her lungs and jugular and the back of her neck, where her spinal cord was severed. Some areas had been stabbed more than once.

It was clear to him that this was a crime of passion. There were no signs of forced entry in or around the house, so he strongly suspected that she had been killed by someone who knew her, rather than a total stranger. But he did not suspect that the anxiety-ridden teen girls, who claimed that their mother was still alive before they departed for school that morning, were involved whatsoever. During the initial phase of the investigation, they began compiling a list of potential suspects. Through the sisters, they learned that Nikki had a couple of boyfriends. Robert Head, whom she had been living with for the past several years, was one of them. On the side, she was secretly seeing someone else, a man by the name of Joe. Robert had apparently caught wind of the infidelity after overhearing a phone call between them and had confronted her about it. This, to the police, might serve as the perfect motive.

Ken Swift decided to bring Jas and Tas to police headquarters where they could chat further and get the whole story. On the drive there, however, he noticed something that raised a red flag in his mind. In the backseat, Tas was biting down hard on her arm. He immediately stopped her in the act and questioned what she was doing. The 16-year-old replied that it was an old habit of hers when she was upset by something.

What he didn't know was that Tas was really trying to mask the teeth marks that were inflicted by Nikki during the quarrel that morning.

Back at the station, the girls were asked to describe exactly how they discovered their dead mother.

"I went into her room and I saw blood all over the floor and I went in there and I seen her and I touched her," Jas said through uncontrolled sobs.[15]

The girls claimed that they had missed the bus that the morning, so they had to walk to school. They departed at 7:30. Nikki was still alive and well at this point. It was just a typical morning.

While the two were left alone in the interrogation room, the girls consoled each other and cried out for their grandma and "mama." They embraced one another and Jas gave her sister a peck on the cheek. Captain Jackie Dunn felt sorry for the twins, who had just lost their mother in an unimaginable way. He wanted to know if there was anything he could do at all to alleviate the pain they were feeling.

The girls perked up: "Can we watch *CSI*?"[16]

Immediately, chills went down the investigator's spine. The girls just discovered their brutally-murdered mother, and their go-to comfort was to watch a show about murder? Something in his mind told him that the sisters were being deceptive.

But this wasn't the first red flag the investigators noticed in their behavior. For two young ladies who had just lost their parent in a traumatic way, they failed to demonstrate the level of grief one might expect. The police became acutely aware that the twins shared a rather tumultuous relationship with their mother. One would expect to hear loving and affectionate descriptors from the victim's children when they were asked to describe what their mother was like, but the sisters had nothing positive to say about her.

Jas and Tas stood by their original story the whole time. Occasionally, investigators would find inconsistencies in their claims and pressure them for the truth. Each time, the sisters would get increasingly defensive and argumentative. Having them in the same room wasn't exactly helping to extract information from them, so investigators decided to separate them and question them individually.

Detectives also noticed that the girls were wearing gloves indoors, presumably to conceal their injuries from the officers. When they were asked to remove them, detectives noted very visible scratches marking their hands, on top of the fresh cuts and bite marks covering their arms, which had naturally been acquired during an obviously vicious struggle. The twins both claimed that the bite marks were self-inflicted and that they acquired the scratches after getting into a physical altercation with one another.

Tasmiyah was placed in a separate room for interrogation. She seemed well aware that she was being watched, at some point even making direct eye contact with the installed surveillance camera, so she put on an act and police listened closely.

"Can't eat. Mom's dead. Stupid scratch," she mumbled to herself, quietly, in a brittle voice. "Gonna blame this whole thing on me … over a stupid scratch."[17]

Staring down at her hands, she prayed, "Please God, I'm really hoping they catch this person."[18]

Back at the crime scene, investigators were discovering physical evidence left behind by the girls. They found bloody clothes stuffed in the washing machine and a pair of shoes hidden in the very back of their closet. They also discovered a shoe box in Tas' bedroom containing a bloody pair of brown boots. There, stuffed in the toe of the boot, was a clump of hair wrapped in tissue. The sink in the bathroom had been completely scrubbed clean, and evidence indicated that the sisters tried to clean the bloody mess they had created around the home, but gave up less than halfway through when they realized that it was too much.

Unfortunately, the evidence was only circumstantial; first and foremost, they needed to test the evidence before they really started pointing the finger at anybody. So, with no grounds to implicate them in the murder of their mother, they released the teenage girls from custody. Jas and Tas were returned to the care of their great-grandmother once again. But that didn't mean that they had gotten away with it.

In the subsequent four months, the girls resumed their life as normal. They enrolled in Tucker High School as sophomores, had a social life, and even attended prom. They had no idea that during this time, police were silently watching them and building their case, assembling all of the damning pieces of evidence that would soon be used against them.

One piece of evidence that showed that the girls were lying about the timeline of that morning was caught on video. Recovered surveillance tape showed the twin sisters walking to a nearby gas station and hitching a ride from someone. Surveillance footage also showed Jas and

Tas entering their school building at roughly 10:40 a.m.—nearly two hours late. The sisters had told police that they were only 10 minutes late, which couldn't have been further from the truth. The more deceptions that the police discovered during the investigation, the more responsible the twins were looking.

They tested the bloody items recovered from the crime scene at FBI labs to try to link the girls to the murder. Their only issue was distinguishing just *who* the blood belonged to, as identical twins share identical DNA.

Police went around to question neighbors and ask if they had seen or heard anything unusual that morning. There was bloody footprint evidence at Nikki's front door, indicating that she had managed to escape briefly. She ran to her next-door neighbor's home, ringing the doorbell and knocking frantically while shouting for help. That neighbor told police that he did recall this occurrence, but it was early in the morning and he was still in bed, so he didn't bother to investigate. This untimely opportunity that slipped by was Nikki's only chance for survival.

There was one significant clue that was missing in this puzzle: the murder weapon. Police officers canvassed the subdivision and used batons to "beat the bushes," but all efforts to locate the murder weapon were futile.

But the most crucial clue would be uncovered during the medical examination, for the wounds that covered Nikki's body from head to toe would tell a story that would give a very important clue that would lead to the twins' ultimate downfall and arrest. The defense wounds indicated that the 34-year-old didn't go down without a fight. Not only did a dental examination of Nikki's teeth prove that it matched the bite mark inflicted on Tas, the one Tas had tried to cover up herself, but a tiny piece of human hair was found lodged between her two front teeth, which she must have acquired while she bit down on her daughter's arm. Sadly, the medical examiner who assessed Nikki Whitehead's body would later say that her wounds were survivable had she received immediate medical treatment.

Arrest and Confession

After months of collecting, examining, and testing evidence, police had grounds to apprehend the twin sisters and charge them with the murder of Nikki Whitehead.

It was the last day of school. The twins had probably been counting down the days for the arrival of their summer break. Very likely they had visions of basking in the sun's warmth, hanging out with friends, going shopping, staying out late—doing whatever they desired, just as they had killed for. Enough time had elapsed between their mother's murder and now for them to even relax about that incident that occurred on January 13. And, indeed, to them, it probably was a minor mishap in their lives, a blip in their timeline that they believed was now in the past. They were only looking forward, not back.

Detectives began driving to Della Frazier's house with two warrants for their arrests, ready to shatter any summer plans that the twins were probably anticipating.

"We decided we were going to arrest them on the last day of school for fear they were going to take flight out of the country to avoid the charges," said Dunn.[19]

They arrested Tas at her home, handcuffed her, and conducted a body search. Jas was still at school, however, so they took a quick detour to Rockdale High where she, too, was cuffed. Now that the police had the girls arrested, they secretly audio recorded their conversations while the girls waited in the cruiser, hoping they might say something incriminating. But the girls kept up their act of innocence.

"They're talking about those damn bite marks," said Jas.

"They're saying I have momma's teeth on my arm," responded Tas.

Their tones got increasingly angry as they criticized the "terrible" evidence that police had stacked against them. "I am not going down for something I did not do!" said Tas.

"Me either!" exclaimed her sister.

Tas continued her rant. "The day that you find a murder weapon with my fingerprints on it or something, please do that. Please find a murder weapon and then it will be different."[20]

The twins were now facing multiple charges, including malicious murder, felony murder, and aggravated assault, all of which carry a potential life sentence without parole. Prosecutors could not push for the death penalty as minors are not eligible for capital punishment. They were held in separate juvenile facilities to prevent them from "comparing notes."

Both sisters pleaded not guilty. But their tones would change four years after the murder, when they gave police yet another account of what happened on that fateful day—only this time, it was no longer denial. In tearful confessions, they were coming clean about everything.

On January 11, the night before the murder, the sisters claimed that their mother came home in a drunken stupor. Usually, the twins said, when their mother was high or intoxicated, she would be plagued with hallucinations and thoughts of paranoia that the police and army were coming, ordering the twins to lock all of the doors, check the windows, and look under their beds. According to the twins, this behavior occurred even when they were younger; whenever their mother was drunk, she would barge into the girls' bedroom and state that there were bugs crawling all over her body or think there was an earthquake happening.

January 11 became another one of those nights. The girls just isolated themselves in their bedrooms, staying up until two or three a.m. and waking up late for school. That's when they encountered a very displeased Nikki in the kitchen, who immediately began shouting and cursing at them for being late. The twins were tired and wanted to stay home for the day. But, as usual, Nikki wasn't going to let them have their way.

She told them, "You're not going to do what you want to do; you have to live by my rules."[21]

A fiery confrontation was ignited, and, according to the twins, their mother threatened them with a pot she had picked up from the stove and swung it at them. It was Tasmiyah who managed to wrestle the pot away from her, but things only escalated from there. Everyone was shouting at each other.

"My state of mind at the time was 'defend yourself,'" said Jasmiyah. "It wasn't like a fight on the street, it was more like a fight until somebody dies."[22]

After grabbing the pot, "that's when she grabbed the knife and kind of turned and said 'get back' but she didn't keep the knife in her hand," said Tasmiyah.

The violent brawl made its way into the living room. Everyone was screaming and shouting at each other; names and curses flew back and forth as they scratched and bit one another. Sometime during the scuffle, Jas took a red vase and smashed it over her mother's head, drawing the first blood. The young mom continued to defend herself, so Jasmiyah picked up the pot and struck her with it.

"She bit me in the chest and like I said, I'm not that big, so when she bit me she latched onto me and I tried to get her off because it hurts," said Jas. "I'm trying to punch her, I guess, and then I think Tas stabbed her."[23]

More fighting ensued. The twins exchanged bites, punches, scratches, and lots of hair-pulling with their mother. At some point during the intense struggle, Jas began strangling her mother with a ribboned medallion. That's when Nikki caught her by surprise with a swift backhand blow. As if on instinct, Jas lunged for the knife and stabbed her. After Nikki's failed attempt to seek refuge at her neighbor's home, she slumped at the kitchen table, battered and exhausted from the scuffle. She tried to reach for the steak knife again, but Jasmiyah was faster. She delivered the final blows that would render her mother powerless. Nikki could no longer fight back. She had lost the battle.

The girls lifted their mom and carried her toward the bathroom, grunting all the while, and dropped her into the water-filled tub.

But Nikki was still drawing breath. And her final words before the lights would go out were coated with a thick layer of hurt, anger and betrayal.

"She hates us ... she hates us," recalled Jas of her mother's last words to them. "I don't know, I guess the same thing, 'we're going to jail, we're going to jail.'"

The only words Jas could muster in response were "I'm sorry."

The twins watched as the woman who gave them life submerged under the water a couple of times and then, in Jasmiyah's own words, "that was it."

"I guess we were shocked," she said. "We couldn't believe what we did. We cried, we cried for a long time. We argued a bit."[24]

But it was the worst time to pick fights with each other, because now they had a bloody crime scene and dead body to take care of. They needed to figure out how they were going to cover it up. After attempting to clean up some of it and hide the evidence, the girls changed their clothes, tossed the old ones in the washer, and collected the pot, knife, Nikki's cell phone and purse in a plastic bag. Then they went to school so they could have an alibi. Upon their return in the afternoon, they fully expected to see police cars parked outside of their house. But there was nobody. The nightmarish scene was completely untouched, just as they had left it.

Whether it was through genuine tears of remorse or crocodile tears from being caught red-handed, the girls expressed regret for how things had escalated beyond control that morning.

"I really wished it didn't happen like that. I wish I could have seen something else to do," said Tas. "It was just confusion. It was like turmoil. It just seemed like it never stopped."

"I'm sorry and I miss her," said Jas. "It's not what Lynda and all them try to make it seem. I didn't hate her. And Tas didn't hate her either. I guess it was just the heat of the moment and built-up anger between all three of us."[25]

Both of the girls said they wished they had called the police during the fight when things began to blow out of proportion.

───

After nearly four years of sitting in a jail cell, the now-20-year-old Tasmiyah Whitehead showed up in court on January 9, 2014. But this wasn't just another court proceeding in preparation for the impending trial. Clad in her orange jump suit, she looked strikingly different from the innocent-looking 16-year-old who had been arrested four years earlier. Gone was her long hair, which had since been lopped off with a star shape shaved into the back of her head. She pleaded guilty to reduced charges of voluntary manslaughter, possession of a knife during the crime, and falsification in government matters. It is unclear whether she took full responsibility for the murder to avoid the taxing process of a trial that she most likely wouldn't win, or, if sometime during her lengthy jail time, she reflected on what she had done. She was sentenced to 30 years in prison.

But for once, her sister was not on the same page. Jas had rejected a plea deal, meaning the case would still go to trial anyway, forcing Tas to testify against her own blood sister. The trial was to commence in March, and it would pit sister against sister. If convicted, she could be sentenced to life in prison.

It didn't take Jasmiyah long to realize that the odds were stacked against her. On February 7, one month after Tas pleaded guilty, Jasmiyah appeared in court again. Garbed in an orange jumpsuit, her hair tied in a modest bun, she followed in her sister's steps and also took responsibility for her role in her mother's murder.

"I just want to say I'm sorry for all that has happened and all the pain it has caused to my family and my sister and especially my mom," she testified before Rockdale County Chief Superior Court Judge David Irwin. "I'm sorry for everything, and I take full responsibility for my actions. I want to thank y'all for the mercy and leniency in my sentencing. This is not where I want to be. I want to contribute to the world. Not hurt my mom."[26]

Jasmiyah had filed for a request for "first offender status" which would essentially have expunged her criminal record once she had served her time behind bars. The judge denied it.

"I don't know who was the leader and who was the follower," he stated as his reason. He believed that the twins were "co-conspirators" and should be treated equally by the law, as he did not give Tasmiyah a first offender status either. He further stated that he believed in redemption and bought into Jasmiyah's expression of remorse, which, to him, indicated a willingness to change. "I believe in redemption; I believe everyone should have a second chance. No question about that."[27]

Prior to handing Jasmiyah her sentence, the judge had some final words of wisdom to offer to the court. "The tragedy doesn't end. I don't think there's a single person here whose heart has not been broken. I know mine has and I know the family's has." He reminded onlookers that it is not the responsibility of the court to provide closure. "Closure has to come from within. People can learn and heal in the process by people stepping up and acknowledging their participation, and I think that's what Ms. Whitehead has done here today."[28]

He then sentenced her to 30 years in prison, as did her sister. As Jasmiyah was escorted out of the courtroom, she waved a final goodbye to her family members. Seated among them was her grandmother, Lynda Whitehead, who was sobbing during and after Jas' testimony. Another relative chastised Della for not consoling her own daughter, making it clear that family tensions remained.

Life in Prison

It has been more than a decade since the tragic murder of Nikki Whitehead, and the Whitehead twins have spent the years imprisoned for causing her death. Some might see it as a double tragedy, both for Nikki, who lost her life, and her two daughters, who lost their future, although through nobody's fault but their own. Nikki was just a broken mother who made mistakes in her past but wanted to turn her life around and make things right by her daughters. Against the advice of her relatives, counselors, boyfriend, and friends, she fought for her girls until the moment she drew her last breath. Jasmiyah and Tasmiyah were intelligent young ladies who had bright and glimmering futures ahead of them that they had just so heedlessly tossed away in the heat of a really bad moment.

The sisters are now separated, leading independent lives and paving their own paths for the future. According to recent reports, the twins are thriving in prison. Jasmiyah is currently being held at Lee Arrendale Prison, where at 21 she earned her high school diploma, along with 19 other women, after completing a prison-based charter school program through the Mountain Education Charter High School. Even though she had already earned her GED earlier in her incarceration, Georgia correctional and educational officials convinced her that earning her high school diploma would take her further upon her release into society, as possession of a high school diploma improves your chances for post-secondary school admissions and employment, as opposed to a GED.[29]

At the forefront of this diploma program is former educator Buster Evans, who was invited into the world of corrections to concentrate on education programs as a method of rehabilitating inmates to increase their chances of success post-release. Their efforts did, indeed, prove effective.

He pointed to a 2013 study at the RAND Corporation, which was supported by the U.S. departments of justice and education. It found that inmates who participated in correctional education programs, be they academic or vocational, saw reduced recidivism rates compared to those who did not participate in the programs. Educated inmates in Georgia had a 43 percent lower risk of re-offending upon their release and a 13 percent higher rate of gaining employment. Those who participated in vocational training were 28 percent more likely to find a job upon their release than those who received no such training.

Nevertheless, this special program had exceeded expectations and saw great success in rehabilitation of offenders since its launch, which had started with the 19 female inmates at Lee Arrendale State Prison. Since then, correctional officials have worked to expand the initiative statewide with the aid of 250 educators and support staff. Next, they would launch a similar program for male inmates at Burress Correctional Training Center in Monroe. As of 2010, about 30 percent of Georgia inmates hold a high school diploma, and the state's recidivism rate is also 30 percent.[30]

"To see our ladies overcome their pasts to create a new future, for me, is one of the greatest experiences of my professional career," said Evans, who now serves as Georgia's assistant commissioner.[31]

On Thursday, July 23, 2015, Jasmiyah Whitehead swapped her prison jumpsuit for her graduation gown and cap and stood before her classmates as the valedictorian of the class of 2015.

"I would love to major in child psychology. I want to be a family counselor or something with kids because I was a kid when I was first incarcerated," she explained. "If I could help kids not make the same mistakes that I made, or help families not make the same mistakes my family made, it would be wonderful."

She concluded: "You can't quit on life!"[32]

What could have been done to prevent this tragedy from occurring? Do the adults in the Whitehead twins' lives bear any sort of responsibility or blame for what had happened? How about the counselors, who advocated the sisters' move back into a toxic environment against the safety and well-being of both Nikki and her daughters? What about the judge, who allowed this to happen, despite the sisters' grim track record of violently assaulting their mother? The family wasn't capable of keeping the peace. Within 10 days, the brewing tension boiled over, and Nikki Whitehead was found viciously beaten and murdered in her own bathtub.

Had the judge denied Nikki's request for custody, might she still be alive today? Possibly. But who is to say that Jasmiyah and Tasmiyah, who resented authority and refused to allow anyone to dictate their lives, might not turn on someone else, perhaps their elderly great-grandmother who was so terrified of them that she had deadbolted her bedroom door? The truth was Jasmiyah and Tasmiyah were a package deal. They operated together and fed off of each other's toxicity. Nobody was safe from the Whitehead twins if they got in their way. Nikki Whitehead is an unfortunate example of that.

Daniel Petric
(2007)

Daniel Petric was a seemingly average 16-year-old boy in all respects. His school grades were not particularly outstanding but not concerning either; he had a 2.7 grade-point average that placed him in the middle of his class at Wellington High School. He was an active young man who played tailback for his school's football team, liked to skateboard, and had a knack for beating a catchy rhythm on a drum set. He had a decent number of friends who affectionately called him "Danny." They described the high school junior as a jokester who was always fun to be around, maintained a cool head and typically kept to himself when he was angry. One area of his life where he prospered was in the youth group at the New Life Assembly of God in Wellington, Ohio, where he was heavily involved. This happened to be the same church where his father, Mark Petric, was a pastor. He participated in the church's Bible quiz team, excelling at reciting lengthy passages from scripture. He could quote every word from the book of Hebrews all the way down to the Gospel of St. John by heart. This virtuosity of his took him to regional competitions and even as far as state competitions, where he tended to outclass his rivals.[1]

His relationship with his family also appeared ordinary. He was the youngest of three siblings, with two older sisters: Holly Petric and Heidi Archer. Holly was just a senior in high school herself. Heidi was the eldest sibling. Before the family made their move to Wellington, Ohio, in 2003, the parents worked as youth and associate pastors at Eastgate and at the Choice Place Boy's Home as "house parents" for troubled teenagers in Ashland. In April 2007, the family moved to their seven-acre property in Brighton Township, Ohio, just outside Wellington.[2]

It was nothing unusual for the Petric home to be fully stocked with different types of guns used for target practice and hunting, a much-loved bonding activity between the father and son. Only one firearm owned by Mark was not used for pleasure and was instead locked away in a safe at all times: a 9mm Taurus PT-92.[3]

His family described him as a loving and caring son, grandson, and brother. Daniel didn't seem to have a violent bone in his body.

And that's why, when this 16-year-old boy became the subject of news headlines for a gruesome crime in October 2007, it would hit everyone who knew him hard. People were naturally quick to ruminate on all of their interactions with the youth, frantically scouring for any red flags in his history that they might have overlooked.

They couldn't find any. And that was perhaps the most daunting aspect of it all.

A Deadly Addiction

Nothing in Daniel's profile seemed to indicate the existence of the pure evil he would display on October 20, 2007, except for one seemingly innocuous hobby in Daniel's life that people were quick to identify as the source of his ostensibly random act of violence.

Everything seemed to go downhill for Daniel after he injured his spine in a snowboarding incident, which also led to a severe staph infection. His back trauma was so severe that the doctor instructed him to avoid any sort of physical activity, including sports or even running, as the slightest injury to his back could leave him paralyzed. Daniel, who was once an active and outgoing boy, became housebound for more than a year during his recovery. Bored and having nothing to do all day, he eventually turned to a hobby that required no movement other than pushing a few buttons. He would become so deeply entrenched in this pastime that it didn't take long for it to develop into a dangerous obsession that his parents would soon see as a cause for concern.

Daniel was first introduced to the *Halo* franchise at his good friend Jonathan Johnson's house. The first-person shooter game, rated "M" for mature players, revolves around a science fiction world where the player has to destroy aliens that have taken over the planet.[4] Whenever he was at his friend's house, Daniel would squander almost eight hours tapping away at his controller, unleashing an onslaught of deadly attacks on the virtual enemies battling across the television screen. When Daniel told his parents that he wanted to purchase a copy of the game for himself, both said no. Video games were nothing new in the adolescent's life. In fact, the Petric family owned a few racing and sports games themselves. But the nature of the games Daniel was now indulging in were a little different from the virtual motocross matches that he and his father used to bond over. They felt these games were just too graphic for a boy of his age. They warned him that if he was caught with any violent video games, they would be confiscated.

But Danny wasn't going to take no for an answer now that he had a taste for shooting games and hungered for more. Like many stubborn teenagers who are met with strong objections from their parents, he found another way to get what he wanted behind their backs. He began routinely sneaking out of his bedroom window at night to purchase more first-person shooter video games, such as *Halo, Gears of War* and *Call of Duty*, with his allowance money.[5] In no time, Daniel found himself sucked into the online world of fantasy, much to his parents' disapproval. His father noticed a drastic change in his youngest child's personality. There seemed to be a cloud of darkness hanging over the boy wherever he went, a strange aura that rendered Daniel unrecognizable, no longer the affable goofball that Mark always knew his son to be. He was more reclusive now, alienating himself in his room for hours on end immersed in the very games his parents forbade him from playing.

Halo 3 was released in North America on September 25, 2007, and the game immediately made groundbreaking sales that would smash the game industry's records. Within the first 24 hours alone, more than one million people were playing *Halo 3* on Xbox Live. It grossed more than $300 million within the first week of its release. The game received high praise from fans and critics worldwide.[6]

Daniel was prepared to get his hands on it as soon as possible. He furtively climbed out of his bedroom window and hiked his way to the nearest retail store that sold the game, making it back home as fast as he could. As he was creeping back into his bedroom, eager to pop the new game into the Xbox console, his secret expedition was foiled when his mother, Susan, caught him during the sneaking-back-in process and inquired what he was doing. Her son caved, showing her the newly-purchased video game in his possession that both of his parents strictly prohibited him from playing.

His parents stood by their promise and took the game away from him. They told him that they didn't care if he spent some $70 on it, he was banned from ever playing the game and was never going to get it back. Mark locked the *Halo 3* game in a safe, the same safe where he also stored his 9mm Taurus PT-92, and stashed the key.

As evidenced by the past, nothing and nobody got in the way of what Daniel wanted. One might think he would go over to his friend's house to play the game for hours on end as usual or perhaps find a way to sneak out of the house again and buy another copy of the game, only this time he would attempt to be more discreet. Surely, he could have figured out a way to get around the video game ban in his household. But the plan Daniel had was far more sinister than the typical manipulative, sneaky behavior he had a history of exhibiting. And what he was about to do would utterly rip his family apart.

Murder

There was a tense atmosphere in the Petric home in the weeks following the incident. Daniel began experiencing the heavy withdrawal symptoms that a drug addict may feel after quitting cold turkey. What started off as an innocent hobby characteristic of adolescents in this day and age evolved into a dangerous obsession. But as time elapsed without having direct and free access to feed his addiction, the more animosity brewed inside him. Confined in his home recovering from a staph infection, faced with the possibility of becoming paralyzed if he so much as ran, he began to resent his parents for taking away the one thing that had by now become his lifeline.

One heated argument occurred in which Mark told his son to leave the house if he could not give up video games. Daniel ended up crashing at his good friend Jonathan Johnson's home, and the pair had a "marathon weekend" wherein they played the *Halo* games for 18 hours straight with no breaks in between except to eat and use the restroom.[7]

Regardless of the now-strained relationship with their son and the constant arguments in the household, Mark and Susan were sticking to their guns. They knew that they could no longer enable their son's dependency on these violent video games that were mentally doing more harm than good. Though they were probably aware of the resentment Daniel was harboring, they had no clue about the seething hatred and evil that was festering deep in his youthful mind. They missed their old son and patiently hoped that eventually this whole thing would blow over, Daniel would conquer his video game addiction, and everything would go back to the way it used to be in the Petric home. The tides may have been rough, but they were a family bonded by faith, so that meant they could overcome any hurdle.

October 20, 2007, was a quiet day. Mark and Susan were seated on separate couches a few feet away from each other in the living room, completely absorbed in the baseball game unfolding on their flat-screen television. Their 17-year-old daughter was working her shift at a fast-food restaurant, and at any time now they were expecting their eldest daughter, 21-year-old Heidi, along with her husband, Andrew, to arrive, as they all planned to watch the Indians play the Boston Red Sox in the Major League Baseball playoffs.

That's when their 16-year-old son approached his parents in the living room.

"Hey, Mom and Dad, would you close your eyes?" he asked. "I have a surprise for you."[8]

Mark and Susan exchanged a curious but agreeable glance. Maybe their boy was going to show them something, an apology that would make up for the family friction that had been pervading the home lately. So, eagerly, they readily complied, allowing their eyes to flutter shut and awaiting whatever pleasant surprise was to come. Daniel shuffled to the other side of the couch where his father was sitting, stopping once he was behind him. That's when he pointed the 9mm semiautomatic pistol at his unsuspecting father and shot him point blank in the head—the same pistol that Mark always kept secured in a safe. Daniel had managed to locate the key to unlock the safe and retrieve the gun and his video game.

Susan's eyes shot wide open the moment she heard the loud gunshot. Mark could feel his entire head go numb and blood gushing from his skull. Their youngest then aimed the firearm at his own mother and fired the gun three times, hitting her twice in the forearms before the final bullet struck her in the head. She was killed almost instantly. Investigators would later comment that the wounds on her forearms appeared to be defensive.

As if what he had just done wasn't already the cruelest, most despicable act of betrayal one could commit against their own parents, he would commit a final act that would render clear the true intentions in his wicked heart. He sat down next to his father, who was still alive, but barely hanging on.

"Hey, Dad, here's your gun," Daniel said, prodding the gun into his hand. "Take it."[9]

Then there was a sudden interruption. A knock on the door. Daniel must have forgotten about his sister's expected arrival to watch the baseball game with their parents, because just minutes after the shooting, Heidi and Andrew were standing on their front porch. Daniel immediately rushed over and denied them access.

"You guys shouldn't come in," he yelled from behind the door. "Mom and Dad had a big argument."[10]

At first, the couple was confused as to what was going on. But then they heard the soft moaning coming from the inside, a guttural yell for help, and they knew they had to force their way in. Andrew and Heidi burst through the door and brushed past Daniel, rushing into the horrifying scene of their wounded parents slumped over separate couches in pools of their own blood.

Immediately, Daniel made a grab for the gun on the couch, but Andrew was able to quickly wrestle it away from him before anyone else met the same fate. Daniel tried to blame his father, but the older Petric named his son as the shooter through his shattered jaw. Andrew then checked his mother-in-law for a pulse but failed to locate one. He turned his attention to Mark, the only one still clinging to life. He immediately began performing CPR while Heidi called 911 at 6:58 p.m.[11]

"I don't know what happened! I just came over to my parents' house because we were going to watch the game," she frantically cried into the phone, her heart pumping rapidly in her chest. "My mom is shot and my dad is shot and my brother's here!"

"Does anybody know what happened? Did your brother shoot your parents?" responded the dispatcher.

"I don't know!" she sobbed, taking a deep breath.[12]

By then, Daniel was already out the door, making his great escape. He had grabbed the keys to the family's Ford Windstar and was speeding down the road. Resting in the passenger seat was the one valuable he took with him: *Halo 3*. With the police surely on the way, Daniel had to get out of there as fast as possible. He already had a destination in mind. He picked up the phone and placed one call to Andrew's 18-year-old brother, Steven, with whom he'd struck up a friendship. Daniel had a brief conversation with him, although the details of that interaction were never disclosed. Daniel was headed toward Litchfield Township, where Steven lived.

But the teenage killer didn't make it very far. The police had put an all-points bulletin out for his vehicle, and within 12 minutes of the 911 call, Wellington police had caught up with him on South Herrick Avenue just a few miles away from the murder scene. Police cruisers barricaded the road, leaving Daniel no other option but to surrender.

While he was being handcuffed against the minivan, Daniel was quick to point the finger at his father. "My dad ... he shot my mom, then he shot himself," he declared.

The 16-year-old was placed in the back of a police cruiser. Whether this was all an act or the reality of the situation now starting to dawn on him, the boy started breaking down. "My dad shot my mom!" he wailed. He pleaded over and over, "Lord, please don't let my dad die."[13]

Back at the police station, Daniel was sitting in the interrogation room directly across from an officer. It was time for him to explain everything that just happened. But Daniel had no intention of telling the truth and continued to blame his father.

"My dad was just yelling, just screaming at my mom, and then I heard my dad walk in the room," he told the officer, explaining that he heard his father walk into his bedroom and then return to the living room. "I ran out there, and my mom was shot. He pointed the gun at me, then said he was sorry and then he shot himself."[14]

But, as guilty people usually do, he began to succumb to the pressure and open up about what really happened. The boy "just snapped," he told the officer. "It wasn't something I really thought about," he said.[15]

With his confession, they detained the teenage boy at the Lorain County Detention Home while they continued to investigate the case.

After the Shooting

Paramedics from southern Lorain County had come to Mark's aid and brought him to MetroHealth Medical Center in Cleveland.[16] Medics tried to communicate with him, as he appeared to be slipping in and out of consciousness, but he was unable to communicate because part of his jaw had been blown off. He was in such critical condition that he had to be put in a medically-induced coma for two weeks. Nobody could predict what was going to happen, but the family hoped and prayed that Mark would have the strength to pull through.

News of the shooting circulated fast throughout the small town of Wellington. Those who were very familiar with the Petric family, particularly members of the close-knit congregation at the New Life Assembly of God, were in disbelief. The regular church-going family just seemed so close that they had no inkling of the problems that were behind closed doors.

Church members attended the New Life Assembly of God the day after the shooting, but this was not your typical Sunday morning service. There was a gloomy atmosphere that swept through the church pews; Pastor Mark's tragic absence was felt in the hearts of all 75 members who had gathered that day to comfort one another.

A former pastor at New Life presided at the morning service in place of Pastor Mark. He encouraged everyone to pray for Pastor Mark's speedy recovery and to also extend their prayers to his two daughters and, yes, even to Daniel; they mustn't forget about him, either. Instead of concerning themselves with the whys and hows, they needed to come together and power through such a terrible crisis. Joel preached love and forgiveness for someone who may not have even deserved it.[17]

On Monday morning, Daniel appeared in court for the first time. He was restrained by red shackles and garbed in his khaki detention home uniform and blue flip flops. He stood before Lorain County juvenile court magistrate Stephen Blake and learned of the charges laid against him: aggravated murder, attempted aggravated murder, and tampering with evidence.

Despite having just killed his mother and severely wounded his father less than 48 hours earlier, Daniel surprisingly had one supporter vouching for his release. It would be a man the court identified as Daniel's paternal grandfather, Michael Brockel.

His grandfather pleaded that the juvenile magistrate release Daniel into his custody, citing that he'd already been forgiven by his family, his church, and even God. He described his grandson as someone who had always been a "loving child" and never caused anybody trouble. If his parents were sitting here in the courtroom, they, too, would forgive him. The magistrate denied this request. The violent offense Daniel committed made him too much of a threat to release back into society. The juvenile magistrate cited state law which required the 16-year-old youth to be tried as an adult. He set a probable cause hearing for November 9, which would be held before Loran County Domestic Relations Judge David Berta.[18]

Susan Petric's funeral was to be held on Saturday, October 27, at the New Life Assembly of God. Judge Berta would make a decision the week after the cruel slayings that would enrage the public.

He granted Daniel the furlough privilege to visit his mother one last time to say his goodbyes before she would be buried the following day. While he had initially requested to attend her funeral, the judge refused to let him visit beyond the viewing. He would be accompanied by a court employee and sheriff's deputies. He was banned from having any sort of contact with family members during the half-hour visit he was allotted just before visiting hours would commence.

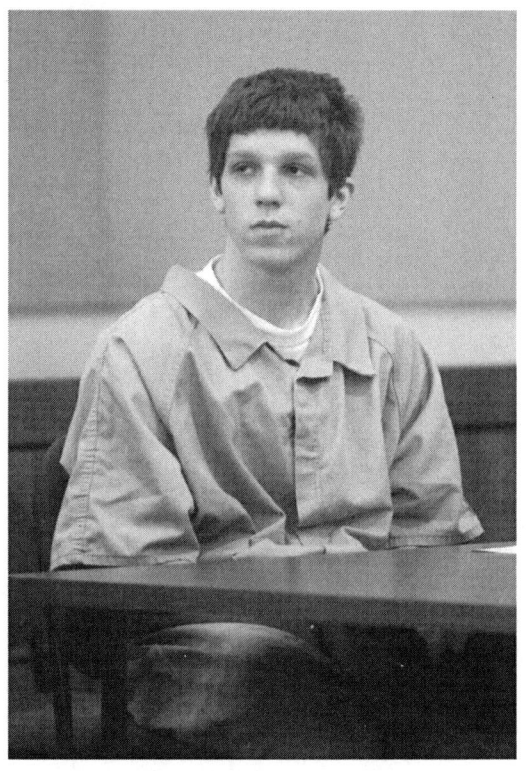

Daniel Petric, 16, shot his parents after his newly-purchased video game, *Halo 3*, was confiscated from him (courtesy Nate Parsons, *Morning Journal*).

Assistant county prosecutor Tony Cillo was adamantly against allowing the teenage killer to be granted his own private viewing while his father, who remained in grave condition at the hospital, would not have the opportunity to do so. The prosecutor called this "distasteful." After all, Daniel's actions were the reason why Susan was even resting in a casket, so why should he even be given this privilege?

Defense lawyer Russ Bensing said, "The court should not draw any conclusion about what this young man is feeling by wanting to see his mother one last time."

The judge had ultimately sided with the defense, stating that she had to protect the juvenile's well-being and consider the long-term psychological effects this would have on him. "He will have to live with this for the rest of his life, no matter what happens." Even the court employee who would supervise the teen during the funeral stated that he failed to find a reason why Daniel shouldn't be allowed the private viewing.

Daniel's paternal grandfather came into the courtroom once again to back his grandson. "The family has forgiven him," he told the judge. "We love him. Love covers a multitude of sins."[19]

With the support of his family, the judge, and his lawyer, Daniel was loaded into a jail van and taken, for the last time in his life, to his father's church, a place where he had made many positive memories and met so many wonderful people who truly loved and cared for him.

Mark woke up from his medically-induced coma two weeks later. When his family came to visit him and informed him that he had missed his own wife's funeral, his heart absolutely broke. Over and over again, like a looped recording, the evening of October 20 replayed in his mind. He vividly remembered the sound of the gunshot reverberating throughout the living room, the bullet penetrating his jaw, and the numbness that followed it. And the more he thought about it, the more his anger for Daniel expanded. Thoughts of that fatal evening and his son tortured his mind every second of the day. There was no escape. His son was now his worst enemy, and he grew to *hate* him. And the next time he ever saw his face, he swore to himself that that would be the end of Daniel's life.

He underwent surgery to rebuild his jaw using a part of his leg bone and a skin graft. Although it did not turn out perfectly symmetrical, and he was left with a deep visible scar on the right side of his jaw, Mark was overall satisfied with the results. He recovered smoothly and could talk, eat, and function like a normal human being again.

On November 9, Daniel appeared in court once again. His attorneys had waived his right to a probable cause hearing the day before, and his case was transferred to the Lorain County Court of Common Pleas. According to state law, it is mandatory for a child age 16 or older to be tried as an adult in cases of serious or violent felony offenses, especially when a firearm is found to have been used during the crime. Since Daniel met all of these circumstances, his case was to be bound to adult court.

Trial, Verdict, and Sentencing

Daniel's trial commenced on December 15, 2008, one year and two months after the shootings, at Lorain County Common Pleas in front of Judge James Burge. Daniel was pleading not guilty by reason of insanity and waived his right to have a jury present, meaning both the defense and prosecutor would have to convince the judge of their arguments.

"Daniel Petric executed a simple plan. It was a plan that was both as simple as it was in its design as heinous it was in its results," stated deputy prosecuting attorney Anthony Cillo during his opening statement. "What he did was decide to kill both parents: his mother Susan Petric and his father Mark Petric. And he did so with the intention of escaping any criminal liability by making it look like a murder-suicide." He described his plan to frame his father for the fatal shooting that was sabotaged by the timely arrival of his older sister and her husband.[20]

The central question hung over the courtroom like a dark cloud: was there prior calculation and design in the evil deed Daniel carried out on October 20, 2007?

Prosecutor Anthony Cillo would say yes, there was, and evidence shown in the courtroom would prove that without a shred of doubt. He illustrated the grim version of events that unfolded on that tragic evening, starting with the meticulous steps Danny had to take in order to achieve this act of cruelty. First, he had to find the key to the lock box in which the Taurus 9mm was stored, which he easily succeeded in doing. He had to load the gun. He then approached his parents under the pretense of a surprise and opened fire on both of them. Then, proving even more calculation and design, he tried coaxing his dad into taking the gun. He immediately took flight from the crime scene once Heidi and Andrew intercepted him, and he pointed the finger at his own father as soon as police caught up with him.

"He purposely, with that prior calculation design, killed his mother with three shots. He shot his father in the head with the intention with prior calculation design, purposely. He caused both of them grievous, serious physical harm and he did cause them physical harm by a deadly weapon. Lastly, he tampered with evidence by trying to stage the scene and to make it look as if it were a murder-suicide; that was tampering with evidence. By grabbing a bucket and a cloth and beginning to clean the scene up, that was tampering with evidence. By taking a *Halo 3* game out of the gun safe that had been taken away from him and leaving the scene with it, that was tampering with evidence. By attempting to keep Andy and Heidi from seeing what had occurred in this house, that was tampering with evidence."[21]

This was not the doing of an insane person, he finally argued. These were the methodical, calculated steps of a cold-blooded murderer. This act was thoroughly thought through in advance; not only did he plan this beforehand, but he also was smart enough to tamper with evidence so as to portray his father as the guilty party and run away from the crime scene he caused. Only an individual who knew their action was immoral and illegal would have the capacity to stage a crime scene, deflect the blame, and lie to police about it, however foolishly they went about it.

Defense attorney James Kersey painted the opposite picture of the kind of young man Daniel Petric was. Instead of depicting him as a cold-blooded murderer who plotted to kill both his parents out of pure selfishness and self-entitlement, he characterized him as one who was under severe delusions influenced by his ever-growing addiction to these violent video games he became fascinated with while convalescing in his home. With his word of honor, he was committed to providing evidence that Daniel was mentally ill and actually suffering from a video game addiction that his parents enabled in the beginning by supplying him with an Xbox in the first place—that was, until they forbade him from playing the *Halo* games and confiscated *Halo 3* immediately after he purchased it behind their backs, which became the final trigger.

"Even though he was prevented from playing the game by his parents' rules, he nevertheless kept an attitude without anger, without threats, without violence toward his parents or anything else," said James Kersey, characterizing his client as a "normal 16-year-old boy" who, despite disliking the strict conditions set against him regarding video games in the household, accepted them and never once acted out his anger or frustration against his parents.

The defense attorney continued, "Instead, he probably tried to explain why the game should be allowed. There was a didactic discussion, the evidence will show, between his father *and* mother, and Danny, as to why that game should be allowed, I think to the extent that he even went into Christian websites in an effort to convince his parents."[22]

And even after Mark had kicked his son out of the house following an argument regarding Danny's overall dissatisfaction with the rules laid out for him, prompting him to spend the weekend with his good friend Jonathan Johnson where they played *Halo* all day and into the night, he never indicated that he was, by any means, irritated with his parents or having homicidal thoughts. In fact, there was no sign that Daniel had a single evil thought lurking in his mind in the weeks and days leading up to the "terrible tragedy" that transpired on October 20, 2007.

"Danny Petric, without the distinct process of reasoning, without a scheme, and after a momentary consideration, shot and killed his mother and shot his father and without prior calculation and design," he said in his final thoughts, drawing the opening statement to a close.[23]

Mark Petric was the first key witness to take the stand and describe what happened to him and Susan on that awful evening. He told the court that he remembered getting ready to watch the Indians game with his wife when his son approached them and instructed them to close their eyes. He expected a pleasant surprise and instead received a bullet to the head. He broke down in tears as he said he firmly believed that if not for the timely arrival of his oldest daughter and her husband, he wouldn't even be in court testifying right now; he would be dead, alongside his beloved wife.

The father testified that Daniel had a very close relationship with Susan, telling the judge, "He was always her little boy." He, too, shared a close bond with his youngest and only son. The problems began once Daniel became addicted to first-person shooter games and refused to give them up, continuing to indulge in these games against his parents' wishes.[24]

Daniel's only surviving parent had been visiting him in jail over the past year. The two had made amends, and Mark mustered courage and strength from God to forgive his son, whom he previously wanted dead when he woke up at the hospital. Mark testified that his son had since expressed remorse and had difficulty living with the guilt of what he had done. The two had shared many tears during the visitations.

"Dad, I'm so sorry for what I did to Mom, to you, and to the family," he quoted Daniel as saying. "I'm so glad you are alive."

"You're my son," Mark had told him. "You're my boy."[25]

James Kersey was prepared to present his defense, which stood entirely on the basis of delusion and addiction. He delivered a short opening statement, claiming that his young client was under a lot of stress after his snowboarding accident, which left him with a spinal injury and a severe staph infection. These physical impairments rendered the boy practically immobile beyond very minor physical activities, such as walking. Because of this, he was housebound for more than a year, unable to do the things he once enjoyed in life, and he had nothing productive to invest his time in except for watching television and playing on his Xbox. He developed a fixation with the *Halo* games that would consume his daily life and, in turn, warp his sense of reality.

In the *Halo* games, a solo- and multi-player game in which you compete to kill as many aliens attacking the earth as possible, the game always resets and the characters in the game respawn after they have died. After becoming so engrossed in this game, playing for up to 18 hours a day with almost no breaks other than to sleep, eat, and use the restroom, this fantasy world crossed lines with reality, making the two practically indistinguishable in Daniel's young, delusional mind. At least, that is what the defense contended. Daniel was suffering from major withdrawal symptoms that would plague anybody suffering from an addiction after his beloved game was taken from him by his parents. Breaking into his father's lock box and grabbing the gun was a spur-of-the-moment decision. When he shot both of his parents, he was not in his right mind. He believed that his parents would respawn, just as they do after characters are gunned down in video games. He hadn't the slightest clue that his actions would result in permanent damage. And when he left? He only brought *Halo 3* with him. This was proof that Daniel's addiction severely impaired his judgment.

Before the trial would resume Tuesday morning, more than 20 adolescents appeared in court to say hello to their old friend and show their love and support for him. Some were from the youth group Daniel once belonged to in his father's church. This surprise visitation broke through his blank exterior, seemingly elevating his mood.

The defense kept their argument short and sweet, introducing friends and family who attested to Daniel's supposed video game addiction. His older sister Heidi told the court that he became obsessed with the *Halo* series and other graphic video games only after the injury and infection he sustained following the snowboarding accident. She told the judge that everyone had forgiven her brother for his wrongdoing and wanted him to come back home so that the family could heal in unison.

Defense attorney James Kersey also introduced his client's 17-year-old friend Jonathan Johnson, the young man responsible for introducing Daniel to the *Halo* franchise. He testified about his friend's increased fascination with the games. Sometimes, he said, when Daniel was over at his house, he would play *Halo* for eight hours straight. Upon cross-examination, when Cillo asked the teen if he truly believed *Halo 3* brainwashed him and propelled his friend to open fire at his parents, he answered, "No."[26]

Kersey didn't bring forward any experts to support his argument about the sort of negative influences that addiction and desensitization caused by video games had on young, impressionable minds. He did, however, supply a pre-trial mental health evaluation report conducted by juvenile psychologist Steven Neuhas. Deputy prosecuting attorney Anthony Cillo would later read something very telling from the report, in which Daniel confided that he had actually plotted the murder for weeks in advance.

"Now that I was 16, I wanted to make my own decisions, not live by their rules," the prosecutor quoted Daniel from the report.[27]

As the trial droned on, it seemed more and more obvious that the entire insanity defense built around Daniel's video game addiction wasn't carrying any weight. So far, Daniel's defense attorney had failed to prove any sort of causative link between the violent video games Daniel was hooked on and shooting his parents. His own friend admitted that he didn't think there was a correlation between the two, and the report supplied by the defense indicated that the teenager was contemplating the heinous act for weeks. During closing arguments Wednesday morning, defense attorney James Kersey argued his client was just a "typical 16-year-old boy" who "just popped." His youth and video game addiction made him less responsible for the murders; therefore he should be found not guilty by reason of insanity. But the prosecutor argued that Daniel was a cold, calculating killer who shot his parents because he was angry that they took his favorite video game from him.[28]

And that just about wrapped up the three-day trial. In the end, Lorain County Commons Pleas Judge James Burge rejected the video game addiction defense, pointing out that evidence provided during the trial indicated that "Daniel Petric did cause the death of his mother purposely and with prior calculation."[29] He cited state law that an individual may only be absolved of guilt if it is proven that at the time of the commission of the offense, the individual did not know about the wrongfulness of their conduct due to a mental disease or defect. He did not find that any of the experts' opinions about Daniel's mental state at the time he opened fire on his parents were cogent enough to warrant an insanity defense.

With that, Judge James Burge announced the dreaded verdict: guilty as charged. As soon as the words left the judge's lips, Daniel's head dropped. His father, a few feet behind his son and surrounded by family members, broke down in tears while Daniel's grandfather rubbed his back to console him.

But then, right after delivering his verdict, Judge Burge said something that would shock the court. He was no longer speaking from the perspective of the law, but from that of an empathetic human being. "That being said, it's my firm belief as a human being and not as a jurist that Daniel does suffer from a serious defect of the mind. This court's opinion is that we don't know enough about these video games." He clarified that he didn't believe so much that the violent nature of the *Halo* series, which revolved around a competition over who could gun down the most aliens, would cause this aggressive behavior that Daniel had demonstrated, but rather that after a certain amount of time playing them, "the same physiological responses occur in the ingestion of some drugs. And I believe that an addiction to these games can do the same thing. The dopamine surge, the stimulation of the nucleus accumbens, the same as an addiction. Such as when you stop, your brain won't stand for it."

He went on to say, "The other dangerous thing about these games, in my opinion, is that when these changes occur, they incur in an environment that is delusional. Because you could shoot these aliens and they're there again the next day! You have to shoot them again. And I firmly believe that Daniel Petric had no idea at the time he hatched this plot that if he killed his parents, they would be dead forever." He stated his belief that there was still hope for young Daniel, and it began right here in the courtroom.[30]

Daniel would be sentenced at a later date. Since he was convicted, Daniel's sentence could carry a harsh maximum of life in prison without the possibility of parole.

Daniel Petric appeared in court before Judge Burge on June 16, 2009, to finally learn his fate and receive the consequences of his fatal actions. But first, the court would hear the defense's reasoning as to why Daniel should receive a lenient sentence, the prosecutor's assertions that the teenage killer should be punished to the full extent of the law, and, lastly, his father's pleas for leniency, before the judge would make his final decision. Who would succeed in swaying the judge?

Defense attorney James Kersey told the judge that Danny was not responsible for the heinous crime he committed due to the combination of video game withdrawal and hormones that "young men have raging in their system."[31]

"In this instance, the video games, the playing of the video games and the reality of shooting someone, in his case, was blinded. It was merged. He had left playing video games. He then went home and he didn't realize, had no thought, that during this process, during the time he was blinded, that his parents might be dead. They might never come back," said the defense attorney, who then asked the judge to consider his words and serve Danny the minimum sentence.[32]

Mark Petric then presented his own statement, inciting mixed emotions in the courtroom. Half reading from his letter, he told the judge that he undoubtedly knew that Daniel felt remorse and guilt for what he had done to his mother and himself.

"I can't count the number of times he has told me that he's so sorry for what he did and he'll never be able to forgive himself. I can't also count the number of times that he is so happy that I survived. He's so glad he's still able to see me. He's told me that numerous times." He stated that his son was "not a throwaway kid" and he indeed had a conscience. Daniel still could not comprehend why he did the horrible thing he did.[33]

Hearing those heartfelt words coming from his own father's mouth in the courtroom, the person whom he hurt the most, had tugged on Daniel's heartstrings. Breaking through the otherwise expressionless exterior he had exhibited so far throughout court proceedings, he looked up at his father tearfully. Mark made eye contact with his son and, moved by his son's tears, also began to cry.

Mark turned to face his youngest child, the very same child that, more than a year ago, he had sworn he hated. "I love you, Danny," he said through tears, then faced the judge once again to say, "I can't count the number of times that he said, 'Dad, I miss mom, I miss mom.' His pain runs very deep and it should. I believe it should run deep. And if his pain did not run deep, I guarantee you I would not be standing here speaking on his behalf." He jabbed a finger to indicate Daniel, then implored the court, on Danny's behalf, for a lenient sentence.

To conclude his poignant speech, he spoke from a believer's point of view about God's boundless ability to forgive and give second chances. He believed that if Danny were given a second chance in his lifetime, he could amount to something great and use his horrible experience to make a positive impact on other struggling youth.

"Danny can set an example for other young people not to get involved and do the things that he did and I believe he can do that," he said. "I believe that may be a call upon his life to do that."

Then it was the prosecutor's turn to speak one last time and push for the maximum sentence to be imposed upon Daniel. First, he wanted to make it clear that he did not intend to belittle Danny's loved ones who had chosen to forgive him for his actions. "I can't speak for whether God will take mercy upon him, but that's not what we're here to decide. There's a separation between the Laws of Man and the Laws of God. I am here to speak for the citizens of Lorain County, and I believe it's incumbent upon me to speak for the memories of Susan Petric."

He began reiterating the events leading up to the shootings, starting from when Daniel's *Halo 3* game was confiscated from him. "Daniel snuck out to buy *Halo 3* on the day it was released. He didn't get to play it. He hadn't been given an opportunity to become addicted *to* it when it was taken away. This is not the case of a drug fiend stash being taken away."

He reminded the court that during an interview some time ago, Mark Petric had described Daniel, in his own words, as a "pathological liar" and expert manipulator who had serious problems telling the truth. He took the court through Danny's thought process on the fateful evening of October 21, 2007, and all the steps he had to take to accomplish the evil action that changed the lives of the Petric family forever, to prove this was not the doing of a delusional addict but a cold, methodical killer. "That he admitted that his mother was likely to allow him to play the games, his father would be the problem. What does that make Susan Petric? Collateral damage? Because he chose to shoot both of them. That to escape what he was going to do, he decided to kill both of them and then make it look like a murder-suicide. That he had to unlock the gun cabinet to accomplish this. The game was in there, and yes, he took it afterwards, but he also had to load the gun. That he was able to pretend that things were going well, walk out of the room, and say, 'I've got a surprise for you, please close your eyes.' And then he opened fire. But he opened fire in a very methodical manner. The father first—the biggest target—also to make it look like a suicide, and then the murder—three shots from across the room. His hand was steady. This is not a shaking addict having trouble with his thought process."

He echoed Daniel's response to Dr. Neuhas during the interview in which he was asked what went wrong. "Well, first my dad didn't die, and then my sister and brother-in-law—I knew they were coming over at 9 p.m.—came over early and it all just blew up in my face."[34]

The attempt to frame his own father by coaxing him to accept the gun, staging the scene to look like a murder-suicide, and cleaning up afterward, deputy prosecuting attorney Anthony Cillo argued, warranted an additional five years to the already life sentence without parole he was pushing for.

The judge then gave Danny the opportunity to speak, if he so wished. The teen rose from his seat, sucking in a huge breath of air. He stood there for a few seconds, seemingly struggling to gather his composure, before he sank back into his chair without uttering a word.

After listening to both sides of the argument, the defense's and Mark's plea for mercy on the young defendant, and the prosecutor's recommendation for life imprisonment, the judge would make his final say. He would keep his thoughts short before announcing the consequences that Daniel would face. It was a nail-biting moment for everyone sitting in the courtroom.

He started off by saying that he could not find anything in Danny's background to indicate sociopathy. "He didn't run away from home, torture small animals, didn't fight with his parents and wasn't a bully, wasn't a predator at all." He admitted that it was difficult to see remorse after the killing of his mother, and the attempted murder of his father, but he added that he didn't "assign that to some aspect of Daniel's character but rather the condition that was probably created by this obsession and addiction."

To conclude his statement, he said he hoped he would impact the future in preventing these types of crimes in youth from recurring. "I feel confident that if there were no such thing as violent video games, I wouldn't know Daniel Petric. In my opinion, Daniel Petric isn't the same young man he was on the evening he attempted to kill both his parents. He will be a different human being, I am certain, twenty years from now."[35]

At the end of the day, Daniel's family and defense attorney got their wish. Judge James Kersey took to heart the cries and pleas of the surviving father of the young defendant seated at the defense table about a dozen feet away from him and sentenced Daniel to 23 years to life in prison. He split up the charges as follows: 20 years for aggravated murder, 10 years for attempted aggravated murder, and five years for tampering with evidence, which would be served simultaneously. The judge tacked on an additional three-year firearm specification, which would also be served concurrently with his prison term. The judge said he would try to get Daniel into the Lorain Correctional Institution as per the defense counsel's recommendation.

Afterword

The odd case of Daniel Petric has once again exhumed the ongoing dispute about the potential correlation between violent video games and aggression in children. But believe it or not, Daniel wasn't the poster boy for the video game controversy. The original poster boys actually date back to the 1999 Columbine school shooters, Eric Harris and Dylan Klebold. In the aftermath of the massacre, people began digging deeply into their past hobbies and interests in search of anything they could find to explain the inexplicable—what propelled two teenage boys to commit such a horrific crime that would devastate the lives of many. And indeed they found a few things. They found out the boys liked wearing dark apparel and had formed a group called "The Trenchcoat Mafia" which, as intimidating as it sounded, was simply an inner circle consisting of other social outcasts at the school. They learned that the boys had a penchant for violent video games, particularly *Doom*. They discovered that they preferred music containing rather violent lyrical content. This caused adults to begin profiling adolescents as potentially dangerous based on their choice of clothing and the type of music they listened to.[36]

It's not new. Before video games came into existence or became such a prevalent pastime for youth, the media blamed and demonized rock music and horror movies for the rise in violence perpetrated by adolescents. In reality, it is a feeble and rather lazy attempt to shift the blame away from the perpetrators instead of looking deep within ourselves to question how we may be partially contributing to a society that breeds criminality and delinquency.

Video game use has become a normal part of the average American kid's daily life. Ninety percent of children play video games, a figure that skyrockets to 97 percent if we are looking at adolescents between the ages of 12 and 17.

Kids have been killing since the beginning of time, and juvenile homicide rates have been steadily on the decline within the past decade in spite of the ubiquitous growth of violent video games. If we consider that the vast majority of video games in today's market contain some form of violence in conjunction with how much of the population indulges in these games, naturally it has begun to inspire some concern from the public about how graphic entertainment may be influencing children and youth for the worse.

The APA has been studying the effects of violent video games for more than two decades in an attempt to settle the debate once and for all. Although research is still limited, they have failed to find any foolproof evidence that violent video games have a direct causality to violent crime. They were, however, able to establish an association between violent video games and increased aggressive thoughts and behavior, heightened physiological arousal, and decreased prosocial behavior. But, again, causation does not equate to correlation and there is a combination of contributing factors, excluding video games, that can lead to aggressive behavior. Perhaps high levels of exposure to violent video games to youth who are already prone to delinquency only exacerbates the aggression that is already there.[37]

More research needs to be done before any conclusions can be drawn. Did violent games play a major role in Daniel Petric's shooting of his parents on the evening of October 20, 2007? Possibly. At the end of the day, who, or what, bears the most responsibility for Daniel's heinous actions: the video games or Daniel Petric himself?

Cristian Fernandez
(2011)

This is the story of a tragic case involving a toddler who was beaten to death, leading to the handcuffing of his older brother. The startlingly young age of the culprit would shock not just the state of Florida but the entire nation. Plastered next to the first-degree murder charge was the mugshot of a curly-haired, cherub-faced 12-year-old child.

Not quite a teenager, this boy was not only being charged with the highest degree murder charge possible, but he was also being tried as an adult before he had even lost his baby fat. Due to the nature of the crime, his charge carried a mandatory life sentence in prison. When details of his grim childhood, involving years of sexual and physical abuse, came to light in the news, it struck a deep chord in the hearts of American citizens, sparking a nationwide moral dilemma. As happened with the cases we've familiarized ourselves with in previous chapters, the public would come to question whether treating a 12-year-old child who grew up in harsh circumstances as a full-fledged adult in the legal system was really serving justice.

Background

Born on January 14, 1999, in Miami, Florida, Cristian Fernandez got off to a rough start in life. His mother, Biannela Marie Susana, did not give birth to her first son under pretty circumstances herself. She was only 12 years old when she had Cristian. The boy's father, Jose Antonio Fernandez, was a 25-year-old man.

Biannela Susana's mother, Sonia Valdez, rarely made an appearance in her early childhood. She was raised primarily by her grandmother in the Dominican Republic from birth until she was eight years old. Her grandmother doted on her; she baked three-tier cakes for her birthdays. Her father lived just across the street from her and taught her how to swim.

When she was eight, Sonia unexpectedly showed up and whisked her daughter away to Miami, Florida. Suddenly, Biannela found herself in a foreign country where she knew no one and didn't even speak the language. The mother and daughter lived in cheap motel rooms, barely scraping by.

Sonia hadn't changed her ways. She was still a heavy drinker, a drug user, and hot tempered, throwing and breaking dishes when she was angry. The first time police got involved in the mother's and daughter's lives was in 1996, when Biannela was just 10 years old. Sonia failed to pick her daughter up from school and left her waiting outside after dark.

When she was 11, Biannela made a new friend. She would frequent this friend's apartment for play time, and there she met the friend's older brother, Jose Fernandez, a man twice her age.[1]

"She would come around to find me … she would not leave me alone," he stated. He further added that he provided her with the love and care that she didn't receive from her mother.[2]

In Biannela's eyes, Jose was the first person to make her feel loved, wanted, and appreciated. The last time she felt that way was with her grandmother back in the Dominican Republic. She was so desperate for Jose's attention and affection that she would do anything to please him.

She had barely reached middle school when he got her pregnant. Jose, for obvious reasons, pushed for her to get an abortion, not wanting to take any sort of accountability for what he had caused. To hide the pregnancy from her mother, who most certainly would have pushed for her to terminate it as well, she began wearing baggy t-shirts. By the time Sonia found out her daughter's secret and took her to a doctor, it was far too late for an abortion. Biannela's baby was much too developed.

When her son entered the world, she decided to name him Cristian, "without an H, to be original."[3]

She loved her son. She sang him songs. She breastfed him. She taught him the names of animals.

"He was my little doll," she said.[4]

Jose was charged with statutory rape. He was let off with

only 10 years of probation when he took a vow to assist in raising his son, a promise he narrowly stood by. He only somewhat stuck around for the first portion of his son's life; for the most part, the young mother was raising him alone with no other support besides her 34-year-old drug-addicted mother, who wasn't a stable presence either. The sole burden of raising a child sat on her 12-year-old shoulders.

Even years later, Jose Fernandez would blame Biannela for pushing the sexual relationship onto him, despite the fact that he was an adult and she was only a child. He remains a registered sexual offender to this day.

Biannela wanted to return to school to continue her education, but Sonia wouldn't allow it. She forced her daughter to stay behind and take care of Cristian while the family continued to live in cheap motel rooms.

Two years later, when Biannela was 14, she left her son in the care of Sonia so she could sleep over at a friend's house. Authorities in South Florida would spot a toddler wandering around a motel parking lot all by himself at four in the morning, completely naked and covered in filth. That toddler was two-year-old Cristian Fernandez. His 34-year-old grandmother, who was supposed to be looking after him, was not too far away. She was cooped up in a filthy motel room, highly intoxicated. Police also found cocaine in her purse and a baby bottle crawling with worms.

Biannela's mother was charged with child neglect and merely given a "case plan" to follow. But Sonia didn't follow it. A year later, she placed her daughter and grandson in a mobile home which lacked bare necessities such as water and electricity. The teenager and toddler lived there alone. Eventually, someone notified the authorities of the situation.

Social workers came to take Cristian to foster care. Biannela, not wanting to part with her son, joined him there.

The thought of abandoning Cristian and allowing someone older, more competent and more financially stable to provide Cristian with love and stability was not one that ever crossed Biannela's mind. She wanted to do whatever it took to provide all of that for Cristian herself. She was committed to being a mother to him.

So she made ends meet. At 15, she landed a job at KFC as a cashier while simultaneously juggling school—all while living in foster care. With her new income, she managed to save $200 monthly. She enrolled in parenting classes, earned her GED, and began tutoring. She even managed to learn Miami's bus system by herself.

In a sense, Biannela practically raised herself her whole life, her innocence and youth having been robbed from her long, long ago. The teen mom must have quickly realized that she was alone from day one and the only person she could depend on was herself. She had to learn to be self-sufficient in order to succeed and build a life for herself and her son.

But, as if Cristian and Biannela hadn't already endured enough trauma, something else would happen to add to the many disturbing and distressing experiences they had suffered.

In 2004, Biannela walked into Cristian's room and witnessed two older foster boys, whom he shared the room with, molesting her five-year-old son. Biannela was horrified. She then moved Cristian to her room, where he was to sleep henceforth, and sought out therapy for him. When he began kindergarten, she made a point of being very involved with his school life and volunteered to chaperone his school trips.

Though this struggling, self-sufficient teen mom tried her best, a foster care counselor had some criticisms of her parenting style.

"Biannela is a very caring mom but needs to be more stern," the counselor wrote.[5]

When she was 18, Biannela moved into her first apartment and bought a vehicle, an old Toyota, using all of the money she had saved up from years of hard work, and taught herself how to drive. Finally, she was an adult, completely independent and liberated from the bounds of the foster care system. She now had complete control over her own life. She constantly envisioned the happy life that she could now build for herself and for Cristian. She promised him that he would never set foot in another foster home again.

At around the same time, Biannela met 25-year-old Luis Galarraga-Blanco, a former minor league ballplayer from Venezuela, at the gas station where he worked. He had given little Cristian some candy, and soon Luis and Biannela started dating. They were quick to get married, which happened at the courthouse, and before they knew it, Biannela gave birth to a baby boy in the summer of that same year. They named him Luis Jr. One year later she had her first girl. Her name was Lyanni.

Cristian was unhappy with the new living situation, to say the least. For all of his six years, it was just him and his mom. Now, suddenly, he found himself struggling to adapt to this new family dynamic—and failing. He didn't like having to share his mother with this new man, and the two frequently butted heads. And once another father figure entered the picture, Jose, Cristian's biological father, decided to step back and completely vanish from his son's life for good.

Biannela made the decision to send Cristian to live with his great-grandmother in the Dominican Republic, the elderly woman who had taken good care of her as a child. It was his first time ever meeting her. He returned to Miami after a year, but things had changed drastically since his departure. He now had a new half-brother, David Galarraga, to share the already-cramped apartment with.

Because bedrooms were limited, and all were occupied by his half-siblings, mother and stepfather, the couch became Cristian's new bed.

The small, two-bedroom apartment that the family lived in was filled with never-ending conflict. Biannela was working two jobs, cleaning motel rooms and answering phones for a tutoring company, while Luis stayed home and took care of the children. Luis was an abusive, intimidating man who often got physical with his kids, including his stepson. Cristian was described by neighbors as a quiet boy who was forced to bear all of the adult responsibilities in the house, such as cleaning and cooking.[6]

After going through so much trauma, neglect, and abandonment during such an early and crucial period in his life, it came as no surprise that Cristian was already showing signs of troubling behavior. At school, he established a worrisome track record. There were documented incidents of him masturbating and simulating sex on a male student twice his age. Furthermore, he admitted to having killed a kitten by punching it and repeatedly slamming its head into the floor because it had scratched his face.

To nobody's surprise, the Department of Children and Families had to intervene more than once. The first time was on a report that Cristian had been molested by his older cousin. The second time would be a much more traumatic experience for all involved, a huge turning point in the lives of everyone.[7]

On October 22, 2010, Cristian showed up at school with a swollen and bruised eye. Staff were so concerned about the extent of this injury that they called the police. When they questioned the young boy as to how he sustained this eye injury, he admitted that his stepfather had punched him in the face. He was then sent to the hospital so his eye could be examined for retinal damage. It was discovered that he indeed had a torn retina as well as a broken rib.

While the boy was in the hospital, the Department of Children and Families was contacted to come by the school. Biannela was just on her way to her motel-cleaning job when she got the urgent phone call from Cristian's school regarding her son. She had no knowledge of what had happened.

Quickly, she called her husband, who explained that, yes, he did punch Cristian, because he caught him changing his clothes in front of Lyanni.

Biannela changed her route and drove to Cristian's school, where she met with staff members and the Department of Children and Families. Together, they tried to reach Luis for questioning on the allegations of abuse, but he wasn't picking up the phone.

Authorities showed up at the family's apartment in Hialeah, a Miami suburb, and knocked on the door. They were fully prepared to put Luis in handcuffs. But it wasn't Luis who answered.

"The door was opened ... by a little girl who got frightened," stated the police report.[8]

The little girl ran off into one of the rear bedrooms, leaving a trail of bloody footprints behind her. As officers advanced into the apartment, they were totally unprepared for the gruesome scene they were about to stumble upon.

They entered the living room and discovered Luis' unmoving, outstretched body lying on the floor, his right hand loosely gripping a 9mm handgun, and blood oozing out of a gaping gunshot wound in his head.

The man had committed suicide in front of his one-year-old son, David, who was covered in the red substance, and his daughter, Lyanni. Clearly it was an attempt—and a very successful one—to evade the well-justified child abuse allegations against him.

Biannela, who was still at the school, raced home as soon as she was notified of what had happened. Since her apartment was now deemed a crime scene, she had to stand in the parking lot. Using baby wipes, she cleaned the blood splatters off her children. Then she picked up Luis Jr. from school and Cristian from the hospital, and she took her kids to the motel where she worked.

For reasons that are unclear, Biannela ended up quitting both of her jobs, leaving behind the life she had worked so hard to build for herself and her family, and relocating north of Jacksonville. Perhaps she was so emotionally scarred by what had happened that she wanted to move far away from the traumatic incident. Or maybe she wanted to distance herself from Miami as a whole, a city that harbored too many painful memories for her, and start fresh in a new city.

But now, she was jobless and knew no one. The family moved into a modest, two-bedroom apartment. Across from the apartment was a small playground and a tennis court situated among beige-colored buildings. Cristian shared a room with Luis Jr. and Lyanni. Cristian and Luis shared a bunk bed and Lyanni slept in a toddler bed, while little David slept in his mom's bed. Every night, all of the kids would pile onto Biannela's bed and eat popsicles.

Things seemed to be looking up for the family of five. Cristian enrolled at Kernan Middle School, where he excelled in all of his classes as a straight-A sixth grader. Biannela was still looking for work. She did, however, have an appointment with a family therapist in December, which she missed for unknown reasons.

Months went by before another incident occurred in January 2011, in which Cristian broke his two-year-old half-brother David's leg while allegedly doing yoga. Biannela wasn't home at the time, leaving Cristian unattended with his siblings. When she returned a couple of minutes later, Cristian made up a story about how David's leg got broken.

The 25-year-old mother waited two days to get her son medical help for his broken leg. She claimed that she wasn't aware of the extent of his injuries because David never cried; he simply had trouble standing up. When she finally took him to the doctor to have his leg examined, the doctor told her that it was the worst broken leg he had ever seen on a toddler.

Not surprisingly, the Department of Children and Families had some concerns. Biannela, of course, covered for her firstborn. She told them that David had fallen off the monkey bars and made Cristian echo the same lie. She feared that Cristian could get into trouble, or worse, that her kids could be taken away from her.

Biannela had another therapy appointment scheduled for February 23, but she missed that one as well.

The next time the mom of four would leave her eldest son alone with his younger siblings would prove to be a more disastrous, fatal mistake.

The Killing

The morning of March 14, 2011, was a semi-typical one.

Five-year-old Luis Jr. had missed his bus, so Biannela put her firstborn in charge of supervising his two youngest siblings, who were sound asleep. He might not have been the most trustworthy babysitter due to January's incident; David's blue cast still swathed his leg from below the hip all the way down to his foot, serving as a daily reminder of the pain he endured at the hands of his older brother.

Perhaps Biannela didn't think anything nearly as bad would happen during her absence this time. It was just a quick errand, after all. But whatever her thought process and justification was would turn out to be dead wrong. This time, there would be a more appalling outcome when Cristian was left alone with the kids. On March 14, 2011, Biannela, Cristian, and the rest of her kids' lives would change forever, shattering any hope of recovery from the trauma they had all experienced months before.

After dropping the kindergartener off at school, she stopped at a nearby bank.

And that's when she received the phone call.

At 9:20 a.m., her eldest called. He told her that David had fallen off his bunk bed while climbing the ladder and was now unconscious. But the injuries he sustained were far too extensive to be explained away by a simple tumble. In truth, Cristian had gotten violent with his youngest half-sibling, savagely bashing his head twice against the bookshelf with no provocation whatsoever.

Within minutes, Biannela dashed through their apartment entrance and made a beeline for Cristian's room, where she discovered David on the bottom bunk, unconscious, blood gushing from his nose. She wiped it away with a baby wipe.

She frantically implored him to wake up. But he didn't.

One might expect a mother's first instinct would be to instantaneously seek medical help for their injured, unconscious child. But the sad reality is, that is not at all how Biannela responded to the sight of David's injuries. She changed the child's clothes and diaper, poured alcohol on a cloth and held it to his nose in an attempt to wake him up. She pressed a bag of ice over his swollen nose to slow down the swelling. But the toddler still did not stir.

One might also expect that her next course of action would be to call 911. But, unfortunately, that is not what happened either. The young mom held on to the hope that he probably had a concussion and would eventually wake up.

In the meantime, she surfed the web on her Toshiba laptop. Occasionally, she would research head trauma on the Internet. The first time was at 10:54 a.m., when she had keyed the words "when someone gets knocked out" into the Google search engine. The first medical website she visited for information about concussions was kidshealth.org. Hours passed before she searched for "concussions on children" at 2:38 p.m. and "unconscious for hours." She perused a Wikipedia page about comas and read more on concussion symptoms on mayoclinic.com. But, apparently, nothing she read prompted her to seek immediate medical attention for her toddler, whose life was slowly withering away in the other room.

In between these searches, she did some online banking, watched YouTube videos, downloaded a reggaeton album by Yom, and searched for popular screensavers. She also found some time to text her friends. At one point, she put David's unconscious body in the vehicle and drove to pick up her other children from school.

When Cristian returned home from school, she ordered him to watch Luis as she wrapped David in a blanket and packed some snacks for when he woke up.

Then, at 3:07 p.m., she conducted her final web search, this time looking up the address for St. Luke's Hospital in Jacksonville. But she still did not seek medical attention; she continued surfing the web for another hour before finally bringing David to the hospital. She arrived at 5:25 in the evening, virtually eight hours after the incident.

Little David was in such critical condition that he had to be transported by helicopter to Shands Hospital, the Jacksonville area's trauma unit, where he was put on life support.[9] His head injuries were extensive. In addition to his skull fracture, he was also suffering from bruising on his left eye and the bridge of his nose, as well as blunt force trauma, subdural hemorrhage and subdural hematoma. Essentially, his brain was bleeding. A subdural hematoma is caused by the bursting of a blood vessel near the brain.[10]

Biannela sat by her lastborn's side, her fingers intertwined with his, and, in a soft whimper, told him she loved him and pleaded for him to wake up.

Doctors felt David's chance of survival was slim. They knew that Biannela's story for how he had sustained this injury didn't add up with the severity of his head trauma. It simply could not have been achieved by falling off a bunk bed. They had their suspicions.

Initially, when a doctor asked Biannela how the injury had happened, she lied and told them she was at home in the kitchen when David fell.

"I thought they were going to think I was crazy for leaving David with Cristian ... after what happened before," she later wrote in her journal.[11]

Police were quick to get involved. They took Cristian into custody and detained him at the Jacksonville Sheriff's Office for questioning.

Biannela signed her consent for police to conduct a search of her apartment. They observed the kids' bedroom where the supposed fall had happened. The bookshelf which David's head was slammed against was unscathed, but there were traces of blood and a pile of vomit on the carpet. There was also blood on the bottom bunk's bedsheet and pillow and on a baseball T-shirt. They also recovered a pair of bloodied tan-colored pants, presumably David's, in the laundry basket, and they discovered blood on the shower curtain as well.

They collected their evidence, including two laptops sitting on the kitchen counter, one an HP and the other a Toshiba.

Detective Mechelle Soehlig was assigned to the case. She personally paid David a visit in the hospital to review his injuries. It quickly became obvious that Cristian's account was fabricated. She observed the blue cast covering his entire leg, from below the hip all the way down to his foot from the broken leg he suffered back in January. She noted his bruised face, lack of body movement, and his partially rolled-back, immobile eyes. A horrible feeling settled in her gut. It would be a miracle if this child survived.

Cristian waited in the interrogation room. It was now early morning on March 15. Detective Soehlig walked in and carefully explained his Miranda rights to him.

The detective then jumped right into questioning. She began by wanting a recap of the January 2011 incident in which Cristian had broken David's leg. Cristian told her that the two had been doing yoga in his bedroom. Using a doll, Cristian demonstrated the upward dog position he had posed his brother in, which resulted in the breaking of his leg.

"When you broke his leg, did you hear it snap?" she asked.

"A pop."

"Did you hear it pop?"

"Well, sort of," he said. "He started crying, then I stopped."

He told her that his mom came home a couple of minutes after the incident, and he made up a lie about how his brother broke his leg. Not surprisingly, the Department of Children and Families had some questions. Biannela told Cristian to lie to them and say that David had broken his leg from falling off the monkey bars.

"And what happened tonight, because I know originally you said that he fell off the bunk bed but that wasn't true, correct?" she asked.

"Mhmm."

"So that was a lie?"

"Mhmm."

"So tell me what really happened tonight," she urged.

Cristian told the detective that David was carrying books over his head to the bookshelf when the books came crashing down on his head, then David "went to sleep." But the detective knew that couldn't be further from the truth given the severity of his head trauma, which couldn't have been caused by books. She repeatedly pushed for Cristian to tell what really happened that night, but he reiterated the same fabricated story.

"I don't think it's the truth. Actually, I know it's not the truth. He's got a really bad head injury. So, if you could tell me how he got that, it would be really helpful for him. And for us," she said. "And then the truth will be known and you don't have to worry about hiding that inside of you anymore, because you already told us."

"So, what happened tonight? Let's just start over," she continued. "It's okay, I'm not angry with you or mad at you or anything like that. We just need to know the truth. You don't have to be scared."

He denied bearing any responsibility for, or aiding in, what happened to David. But Detective Soehlig, remaining as soft-spoken and patient as ever, knew the right strings to pull in order to lure the real story out of him. She asked if his mother and siblings were going to corroborate Cristian's version of events once she questioned them, too. She wanted to give Cristian the opportunity to be the first to tell the truth.

"Just take a deep breath, and just be honest, and everything's going to be okay," she said in a soft, lulling voice. "You have to be honest with yourself, too. And you need to be honest for little David's sake. Cause David's not feeling too good right now. He deserves for you to tell us the truth."

But still, getting answers out of Cristian was very difficult. The young boy sat there, tight-lipped, his eyes shifting from the detective sitting across the table from him and the doll resting atop the surface between them.

"Do you feel bad about what happened tonight? Is that why it's hard for you to tell me?"

"Yes," he murmured just above a whisper.

"I understand that. I can see why it's really hard for you to tell me. But if we do things that are wrong, Cristian, and we feel bad about it, then we need to tell the truth about it. So, tell me what happened tonight."

Finally, Cristian became responsive. "I pushed him against a bookshelf." He described to the detective that he had slammed David's head twice into the bookshelf in his bedroom. He used the bookshelf located in front of his sister's bed. After the first shove, David was crying in pain. The second shove knocked him out. Blood trickled out of David's mouth, and his eyelids remained half closed. Cristian then carried him to the bed and called his mother.

"Why'd you push him?" she asked the 12-year-old. "Were you angry about something?"

"Yes."

"What were you angry about?"

"What my stepdad did to me," he responded, although it is unknown if he was referring to the isolated incident from October 2010 or the overall abuse and torment he was subjected to by his stepfather for years.

Cristian told the detective that he had been thinking about his stepfather in the moment, but he could only shrug in response when asked why he took his rage out on his baby brother.

After he confessed everything, she asked how he was feeling.

"Pretty bad," he replied.

"Do you feel better about telling me what happened?"

"No."

The detective then stepped out of the interrogation room for a while, leaving Cristian to himself. As soon as she left, he dropped his head into his hand and sniffled. For the next six minutes, he played with his curly locks and squirmed incessantly in his chair. He then got up for a bathroom break. Upon his return, he remained alone for a few more minutes until the detective rejoined him with some more questions. She told him that she had just spoken with the doctors and they wanted to know if anything else had happened that could explain the other injuries David had sustained on his body. But he denied doing anything other than bashing David's head against the bookshelf twice.

"Did you know what you did was wrong?" she asked.

"Mhmm," he said. "I felt bad because then I realized what I'd actually done. 'Cause I wasn't really thinking about what I was doing when I pushed him, I was just thinking about myself then."

"And then when you realized what you'd done, you said you felt bad. What did you feel bad about?"

"About what I did, and what was going to happen later."

"To him or to you?"

"To him. I wasn't worried about me," he admitted.[12]

Whether this was the truth remained unclear. Was it really the case that Cristian, who never once expressed remorse or shed a tear for his baby brother, who was fighting for his life at the hospital, his brain swelling more and more with each passing hour, was more concerned for David's well-being than his own? Did Cristian really lack the foresight to consider the consequences of his actions?

Cristian only expressed some concern about his brother. He asked the detective if David was going to wake up. The detective responded that the doctors hoped he would, but they didn't know if he was going to live.

Biannela was informed of Cristian's confession and was escorted to the police station to be questioned as well. She sat in the room next to Cristian's.

The detective then left Cristian alone again to speak with Biannela in the next room.

The young mother told varying accounts of what happened on the morning of March 14. First, she told police that she was in the kitchen when her toddler son got hurt. Then she changed her story again, saying that she wasn't home at the time. When asked why she waited several hours to take David to the hospital, she explained that she thought he simply had a concussion and would eventually wake up. The mother also admitted that she had previously covered up the January 2011 incident.[13]

At one point, Cristian was sent to the interrogation room next door to speak with his mother. Biannela sobbed and told him to go away.[14]

The night ended with Cristian being led out of the interrogation room in handcuffs.

Another Arrest

After two days, doctors shut off David's life support machines when they were certain that he wasn't going to regain consciousness. Those several hours Biannela waited to seek medical attention for David could have been what cost him his life, for a physician would later inform police that there was still hope of resuscitation had she brought him to the hospital right away. But instead she waited, and by the time she took action, it was too late. The damage was irreversible.[15]

Biannela had driven to the hospital as soon as she left the police station and held her youngest until he took his last breath. For the next two weeks, she ruminated over what her life had become. Her youngest was in a coffin, her firstborn was in jail, and her remaining children were in foster care. She was now at an all-time low. In just one day, Biannela had lost her entire family.

She had the chance to meet with Cristian on visiting day, still not believing that he had any intention of killing his brother.

"He said he didn't think I would still want him as my son," Biannela wrote in her journal. "That broke my heart. Or what little I had left of my heart."[16]

On April 1, 2011, Biannela Susana was arrested for her role in her son's death. After all, it wasn't only Cristian's actions that killed him; his mother's negligence, too, cost him his life. She was charged with aggravated manslaughter of a child under 18 years by culpable negligence. This wasn't only for her lack of action but also due to the fact that she left her eldest alone with David even though he had previously broken his leg. In the law's eyes, this was negligent, too.

Her bail was set at $1 million.

In the months following Cristian's arrest, state attorney Angela Corey, the prosecutor in charge of his fate, and her staff (including assistant state attorneys Mark Caliel and Alan Mizrahi) looked into Cristian's background, had him evaluated by experts, and met with the defense to discuss their options.[17] The two forensic psychologists that assessed Cristian concluded that the boy was emotionally underdeveloped; however, he had a high likelihood of successful rehabilitation.

On June 2 of that year, under Angela Corey's orders, assistant state attorney Mark Caliel, would raise the boy's charge to first-degree murder. It was also decided that he would be tried as an adult, making him the youngest person in the history of Jacksonville to be charged with murder in the first degree. Additionally, he would be transferred from the juvenile detention center he had been held in for the past few months to the Duval County Jail, the same jail that housed his mother. He would, however, be placed with the juvenile inmate population there.

Cristian's indictment sparked an international public outcry which left both ordinary citizens and legal experts wondering if the 12-year-old even possessed the mental capacity to comprehend and predict that his actions would result in his half-brother's death. A first-degree murder charge implies that the accused willfully and purposefully committed homicide, knowing full well that their actions would result in death. First-degree murder is premeditated and intentional.

Were Cristian's actions premeditated and intentional?

Professor Robert Batey, who teaches criminal law at Stetson University College of Law, was among the dubious demographic.

"Especially if it's a beating death, you could argue that the child did not have the intent to kill, which would be necessary even for second-degree murder," he commented, "or that the child was not capable of the cool thinking beforehand that's implied by the notion of premeditation."[18]

But assistant state attorney Mark Caliel voiced his disagreement. "It was something that was done with a lot of reflection."[19]

State attorney Angela Corey especially received a lot of backlash for her decision to try a child as an adult for first-degree murder. Her reasoning was that juvenile jurisdiction ends at age 21, meaning he would only be incarcerated for eight years—which was not enough time to undo the years of abuse and trauma that Cristian had previously endured and successfully rehabilitate him.

"My fear is that whatever has happened to this young man in his short time on Earth cannot be solved in eight years," she expressed.[20]

She stated that she had no other choice but to try him as an adult and that many children who emerged from even more horrific backgrounds than Cristian have never committed such violent offenses. Cristian's childhood, she said, should not serve as an "excuse" for what he did.

"The whole system has failed him. This child clearly is a victim," said public defender Rob Mason, who was the director of the public defender's juvenile division and was assisting Matt Shirk with Cristian's case. "We think he can be rehabilitated and, as his lawyers, we will fight for that."[21]

In later court hearings, questions would be raised about the individual who was behind the computer searches on March 14, 2011, between the time David was injured until the time he was brought to the hospital. Defense attorney Shawn Arnold, who represented Biannela, noted that the Toshiba laptop, on which the web searches were conducted, belonged to Cristian. While neither of the two laptops owned by Biannela were password-protected, and both were under her name, the Toshiba laptop specifically listed "Cool Kids Learn" as its user-defined account. Furthermore, one of the first medical sites about concussions that was visited was "kidshealth.org" which he described as a "child-friendly site."

Biannela's attorney insisted that the Toshiba laptop belonged to Cristian and that Cristian was the one who made those Internet searches about head trauma during those hours, not his mother.

Assistant state attorney Mark Caliel was quick to point out that among the websites visited was a banking site. Why would a 12-year-old have any business doing online banking?

Matt Shirk, Cristian's public defender, saw this as Biannela's feeble attempt to shift the blame to her own son and minimize her own role in the slaying.

More Charges

On January 5, 2012, Cristian Fernandez, just a week shy of turning 13, appeared in court again not only to seek the dismissal of his first-degree murder charge but to also be indicted by a grand jury of a brand-new charge: sexual battery by a person under the age of 18 upon a person under the age of 12.

Victim #2 was also someone who was very close to Cristian: his five-year-old half-brother. The youngster had told police that his brother had sexually molested him more than once between October 22, 2010, and March 14, 2011. It was a claim that was corroborated by Cristian himself while in custody for first-degree murder and aggravated child abuse.

The state was aware of these serious allegations and had been prepping the sexual battery case as early as June 2011. The defense had requested that they postpone the indictment during plea negotiations for the murder case. If the defense and prosecution settled on a plea agreement, the prosecution planned to merely incorporate the case into the murder trial. In the month prior to Cristian's sexual battery charge,

Angela Corey sent him a plea agreement of second-degree murder. This charge would have still led to a lengthy prison term for Cristian, but nevertheless, it was a plea which appealed to Matt Shirk.[22]

Just as all hope seemed to be dwindling, three Jacksonville attorneys swooped in to rescue Cristian. They were Hank Coxe, George "Buddy" Schulz, and Melissa Nelson. The trio had previously been working on the Terrance Graham case. Graham, at the age of 16, had attempted to rob a barbecue restaurant in Jacksonville in July 2003.

They consulted with Matt Shirk, and the defense ultimately rejected Corey's plea deal, leaving the state with no other option but to proceed with the sexual battery indictment against Cristian.

Public defender Matt Shirk called the sexual battery case against Cristian "weak" and accused the state of trying to ruin his young client's life in as many ways as they could think of.

"We can't ignore our additional victim," stated prosecutor Mark Caliel.[23]

The prosecution also said that they would not be seeking the maximum sentence for the soon-to-be-13-year-old in either of the cases against him and expressed their hope for his positive treatment and rehabilitation while he served time behind bars, a contradictory statement at best given that a first-degree murder charge in Florida carries a mandatory life without parole sentence.

But the three Jacksonville attorneys didn't discontinue their involvement from there. In fact, Cristian's court-appointed guardian ad litem filed to remove Matt Shirk as Cristian's public defender and replace the teen's representatives with a private pro bono counsel. The counsel would consist of Melissa Nelson, Hank Coxe, and George Schulz.

Matt Shirk was characterized as an incompetent attorney who only took on the Fernandez case for the attention. In the previous year, he had only paid his young client three visits and held copious amounts of evidence in storage that he had never reviewed. It was time for him to be replaced with a more adequate team of lawyers.

With the takeover of the new private counsel consisting of competent and highly experienced attorneys representing Cristian, a positive ray of light for a better outcome in the case began to shine through the cracks of despair. But these new attorneys knew they had a lot of work to do. They began by rummaging through boxes upon boxes of evidence that Shirk had been neglecting for the past several months and started piecing together their defense from scratch.

A Guilty Plea

After nearly a year since her arrest, the now-26-year-old Biannela Susana showed up for her pre-trial court hearing clad in a gray jail jumpsuit, her hands and feet bound by shiny silver shackles. To everybody's surprise, she pleaded guilty to aggravated manslaughter before Circuit Judge James H. Daniel. When he asked whether she wanted to plead guilty because she truly was guilty and wanted to take responsibility for her role in her toddler son's death, she simply replied that it was in her "best interest."[24]

Prosecutor Mark Caliel said that Biannela's failure to seek medical attention for her son as soon as she discovered him unconscious was a huge contributing factor to his death. Her willful negligence while David lay there for several hours meant that she too bore some responsibility for his death.

Not only that, but she also had a fixed pattern of negligence which she'd demonstrated in the past, first by lying to authorities about how David broke his leg back in January 2011 *and* waiting two days to seek medical attention for it. Her second demonstration of irresponsible and inexcusable parenting happened when she permitted Cristian to be left alone, unsupervised, around David and the other siblings despite what had happened the previous time.

Prosecutors offered nothing in exchange for the mother's guilty plea. She was now facing 13 years to a maximum of 30 years in jail.[25]

A Dismissed Charge

Cristian Fernandez's defense team ultimately got their wish, for on November 8, 2012, prosecutors made the decision to drop the sexual battery charge against the 13-year-old defendant. By doing so, they were authenticating public defender Matt Shirk's claim that the case they had against Cristian regarding the sexual allegations was, in fact, implausible.

Previously, Judge Mallory Cooper had thrown out all statements Cristian had made to police (including the sexual assault interrogation) as he didn't believe Cristian, being just 12 at the time, was able to fully understand his Miranda rights and what he was doing when he waived his constitutional rights. In addition to Cristian's age, Cooper considered the boy's clarifying questions about his rights when he made this decision.

With no statements to go on, the judge's move eradicated the bulk of the sexual battery case against Cristian. That, on top of the victim's conflicting statements and lack of physical evidence to corroborate his accusations, meant the state was no longer able to prosecute Cristian and had no alternative but to drop the charge against him.[26]

The defense had been pushing for the dismissal of Cristian's first-degree murder charge following the 2012 U.S. Supreme Court ruling in *Miller v. Alabama* that it is unconstitutional to sentence juvenile offenders to mandatory life sentences without the possibility of parole. According to the Florida Criminal Punishment Code (a.k.a. the Sentencing Guideline), a first-degree murder conviction mandates the death penalty or a life sentence without the possibility of parole.

This request was later denied by the judge, who, in her three-paragraph explanation to defend her decision, wrote that only life sentences without the possibility of parole are forbidden in *Miller*. As long as certain mitigating factors, such as one's age, were largely taken into consideration during the sentencing phase, then the juvenile in question (in this case, Cristian) could constitutionally face a life sentence if convicted of first-degree murder.[27]

Public defender Hank Coxe, also representing Cristian, had accepted Judge Cooper's final say in the ordeal and vowed to continue fighting for Cristian's fate against the prosecution, which continued seeking to put the youth in an adult prison for the rest of his life.

Harry Shorstein, a former state attorney for Florida's Fourth Circuit who, as we remember from a previous chapter, had prosecuted 14-year-old Joshua Phillips back in the 1990s and was now an avid proponent for less harsh sentences for juvenile offenders, stated that the judge's decision might actually work in the defense's favor. If Judge Cooper had heeded the defense team's request and dismissed Cristian's charges, then Cristian would have to undergo a lengthy appeals process, which entailed extra time behind bars. Now that they were to proceed with the first-degree murder charge, Cristian had a much better chance of walking out of prison sooner than if they had ventured down the appeals route.[28]

Cristian didn't have only his public defense team and influential Floridian attorneys backing him up. He also had the most important advocates in his corner, fighting for his freedom: the people of America. To them, Cristian Fernandez encapsulated everything that was wrong with America's justice system. His case garnered a monumental amount of attention outside of Florida, inspiring nationwide support, including a Facebook page and a change.org petition calling for the state and Judge Mallory Cooper to reverse the decision to try him as an adult.

"The system failed him his entire life and now it stands to repeat history by refusing Cristian the right to be tried in juvenile court," wrote Melissa Higgins, who started the petition. "Cristian has demonstrated he is amenable to rehabilitation. There is no logical reason to deny this child his right to the programs and treatment provided through the juvenile court system. Help Cristian receive the justice he deserves as a juvenile."[29]

The petition gained nearly 193,000 signatures. But neither the state nor Judge Cooper granted their pleas. Cristian's trial date was set for March 4, 2013.

Plea and Sentencing

Cristian's attorneys' hard work had really paid off. On February 8, 2013, during a court hearing that was set for pre-trial motions, the 14-year-old youth, wedged between his attorneys, pleaded guilty as a juvenile as part of a plea agreement to reduced charges of manslaughter and aggravated battery in connection with his half-brother's death.

The plea deal was established between Angela Corey's office and Cristian's private lawyers shortly before the hearing, as his trial date was inching dangerously closer.

This plea agreement entailed that he would be serving time in a juvenile detention center where conditions such as continuing education and therapy treatment would apply. If all went well, Cristian could be released as early as his 19th birthday in January 2018.

The sentence for the manslaughter charge was to run consecutively with the one for the aggravated battery charge. Another part of the plea agreement stated that upon his release Cristian would have to serve an additional eight years of probation for the aggravated battery charge. He would be subjected to certain conditions he must comply with, such as seeking employment and avoiding contact with his remaining younger half-siblings unless they sought him out first. As per his probation, he must also not be left alone unsupervised with children under the age of 16.

His probation would expire after five years unless he violated it, in which case he would be sentenced as an adult in connection for the aggravated battery charge and be forced to spend it in an adult prison.[30]

On August 14, 2013, Biannela Susana, now 27, also appeared in court to finally hear her sentence after months of waiting once she pleaded guilty to her charge. It was decided that she would be sentenced after Cristian.

Circuit Judge James Daniel would give her a sentence of 10 years in prison, although she was given credit for the two years she had already served and saw the remainder of her sentence suspended to probation, much to Mark Caliel's dismay. He had been pushing for a 15-year sentence for her constant neglect of her children, which led to David's death.

Her sentence essentially meant that she would not have to spend any more time behind prison bars if she complied with the specific set of conditions imposed upon her. For example, once she was released, she would have to spend 90 days in the Hubbard House domestic violence shelter and then an additional two years in a halfway house, where she would receive therapy and learn life skills. She would also be required to obtain a job or be actively seeking employment for the next seven years, and she must *not* test positive for drugs or commit any crime.

Judge Daniel also examined her background and the rather grim circumstances she grew up in. Raising a child as a product of rape when she was barely a teenager herself put her at a serious disadvantage in life. Another factor considered by Judge Daniel was that there was no evidence that David's life could've been saved by prompt action from Biannela.

Psychologist Jacqueline Brown had testified in a court hearing the previous month that Biannela suffered from post-traumatic stress disorder after her husband shot himself in front of his children, a strong mitigating factor cited by Judge Daniel who believed that, since Biannela was not a threat to society and had taken responsibility for her actions (or lack thereof), she would benefit strongly from mental health counseling.

Lawanda Ravoira, founder and CEO of Jacksonville's Delores Barr Weaver Policy Center, a nonprofit organization and social service advocates for the rights of at-risk girls and women, had been visiting Biannela weekly for the past year. She vowed to hire the woman after Biannela completed her time at the halfway house. Judge Daniel said that Biannela must work for the Weaver Center for three years.

"I've come to realize the incredible potential that Biannela has. She needs intervention and treatment, not prison," said Lawanda Ravoira.[31]

Biannela gave up her parental rights, and her surviving daughter and son were adopted by the same family in August 2012. Biannela is not allowed to maintain any sort of relationship with her children, and she may only have contact with Cristian with the state's permission.

Mark Caliel stated that Biannela did not deserve to be freed, but he wished her the best in her journey to rehabilitation. He urged people to focus more on David Galarraga, the true victim in all of this.

"It's very easy to judge when you're not in the middle of it," said Jessica Callow, Biannela's half-sister. "But I hope people know my sister is a good human being who needs help."[32]

Afterword

Since the case's closure, Cristian Fernandez's story continues to be discussed when the subject turns to how juveniles are prosecuted in the criminal justice system. Is it cruel and unusual punishment to make someone pay for a crime they committed as a child for the rest of their life? And, even more importantly, can someone like Cristian Fernandez, who is susceptible to extreme violence, be successfully rehabilitated and become a productive member of society?

Cristian Fernandez spent his entire adolescence in the Cypress Creek Juvenile Offender Correctional Center completely surrounded by 12-foot fences with razor wire. Every Saturday, Mary Coxe, the wife of Hank Coxe, who was part of the "dream team" of pro bono attorneys that represented Cristian and spared him from spending a lifetime in adult prison, made the long drive to visit Cristian. She has become his self-proclaimed "honorary grandmother" and court-appointed ad litem. She gives him a touch of hope, laughter, and love in his otherwise bleak life, all vital forms of affection that Cristian lacked in his childhood, for a mere three hours a week.[33]

In a bittersweet sense of irony, Cristian's quality of life was far improved from the circumstances he grew up in. He was well fed, went to school, received counseling, and had his own room with a bed. But it could get lonely.

He often mused about getting a job so that he could pay his lawyers back for everything they had done for him.

But Mary Coxe told him the same thing every time: "The way you pay them back is to do well. Be somebody."[34]

Cristian was released from prison on January 15, 2018, just one day after he turned 19. Nothing about his progress since his release has come to light.[35]

And what has come of Biannela Susana? The young woman kept a relatively low profile once the case ceased to be featured in national headlines. However, in 2019, an updated mugshot would find its way into the public's online news feeds after it was reported that she had been arrested for a DUI.[36]

Biannela Susana was villainized and dubbed the "worst mother in the world" by the media and the people of America. However, Biannela's story continues to serve as a glaring reminder of the daily disadvantages and lack of support that thousands of teen moms in the United States continue to face today, in addition to the numerous risk factors that should be addressed before more young moms find themselves in tragic situations.

There were multiple critical instances in the young mom's life that would have warranted early intervention, but she was failed by a system that had pledged to provide protection and avenues of assistance for girls and women like her. Raising a child is one of the most challenging jobs, but raising a child—*alone*—as a child yourself with limited access to external support systems only exacerbates the struggles that accompany parenting tasks. Life experience and maturity are the two integral elements of healthy parenting, but they are also elements that teen moms may be lacking. These missing elements put teen moms at a disadvantage for supporting their own children's development. Children who are the product of teen pregnancy may be at increased risk of academic problems, early parenthood, dropping out of school, and unemployment.[37] They may also be more prone to social problems and delinquency.[38]

An article written in *The Nation* called into question whether Angela Corey was the "cruelest prosecutor in America." Corey began her career in law under the supervision of Ed Austin, who served as state attorney for the Fourth Judicial Circuit before resigning in 1991 to run for mayor of Jacksonville. He was succeeded by Harry Shorstein, who resigned to return to private practice in 2008. Angela Corey then took his place, achieving the status of the first woman to hold the position. She was defeated by Melissa Nelson on August 30, 2016.

Angela Corey has since become something of a nationally controversial figure after failing to convict George Zimmerman in the murder of Trayvon Martin, an unarmed black teen. Aside from that, she has also been slammed by the public for her failure to change the unmerciful system that handles juvenile offenders. The Fourth Circuit, which encompasses the counties of Duval, Clay, and Nassau, sends 75 percent of juveniles being tried as adults to adult prison or jail.

Because minors are more likely to be targeted for physical assault and rape, they are normally kept in solitary confinement, where they receive minimal access to yard time, virtually no access to educational and counseling facilities, and limited if any visitation from family—all of which are vital components in the successful rehabilitation of youth offenders. In January 2016, President Barack Obama banned the practice of solitary confinement for juveniles incarcerated in federal prison, citing research that isolating prisoners leads to long-term psychological consequences which may exacerbate existing mental illness or even trigger new ones. Juveniles, in particular, are more prone to suicide while held in isolation.

The former president said that solitary confinement should only be used as a last resort.

"How can we subject prisoners to unnecessary solitary confinement, knowing its effects, and then expect them to return to our communities as whole people? It doesn't make us safer. It's an affront to our common humanity."[39]

Melinda Loveless, Laurie Tackett, Hope Rippey and Toni Lawrence
(1992)

Near the small town of Canaan, Indiana, on a brisk Saturday morning, two bird hunters, Vietnam veteran Donn Foley and his brother Ralph, loaded up their dogs in the back of the truck and cruised along the narrow and winding Lemon Road between dense patches of woods and soybean fields. Donn kept his eyes peeled for prey.

Something caught Ralph's attention. It was a grim sight that he hoped he would never have to see again after coming home from his military service. He promptly slammed his foot on the brake, stopping the truck, and got out to get a closer look.

The scent of gasoline and burnt flesh lingered in the air. There, lying stiffly on the frozen ground just off the side of the road, appeared to be a blackened figure. The brothers briefly speculated that perhaps it was just a mannequin or one of those blow-up dolls that someone had burned and placed there as a twisted prank. But they weren't sure of that.[1]

Together they approached the peculiar figure with trepidation until both of them loomed over it. They guessed that the charred body, blackened from the waist up and completely nude save for a pair of torn-up underwear, was a young lady. Underneath the thick, filthy gray substance coating her wavy hair were perceptible traces of blond strands. Her pale legs were spread out and bent upward. Her clenched fists, tightly holding fragments of what appeared to be a red cloth, were raised in the air in a boxer-like "defensive" position.

This strange pose is what forensic pathologists commonly refer to as the "pugilistic stance." Seen exclusively in burn victims, it is characterized by shrinkage of body tissues and muscles due to high temperatures in a fire.[2]

All at once, the hairs on the back of Donn's neck stood up and his stomach flipped. He was now almost certain that this was, in fact, real. As a war veteran, he knew a dead body when he saw one. Donn and Ralph urgently drove back home to phone the police.

Chief deputy Randy Spry and Indiana state trooper Stephen Henry were among the first to arrive at the scene. Their first impressions, too, were that this severely-burned figure was a mannequin that someone staged as a prank. But the closer they came to it, the more unsure they became.

"I've never seen anything that horrible and I don't think I ever will," one of the men would later remark.[3]

This woman had been more than just lit on fire; she suffered from all sorts of horrific injuries, ranging from stab wounds, cuts on her legs, and ligature marks from head to toe. Soon, more officers arrived.

When Richard Shipley, sheriff of Jefferson County, arrived at the scene and first saw the body, he was taken aback. This was unlike any dead body he had ever seen in his entire career in law enforcement. His first impression was that this was an older adolescent or a young woman in her early 20s, judging by how mature and developed she looked. He also didn't think this young woman lived locally as they had not received any missing persons reports in the Madison area.

In his mind, he theorized that this poor victim's death was the result of a drug deal gone wrong and that she was perhaps brought over from a big city like Indianapolis and pushed out of a car. One factor of the crime that struck him as odd, however, was that the perpetrator, or perpetrators, didn't do anything to conceal the body. The victim was dumped on the side of a rural road, in a cornfield that lacked vegetation during mid-winter, when there was a dense patch of forest consisting of thick, towering trees just 20 yards over.[4] Had the culprit(s) left her body there, it might not have been discovered for a long time. Why leave her out in the open, for the first passerby to find? Did whoever leave her here perhaps want her to be found? Or did they just not care?

Investigators began the unpleasant task of photographing and videotaping the grisly crime scene, collecting evidence, and cleaning up the mess. They were careful to not disturb the fresh tire marks or footprints in the gravel. A melted plastic two-liter Pepsi bottle rested near the body. Overall, the entire process took several hours. When they were finished with their work, they carefully lifted the victim's body from the ground and into an ambulance, which would transport her to a morgue.

As dreadful as the whole day had been, the officers took a touch of comfort from the assumption that the person(s) responsible for this sick, stomach-twisting murder was probably not a local, for these types of violent crimes were just not heard of here. There hadn't been a single murder in Jefferson County in the past three years.

All the while, one daunting question would haunt these investigators' minds.

What kind of animal was capable of doing such a thing?

Things were looking hopeless for the officers. Here they had a Jane Doe who suffered an unimaginable death and zero suspects. Their chances of ever solving this murder seemed dim. But just as all hope seemed lost, police were about to get their first big break in the case when a 15-year-old boy entered the Jefferson County police station with some important information to share. Although the authorities didn't know it at the time, this boy was the first vital nudge that would push them closer to finding the truth.

The teenage boy claimed that he heard about a girl who was burned and killed earlier that morning. He said a couple of girls at the Anderson Bowling Alley, a common hangout for teens, had tearfully told him and his friend all about it. The girls claimed they were there to witness it all.

When Steve Henry asked for their names, he uttered two: Toni Lawrence and Hope Rippey.

Even though the police were edging closer to finding the truth, they still had yet to uncover the identity of the girl, and that was frustrating. Still there were no missing persons reports. The interview at some point was interrupted by a knock on the door. Henry was informed that a 15-year-old girl had shown up at the police station with her parents and she was in absolute hysterics. It was Toni Lawrence.

"I was shocked," he would later say. "It was the participants' age that shocks your imagination most. It's hard to put into words what I felt when I learned what happened."[5]

What they didn't know was that, while all of this was unfolding, the answer was hidden in a city some 40 miles away, where two worried parents were desperately searching for their missing daughter. But soon, all of the missing puzzle pieces would fall into place. When the true age of the victim came to be revealed, it would shock investigators when they learned that this "woman" was not a woman at all. In fact, the girl was barely in her teens. They were not at all prepared for the jarring story behind what led up to this poor child's heinous murder, a tragedy that would bring two cities together in mourning.

The New Girl

It was weeks before the school year would start again, and students at Hazelwood Junior High were about to see a bunch of fresh faces roaming the halls. One of these faces would belong to Shanda Sharer, a five-foot-tall beauty who had bushy 80s-style honey blond hair and bangs that would frame her blue eyes, dark eyebrows, and big, contagious smile. She had recently moved to New Albany, Indiana, a small city of roughly 36,000 people, all the way across the Ohio River from the much more populated city of Louisville, Kentucky. Before, she had attended St. Paul Catholic School for fifth and sixth grades, where she had no shortage of friends. An active young girl, she participated in several team sports at her old school, including volleyball, softball and cheerleading.[6]

Her mother, Jacqueline (commonly called Jacque), and father, Steve Sharer, divorced when Shanda was young; however, she lived with her mom but remained in frequent contact with her father. After the move to New Albany, Shanda was ecstatic to live much closer to Steve, who lived in Jeffersonville, just eight miles away. She typically spent weekends with him.

But still, moving to entirely new city and enrolling in a new school with twice as many kids is stressful. Shanda, being so outgoing, never had issues adapting to new environments. Initially, Jacque wanted to enroll Shanda in Our Lady of Perpetual Help, but Shanda begged to be enrolled in a public school this time. She was tired of wearing uniforms, she said. Jacque was a bit tight on money after her recent divorce, so she gave in, but only under the condition that Shanda kept her grades up. By fall, Shanda had started her first day at Hazelwood Junior High, and all her fears and anxieties about not fitting in had crumbled. She loved her new school and got along with her new classmates. Jacque thought she no longer had anything to worry about and neither did Shanda. But just as things seemed to be going well, Shanda ran into some trouble.

Within a couple of weeks, Jacque got a phone call from Shanda's new school that she had gotten into a scuffle with another student. She was shocked; Shanda was not the kind of girl to get into fights. The other student was a 15-year-old girl named Amanda Heavrin, an intimidating eighth-grader on the basketball team with a tall, lean figure and short-cropped hair that she often kept tucked beneath a baseball cap. Both girls were given in-school suspension (ISS) for a week, meaning they would have to spend the school day in a separate room with other kids serving ISS as punishment. Shanda was not the type to get into physical altercations with others. This was when Jacque began having reservations about Hazelwood Junior High.

During in-school suspension, Amanda and Shanda made up. The girls quickly struck up a friendship and continued to exchange letters and notes throughout the week that they were forced to spend together as punishment. Amanda revealed to Shanda in these letters that she was a lesbian and asked if Shanda had an interest in girls. Amanda made several passes at the seventh grader, her written letters often having flirtatious undertones.

And this is when Shanda would first cross paths with 15-year-old Melinda Loveless.

Melinda Loveless was a striking brunette with long, thick curls, skin like a porcelain doll, and a slim figure. Melinda was also a student at Hazelwood, even though she was turning 16 in October. She had been held back a couple of grades. She and Amanda had become lovers two years before and had been inseparable since. Melinda was known to have a jealous streak and felt very possessive of her lover. She could get anyone she wanted, as beautiful as she was, but her heart belonged to Amanda.

Sometime during that week, Melinda wound up in detention as well. She sat on the right side of the room, while Amanda and Shanda sat together on the left side. Melinda watched as Shanda walked to the desk to get some homework. The whole time, Amanda was staring at her. When Shanda returned to her desk, the girls began passing notes to each other.

At the end of the day, the three walked out of the room together.

"Shanda and Amanda were laughing and talking," Melinda remembered. "Amanda introduced me to Shanda. That's when I first met her." She described Shanda as a "sweet, sweet girl."[7]

After school, Shanda and Amanda went to Melinda's house. Melinda confronted Amanda and demanded to see the letters she received from Shanda. She refused, but finally gave in after Melinda smacked her and screamed at her. In one of the perfume-scented letters, Shanda called Amanda cute. A jealous flame flared up inside her, and Melinda forbade Amanda from further pursuing this friendship with Shanda.

Normally, Melinda was able to successfully run off other girls, but her attempts to separate Amanda and Shanda would be ineffective. In the following days, Melinda would spot them hanging out in the hallways, laughing and passing notes. She began feeling a growing sense of unease at their budding friendship. In an attempt to scare Shanda away, she confronted her one day in Hazelwood's corridor and threatened to beat her up if she didn't back off. Shanda, feeling intimidated by the older girl, weakly promised that she'd stay away from Amanda. But that didn't happen at all. Amanda and Shanda spent an increasing amount of time together. The older girl continued to relentlessly pursue Shanda in secret, exchanging letters with her new love interest, which became more and more flirtatious and sexually suggestive in nature. She wrote to Shanda that she loved both girls and didn't know who to choose, expressing that she was afraid that Melinda might hurt Shanda.

Jacque was well aware that Shanda and Amanda had made up. Initially, she didn't approve of their friendship because of the altercation between them and the age gap. This was not the kind of girl she felt comfortable about her daughter hanging around with. Although still cautious, she eventually succumbed to Shanda's pleas. She was the new girl, and she didn't know anyone. Amanda had offered her friendship, and Shanda seemed to really like her, so Jacque wanted to give her a chance.

But in the span of a month, Shanda changed from a sweet, upbeat girl who would spend hours in the mirror fixing her hair and doing her makeup to a child who was less sociable, preferring to lock herself in her room and not come out all night. Once a girly girl, she suddenly stopped taking care of her physical appearance, opting to wear baggy shirts and unsightly jeans. She was failing all of her classes. This was unlike Shanda—she was always on top of her schoolwork. Since her fight with Amanda, she had been placed in detention several more times for skipping class.

All of the warning signs made it clear to Jacque that something was deeply troubling her daughter; she just didn't know what it was. That was until she came across a letter from Amanda instructing

Shanda how to forge her mother's signature on detention slips. Jacque urgently arranged a meeting with Shanda and school officials to get to the bottom of it all. She learned that Melinda and Amanda had a record of disciplinary problems, making it clear that Shanda had fallen in with the wrong crowd. Shanda told her mother that she wanted to distance herself from these new friends but was afraid of potential consequences.

Jacque forbade her daughter from hanging out with those girls and hired a tutor to help Shanda get back on track.

Melinda Loveless

Adolescent love may seem trivial. But nobody was capable of fully comprehending how significant Amanda's presence was in Melinda Loveless' life. Not unless they knew her story.

Melinda Loveless was born on October 28, 1975, in New Albany, Indiana, the youngest of three sisters; her older siblings were Michelle and Melissa. Her mother, Marjorie "Margie" Loveless, worked as a nurse and her father, Larry Eugene Loveless, was a Vietnam War veteran and worked a series of menial jobs upon his return from his military service.

Described as a sexual deviant, he had more than once raped his wife and often abused her both physically and verbally behind closed doors. He had a sick penchant for "sharing" her with others, often bringing home men and women from bars and coercing Margie into participating in orgies. Any refusal or hesitation to engage in these depraved sexual fantasies of his would lead to more threats and beatings, so she played the dutiful wife and did as she was told. Many times, the doors would be wide open for her children to see what was going on.[8]

The young father didn't care for his own children either. The eldest Loveless sister, Michelle, could only encapsulate her upbringing with two words: a nightmare.

"I hated my father. He told me I was ugly and a bitch," Michelle said, describing her father as a monster and a heartless man who knew she was terrified of the dark, so he would remove the light bulbs in her room and lock her in. She would frequently scream and scratch at her door, begging all night to be let out. She would eventually fall asleep at the door.[9]

Larry had a fascination with guns and often talked about wanting to live in the Old West so he could walk up to any random person on the street and blow their head off. One day, he decided he wanted to teach Michelle how to clean a gun. After they finished, he aimed the loaded weapon at her and shot at her. The bullet missed her, and the young girl ended up urinating on herself. The father of three would frequently beat and choke his wife in front of all of the kids. More than once he would point a gun at Marjorie's head and threaten to kill her and the whole family if she dared leave him.

Both Michelle and Melissa would later share disturbing tales of how Larry had sexually abused them throughout their childhood. Larry's abuse extended toward his nieces, Edie and Teddie, as well. Teddie babysat the Loveless sisters from the age of 10 up until she was 16, while Melinda was still a little girl. Larry raped her countless times throughout those six years. A sick man, he would often take her underwear, sniff them, and walk around the house with them while spewing crude remarks. He once inserted a loaded pistol in her vagina as well as sodomized her. He made sure that she would keep her mouth shut about the abuse by threatening to kill her if she dared tell a soul.

One time, Teddie claimed, Larry had taken her and all three daughters into the garage, chained them up, and raped each of them. After the traumatic incident, Teddie went back into the house and sat on the couch. A whimpering Melinda crawled into her lap and asked to be held.

In another terrifying incident, when Edie was around eight years old, she was sleeping in bed with Larry and Marjorie when she felt a nightmare coming on. But what was happening was not a simple case of a horrible dream. When she opened her eyes, Larry had one hand clapped over her mouth and the other wrapped around her arms. He was sodomizing her.

Teddie would end up telling their mother about all of the nightmarish happenings going on in the Loveless home, but nothing was done about it.[10]

When Melinda was a toddler, the family moved into a bigger house in upscale Floyd Knobs. But things didn't change for the better. Larry spent most of his time bumming around the house and drinking. The family suffered financially and struggled to even put food on the table. They were on the verge of being evicted.

But then, a miracle happened.

Larry decided he was going to clean up his act, practice strict monogamy, and quit drinking. He decided that he was now a man of God. Guided by newfound faith, he went to Graceland Baptist Church to confess his sins, and the church welcomed the Loveless family with warm and loving arms. Larry became a lay preacher at Graceland Baptist Church and delivered inspiring speeches detailing his past sins of drinking and affairs, which came to an end once he saw the light of God.

But it was all lies. Religion didn't change Larry. It only gave him new ways to control his family. He tossed out all of Marjorie's provocative clothing and makeup and forced her to dress more modestly. He burned the kids' beloved toys and stuffed animals that he believed were evil and Satanic. Larry had his entire family exorcised at the church. When Melinda was five, it was her turn to get exorcised. Larry dropped her off at a motel room with a 50-year-old man for five hours. Soon, he began counseling many women at the church who were going through marital struggles. Many of these women were sexually assaulted by Larry.

Eventually, Larry quit his position at Graceland. The family moved back to New Albany, and he reverted to his old ways of abuse, alcoholism and sex parties.[11]

Melinda was a daddy's girl and Larry's favorite daughter, although Michelle would later say that their relationship dynamic played out more like a husband and wife. Melinda idolized her father and thought of him as her hero. She did everything he asked her to do. Both Michelle and Melissa strongly suspected that their little sister, too, was being molested by Larry. Sometimes, he would call Melinda, whom he nicknamed Lindy Star, up to his room despite his older daughters' pleas to stop. Every night, up until she was a teenager, they slept in the same bed together.[12]

Melinda was desperately afraid of losing her father; he was her rock. But that fear was about to come true. In March of 1989, a drunken Larry took Melinda and her cousin to the Holiday Inn's indoor pool. Larry repeatedly prodded at their breasts and buttocks with a cane. When the girls went to go change out of their swimwear in the changing room, they noticed Larry was peeking at them while they were unclothed.

Feeling completely humiliated and shaken up, Melinda's cousin told Marjorie as soon as they got back home.

The mother of three finally had enough. She confronted Larry by chasing him out of the house with a kitchen knife. When he shielded himself with his arm, she accidentally slashed him. Larry was taken to the hospital and Margie attempted suicide. And that would mark the end of their marriage. Larry subsequently moved to Florida, abandoning his entire family.[13]

Larry was not missed by anyone except his youngest. Melinda sank into a deep depression. She cried and felt empty every day. The two kept in contact via letters and phone calls, but, slowly, Larry faded away from Melinda's life. She began acting out, dating and becoming promiscuous, desperately trying to fill the void that her father left in her heart.[14]

Shortly after, however, she met Amanda Heavrin at Hazelwood Junior High and immediately latched on. She was drawn to her masculine appearance, tough-girl attitude, and swaggering gait. Amanda bore a striking resemblance to Melinda's father.[15]

Melinda had done her fair share of fooling around with boys in the past, but she was often treated like dirt. She came to the realization that she liked girls much, much more. After the two became a couple, Melinda followed in her sisters' footsteps and came out to her family as a lesbian. Melinda confided in a school counselor that her mother disapproved of her same-sex relationship and that she was depressed over her parents' divorce. She was then referred to counseling at LifeSpring Mental Health in February 1991.

From the beginning, Melinda knew that Amanda was a rare find. She was not going to let someone so special go so easily.

Brewing Jealousy

Shanda and Amanda's relationship continued to progress behind Melinda's back, but she was not completely unaware. She had a strong suspicion that something more serious was going on between them. Soon, the 16-year-old's jealousy engulfed her, and she escalated to direct harassment, such as name-calling and threats toward her 12-year-old rival in the school halls. She began thinking about how much easier her life would be if Shanda were gone. Soon, she was ranting to her friends about how she wanted her dead.

One day, Jacque came across a letter in the mailbox. It was written to Amanda, by Shanda. She had forgotten to put a stamp on it, so the letter was returned to sender. Shanda's writing suggested that the two had been intimate. Both disturbed and worried, Jacque immediately staged an intervention and got Shanda's father and stepmother involved. Jacque invited Amanda and her father over so they could discuss the matter as well, but neither of them showed up.

Jacque knew she had to be gentle when confronting Shanda with the letter. She wanted her to know that she wasn't upset with her and simply wanted to be there for her. She sat on the floor with Shanda and urged her to tell her mother, father, and stepmother the truth.

"Shanda, we will always love you. Whatever you have done, it's not unforgivable," she told her gently. "It's nothing you should be ashamed of. You are only 12 years old. You are just a little girl."

Shanda denied to her mother that Amanda had ever touched her inappropriately. But Jacque wasn't buying it.

"This letter leads me to believe that you and Amanda have more than just a friendship," Jacque said.

"No, Mom, we don't," Shanda replied. "It's just that Amanda needed a friend, and I wanted to be a good friend."[16]

Now that Jacque knew the source of Shanda's behavior change, everything started making sense. Amanda was a bad influence on Shanda, and it was only going to get worse unless she separated the two for good. She decided to pull Shanda out of Hazelwood and enroll her in Our Lady of Perpetual Help, as was her original plan.

When Melinda heard the news about Shanda's transfer, she couldn't have been happier. She felt like this was finally going to put an end to all of her problems. Finally, her competition was gone, and she would have Amanda all to herself again.

But that was not quite the case, she would discover. Even though Shanda was at a new school now, she still occupied much of Amanda's attention and thoughts, and the girls continued to carry on their relationship in secret. Melinda had thought that Shanda's transfer would put an end to all of her worries, and she was sick and tired of Shanda standing in the way of her and Amanda's love.

"Shanda is not gone! You haven't got rid of her," Melinda angrily vented in a letter to Amanda dated on November 26, 1991. "I'm real mad at you! I feel like I need to cry! I want Shanda dead!"[17]

Amanda Heavrin's father came across that letter among many others and was disturbed by their romantic and sexual tone. He turned all of the letters in to the Floyd County Probation Department, and a probation officer went to the Loveless home and ordered Melinda not to contact Amanda anymore. However, Shanda's mother was never informed about the letter containing the death wish against her daughter. Had she known, perhaps she would have kept a more watchful eye on Shanda.

This restriction only further drove a wedge between Melinda and Amanda. It seemed like there was no winning for Melinda. No amount of pleading, promises and tantrums seemed to drive Amanda and Shanda apart. She needed to figure out a way to get rid of Shanda permanently. She began endlessly ranting about her love rival to her friends and asking about the best way to dispose of a dead body.

That was when her 15-year-old friend Kristin Brodfuehrer convinced Melinda that she should reorient her anger to Amanda. Amanda was the bad guy here. She was the one who cast her aside for someone else.

The two hatched a plot to teach Amanda a lesson. Since neither of the teenagers had a car, they talked some boys into driving them to Amanda's house with the plan of luring Amanda out and beating her up, but by then, it was already 4 a.m. and Amanda had fallen asleep.

Back at Shanda's new school, the 12-year-old was flourishing. Her grades drastically improved and she was making new friends. Slowly but surely Shanda was becoming her old self again. Shanda and Jacque's relationship was close to being repaired. Instead of hiding in her room every day, Shanda would spend more time with her mother, and the two shared lots of long talks. Every night, Shanda slept in bed with her mother.

One evening, during another one of those long talks in the kitchen, the conversation took an emotional turn when Shanda expressed gratitude to her mother for pulling her out of Hazelwood. She told her that she understood why she made that decision and said she felt like she was given a second chance.

"I had done so many bad things that I had never done before," Shanda tearfully told her mother. "I just couldn't find my way back, and you helped me find my way back."[18]

By then, though, it was too late. The wheels in Melinda's head were already turning. It was around this time that Melinda made a new friend.

Laurie Tackett (full name Mary Laurine Tackett) was a rather eccentric young woman. She had short, unkempt blond hair, blue eyes, a somewhat crooked jaw, and a stare that was as cold as ice. She was deeply into devil worship and the occult, and she claimed to have the ability to communicate with the dead. She would frequently channel a spirit named Deanna the Vampire and talk about how she could bring people back to life. She once self-mutilated at a party and drank her own blood. She liked to share her murder fantasies with others and often mused about what it would feel like to burn another human being alive. She would relish the publicity, she said. It was clear to everyone who knew her: this girl was a nutcase.[19]

Laurie was born on October 5, 1974, in Madison, Indiana, to Peggy and George Tackett. From an early age, Laurie was a social outcast. Her parents were devout Christians who belonged to a strict, fundamentalist church that often spoke in tongues and had visions and forbade women and girls from wearing makeup, jewelry and jeans. As a child, Laurie had long, dark hair and was forced to wear modest dresses that went down to her ankles. Her mother also barred her from participating in gym class, as the church did not allow girls to wear shorts or sweatpants. She wasn't allowed to listen to any music that wasn't gospel, and Peggy tossed out the family's TV set after making a vow to God that she would no longer watch television.

"Other kids joked about me and teased me because I was different," Laurie said.[20]

When Laurie was a child, she was molested countless times by a male cousin, which ceased by the time she reached 11 years old. Growing up, she had frequent spats with her mother; Laurie was beaten and choked whenever she refused to go to church, which held services four times a week. The beatings came to a stop when Laurie was 14, after school officials reported Laurie's facial bruising to the county's welfare department.

Once she reached the eighth grade, she finally refused to play by her mother's controlling rules any longer. She decided that from now on she was going to live her life however the hell she wanted, even if it was at the expense of her mother's approval. She was now at the age where she wanted to ditch the dresses and wear more socially appropriate clothes for a teenage girl. She began rebelling against her mother's conservative lifestyle by wearing jeans, cutting her hair short and dyeing it wild colors, once even shaving it off entirely. She sported dark apparel and hung around a group of like-minded social outcasts at Madison High School called the "Alternatives." She drank a bottle of whiskey four times a week and took up self-mutilation, which became a tension release for her.

Outside of the Alternatives, Laurie spent time with two 15-year-old girls, Hope Rippey and her friend Toni Lawrence, a timid sophomore with short brown hair and thick-framed glasses. Although Laurie was quite close with Hope, she simply tolerated Toni. Toni was a bit too preppy for her taste.[21] One time, however, Laurie was spending the night at Toni's house when she cut her hand a little too deeply with a razor blade. After this incident, Laurie was placed in psychiatric care.

The atmosphere in the Tackett home only grew more toxic. An incident in which her brother pried into her diary and found a passage written by Laurie stating that she wanted to be a boy sparked an angry confrontation with Peggy, who asked her daughter why she couldn't just be normal. She invited a minister over to the house to pray for Laurie, who had barricaded herself in her room and slit her wrist, as the minister stood outside her door and prayed for the devil to leave her alone.

Later, her mother dragged her to a prayer meeting where it was preached that homosexuals would burn in hell.

Tired of being condemned by her family and harassed by other kids at school for dressing and behaving differently, Laurie, at the age of 16, decided to move in with her cousin in New York in the hope that she could start fresh. People in New York were rumored to be more open-minded, and maybe, just maybe, she would finally find her crowd and fit in for once in her life. But after a few weeks, the arrangement failed and she wound up in Madison again. In September 1991, she officially dropped out of high school and got a job at Kroger.

But Laurie didn't give up on her search for a fresh start and new friends. She was absolutely miserable in Madison. She had heard of a group of people in New Albany who would accept someone like her. One of these people was Carrie Pope. She got in touch with her and the two arranged a meet-up. Carrie brought Melinda along.

Laurie's first impression of Melinda was that she was hyper. She had boldly asked Laurie if she liked girls, and the older girl responded that she did.

For a while, Laurie and Melinda didn't talk much and hardly knew each other. But towards the end of 1991, the two started hitting it off.

On January 8, 1992, Laurie phoned Melinda and invited her to a punk-style slam-dance on Friday night.

Knowing that Laurie had a taste for blood and violence, Melinda saw this as a perfect opportunity to use her as a tool in a revenge plot she had secretly been scheming. She told Laurie she would go, but only if they made one stop beforehand: Shanda's house. She wanted to kill her, she said.

Laurie simply responded, "Okay."[22]

January 10, 1992

On the evening of January 10, 1992, Laurie Tackett picked up Hope and Toni from school. Hope was already aware of Laurie's sinister plan for the night, but Toni was blissfully unaware, under the impression that they would just be picking up another girl, a friend of Laurie's, and attending a punk rock concert. Toni had asked her parents for permission to go to the event with Laurie, but they objected. To get around their refusal, she asked a friend to cover for her by saying she would spend the night with her instead.

En route to Melinda's New Albany home, Laurie told Toni, "We're going to kill a little girl."[23] Toni, however, thought Laurie was just being Laurie and didn't take her seriously. They made one quick stop at the Witches' Castle, which stands on a hillside overlooking the Ohio River in Utica. The ruined remains of what used to be an old stone castle, it appears less intimidating in broad daylight, but, in the dead of night, it looks about as ominous as its name.[24] According to urban legend, a coven of witches once lived in this hillside structure—that was until some locals who didn't trust the women decided to burn it down some 20 years before, earning it the eerie moniker "Witches' Castle." This small, standing structure was rumored to be haunted by old spirits, and it was a common place for youths to meet for occult practices, making it a subject of fascination for paranormal investigators and a draw for thrill-seeking teenagers with a sense of morbid curiosity who wanted to explore and sometimes vandalize the property.[25] To Utica residents, however, this derelict home bore a much less menacing name—Mistletoe Falls—as it rested by a spring and mistletoe.

After exploring the area some, the girls piled back into Laurie's car and drove the rest of the way to Melinda's house.

Melinda had met Hope once before, but this was her first time meeting Toni. To Toni, Melinda just seemed like your average teenage girl, and they all immediately clicked. The girls went up to Melinda's bedroom, and Toni and Hope admired her closet full of beautiful clothes. In between trying on her clothing and gushing excitedly about the slam dance that was just a few hours away, Melinda suddenly dropped a bomb on them. She pulled out a kitchen knife and started discussing her plan to beat up her love rival and "tease her with the knife." Melinda began her tirade about the 12-year-old, explaining that Shanda had stolen her girlfriend Amanda away and she needed to teach her a lesson. Toni gulped and glanced between the other two girls to see if their eyes reflected the same fear that she was feeling. But they didn't. In fact, Laurie and Hope looked excited. It began to dawn on Toni that Laurie may have been telling the truth after all. Suddenly, she found herself in a situation she did not want to be in.

The girls piled into Laurie's car and headed over to Shanda's father's house in Jeffersonville, where Melinda knew she regularly spent the weekends. Laurie parked a few houses away, knowing that the plan would be foiled if Shanda spotted Melinda in the car. Then, Laurie and Melinda quickly came up with a ruse to lure Shanda out of the house. They both carefully instructed Hope and Toni to knock on the door, introduce themselves as friends of Amanda, and tell her that Amanda wanted to meet her somewhere.

At first, Toni was reluctant to get herself involved. But after much pressure, she finally gave in and got out of the car with Hope. They approached Shanda's house, knocked, and waited.

That Friday was a typical one for Shanda. Her father had picked her up from Jacque's house after school ended and brought her over to his Jeffersonville home, where she would spend the weekend. That evening, she had plans to attend a party at a neighborhood girl's house. She was helping her father around the house when she heard the knock on the door. Before anyone else could react, she ran over to open it. Before her stood two unfamiliar faces. One of them asked if she was Shanda.

Hope and Toni stuck to the script they were fed by Laurie and Melinda. They explained to the much younger girl that they were friends of Amanda and that she wanted to meet with her somewhere to talk.

Regardless of the effort that her parents had made to build a wall between Shanda and Amanda, old feelings came rushing back. Amanda still had a pull on her, clearly, and Shanda found herself unable to resist the offer. She informed the girls that she was about to leave and suggested that they return after 11 p.m., when her father would be sound asleep.

After the strange girls left, Shanda was immediately confronted by her father. Steve had heard the girls inquiring if she was Shanda, implying that they didn't know who she was. Shanda feigned innocence and explained that they were just some friends who wanted to know if she'd be interested in going to the mall with them, which she declined. Steve, still skeptical about the bizarre encounter, dropped the subject.

Meanwhile, Laurie, Melinda, Toni and Hope attended the concert, which was held at Audubon Skatepark. There, the group of four split into two groups of two. Melinda and Laurie went one way, and Hope and Toni stuck together. At one point during the night, Melinda found a phone and used it to call Amanda and inform her of the sinister plan she devised.

"Don't do it, you'll get arrested," Amanda pleaded. "Don't kill her."[26]

But Melinda told her she had already made up her mind and hung up the phone.

Meanwhile, Toni and Hope spent the majority of the night in Laurie's car with a couple of boys they had just hooked up with named Lloyd and Jimmy.

But Toni couldn't get her mind off of her friends' evil scheme for the night, and the boys could tell she was anxious about something. After much prodding to get it off her chest, she finally revealed the truth: those other girls that accompanied her to the concert had a plan to kill a little girl tonight.

The teenage boys were shocked. They offered to find the girls a ride home. Hope immediately interjected with a resounding "no." Laurie would be livid if they just abandoned her like that, she told Toni. Passing up an opportunity that would have, without a doubt, saved her a lot of future trouble, Toni decided to stick with her friend.[27]

At 11 p.m., Shanda returned from the neighborhood party and asked her father if one of her friends could sleep over. Because he had some plans for a home repair the following morning, he told her another night would be better. Before going to sleep himself, he told Shanda she could watch television for half an hour, but then she'd better climb into bed too.

After the concert was over, Laurie and Melinda regrouped with Toni and Hope, and they made the trip to Steve Sharer's house once again. This time, Toni flat-out refused to leave the car, so, instead, Laurie voluntarily accompanied Hope to retrieve Shanda. Shanda answered the door and told them she just needed a minute to freshen up. While Hope waited with her, Laurie ran back to the car and helped obscure Melinda's presence. She was crouched in the back seat. Laurie quickly covered her with a red blanket.

Hope and Shanda crammed into the car shortly after—Hope behind the wheel this time—and they hit the road. Hope began innocently asking Shanda questions about her relationship with Amanda, hoping to strike a nerve in Melinda. Shanda was notably excited about seeing Amanda and wanted to know where she was and what she was wearing.

They didn't get very far before Melinda sprang from her hiding spot, pulled back Shanda's hair and pressed the dull blade of the knife against her throat.

"Surprise! I guess you didn't know I was here," she exclaimed.[28]

Melinda began to interrogate her about her relationship with Amanda and threatened to slit her throat if she dared lie. Shanda cried and begged the older girl not to hurt her.

When they arrived at the Witches' Castle, Laurie and Melinda, each gripping Shanda's arms, escorted her into the castle and bound her wrists and ankles with a rope. Melinda took off Shanda's rings, and Hope removed her Mickey Mouse watch. Melinda threatened to cut off the younger girl's hair, accusing her of copying her hairstyle in order to impress Amanda. Laurie pointed to a dungeon-like room and told Shanda that there were human bones there and that hers would be next.[29] The girls continued to taunt her with threats while Toni watched passively.

But Shanda was never harmed. Worried about the many cars that were passing by, they ended up forcing her back into the car and searched for another place where they could continue their torment, somewhere more discreet. But first, they made a stop at the gas station to fill up on gas and ask for directions.

Toni walked into the gas station and decided to make a phone call. Not to the police, not even to her parents, but to a boy.

Throughout the phone conversation, she made no mention of the little girl tied up in the backseat, crying and begging to be taken home. After some casual small talk, she hung up and headed back to the car where Shanda remained held captive, once again passing up the perfect opportunity to summon help and prevent the impending tragedy.

The girls headed toward Madison and drove down a rural road near Laurie's home, stopping at the edge of some woods. They all got out of the car, while Melinda and Laurie dragged Shanda out with them. Toni watched as Shanda begged Melinda not to hurt her once more, and Toni gave Shanda a hug and asked Melinda to take the little girl home. Melinda simply told her to shut up.

Laurie forced Shanda to strip down to her t-shirt and panties. Shanda readily complied, and while she stood there, shivering in the cold, Laurie suddenly restrained her from behind and encouraged Melinda to hit her. Melinda violently punched her in the stomach.

"Please stop," Shanda cried. "I have asthma."[30]

Blinded by hate, Melinda ignored Shanda's pleas. She grabbed the 12-year-old by the head and rammed her knee into her face. Shanda went down bleeding.

Shanda was suddenly pinned to the cold ground by both Laurie and Melinda, who attempted to slit her throat using the knife Melinda had brought along. They were having little luck, for the blade was too dull to do any real damage. All they managed to do was jab the knife's pointed end into the back of her neck, leaving a puncture wound.

Toni and Hope watched the entire scene unfold from inside the car in complete horror, playing the radio loud to drown out the sounds of Shanda's screams as she fought desperately for her life. Suddenly, Hope bolted out of the car and ran over to the girls. Toni couldn't quite make out what she was doing, but it appeared as though Hope was helping her friends hold Shanda down. Just as quickly, she was back in the car. She swore to Toni that she was actually trying to help Shanda by pulling her away.

And this is where the stories would conflict.

According to Melinda, Laurie asked her to retrieve the rope. She slipped it around Shanda's neck and began tugging as hard as she could. Shanda began to show signs of struggling. As she gasped for breath and frantically flailed about, she called out to Melinda for help, promising to stay away from Amanda for good this time. But Melinda just told her to shut up and watched as the girl was slowly losing consciousness, the strength that propelled her to fight for her life dwindling. Eventually, she blacked out; all movements ceased, and her limbs went slack.

However, Laurie would later claim that Melinda held one end of the rope, while Laurie grabbed the other, and they both yanked on it together.

Whatever the case may have been, they now had an unconscious girl on their hands. Melinda and Laurie had no idea if she was even alive or dead. Together, they hauled her body into the trunk, and Hope sped toward the Tackett home.

Careful not to make a sound and inadvertently awaken Laurie's parents, all four girls quietly shuffled through the back door, abandoning Shanda in the trunk. The 12-year-old still showed no signs of life.

They tiptoed up to Laurie's bedroom and remained there for a while. To Laurie, this whole thing was just a thrilling escapade, a stark contrast to the remaining girls' nervous whispers and skittish demeanors.

As she comforted the others, she suddenly heard the muffled screams of their young hostage in the trunk, along with her barking dog. Laurie immediately got up, determined to take care of things. She went into the kitchen, grabbed a knife, and stepped back outside, into the cold winter air. She opened the trunk in which Shanda was held prisoner and stabbed her once in the head. She fell silent and stopped moving.

When Laurie headed back to her room, the girls noticed that the noise had stopped and she was covered in blood. To assuage their worries, Laurie decided to read Melinda's stones, an occult ceremony that tells one's future. She assured her friend that everything was going to be all right.

Afterward, she asked the girls if they wanted to go "country cruising." Immediately, Toni and Hope backed out, opting to stay behind. Only Melinda volunteered to come with her.

The Final Breath

It was almost 2:30 in the morning. Laurie and Melinda climbed back into Laurie's car and drove off, all the while trying to decide how to get rid of their hostage once and for all. They whizzed past farmhouses and forests, scoping out places where they could dump Shanda.

At one point, Melinda suggested that they stop. They opened the trunk to see if Shanda had enough strength to climb out of the car herself, hoping they could just run her over and be done with it. But Shanda was too weak to even sit up, so they got back in the car and kept on driving. Then, they thought of another idea. They stopped on a bridge and considered tossing her into the creek. Possibly realizing that someone would see her floating body, they decided against it and continued driving around aimlessly.[31]

Each time they heard Shanda yelling and pounding in the trunk, they would slam on the brakes, make their way around to the rear of the vehicle, and repeatedly strike her with a tire iron to silence her cries. (Later, Melinda would claim she took no part in this.) During one of these vicious beatings, which continued for hours, she was also sodomized with the tire iron.

Shanda was covered in blood from head to toe. She could no longer string together a coherent sentence. She no longer had the strength to defend herself. She was barely holding on. With her eyes rolled back, the only lasting cry for help that would fall from her lips was the only word she could muster: "Mommy."[32]

Back at the Tackett home, Toni and Hope tried to sleep off their anxiety. At one point, Laurie's father entered the bedroom and inquired where his daughter was. They were quick to cover for her—once again, another opportunity passed up to alert someone as to what was really going on.

Once dawn came, Melinda and Laurie returned to the Tackett home with a still-alive Shanda imprisoned in the trunk.

"When we left my house, it was dark, and when we came back, it was light. That's how I know it was a long time," Laurie later said. "It seems like eternity when I try to remember it. It seems like we were out there forever."[33]

They washed up and told the girls how they would strike Shanda with the tire iron every time she made noise, both of them laughing about the whole ordeal.

Laurie and Melinda led the girls out to the back to show them the horrible condition Shanda was in. But Toni refused to look. When Laurie opened the trunk, Hope grabbed a bottle of window cleaner from the trunk and sprayed it all over Shanda's wounds. She stared in fascination as the dazed Shanda sat upright, her eyes rolled to the back of her head. Just like that, Hope went from being a semi-passive onlooker to an active participant.

But the torture couldn't go on forever. They were desperate to finally rid the car of Shanda and end this whole nightmare already. The teenagers piled into the sedan and hit the road once again. Laurie told the others that they would have to finally finish the job this morning and told them of her plan to burn Shanda alive. They stopped at a gas station and bought a two-liter bottle of Pepsi. They emptied it and filled it with gasoline. Hope recommended the perfect place to burn Shanda—Lemon Road, only a 20-minute drive away.

When they arrived, the gravel road was completely deserted. They stopped the car just after they passed a thick patch of woods, and everyone got out except for Toni. Hope helped Laurie wrap Shanda in a red blanket. At this point, Shanda was still drawing breath. They carefully set her down on the side of the road. Shanda was still crying and trying to speak, but her garbled words could hardly form a coherent sentence.

Hope doused her with gasoline. Laurie lit a match and threw it on Shanda.

All of the girls leapt backward as her body erupted in flames. They crammed into the car and began driving away. As the gulf between Shanda's burning, wrapped-up body and the sedan widened, Melinda looked back and noticed that the flames were already dying down.

Melinda immediately demanded that they turn back.

Heeding her concerns, Laurie spun the car around and pulled up beside Shanda. This time, only Melinda got out of the car.

For a few moments, she loomed over her enemy's blazing body, observing the way her tongue flickered in and out of her mouth. Then she poured the remaining gasoline left in the bottle over Shanda and heedlessly tossed the empty bottle to the side. The fire aggressively surged, doubling in intensity, and Melinda quickly scrambled back into the sedan. As they sped away, she laughed and told the other girls she was glad Shanda was dead and permanently out of her and Amanda's lives.

The girls completed that harrowing morning by eating breakfast at McDonald's, where they joked that Shanda resembled the sausages.[34]

Aftermath and Arrests

When Steve Sharer awoke at 7 a.m., only to find his daughter missing, he immediately went into panic mode. Just three hours earlier, when he woke up and stumbled into the kitchen, he noticed something strange. The back door was ajar. He closed and locked it, then quickly peeked into Shanda's bedroom. She wasn't there. Figuring she was sleeping in the basement as she sometimes did, he shrugged it off and went back to bed.

But now, alarms were blaring in his head. He worried that he might have locked Shanda out. He searched the house and around his property, peering into cars, but still saw no sign of Shanda. He called all of the neighbors and her friends, but nobody had seen or heard from Shanda since the night before. He had absolutely no idea what was going on or where she might be. It was unlike Shanda to run away and disappear without telling anybody.

Once it became obvious that Shanda might actually be in imminent danger, he finally gave Jacque a call and broke the news: their beloved daughter was missing.

In no time, Jacque pulled up in front of her ex-husband's Jeffersonville home. By then, the driveway was packed with relatives and friends who had heard about Shanda's disappearance and were equally as concerned for her safety and eager to find her. By noon, they filed a missing person report and began the search for the little girl. With the help of volunteers, they combed through the local neighborhoods, stopped by Hazelwood Middle School, and even called Amanda Heavrin, who claimed she had no idea where Shanda might be—which would later turn out to be a lie.

After dropping off both Hope and Toni at their homes, Melinda and Laurie headed back to Laurie's house and tried to erase any existence of Shanda's former presence in the trunk of the car. They washed the bloody hand prints off of the trunk with a hose. Laurie discovered what appeared to be a chunk of Shanda's head and tossed it out onto the lawn for her dog to eat.[35] They then drove back to New Albany, where they spent the rest of the day together. They ended up meeting with one of Melinda's best friends, Crystal Wathen, and drove around in Laurie's car for a while. Laurie laughed as she gleefully bragged about the gruesome details of Shanda's slow torture and death. She suggested holding a seance to summon Shanda's ghost and ask what it felt like to die in a fire.

At one point, Laurie pulled out the tire iron and beat it against the dashboard to demonstrate how she had struck Shanda.

"She stuck it in my face and told me to smell it," Crystal later said.[36]

They eventually got in touch with Amanda at the mall, where Melinda paged her over the public address system. When Amanda picked up an emergency phone, Melinda revealed over the line that Shanda was dead. Amanda ended up leaving the mall with Melinda, Crystal, and Laurie. They, too, filled her in on the night of torture.

Amanda was internally freaking out but tried to maintain a calm composure. In truth, she didn't believe a word she was hearing. She thought Melinda was playing a sick joke on her, and after she was dropped off at her home, she still didn't notify her family or the authorities.

Back in Madison, Toni and Hope were struggling to cope with what had happened. The first wave of panic rolled over them, and Hope couldn't handle being alone with images of Shanda's mutilated body playing over and over in her mind. She frantically called Laurie.

"I need you guys to come over," she said. "I can't stand being alone. I came into my house and nobody was home and I started screaming."[37]

Toni, too, was freaking out. With nobody to talk to, she met up with Hope, seeking out the comfort of familiarity, knowing that none of her other friends could possibly understand how she was feeling right now.

The two girls hit a pool hall at the Anderson Bowling Alley, a common hangout for teens, where they joined up with two boys from school. Whatever oath to secrecy they had previously made to both Laurie and Melinda went out the window. They were traumatized, scared, and needed to talk to someone. Tearfully, they both told the boys the gist of what had happened the night before and in the early morning.

The boys could hardly believe what they were hearing. They encouraged the girls to go to the police, and the girls both gave them their word.

Toni went to the Rippey home with Hope and told her parents that they witnessed Laurie and another girl kill someone. In the evening of the day of the murder, Hope, along with her parents, brought Toni back home. Immediately, a sobbing Toni ran to her dad, wrapped her arms around him, and said, "You're going to hate me."

"She was crying so much, I thought she was going to tell me that she was pregnant," Clifton Lawrence, Toni's father, later said. "I guess that's the worst thing a father can think his daughter will tell him."[38]

When Hope's parents explained what the girls had just told them, his eyes went wide. He told Toni that they needed to go to the police this instant. There might be a chance that this little girl was still alive, and they might be able to save her. However, Hope's parents declined to go with them, saying they had already made an appointment with an attorney for Monday, and they were going to hide out in a motel for the time being.

After the Rippeys left, Toni and Clifton got into their vehicle and made their way to the police station.

"All the way down the hill to the police station, I was waiting for Toni to tell me she was lying and to turn around and take her back home. I was still thinking she was pregnant."[39]

In the interrogation room, Toni waived her rights and gave her statement to Steve Henry, detailing everything that had happened while downplaying her role in the torture and slaying as much as possible. She was truthful until the end, when she told one little lie—she stated that Laurie and Melinda dropped both Toni and Hope off at home just before they went on to set Shanda on fire, making it seem that she wasn't actually present during the final evil act. The entire time, Toni portrayed herself as an innocent bystander.

Steve Henry looked into missing person reports in Jeffersonville, and, as it turned out, a report had been made earlier in the afternoon, a 12-year-old girl named Shanda Sharer. The investigators practically gaped when they discovered how young the victim really was.

But now that they had a confession, a body, and names, they had sufficient grounds to make some arrests. Less than 15 hours before, the case seemed like a lost cause, but somehow, they managed to solve it in less than a day. The authorities obtained warrants for the arrests of Melinda Loveless and Laurie Tackett and drove all the way to Melinda's home in New Albany.

It was past two in the morning when police forced their way into the Loveless home, barged into Melinda's bedroom and woke up the girls. Within seconds, they escorted the handcuffed teens into their police cruisers.

A few hours earlier, two Indiana State Police officers had carried out one of the most heart-wrenching tasks in a law enforcement officer's career: delivering the awful news to a deceased's family that their loved one has passed.

Steve and Jacque entered a state of shock. They thought that, at most, Shanda had been found injured. They never allowed themselves to consider the unfathomable: that their beloved baby girl had been viciously murdered. They had tried hard to keep tabs on their little girl after they removed her from the negativity associated with Hazelwood. They had watched Shanda revert to her old, bubbly self: the Shanda who stood in front of her bathroom mirror fixing her hair and makeup for hours on end, who participated in extra-curricular activities, who was popular.

And just as they got their old Shanda back, some monsters senselessly took her away.

Investigation

It was Guy M. Townsend, the chief prosecutor for Indiana's Fifth Judicial Circuit, who would be the prosecuting attorney for the case. He had only been in office for a little over a year and didn't yet have much experience in prosecuting cases. Previously, he had been a newspaper reporter with a Ph.D. in British history when he made the drastic decision later in his life to attend law school and become an attorney. Now, he would be prosecuting his first murder case.

It was Sunday afternoon when both Melinda and Laurie made their first court appearances to be arraigned on murder charges before Jefferson Circuit Judge Ted Todd.[40]

Earlier in the morning, Shanda's body was assessed by Kentucky's chief medical examiner, Dr. George R. Nichols II, in Louisville. He had years of experience and was no stranger to having burn victims on his table for examination. Shanda's body would be in reliable hands, and her loved ones would undoubtedly find out what really happened to her.

In his findings, he noted the ligature marks that remained around her wrists and ankles, leading him to conclude that she had been bound with a rope. Her upper body had severe third- and fourth-degree burns. She had lacerations on her legs consistent with knife cuts, and she had been stabbed and repeatedly bludgeoned with a blunt instrument. She had also been sodomized with this same blunt instrument (later identified as the tire iron) three and a half inches into her anus, which caused substantial damage to her anal cavity. However, she survived the torture and was still alive when she was set on fire. He could confirm that she was alive because her upper airway was coated with black soot from inhaling the fumes. He concluded in the autopsy report that her cause of death was burns and inhalation of smoke.

Although the head and anal cavity injuries she had sustained during the torture were severe, she could have recovered from them had she not been set on fire—she only would have required a colostomy. If, at any point, one of the girls had interceded, Shanda would probably still be here today. This very chilling reality would come to haunt Shanda's parents for years.

⁓

On January 16, more than 300 mourners gathered at Our Lady of Perpetual Help's chapel for Shanda's funeral service. Previously, Jacque and Steve had picked out the casket that would house their daughter's body forever; now, they waited inside the funeral home to see their daughter's body. They had no idea what was waiting for them but had gotten very emotional after seeing the extent of her injuries. She was burned beyond recognition. She didn't even look human.

It would have to be a closed casket funeral due to her body's terrible condition. Among the hundreds of mourners attending Shanda's funeral were family members, old friends from Hazelwood, and most of the student body from Our Lady of Perpetual Help. The school banded together to grieve the loss of a friend, peer, and loved one.

"We're going to miss her. I just can't believe she's gone," said April O'Rafferty, a student at Our Lady of Perpetual Help. "It's just so hard to let go." Even though they hadn't known Shanda for very long, it was a poignant feeling that they would no longer see Shanda's smiling face in the school hallways. They had accepted her as quickly as she came, and, just like that, she was gone.

Hazelwood student Brandi Dalton said, "She was a good friend. I just miss her."

The Rev. John Fink stood before the hundreds of grievers that Wednesday and told them to extend their hands outward. When they obliged, he asked, "Can you let Shanda go?"

He then instructed them to imagine that they were setting a butterfly, Shanda, into a new life. "Somewhere along that line you have to let go of that butterfly, of that life," said the priest. Toward the end of the service, he read aloud an excerpt from a poem that Steve Sharer carried around in his wallet titled "Why God Made Little Girls."

"God made the world with its towering trees, majestic mountains and restless seas and then paused and He said, it needs one more thing, someone to laugh and dance and sing ... so God made little girls."[41]

She was laid to rest in Big Spring Cemetery in Kentucky, right next to her grandmother.

Students from Madison High School also felt the same shock and disbelief that their own would be involved in such a heinous crime. But nobody was surprised to hear that Laurie was being accused of murdering a little girl. Most students at Madison High School were aware of Laurie's grim reputation and her supposed involvement in witchcraft and the occult. But Toni and Hope were accepted and well liked among the student body. There were no warning signs with them.

"Hope was real shy. From what I know, this was the first time she'd met this girl, and she tried to kill her? I can't believe it," said Roy Newby, the boyfriend of Hope's older sister. "And Toni Lawrence, she's scared of a bug. I can't believe she would even be in the car. You throw a frog at her and she'd scream."[42]

While Laurie and Melinda were now in custody, Toni and Hope had so far evaded charges for their role in Shanda's slaying. The media at the time was still not aware that both Hope and Toni were actually present at the time Shanda's life was snuffed out by flames.

When the news broke about the grisly murder of a 12-year-old girl committed by local teenage girls, the shock was enough to numb the towns of New Albany and Madison. The tight-knit communities that never experienced violent crime felt their security being threatened.

"When you first hear it, it stuns everybody. I guess we never think something like that will happen in a small town like this. Pretty frightening, isn't it?" said Madison resident Damon Welch, as he worked the griddle at his restaurant.[43]

Melinda and Laurie already had public defenders appointed for them. They both stood before Judge Ted R. Todd and pleaded not guilty to the murder, rejecting the plea bargain offered by Townsend that, if they pleaded guilty to just one count of murder, he would only seek a sentence of 60 years for both of them. Townsend stated that, under Indiana state law, both of the teenage girls would be tried as adults.

A month had gone by since Melinda and Laurie's arrests, and Hope and Toni were still stonewalling the police. By June, the state was left with no other option but to slap Hope and Toni with charges of murder, arson, battery with a deadly weapon, aggravated battery, criminal confinement, and intimidation.

On the same day, Melinda and Laurie faced new charges. On top of murder, they now stood accused of arson and child molestation, among other crimes. Prosecutor Guy Townsend also made it known to the public that he would consider seeking the death penalty for Melinda and Laurie as well.

On April 22, as part of a plea bargain, Toni pleaded guilty to criminal confinement in exchange for the rest of the charges against her being dropped. She also agreed to testify against the other girls. Toni was facing six to 20 years in prison. Indiana state law for criminal confinement carries a prison term of 10 years; however, mitigating factors could deduct four years, whereas aggravating factors could add an extra 10 years.[44]

The plea bargain for both Melinda and Laurie still stood. If they both took responsibility for their actions and pleaded guilty, Townsend stated that he would drop all of the other charges except for murder, and they would receive 60 years in prison. They would most likely serve only half of that time, due to Indiana's law stating that inmates get one day taken off their sentence for good behavior each day. Both of the girls' defense teams objected. But to Townsend, this was non-negotiable. He needed to find a way to get them to accept the plea deal. Deciding to pull out the big stick, he filed for the death penalty in the second week of June.[45]

Under Indiana state law at the time, the minimum eligible age for capital punishment was 16 (pushed to 18 on July 1, 2003), and the death penalty remains legal to this day.[46] In Indiana state history, of 133 people who had been executed, only three were underage. This made Townsend's decision an especially bold move due to the extremely low success rate of executing minors. In fact, the last minor in the state of Indiana to be sent to death row was Paula Cooper, a 15-year-old African American who stabbed 78-year-old Bible teacher Ruth Pelke to death in Gary, Indiana, back in 1985, making her the nation's youngest death row inmate.

At the time, the minimum age for the death penalty was 10 years old, a law that a *New York Times* editorial deemed "medieval."[47] After an international outcry, which included an organized campaign for an appeal started by attorney Monica Foster that garnered more than two million signatures, as well as a plea for clemency by Pope John Paul II, the Indiana legislature passed a new bill that would raise the minimum age for the death penalty from 10 to 16 years old in 1987. Two years after the new bill, Paula Cooper's death sentence was commuted to 60 years in prison.[48]

Neither of the teenage defendants' court-appointed attorneys were legally qualified to represent them due to their lack of experience in handling death penalty cases. Although Judge Todd elected to keep them on the case, the girls would have new lead defense counsels.[49] It was determined that Russ Johnson would represent Melinda and Wil Goering would defend Laurie.

With the threat of death now looming over their heads like a dark cloud, Guy Townsend gave them one last chance to accept his final plea bargain. If they pleaded guilty to murder, criminal confinement, and arson, he would drop the rest of the charges against them and withdraw the death penalty. They would only be facing a sentencing range of 30 to 60 years. As part of the deal, Melinda and Laurie would also have to agree to testify against each other.

The girls' defense teams were scrambling to find a solution, but, admittedly, there wasn't one. The evidence gathered against them was too potent, not to mention Toni's damning eyewitness testimony. If they were convicted, which was a near certain possibility, both of them could find themselves on death row. They needed the death penalty off the table.

After months of being backed into a corner, Melinda and Laurie popped under the pressure and pleaded guilty.[50]

Out of all four girls, Hope Rippey was the only one who had yet to fold to Townsend's plea bargain. Since she was under 16, she was not eligible for the death penalty. Her trial was set for March 1993.

Melinda's Sentencing Hearing

Melinda's attorneys knew that the odds were against them. After she had pled guilty to possibly one of the most heinous murders committed in Indiana, they knew they would have to come up with a plan to soften the heart of Judge Todd if they wanted any chance of achieving the lightest sentence possible. They, along with Melinda's family, decided that if they wanted to help Melinda at all, the family would need to testify about her horrible childhood, filled with abuse and neglect. They also knew they would have to diminish Melinda's role in the murder as much as possible and portray Laurie in a negative light; they would need to push the idea that Melinda simply wanted to beat up the girl and Laurie was the aggressor. It was Laurie who escalated it to torture and murder.

Melinda's sentencing hearing began on December 14, 1992. Television trucks were parked along the street outside of the Jefferson County courthouse in Madison, Indiana, where dozens of camera crews and reporters eagerly waited for her to make an appearance. She then emerged with her wrists bound together by silver handcuffs, wearing a blue blouse coupled with beige pants. The wind blew through her long, beautiful curls as she swiftly walked the short distance from the Jefferson County Jail to the courthouse, accompanied by her attorneys and two sheriffs. Reporters besieged her and bombarded her with questions; she said nothing as she disappeared into the building.

In the courtroom where Melinda, her family, and Shanda's loved ones sat among the 50 spectators, both groups silently praying for completely opposite outcomes, prosecutor Guy Townsend did not start off on a lighthearted note.

"Shanda Sharer is dead because she dared to be a friend to Melinda

Loveless' girlfriend," Townsend began before diving right into his opening statement.[51]

He told the judge that this tragic tale all started when Shanda made the move from Louisville to New Albany and enrolled in Hazelwood Junior High. Shanda first crossed paths with Melinda Loveless when Shanda had gotten into an altercation with her lover, Amanda Heavrin. The two were placed in detention together, but they ended up becoming friends, thus sparking the first sign of Melinda's envy. He described how Melinda had frequently confronted Shanda and discussed wanting her dead with her friends.

He then went into the details of how Melinda recruited three other teenage girls to entice Shanda from her father's home under the pretense that she would be meeting with Amanda, but instead she was terrorized, stabbed, strangled, and severely beaten for several hours, to the point of being bloodied from head to toe and incoherent.

"One time, they opened up the trunk and her eyes were rolled up in her head. She could not articulate and all she could say was 'Mommy,'" he said.[52]

By morning, she would be burned to death on an isolated backroad.

As the lit match dropped onto Shanda's gasoline-soaked, wrapped-up body, "Shanda was still alive, her arm came up," said Townsend.[53]

He told the judge about Melinda forcing Laurie Tackett to turn the vehicle around because she wanted to make sure that Shanda was "burning all the way" and how she got out of the car and poured the remainder of the gasoline on Shanda's body. He described how she had laughed about the murder afterward and expressed joy that Shanda was finally out of her life, never once displaying any remorse for the little girl she caused to suffer and die.

The state then showed a video and photographs of Shanda's charred body, which brought a court aide to tears.

State Police Detective Steve Henry testified for the state that after Melinda's arrest, he allowed her to make one phone call, so she contacted her mother. Catching snippets of their brief conversation, he heard her say over the phone, "I meant to feel good and I beat her up, but it went too far."[54]

Over the course of the next few days, the courtroom heard gut-wrenching testimony from Melinda's family members as they narrated the horrid circumstances that they all had to grow up in. Michelle, the eldest Loveless sister, described her dysfunctional family and the sexual, physical, and mental abuse they were all subjected to at the hands of their alcoholic father.

"When she got involved with Amanda Heavrin we told her she was too young to be involved with anyone, male or female," she told the court. "But she said, 'I like Amanda because she reminds me of Larry Loveless.'"[55]

Edie and Teddie, Melinda's cousins who babysat the girls when they themselves were just children, also attested to Melinda's horrible upbringing with their own graphic tales of the sexual abuse that Larry had exposed them to.

Lifespring Mental Health Services therapist Mina Thevenin testified that after Shanda's murder, she had interviewed Melinda along with her sisters about the sexual abuse allegations. Melinda adamantly denied ever being abused by her father and was unsure about believing her sisters' claims.

The heart-wrenching details of Melinda's past failed to pull a sympathetic string in Jacque's heart.

"Millions of children have been abused and have not become murderers," she asserted. "She may have had a difficult home life. From what I heard today, she probably did. But that does not excuse her for what she did to my daughter."[56]

Amanda Heavrin was also called to testify on Melinda's behalf. She said Melinda did admit to her that Larry molested her growing up and "that's why she hates boys." She also claimed that Melinda had told her she wanted to take Shanda home after beating her up, but it was Laurie who insisted that they "finish the job."[57]

Laurie Tackett, as per the plea deal, was called to the stand to testify against Melinda. When questioned about who sodomized Shanda with the tire iron, Laurie denied responsibility.

Johnson began grilling her about her past involvement in witchcraft and the occult. Laurie denied that it was something she actually believed in. She stated that she was never a devil worshiper, but rather she used it as a facade to "try to portray myself that way so people would leave me alone about my past religion."

Johnson also inquired if she had ever told a friend that she wanted to know what it would be like to burn someone alive.

"No, I didn't say that," she answered.

"You know what it feels like now, don't you?" he asked.

"Yes," she replied softly.[58]

Steve Sharer said during the five-day hearing's closing that ever since the moment officers showed up at his door asking for Shanda's dental records to identify her burned body, his life was filled with pain and anguish. "This was my only child," he said. "I've suffered from the first day. I wish you could feel how I feel. There's a big void in my life."[59]

Laurie's Sentencing

Laurie Tackett's sentencing hearing would commence two weeks after Melinda's, and the ongoing question as to who was the true ringleader in Shanda's torture and death continued to be the subject of dispute. As expected, Laurie's defense team made certain to push as much of the blame onto Melinda as possible and paint a picture of Laurie as a mere pawn of Melinda's jealous rage.

Now 18, Laurie would testify that she was subjected to all sorts of different abuse starting from age six and continuing until she was 16. Displaying very little, if any, emotion, she claimed that her mother would physically attack her whenever she resisted her attempts to indoctrinate her by forcing her to attend a fundamentalist church that held service four days a week.

"So you're saying that you were hit four times a week and once a week you were strangled because you didn't want to go to church, correct?" asked Prosecutor Townsend skeptically.

"Yes," Laurie responded. "I don't have any memories of sunny days. All my memories are black like night."[60]

She also revealed that she had been sexually abused by a male cousin between the ages of six and 11, although she obstinately remained tight-lipped when repeatedly questioned about his identity, claiming she didn't want to cause any pain or shame for his family. Eventually, the court allowed her to write her abuser's name on a piece of paper which was handed to the judge.

Furthermore, she disclosed that she had been raped by a male classmate at the age of 16 after she had inhaled fumes from a bottle of gasoline, causing the memories surrounding the incident to be a little hazy.

"I was dizzy and lightheaded," she said.[61]

Laurie Tackett testified that the best thing to ever happen to her was going to prison and the worst thing to happen to her was being born.

Ellen O'Connor, in her opening statement, described Laurie as someone who had been victimized all of her life. "The public looks at this murder and asks how it could have happened," she said. "Clearly these are not normal children. They come from dysfunctional homes. People say that's not an excuse. Well, it's not an excuse. It's an explanation."[62]

Melinda Loveless, again as part of the plea agreement she made to testify against Laurie, took the stand and pointed the finger at Laurie for her role in the final act of torture. Laurie had always denied being the one to strike the match that set Shanda's body on fire. Instead, she claimed that it spontaneously combusted as she was leaning over Shanda's gasoline-soaked body while holding a cigarette between her fingers.

A member of Laurie's defense team, Ellen M. O'Connor, tried to present photos of Shanda's charred body to Melinda so she could point out the exact locations she saw Laurie inflicting the lacerations on her legs. That's when she became emotional, sobbing, "Oh, God!" when her eyes settled on the photographs.[63]

The defense called two witnesses who once served some time at the Jefferson County Jail with Melinda. Both testified that she relished her notoriety and thought of herself as something of a celebrity in the jail due to the massive media attention that the murder had drawn nationally and internationally. She once handed out an autograph and kept photos of herself and Shanda plastered around her cell. Under her own picture she wrote, "Most Wanted." Over Shanda's school photo she scrawled, "So young. So pretty. Had to die early."[64]

Defense attorney Ellen O'Connor tried to convince the jury that Melinda was trying to diminish her culpability, making Laurie out to be the dominant one so as to evade a harsh sentence. In fact, it was Melinda who had ranted and raved to everybody about how much she wanted Shanda dead. Laurie didn't even know the girl.

∽

January 5, 1993, marked the day that Laurie and Melinda would learn just how long they would be locked up. Both the prosecution and defense would be granted one last statement in an attempt to sway the judge's final decision. Townsend took that opportunity, arguing that Melinda's guilt didn't necessarily negate Laurie's role in Shanda's murder. Laurie was just as culpable as the other girl.

"Melinda Loveless wanted somebody killed, and Laurie Tackett wanted to kill somebody. They each got what they wanted," he contended. "It wasn't until Melinda Loveless' hatred combined with Laurie Tackett's bloodlust that Shanda Sharer's fate was sealed."[65]

He spoke about how it was Melinda's motive of jealousy that fueled the horrendous crime, but there was no explanation for why Laurie wanted Shanda killed—and that's what made her more dangerous.

"That Laurie Tackett was willing to take the life of a complete stranger is a far greater horror than the fact that Melinda Loveless was willing to take the life of someone she hated," he said. "Laurie Tackett is a murderer precisely because she holds the lives of other people in such low regard that she is willing to snuff out the life of a twelve-year-old stranger to see how it feels to burn someone alive."[66]

When it was the defense team's turn to argue one last time in their client's favor, defense attorney Goering made sure to shift all accountability to Melinda.

He argued that Laurie "was a weapon used by Melinda Loveless for Loveless' purposes. Who is more responsible for the damage done by the tiger—the tiger or the person who put the tiger in the house?"[67]

He pleaded for the judge to be lenient with Laurie and demonstrate the compassion and empathy that she could not feel so that she could get the psychological help she so direly needed. Townsend implored the judge to think about the little girl's life that was lost and all the things she had been deprived of because of Melinda Loveless and Laurie Tackett.

"Laurie Tackett being born wasn't the worst thing to happen to Laurie Tackett. Laurie Tackett being born was the worst thing to happen to Shanda Sharer," said Townsend, who then asked the judge to impose the maximum sentence—nothing less than 60 years.[68]

Laurie was then escorted from the courtroom, and after a short recess, Melinda entered through the exact same door that Laurie had exited. She sat down at the defense table, her muscles tense as she nervously waited to hear her sentence.

Immediately, she began to sob when Judge Todd sentenced her to the maximum of 60 years in prison. As soon as the sentence was announced, at least two dozen of Shanda's supporters—including her family—began applauding loudly within the courtroom, prompting the judge to bang his gavel to silence the room. On the opposite end of the rowdy courtroom, Margie let out a moan of anguish and left the courtroom in tears.

Judge Todd told a weeping Melinda about her lengthy sentence,

"You may think this is a very long sentence, but you still have the power to turn your life into something useful and good—something that Shanda Sharer cannot do."[69]

After Melinda was ushered out, Laurie was brought back in. She received the same sentence. She shook her head slowly but maintained the stolid expression that had been etched into her features since the beginning of the legal proceedings.

Half an hour after the sentencing hearing was concluded, Jacque was still shedding bittersweet tears. She was more than pleased with the sentence her daughter's killers received, but it still did not mend her broken heart. "I keep thinking that I want my baby back but I can never have her back," she said.[70]

Steve Sharer, Shanda's father, expressed satisfaction with the sentencing. "I feel like I've been walking on eggshells the past few weeks. I feel so much better now that they got the maximum. I feel like I can breathe again. I feel no sympathy for the families of those girls. They can still visit their child in jail. We'll never see Shanda again."[71]

Toni's Sentencing

Toni's sentencing hearing began on January 26, a couple of weeks after Melinda and Laurie were handed their near-life sentences. As terrible as Toni's reputation was now, with her name being tied to possibly one of the most gruesome crimes in Indiana state history, people still viewed her through a somewhat more sympathetic lens compared to Melinda, Laurie, and even Hope. Her attorney, Paul Baugh, had invested lots of time in building up her defense, and he was confident that she would get off easy.

In his opening statement, he did his best to depict Toni as a timid teenage girl who was simply in the wrong place at the wrong time. He talked about the instance in which Toni had tried to convince Melinda to bring Shanda back home before things escalated any further and was simply told to "shut up," causing Toni to recede into her shell and continue to be passive throughout the entire night and early morning because she feared for her own life. He made sure to emphasize that Toni never once participated in or encouraged any of the mental torture and injuries that were inflicted on Shanda. Furthermore, she was the first to report the crime to the police on the day Shanda was burned to death and remained fully cooperative.[72]

But Townsend wasn't having any of it, contending that it was Toni's inaction that also made her complicit in Shanda's killing. "Just distancing yourself isn't enough," he said. "She had an obligation to prevent this from going forward and she didn't."[73]

He highlighted the numerous occasions Toni could have used to escape the situation before it happened or call for help, from the moment when the boys at the punk rock concert offered her a ride home, to when the girls stopped at the gas station after they left the Witches' Castle, to when she spent hours with Hope at the Tackett home while Melinda and Laurie were driving around. She failed to notify anybody about what was going on. There were no excuses for being afraid and docile during these moments, argued Townsend.

Defense attorney Baugh began to call several witnesses who would corroborate Toni's supposed good character. Among these witnesses were a couple of teachers who testified that Toni was a shy, unproblematic child who made above-average grades. Her former French teacher commented that Toni was "the person I'd have least picked to be involved in something like this."[74]

Clifton Lawrence, Toni's father, also took the stand to testify on behalf of his daughter. He stated that even after Melinda and Laurie were thrown in jail, Toni's fears didn't waver. She ended up dropping out of school and was too anxious to even set foot out of her house without the company of a relative. Every night, he said, she slept in her parents' bedroom in fear that Melinda and Laurie's friends would come after her and kill her for turning them in to the police.

Melinda and Laurie were also called to testify against Toni on the stand. Their statements aligned. They agreed that Toni never was involved in the actual torture and killing of Shanda and that she seemed very frightened and in shock the whole time. On a few occasions, she had even screamed and cried.

"She was there but in mind she didn't want to be there. She was scared," said Melinda on the stand.[75]

After a brief cross-examination between Townsend and Toni, he finally dismissed her from the stand after getting her to acknowledge that she had allowed numerous opportunities to summon help for Shanda to slip by.

At the end of the hearing, reading directly from a written statement, she delivered an apology to Shanda's parents. "I'm so sorry about your little girl," she read aloud. "I know you can never forgive me. But I want you to know it has been a living hell for me. I was terrified. Seeing her tortured and burning is punishment itself."

She then continued, "I know you have the right to hate me. I wish I could bring her back, but I can't. All I can say is how sorry I am."[76]

Jacque, who appeared as a victim's advocate, was allowed to blow off some steam when she rebuffed Toni's apology. "Toni could have saved my daughter's life at any time but she chose not to. She should get the same sixty years as the others. Her disregard for human life is a crime that cannot be taken lightly."[77]

In his closing statement, Townsend once again insisted that Toni had a duty to report what was happening and had happened to someone when she had multiple opportunities to do so. She failed to, however, and for that, she should still be held accountable just like the other girls, as her nonintervention still sealed Shanda's fate.

In the defense's closing statement, Baugh once again stood up for Toni. "Toni feared for her life. She didn't have it within herself to overcome the fear she was experiencing." He further contended that the girl was "at the wrong place, at the wrong time, with the wrong people."[78]

At the end of the day, Judge Todd was not particularly moved by the defense's arguments. He told Toni that due to the gruesome nature of the crime, and her knowledge that the murder was going to take place prior to meeting Shanda and failing to report it to anyone, anything less than 20 years would serve as an injustice to Shanda. He sentenced her to 20 years in prison.

Hope's Sentencing

Hope would eventually follow in the rest of the girls' footsteps and plead guilty in April to the following charges against her: felony murder, arson and criminal confinement. Her sentencing hearing was initially going to be held at the Jefferson County Circuit Court like the others', but, at the request of her lawyer, it was relocated to St. Joseph County Superior Court to escape the widespread publicity the case had drawn, which could potentially inject bias into her sentencing.

Unlike her good friend Toni, who was guilty of failing to stop the crime, Hope couldn't play the innocent bystander card. She did contribute to the brutal torture that led to Shanda's death. It was Hope who had agreed to lure Shanda from her home; it was Hope who joined in on taunting the 12-year-old at the Witches' Castle; it was Hope who sprayed cleaning spray over her wounds; and, lastly, and it was Hope who guided the girls to Lemon Road, where she would eventually soak Shanda's body with gasoline. It was the last thing Shanda would see before her body went up in flames. The teen had repeatedly lent a hand in Shanda's slow torture and killing, and those hands were most definitely not clean. Now she faced between 30 and 60 years in prison. Even so, her attorney, Darryl Auxier, was confident that he could somehow persuade Judge Jeanne Jourdan to sentence her to the lower end of that range.

The sentencing hearing began on June 1, 1993. As per usual, it opened with prosecutor Guy Townsend outlining all of the reasons why Hope was just as guilty as the other girls involved in the slaying due to her active participation. He mentioned the fact that Hope knew about Laurie's plans to kill a little girl on the night of January 10 before they even picked up Melinda and still agreed to join her anyway. He mentioned that Hope was an eager and willing participant who threatened Shanda with a knife and stole her jewelry. He also pointed out that Hope had sprayed window cleaner on her body to test its reaction to blood, a sadistic telltale sign indicating Hope's enjoyment of the whole thing.

And if that didn't make matters worse, he said, Hope "was disgusted" that Melinda didn't lend Hope and Laurie a hand in unloading Shanda from the trunk and dousing her in gasoline.

Quoted from Hope's statement to police about Melinda, she said, "I don't know why she didn't help. She started the whole thing."[79]

In order to assist his client, defense attorney Darryl Auxier had hired Dr. Michael Sheehan, who spent 10 hours picking Hope A. Rippey's brain. What he gleaned from her personality and thought process on the night and morning of Shanda's murder would conflict with the prosecutor's demonizing tale.

His findings would lead him to describe Hope as a "tender, shy person" who was a "reluctant participant" that sought the approval of her peer group. She especially did not want to let down her longtime friend Laurie Tackett, whom she had trouble saying no to as the older girl filled a sort of "big sister" role in her life.

The psychologist maintained that Hope was simply swept up in circumstances beyond her control and that the then-15-year-old couldn't have fathomed that the night would ultimately lead to Shanda's death. She thought, if anything, they were just going to give Shanda a good scare and then bring her home unscathed. But once the confrontation escalated into violence and it dawned on her that Laurie and Melinda intended to kill Shanda, she went into panic mode and "experienced a diminished capacity to function."

"There's no doubt in my mind she had no intention to harm her, even though she poured the gasoline on her," he said.

He asserted that Hope had only reluctantly agreed to be the one to pour the gasoline on Shanda after refusing once when the ever-intimidating Laurie insisted. "At that point she's in a state of shock," said the psychologist. "She was having a very difficult time knowing what to do." He blamed Hope's actions on peer pressure.[80]

The only other witness Hope's attorney would call to the stand on Hope's behalf was Carl Rippey. He described his teenage daughter as something of a "peacemaker" during family tensions within the Rippey household, including arguments between her parents and fistfights between her brothers.

"She would try and be a mediator and separate us and send us to our rooms. Then she would talk to Gloria and I separately," said Carl, who divorced his wife in 1984 but rekindled their romance two years later. "She would tell me to drop it, and I'm sure that's what she told Gloria," he said.[81]

On the afternoon of June 2, the last day of the sentencing hearing, Hope Rippey's family were the first to file into the third-floor courtroom. When Hope entered the now-packed room of spectators, she shot her parents and 18-year-old sister, Tina, a timid smile and sank into the wooden chair at the defense table.

Before Hope's sentencing, Shanda's parents had the opportunity to speak.

Steve Sharer described his daughter as a "daddy's girl."

"Now all the special things we do together are gone forever," he said, then turned to Hope. "There is no way you can understand the love. May you rot in hell for the rest of your murdering life."

Jacque then played a couple of videotapes for the court displaying the highlights of Shanda's short life. Clips of her enthusiastically leading cheers at a basketball game and gleefully screaming when being splashed with water at a pool party played on the television screen. Hope broke into uncontrollable sobs.

Jacque told the court that her daughter was one of God's most precious creations and that Hope "isn't capable of remorse of any kind" and "doesn't even deserve to breathe air."[82]

To a courtroom full of spectators, Superior Court Judge Jeanne

Jourdan made her final statement on her thoughts and reasoning regarding the case and testimony that had been presented to her during the past couple of days, taking into careful consideration the substantial role Hope played in Shanda's death. She rejected Dr. Michael Sheehan's theory that Hope allowed Shanda's prolonged torture and death out of peer pressure and fear of the other girls, citing the many opportunities she had to get help but didn't.

Judge Jourdan told the court that Hope Rippey "thinks of herself as tough on the outside and tender on the inside. Neither are true."[83]

She proceeded to say that "Hope had choices. There were avenues for escape, ways to help herself, ways to help Shanda. Her lack of mercy, of tender courage, is a horrifying lesson to us all."[84]

Shortly after the judge's speech, the 16-year-old's tears would be followed by those of Gloria and Tina Rippey when Judge Jourdan imposed the maximum sentence on Hope Rippey, but suspended 10 of the 60 years. Hope would serve those remaining 10 years during her probation.

On the right side of the courtroom, opposite where Hope's relatives were sitting, Shanda's family could only breathe a sigh of relief.

Both Steve Sharer and Jacque Vaught (she had remarried after Shanda's death) stated later that they were satisfied with Judge Jourdan's decision to give Hope the maximum sentence. Jacque revealed just how tremendously her daughter's death had shattered her once-comfortable life. She was currently out of work, had been hospitalized for a suicide attempt and was now on medication to cope. She stated that she was not the same person that she was before Shanda was ruthlessly killed.

But at the end of the dark tunnel, a sliver of light beamed through. Her eldest daughter, Paije, was pregnant. She was going to be a grandmother soon.

Prosecutor Guy Townsend was particularly tired after scoring four major victories in the cases he prosecuted. He too felt deeply impacted by all of the details and evidence that had come to light.

"I'm numb. After a year and a half there isn't anybody involved that hasn't been affected." He said that the judge's decision to hand down the maximum sentence to Hope was certainly not an easy one, but at the end of the day, she made the right choice while also finding mitigating factors to suspend some of the time.[85]

To everyone, it seemed like justice had finally been served, and while the individuals who were particularly close to the case weren't even remotely ready to move on and forget about this vicious crime that pierced the hearts of Madison and New Albany locals, it did move them a few steps forward in the healing process.

Afterword

On January 11, 1992, the world would come to find out how monstrous children could be.

To this day, Shanda's story continues to make people's blood run cold—however, the chill comes not so much from its sheer animal-like cruelty. The goosebumps rise because the crime was committed not by an adult predator as one would normally expect, but by the girls next door. It is a harsh reality to accept.

But what could possibly possess these teenagers to abduct a girl, stab and beat her, sexually assault her, and light her on fire? Although there are many complex factors that need to be considered, the ultimate answer, their defense attorneys and psychologists argued, stems from their deeply traumatic upbringings.

As was explained throughout this chapter, at least three of the four girls were products of violent and broken homes. Psychologists who closely followed the case all agreed that children who are subjected to abuse are much more likely to repeat that cycle of abuse than kids who grow up in healthy and loving home environments. However, most children who are victims of abuse are able to come to terms with their past trauma and don't feel the urge to express their bottled-up pain, frustration and hurt in violent ways, especially if they undergo therapy.

What sets Shanda's killers apart from other child abuse victims who would never conceive of doing something as horrible to another human being?

Both Melinda and Laurie were riddled with mental health issues, particularly borderline personality disorder (BPD), which, according to the *DSM-5*, entails extreme fear of abandonment, sudden mood swings, impulsivity and recklessness, and unstable and stormy relationships with others. Many, if not most, sufferers of BPD have been physically or sexually abused in their childhood and experienced abandonment by a close loved one.

As we know, Melinda was undoubtedly dealt an extremely unhappy childhood at the hands of a sadistic man who sexually preyed on both women and children. He most likely forced his perversion onto Melinda as well, even though she would later deny having any sort of memory of being molested growing up. After Melinda was abandoned by her father, to whom she was very attached, Amanda became her new object of affection. When she was jilted by Amanda, it was only a matter of time before Melinda would erupt.

Dr. Eric Engum, the psychologist who evaluated Laurie and testified on her behalf, said that her home life impaired her self-esteem and caused her to lose the ability to have empathy for others. He claimed that she had lost her conscience and "the angel on her shoulder was absent" on the night of Shanda's murder.[86]

Dr. Nancy Moore, a Louisville psychologist, called fundamentalism a "breeding ground" for borderlines. "You have to behave in a certain way in order to be considered good. If you act differently, you are evil."[87] Laurie's fascination with witchcraft and the occult was her way of rebelling against the fundamentalist ideologies that had been imposed on her throughout her life.

And what does one make of a girl who was peer pressured into participating and another who was too afraid to speak up and lift a finger to stop what was happening? Psychologists would later blame it on "mob mentality."

Dr. Richard Coomer, another Louisville psychiatrist, stated that during the night of Shanda's abduction, each girl likely felt that they had crossed the point of no return.

"For one, it may have been the kidnapping. For another, the beating. But there was a point where each of them should have said: 'Oops, I messed up. I made a mistake in getting involved. This is enough,'" he said. "But they didn't, and once they crossed that line, they felt they were in too much trouble."[88]

When kids commit homicide, they tend to overkill. Boys are 20 times more likely to kill than girls, but girls that do kill typically have a male accomplice. That's what makes Shanda's murder so unique—there was no male presence; it was carried out by adolescent females. When a murder is being committed by more than one person, a group mentality kicks in and each member feels obligated to "do their part." Girls are especially more likely than boys to seek group acceptance.

And how a girl like Toni can just sit by and watch passively while a helpless 12-year-old is being punched, strangled, stabbed, and set on fire may likely be attributed to a phenomenon called the bystander effect, otherwise known as "bystander apathy." This idea is founded upon the social psychological theory that in the event of an emergency, when someone's life is in immediate danger, the more bystanders that are present, the less likely it is that anyone is going to intervene to help the victim based on the belief that others will take action instead.

Social psychology researchers Bibb Latané and John Darley conducted several experiments to explore this theory. They have concluded that there are five characteristics of emergencies that affect bystanders:

1. Emergencies involve a threat of harm or actual harm
2. Emergencies are unusual and rare
3. The type of action differs from situation to situation
4. Emergencies cannot be predicted or expected
5. Emergencies require immediate action

As a result of these characteristics, bystanders will undergo a cognitive and behavioral process as follows:

1. Notice that something is going on
2. Interpret the situation as being an emergency
3. Feel a degree of responsibility
4. Form of assistance
5. Implement the action choice

The degree of responsibility felt by the bystander is largely dependent on their relationship to the victim, whether they think the victim is deserving of assistance, and the competency of the bystander. According to Latané and Darley, there are two categories of assistance: direct intervention, meaning physically helping the victim, and indirect intervention, like calling the police.[89]

Karma would soon catch up with Larry Loveless too. On the one-year anniversary of Shanda's murder, Larry would be charged with sex crimes committed against his three daughters and two nieces, all of whom were children at the time of the offenses. He was now facing six counts of sodomy, three counts of rape and two counts of sexual battery.[90] After serving more than two years in jail awaiting trial, he was freed after a plea agreement.[91] In 1998, he died after being struck by an automobile.

Steve Sharer never found a way to cope with his daughter's tragic loss. He drank himself to death in 2005 and was buried in Big Springs Methodist Church Cemetery in Kentucky alongside Shanda.

Jacque, on the other hand, has used Shanda to stay strong. After her daughter's death, she found a new purpose in life: becoming a victim's advocate in the prosecutor's office in Floyd County, Indiana. She now serves as Shanda's only voice and has since delivered many speeches titled "No Silence About Violence" in the hope that Shanda's story will impact the lives of many others and teach other kids to always stand up for victims no matter what.[92]

All four girls who were convicted of contributing to Shanda's murder one way or another have been granted something that many child killers serving time in prison could only dream of: a second chance.

Toni Lawrence was released from prison on December 14, 2000, at the age of 24, followed by Hope Rippey in 2006 after serving only 14 years in prison.[93] Laurie Tackett walked free on January 11, 2018, on the 26th anniversary of Shanda's death.[94]

Melinda would be the last one to get her first taste of the outside world in 23 years on September 5, 2019. During her time in prison, Melinda appeared to demonstrate impressive strides in her own personal growth. She joined the Indiana Canine Assistant Network (ICAN) program, in which she trained dogs for the disabled as well as traumatized and abused children who show up to court. Charlie Petrizzo, a burn victim who supplies dogs to the ICAN program, interviewed Melinda and was taken aback by her development. Melinda confided that training these dogs was her way of giving back to the community and has helped her learn to love and value a living being's life. Charlie decided to show Jacque the tape of the interview and she too was impressed. An unprecedented alliance then formed when Jacque agreed to donate a puppy, whom she named Angel, to the ICAN program in honor of Shanda and allow her daughter's killer to train her.[95]

Melinda and Laurie both had their demons; Laurie's anger stemmed from her mother and Melinda's inner turmoil originated from her father. Ultimately, it was the merging of those two broken personalities that created the perfect storm on January 11, 1992. On that night, all of their built-up hatred, hurt and rage flared and consumed poor Shanda Sharer.

Despite Jacque's and Steve's best efforts to shield their daughter from negative influences, Shanda was unable to escape Melinda's wrath. Shanda's story exemplifies why it is vital for parents to always be keenly aware of what is going on in their children's lives. And Melinda and Laurie are both striking examples of how the environment in which children are brought up plays an immense role in the shaping of their psyche. But not just their psyche—parents are also responsible for paving the path for their kids' futures.

As time passes, and more cases of kids who kill make global headlines, one very enduring truth comes to light: from birth, it is imperative that children receive loving affection and support from those that look after them.

Chapter Notes

Introduction

1. Helde, K.M. "A Taxonomy of Murder: Motivational Dynamics Behind the Homicidal Acts of Adolescents." *Justice Issues* 1 (1986): 3–19.
2. DiLulio, J. "The Coming of the Super-Predators." *Washington Examiner*, November 27, 1995.
3. Heide, K.M. "Juvenile Homicide Offenders Look Back 35 Years Later: Reasons They Were Involved in Murder." *International Journal of Environmental Research and Public Health* 17, no. 11 (2020): 3932.
4. "Juvenile Arrests." *OJJDP Statistical Briefing Book*, https://www.ojjdp.gov/Ojstatbb/Crime/qa05101.Asp?QaDate=2017.
5. Heide, K.M. "Juvenile Homicide Offenders Look Back 35 Years Later."
6. "Children's Exposure to Violence: A Comprehensive National Survey." U.S. Department of Justice, 2008, https://www.apa.org/pi/families/review-video-games.pdf.
7. Lippard, Elizabeth T.C., and Charles B. Nemeroff. "The Devastating Clinical Consequences of Child Abuse and Neglect: Increased Disease Vulnerability and Poor Treatment Response in Mood Disorders." *American Journal of Psychology* 177, no. 1 (2020): 20–36.
8. "Brain Development During Adolescence." *Lumen Learning*, https://courses.lumenlearning.com/wm-lifespandevelopment/chapter/brain-development-during-adolescence/.
9. "Understanding the Teen Brain." University of Rochester Medical Center, https://www.urmc.rochester.edu/Encyclopedia/Content.aspx?ContentTypeID=1&ContentID=3051.
10. "Teen Brain: Behavior, Problem Solving, and Decision Making." American Academy of Child & Adolescent Psychiatry, https://www.aacap.org/AACAP/Families_and_Youth/Facts_for_Families/FFF-Guide/The-Teen-Brain-Behavior-Problem-Solving-and-Decision-Making-095.aspx.
11. De Bellis, Michael D. "The Biological Effects of Childhood Trauma." *Childhood and Adolescent Psychiatric Clinics of North America* 23, no. 2 (2014): 185–222.
12. Cope, L.M., et al. "Abnormal Brain Structure in Youth Who Commit Homicide." *NeuroImage: Clinical* 4 (2014): 800–807.
13. Teicher, Martin H., et al. "Childhood Maltreatment: Altered Network Centrality of Cingulate, Precuneus, Temporal Pole and Insula." *Biological Psychiatry* 76, no. 4 (2013): 297–305.
14. Reif, Andreas, et al. "Nature and Nurture Predispose to Violent Behavior: Serotonergic Genes and Adverse Childhood Environment." *Neuropsychopharmacology* 32 (2007): 2375–2383.
15. "Family Life and Delinquency and Crime." Office of Juvenile Justice and Delinquency Prevention, 1993.

Eric Smith

1. "Boy's Death Grieves N.Y. Town; Arrest Is Even More Shocking; Teen's Confession Stuns Neighbors." *The Baltimore Sun*, 23 Aug. 1993.
2. "Why Did Eric Kill?" *48 Hours*, 2004.
3. "Boy's Death Devastates Town, but

Memories of His Life Sustain It." *Los Angeles Times*, 3 Apr. 1994.
    4. *Ibid.*
    5. "Why Did Eric Kill?" *48 Hours*, 2004.
    6. "Boy's Death Grieves N.Y. Town Arrest Is Even More Shocking Teen's Confession Stuns Neighbors." *The Baltimore Sun*, 23 Aug. 1993.
    7. *People v. Smith*, 217 A.D.2d 221 (1995).
    8. "Town Tries to Make Sense of Murder." *Tampa Bay Times*, 15 Aug. 1993.
    9. Hibsch, John. Personal communication, 7 Oct. 2018.
    10. *Ibid.*
    11. *Ibid.*
    12. *Ibid.*
    13. *Ibid.*
    14. "Odd Behavior Marked Eric." *Democrat and Chronicle*, 3 Aug. 1994.
    15. "Boy's Death Grieves N.Y. Town Arrest Is Even More Shocking Teen's Confession Stuns Neighbors." *The Baltimore Sun*, 23 Aug. 1993.
    16. 217 A.D.2d 221, *People v. Smith*, 1995.
    17. *Ibid.*
    18. *Ibid.*
    19. "Why Did Eric Kill?" *48 Hours*, 2004.
    20. Soles, Holly. Personal communication, 14 Apr. 2019.
    21. *Ibid.*
    22. "Why Did Eric Kill?" *48 Hours*, 2004.
    23. "Smith's Sister Says Life at Home Was 'hell.'" *Star-Gazette*, 10 Aug. 1994.
    24. "A Second Tragedy Comes in Wake of Savona Trial." *The Buffalo News*, 18 Aug. 1994.
    25. "Smith's Sister Says Life at Home Was 'Hell.'" *Star-Gazette*, 10 Aug. 1994.
    26. "Why Did Eric Kill?" *48 Hours*, 2004.
    27. Soles, Holly. Personal communication, 14 Apr. 2019.
    28. Hevner, Stacy. Personal communication, 1 Oct. 2018.
    29. "Smith's Sister Says Life at Home Was 'Hell.'" *Star-Gazette*, 10 Aug. 1994.
    30. Hevner, Stacy. Personal communication, 1 Oct. 2018.
    31. "Murder Trial Begins for Teen-Ager." *The New York Times*, 2 Aug. 1994.
    32. *Ibid.*
    33. *Ibid.*
    34. "Why Did Eric Kill?" *48 Hours*, 2004.
    35. "A 'Mad Switch' Led Teen-Ager to Kill Child, Psychiatrist Testifies." *The New York Times*, 11 Aug. 1994.
    36. *Ibid.*
    37. "Teen Says Sight of Lone Boy Drove Him to Kill." *The Record*, 10 Aug. 1994.
    38. *Ibid.*
    39. "Diseased or Evil? Teen Faces Trial in Sadistic Killing of Pre-Schooler." *The Ottawa Citizen*, 25 July 1994.
    40. "Teen Says Sight of Lone Boy Drove Him to Kill." *The Record*, 10 Aug. 1994.
    41. "Prosecutor Chips Away at Defense as Doctor Continues His Testimony." *Star-Gazette*, 10 Aug. 1994.
    42. "A Second Tragedy Comes in Wake of Savona Trial." *The Buffalo News*, 18 Aug. 1994.
    43. "Smith 'Not Be Able to Be in Society,' Doctor Says." *Star-Gazette*, 9 Aug. 1994.
    44. "Diseased or Evil? Teen Faces Trial in Sadistic Killing of Pre-Schooler." *The Ottawa Citizen*, 25 July 1994.
    45. "'I Wanted to Kill Him, I Guess,' Smith Told Psychiatrist." *The Ithaca Journal*, 12 Aug. 1994.
    46. "Envy Drove Smith to Kill, Doctor Says." *Star-Gazette*, 12 Aug. 1994.
    47. "'I Wanted to Kill Him, I Guess,' Smith Told Psychiatrist." *The Ithaca Journal*, 12 Aug. 1994.
    48. *Ibid.*
    49. *Ibid.*
    50. "14-Year-Old Convicted in Murder of Preschooler in Upstate Town." *The New York Times*, 17 Aug. 1994.
    51. "Fate of Teen Lies in Jury's Hands." *The Post-Star*, 16 Aug. 1994.
    52. "14-Year-Old Convicted in Murder of Preschooler in Upstate Town." *The New York Times*, 17 Aug. 1994.
    53. *Ibid.*
    54. "Fate of Teen Lies in Jury's Hands." *The Post-Star*, 16 Aug. 1994.
    55. "Boy, 14, Sentenced to 9 Years in Prison for Killing Child." *Los Angeles Times*, 8 Nov. 1994.
    56. "14-Year-Old Convicted in Murder of Preschooler in Upstate Town." *The New York Times*, 17 Aug. 1994.
    57. *Ibid.*
    58. "Boy's Killer Gets Maximum." *The Free-Lance Star*, 8 Nov. 1994.

59. "Youth, 14, Draws 9 Years to Life in Prison in Killing of 4-Year Old." *The New York Times*, 8 Nov. 1994.
60. "Boy's Death Devastates Town, but Memories of His Life Sustain It." *Los Angeles Times*, 3 Apr. 1994.
61. "Anguish Lingers Over Boys Slaying One Year Later, Savona Remains Small Town with Big Heartache." *The Buffalo News*, 15 Aug. 1994.
62. "Why Did Eric Kill?" *48 Hours*, 2004.
63. *Ibid.*
64. *Ibid.*
65. "Eleven Years After 13-Year-Old Eric Smith Murdered Four-Year-Old Derrick Robie, Smith Explains Why He Killed." *CBS News*, 9 Dec. 2004.
66. "Why Did Eric Kill?" *48 Hours*, 2004.
67. "Penny Brown." National Organization of Victims of Juvenile Murderers, 14 Aug. 2020, www.teenkillers.org/index.php/memorials/york-victims/penny-brown-2/.
68. "Eric Smith, Who Was 13 When He Killed a 4-Year-Old in 1993, Gets Parole." *Democrat & Chronicle*, 15 Oct. 2021.
69. NYS Department of Corrections and Community Supervision. Parole Board Interview in the Matter of Eric M. Smith, 5 Oct. 2021.
70. *Ibid.*
71. *Ibid.*
72. *Ibid.*
73. Tunny, John. Personal Communication, 15 Sept. 2018.
74. *Ibid.*
75. *Ibid.*
76. "A Second Tragedy Comes in Wake of Savona Trial." *The Buffalo News*, 18 Aug. 1994.

Holly Harvey and Sandy Ketchum

1. Bell, Rachael. "Holly Harvey and Sandra Ketchum: 'Kill, Keys, Money and Jewelry,'" www.murderpedia.org/female.H/h/harvey-holly.htm.
2. "Hell to Pay." *ID Twisted Love*, 2020.
3. "Killer Grandkid?" *People*, 20 September, 2004.
4. Collier, Kevin. Personal communication, 12 Mar. 2020.
5. "Devil Child Slaughters Her Grandparents, Steals Their Car to Pick Up More Pot, Cocaine." *Daily News*, 4 Feb. 2017.
6. "Religion in America: U.S. Religious Data, Demographics and Statistics." Pew Research Center, Religious Landscape Study, 9 Sept. 2020, www.pewforum.org/religious-landscape-study/state/.
7. "Killer Grandkid?" *People*, 20 Sept. 2004.
8. "Hell to Pay." *ID Twisted Love*, 2020.
9. *Ibid.*
10. "Murder File Yields Chilling Details." *The Citizen*, 20 Apr. 2005.
11. "Teen Girl, Ex Girlfriend Admit Killing Grandparents So They Could be Together." *The Index-Journal*, 15 Apr. 2005.
12. "Teen Killers Confess, Get Life." *The Atlanta Constitution*, 15 Apr. 2005.
13. "Murder File Yields Chilling Details." *The Citizen*, 20 Apr. 2005.
14. *Ibid.*
15. "Hell to Pay." *ID Twisted Love*, 2020.
16. *Ibid.*
17. "Murder File Yields Chilling Details." *The Citizen*, 20 Apr. 2005.
18. "Lesbian Accused of Stabbing Grandparents Had Kill on 'To Do' List." *Advocate*, 6 Aug. 2004.
19. "Murder File Yields Chilling Details." *The Citizen*, 20 Apr. 2005.
20. "Accused Teen had 'Kill' on To-Do List." *The Charlotte Observer*, 5 Aug. 2004.
21. "Killer Grandkid?" *People*, 20 Sept. 2004.
22. "Accused Teen had 'Kill' on To-Do List." *The Charlotte Observer*, 5 Aug. 2004.
23. "Judge Denies Bond for Girls Accused of Stabbing Grandparents." *The Item*, 20 Aug. 2004.
24. *Ibid.*
25. "Teen Girl, Ex-Girlfriend Admit Killing Grandparents So They Could Be Bogether." *The Index-Journal*, 15 Apr. 2005.
26. "Teen Killers Confess, Get Life." *The Atlanta Constitution*, 15 Apr. 2005.
27. "Teen Girl, Ex-Girlfriend Admit Killing Grandparents So They Could Be Together." *The Index-Journal*, 15 Apr. 2005.
28. *Ibid.*
29. "Hell to Pay." *ID Twisted Love*, 2020.
30. "Georgia Girls Admit to Killing Grandparents." *News4JAX*, 14 Apr. 2005

31. *Ibid.*
32. "Mother Says Not Responsible for Daughter's Actions." *The Citizen*, 14 Apr. 2005.
33. *Ibid.*
34. "Convicted Killer Gets Behind-Bars GED." *The Atlanta Constitution*, 23 Apr. 2007.
35. *Ibid.*
36. *Ibid.*
37. "Killer Grandkid?" *People*, 20 Sept. 2004.

Derek and Alex King

1. "'It's Tragic; It's Unthinkable.'" *Pensacola News Journal*, 30 Nov. 2001.
2. "Blood Brothers: The Derek & Alex King Case." *American Justice*, 2004.
3. "Slain Father Was Getting Along with Sons, Some Say." *Pensacola News Journal*, 2 Dec. 2001.
4. King, Gary C. *Angels of Death: A True Story of Murder and Innocence Lost* (New York: St. Martin's True Crime, 2003), pp. 5–6.
5. "Past History May Haunt Accused Molester at Trial." *The Ledger*, 10 Feb. 2003.
6. "King Brothers Confessed, Say Investigators." *Pensacola News Journal*, 29 Dec. 2001.
7. *Ibid.*
8. "Blood Brothers: The Derek & Alex King Case." *American Justice*, 2004.
9. *Ibid.*
10. *Ibid.*
11. "Chavis Guilty in King Case." *Pensacola News Journal*, 6 Mar. 2003.
12. "Answers Not Clear-Cut in King Tragedy." *Pensacola News Journal*, 13 Jan. 2002.
13. "Brothers' Arrests Shock Community." *Pensacola News Journal*, 30 Nov. 2001.
14. "Teen Says He Had Sex with Chavis 10 Times." *Herald-Tribune*, 12 Feb. 2003.
15. "Fate of Chavis Rests in Jury's Hands Today." *Pensacola News Journal*, 30 Aug. 2002.
16. Montaldo, Charles. "Children Who Kill: Alex and Derek King." *ThoughtCo*, 22 Oct. 2019, www.thoughtco.com/alex-and-derek-king-972684.
17. "Family, Friends Grapple with Final Outcome." *Pensacola News Journal*, 15 Nov. 2002.
18. "Fate of Chavis Rests in Jury's Hands Today." *Pensacola News Journal*, 30 Aug. 2002.
19. *Ibid.*
20. *Ibid.*
21. "Brothers Convicted of Killing Father." *The Washington Post*, 7 Sept. 2002.
22. "The 2019 Florida Statutes." *Statutes & Constitution: View Statutes: Online Sunshine*, 2019, www.leg.state.fl.us/Statutes/index.cfm?App_mode=Display_Statute.
23. asyob. "Alex King Testifies (Live on Court-TV)." Online video clip. *YouTube*, 3 Sept. 2009.
24. *Ibid.*
25. "Florida Brothers Blame Father's Murder on Family Friend." *CNN*, 28 Aug. 2002.
26. *Ibid.*
27. *Ibid.*
28. *Ibid.*
29. "Tape Recordings of Confessions from Alex and Derek King Were Played for Jurors." *The Associated Press*, 29 Aug. 2002.
30. "Fate of Chavis Rests in Jury's Hands Today." *Pensacola News Journal*, 30 Aug. 2002.
31. *Ibid.*
32. Colb, Sherry F. "Two Florida Murder Trials for the Killing of Terry King." *Findlaw*, 10 Sept. 2002, supreme.findlaw.com/legal-commentary/two-florida-murder-trials-for-the-killing-of-terry-king.html.
33. "Blood Brothers: The Derek & Alex King Case." *American Justice*, 2004.
34. "Brothers Convicted of Killing Father." *The Washington Post*, 7 Sept. 2002.
35. "Florida Boys Convicted in Father's Death; Family Friend Is Acquitted in Separate Trial." *The New York Times*, 7 Sept. 2002.
36. "Judge Throws Out Brothers' Murder Convictions." *The New York Times*, 18 Oct. 2002.
37. "King Brothers Sentenced." *Pensacola News Journal*, 15 Nov. 2002.
38. "Teenage Brothers in Florida Plead Guilty to Killing Father." *The Globe and Mail*, 15 Nov. 2002.
39. "Florida Boys Admit They Killed Father; Shorter Term Is Set." *The New York Times*, 15 Nov. 2002.

40. "Teenage Brothers in Florida Plead Guilty to Killing Father." *The Globe and Mail*, 15 Nov. 2002.
41. "Convictions of Boys in Father's Death Overturned." *Los Angeles Times*, 18 Oct. 2002.
42. Ibid.
43. "Lawyers in King Brothers Case Speak Out." *CNN*, 15 Nov. 2002.
44. Ibid.
45. "Parricides: Characteristics of Offenders and Victims, Legal Factors, and Treatment Issues." *Aggression and Violent Behavior* 4, no. 2 (1999): 179–190. www.ncjrs.gov/App/Publications/abstract.aspx?ID=177924.
46. "Parricide: An Introduction for Clinical and Forensic Mental Health Professionals." *Forensic Scholars Today*, 4 June 2019, online.csp.edu/blog/forensic-scholars-today/introduction-to-parricide.
47. Aguilar, Claudia. "A Comparative Study of Sons and Daughters Who Commit Parricide: A Pilot Study." California State University, Long Beach, ProQuest Dissertations Publishing, December 2019, https://search.proquest.com/openview/c11474e59275db4656f-994cf2b20e913/1?pq-origsite=gscholar&cbl=18750&diss=y.
48. "Brothers' Murder Case Has Bizarre Twists." *South Florida Sun-Sentinel*, 4 Nov. 2002.
49. "Second Chances: Dateline Checks in with Brothers Accused of Killing Their Father in 2001." *Dateline NBC*, 7 Sept. 2009.
50. Ibid.
51. Ibid.
52. Ibid.
53. "Life After Murder." *People*, 21 Oct. 2013.
54. "Inside the West Texas Sanctuary for Kids Who Killed Their Parents." *Vice News*, 28 Apr. 2016.
55. Ibid.
56. Ibid.
57. "Life After Murder." *People*, 21 Oct. 2013.

Josh Phillips

58. "Trial Approaches for Teen Charged with Killing Child." *Pensacola News Journal*, 5 July 1999.
59. "The Search for Maddie." *CBS News*, 12 June 2000.
60. "Clifton Family Calls Maddie's Disappearance, Death 'a Nightmare.'" *News4JAX*, 9 Aug. 2017.
61. "Harrowing Story of Child Murderer Joshua Phillips Who Killed His Eight-Year-Old Pal Maddie Clifton Aged Just 14 and Left Susanna Reid in Tears on ITV's Children Who Kill." *The Sun*, 14 Feb. 2018.
62. "A Look Back: The Disappearance and Murder of Maddie Clifton." *Florida Times-Union*, 3 Nov. 2018.
63. Monacelli, Antonia. "Murderous Children: Joshua Phillips (14) Murdered His 8-Year-Old Neighbour." *Soapboxie*, 27 Feb. 2020, soapboxie.com/government/Murderous-Children-Joshua-Phillips.
64. Mills, Gary. *Sutori*, www.sutori.com/story/the-murder-of-maddie-clifton--8rtVFLKHAxZAhZnVsdWXY3Yh.
65. "Teen Indicted in Slaying of 8-Year-Old Neighbor." *Florida Today*, 20 Nov. 1998.
66. "The Search for Maddie." *CBS News*, 12 June 2000.
67. "Teen Charged in Missing Girl's Grisly Slaying." *The Orlando Sentinel*, 11 Nov. 1998.
68. "Emotions Run High During Killer Joshua Phillips' Re-Sentencing Hearing." *Florida Times-Union*, 7 Aug. 2017.
69. "Pornography and Missing Underwear: Child Killer Joshua Phillips' Trial Reveals Disturbing Details of 8-Year-Old Maddie Clifton's Murder." *Daily Mirror*, 15 Feb. 2018.
70. "Clifton Family Calls Maddie's Disappearance, Death 'a Nightmare.'" *News4JAX*, 9 Aug. 2017.
71. "The Search for Maddie." *CBS News*, 12 June 2000.
72. "The Chilling Case of Joshua Phillips and How the Teen Murderer Was Finally Caught as His Story Airs on Children Who Kill." *Daily Mirror*, 18 Feb. 2018.
73. "A Look Back: The Disappearance and Murder of Maddie Clifton." *Florida Times-Union*, 3 Nov. 2018.
74. "Neighbor, 14, Charged in Missing Girl's Murder." *Tampa Bay Times*, 11 Nov. 1998.
75. "Youth to Be Tried as Adult in Slaying." *Los Angeles Times*, 17 Nov. 1998.
76. "Teen Guilty of Killing Girl, Hiding Her in Bed." *Tampa Bay Times*, 9 July 1999.

77. "15-Year-Old's Murder Trial Moved to Polk County." *Tampa Bay Times*, 23 April 1999.
78. "Teen Guilty of Killing Girl, Hiding Her in Bed." *Tampa Bay Times*, 9 July 1999.
79. *Ibid.*
80. *Ibid.*
81. *Ibid.*
82. "Behind the Facade." *CBS News*, 12 June 2000.
83. *Ibid.*
84. *Ibid.*
85. *Ibid.*
86. "Prosecution Rests in Trial of Teen Accused of Killing Neighbor Girl." *CNN International*, 7 July 1999.
87. "Phillips Sentenced to Life." *Florida Times-Union*, 21 Aug. 1999.
88. *Ibid.*
89. *Ibid.*
90. *Ibid.*
91. *Ibid.*
92. *Ibid.*
93. *Ibid.*
94. *Ibid.*
95. "Boy Grows Up in Prison After Killing Young Neighbor." *News4JAX*, 30 Oct. 2008.
96. "Phillips Sentenced to Life." *Florida Times-Union*, 21 Aug. 1999.
97. "Conviction, Sentence Upheld for Maddie's Killer." *News4JAX*, 6 Feb. 2002, web.archive.org/web/20110927152000/www.news4jax.com/news/1223416/detail.html.
98. "New Trial Sought in 1998 Slaying of Maddie Clifton." *News4JAX*, 16 Dec. 2004, web.archive.org/web/20110927151951/www.news4jax.com/news/4002159/detail.html.
99. "Her Killer Fights Back Tears When Asked About Maddie and Her Family." *The Times-Union*, 8 Nov. 2008.
100. Rovner, Josh, and Henderson Hill. "Juvenile Life Without Parole: An Overview." *The Sentencing Project*, 25 Feb. 2020, www.sentencingproject.org/publications/juvenile-life-without-parole/.
101. "Man Serving Life in Maddie Clifton Murder Gets New Sentencing Hearing." *WJCT News*, 8 Aug. 2017.
102. "Emotions Run High During Killer Joshua Phillips' Re-Sentencing Hearing." *Florida Times-Union*, 7 Aug. 2017.
103. "Family Returns to Court for Possible Resentencing of Daughter's Killer." *First Coast News*, 8 Aug., 2017.
104. News4JAX. "UNCUT: Josh Phillips Read Letter of Apology for 1998 Murder of Maddie Clifton." Online video clip. YouTube, 5 Apr. 2018.
105. *Ibid.*
106. "19 Years Later, the Narrative Behind Maddie Clifton's Demise Gets Even Worse." *Florida Times-Union*, 10 Aug. 2017.
107. "Harrowing Story of Child Murderer Joshua Phillips Who Killed His Eight-Year-Old Pal Maddie Clifton Aged Just 14 and Left Susanna Reid in Tears on ITV's Children Who Kill." *The Sun*, 14 Feb. 2018.
108. "After 4-Day Hearing, Josh Phillips Returning to Prison." *News4JAX*, 10 Aug. 2017.
109. "Judge Decides Life Sentence Is Warranted for Joshua Phillips in Maddie Clifton's Shocking Death." *Florida Times-Union*, 17 Nov. 2017.
110. Furbish, Lawrence K. Jacksonville Florida Juvenile Justice Program, 10 July 1998, www.cga.ct.gov/PS98/rpt/olr/htm/98-R-0787.htm.
111. Shorstein, Henry. Personal communication, 17 Dec. 2019.
112. *Ibid.*
113. Sabrina, Chiara, et al. "The Nature and Dynamics of Internet Pornography Exposure for Youth." *Cyberpsychology, Behavior, and Social* Networking 11, no. 6 (2008) 691–93.
114. Ybarra, Michele L., and Kimberly J. Mitchell. "X-Rated Material and Perpetration of Sexually Aggressive Behavior Among Children and Adolescents: Is There a Link?" *Aggressive Behavior* 37, no. 1 (2011): 1–18.
115. Voon, Valerie B., et al. "Neural Correlates of Sexual Cue Reactivity in Individuals with and Without Compulsive Sexual Behaviours." *PLoS One* 9, no. 7 (2014)2014.
116. Ferguson, C.J., and R.D. Hartley. "The Pleasure Is Momentary ... the Expense Damnable? The Influence of Pornography on Rape and Sexual Assault." *Aggressive and Violent Behavior* 14, no. 5 (2009): 323–29.
117. D'Amato, Anthony. "Porn Up, Rape Down." *Northwestern Public Law Research Paper* No. 913013 (2006).
118. "Age Verification for Online

Pornography." *Home—Parliament of Australia*, 4 Mar. 2020, https://www.aph.gov.au/Parliamentary_Business/Committees/House/Social_Policy_and_Legal_Affairs/Onlineageverification/Report/section?id=committees/reportrep/024436/72615#footnote8target.

Alyssa Bustamante

1. "Elizabeth Kay Olten (1999–2009)—Find a Grave..." Find a Grave, www.findagrave.com/memorial/43450313/elizabeth-kay-olten.
2. "Diary of a 'Thrill-Kill: Missouri Teen Murders Neighbor Girl." *Crime Watch Daily*, 2018.
3. *Systematic Search for Evidence*, flashmedia.glynn.k12.ga.us/webpages/rchunn/index.cfm?subpage=49750.
4. "Processing a Crime Scene." *UniversalClass.com*, www.universalclass.com/articles/law/processing-a-crime-scene.htm.
5. "Search for 9-Year-Old Resumes Today." *The Springfield News-Leader*, 23 Oct. 2009.
6. "Search Under Way for Missing 9-Year-Old." *The News Tribune*, 22 Oct. 2004.
7. "Missing St. Martin Girl Found Dead." *The Springfield News Leader*, 24 Oct. 2009.
8. "Authorities Searching for Missing Girl." *The Associated Press*, 22 Oct. 2009.
9. "Hundreds Turn Out for Search." *The News Tribune*, 22 Oct. 2009.
10. "Diary of a 'Thrill-Kill': Missouri Teen Murders Neighbor Girl." *Crime Watch Daily*, 2018.
11. FBI records (used for background).
12. "Diary of a 'Thrill-Kill': Missouri Teen Murders Neighbor Girl." *Crime Watch Daily*, 2018.
13. "Girl Still Missing: 9-Year-Old's Family Frustrated by Pace of Search." *The News Tribune*, 22 Oct. 2009.
14. "How Were Amber Alerts Created? The Amber Hagerman Cold Case." *A&E*, Oct. 11, 2019.
15. "Guidance on Criteria for Issuing AMBER Alerts." *Wayback Machine*, Apr. 2004, web.archive.org/web/20041015003050/amberalert.gov/docs/AMBERCriteria.pdf.
16. "Girl Still Missing: 9-Year-Old's Family Frustrated by Pace of Search." *The News Tribune*, 22 Oct. 2009.
17. *Ibid.*
18. "Diary of a 'Thrill-Kill': Missouri Teen Murders Neighbor Girl." *Crime Watch Daily*, 20 March 2018.
19. *Ibid.*
20. *Ibid.*
21. "Confessed Child Killer to Learn Her Fate." *KRCG*, 6 Feb. 2012.
22. "Alyssa Bustamante Sentence: Missouri Teen's Diary Says Killing Elizabeth Olten Felt Ahmazing."*Daily Mail*, 6 Feb. 2012.
23. "Girl's Body Found." *News Tribune*, 24 Oct. 2009.
24. "Juvenile Faces Murder Charge." *News Tribune*, 25 Oct. 2009.
25. *Ibid.*
26. *Ibid.*
27. "Sentence Could Vary for Juvenile." *News Tribune*, Oct. 2009.
28. "Cole County Grand Jury Returns Two-Count Indictment Against Alyssa Bustamante in Elizabeth Olten Murder Case." *Office of the Cole County Prosecuting Attorney*, 18 Nov. 2009.
29. "Alleged 15-Year-Old Alyssa Bustamante Confounds Missouri Justice System." *Daily News*, 23 Nov. 2009.
30. "Elizabeth Olten Murder Suspect, Alyssa Bustamante, Sent to Mental Hospital." *CBS News*, 20 Nov. 2009.
31. "Evidence in Bustamante Case Detailed." *Columbia Daily Tribune*, 15 Feb. 2012.
32. "Father of Alleged Elizabeth Olten Killer Alyssa Bustamante Has Violent Past." *CBC News*, 25 Nov. 2009.
33. "Confessed Child Killer to Learn Her Fate." *KRCG*, 6 Feb. 2012.
34. DeLong, William. "This 15-Year-Old YouTuber Murdered Her 9-Year-Old Neighbor Just to Feel What It Was Like to Kill." *All That's Interesting*, 11 Mar. 2019, allthatsinteresting.com/alyssa-bustamante.
35. "Understanding Self-Injury/Self-Harm." *Teen Mental Health*, teenmentalhealth.org/understanding-self-injury-self-harm/.
36. "Self-Injury (Cutting, Self-Harm or Self-Mutilation)." *Mental Health America*, www.mhanational.org/conditions/self-injury-cutting-self-harm-or-self-mutilation.

37. Romano, Tricia. "Alyssa Bustamante and the Murder of Elizabeth Olten." *Murderpedia*, murderpedia.org/female.B/b/bustamante-alyssa.htm.
38. "Diary of a 'Thrill-Kill': Missouri Teen Murders Neighbor Girl." *Crime Watch Daily*, 2018.
39. *Ibid.*
40. "Alyssa Bustamante Had Troubled Family, History of Depression." *Columbia Missourian*, 20 Feb. 2012.
41. "Alyssa Bustamante, 15, Pleads Not Guilty in 9-Year-Old's Stabbing." *ABC News*, 8 Dec. 2009.
42. "Judge Blocks Missouri Teen's Statement in Her Murder Trial." *St. Louis Post-Dispatch*, 22 June 2011.
43. "Teen Admits Murdering Neighbor, 9, 'Because She Wanted to Know What It Felt Like to Kill.'" *Daily Mail*, 10 Jan. 2012.
44. "Teenage 'Thrill Killer' Breaks Down in Tears as She Is Jailed for Life for Choking and Stabbing Her 9-Year-Old Neighbor." *Daily Mail*, 8 Feb. 2012.
45. "Prosecutors: Prozac No Defense for Mo. Teen Killer." *St. Louis Post-Dispatch*, 7 Feb. 2012.
46. "Teenage 'Thrill Killer' Breaks Down in Tears as She Is Jailed for Life for Choking and Stabbing Her 9-Year-Old Neighbor." *Daily Mail*, 8 Feb. 2012.
47. *Ibid.*
48. *Ibid.*
49. *Ibid.*
50. *Ibid.*
51. "Self-Injury (Cutting, Self-Harm Or Self-Mutilation)." *NHS Choices*, NHS, www.nhs.uk/conditions/ssri-antidepresants/.
52. Herring, Angela. "A Complicated Link Between Aggression and Antidepressant Drugs." *News@Northeastern*, 9 Oct. 2012, news.northeastern.edu/2012/10/09/antidepressant/.
53. Rettew, David. "Antidepressants and Violence: A Link in Search of a Cause." *Psychology Today*, 30 Sept. 2015, www.psychologytoday.com/ca/blog/abcs-child-psychiatry/201509/antidepressants-and-violence-link-in-search-cause.
54. "Bustamante Civil Case Settled." *News Tribune*, 25 July 2017

Cody Posey

1. "Cody Posey." *Academic Dictionaries and Encyclopedias*, enacademic.com/dic.nsf/enwiki/409520.
2. "Prosecutors Play Boy's Confession; Trial Starts in Triple Slaying." *Albuquerque Journal*, 18 Jan. 2016.
3. "Canyon of Secrets." *NBC News*, 6 May 2006.
4. *Ibid.*
5. *Ibid.*
6. *Ibid.*
7. *Ibid.*
8. "Relatives, Friends Testify About Cody Posey's Abusive History." *Albuquerque Journal*, 24 Jan. 2006.
9. "Posey's Defense Offers Abuse Support." *Albuquerque Journal*, 24 Jan. 2006.
10. "Teen Cody Posey Convicted of Murder, Manslaughter for Killing His Family." *Court TV*, 8 Feb. 2006.
11. "Posey Trial Begins." *Alamogordo Daily New*, 12 Jan. 2006.
12. *Ibid.*
13. "Canyon of Secrets." *NBC News*, May 6, 2006.
14. *Ibid.*
15. *Ibid.*
16. *Ibid.*
17. "Accused Teen 'Tired of Being Hit.'" *Albuquerque Journal*, 9 July 2004.
18. "Canyon of secrets." *NBC News*, 6 May 2006.
19. *Ibid.*
20. "Boy Denies Killing Family at Ranch." *The Associated Press*, 9 July 2004.
21. "Deaths Bring Hondo Teen to Court; Lawyer Denies Charges." *Albuquerque Journal*, 9 July 2004.
22. "Canyon of Secrets." *NBC News*, 6 May 2006.
23. "Posey Trial Begins." *Alamogordo Daily New*, 12 Jan. 2006.
24. "Canyon of Secrets." *NBC News*, 6 May 2006.
25. *Ibid.*
26. *Ibid.*
27. "Psychiatrist: Posey Didn't Have PTSD." *Albuquerque Journal*, 31 Jan. 2006.
28. "Psychopathic Traits Differ Between Cultures, Experts Claim." *The Independent*, 12 Feb. 2018.
29. "Posey Scored High on Psychopath Test." *Albuquerque Journal*, 1 Feb. 2006.
30. *Ibid.*

31. "Canyon of Secrets." *NBC News*, 6 May 2006.
32. "Posey Trial Begins." *Alamogordo Daily New*, 12 Jan. 2006.
33. Ibid.
34. "Canyon of Secrets." *NBC News*, 6 May 2006.
35. Ibid.
36. "Posey Trial Begins." *Alamogordo Daily New*, 12 Jan. 2006.
37. Ibid.
38. "Canyon of Secrets." *NBC News*, May 6, 2006.
39. Ibid.
40. Ibid.
41. "Father of Teen Who Shot Family Searched for Incest Porn on Computer." *Court TV*, 25 Jan. 2006.
42. "Incest Sites on Posey Computer." *Albuquerque Journal*, 26 Jan. 2006.
43. "Canyon of Secrets." *NBC News*, 6 May 2006.
44. "Posey Says He Was Often Abused." *Albuquerque Journal*, 20 Jan. 2006.
45. "Canyon of Secrets." *NBC News*, 6 May 2006.
46. Ibid.
47. Ibid.
48. "Prosecution Calls Posey 'Cold-Blooded Killer.'" *Albuquerque Journal*, 6 Feb. 2006.
49. "Posey Says He Was Often Abused." *Albuquerque Journal*, 20 Jan. 2006.
50. "Canyon of Secrets." *NBC News*, 6 May 2006.
51. "Teen Convicted in 2004 Triple Homicide." *Albuquerque Journal*, 8 Feb. 2006.
52. "Teen Cody Posey Convicted of Murder, Manslaughter for Killing His Family." *Court TV*, 8 Feb. 2006.
53. "Teen Guilty in Ranch Killings." *CBS News*, 8 Feb. 2006.
54. "Teen Cody Posey Convicted of Murder, Manslaughter for Killing His Family." *Court TV*, 8 Feb. 2006.
55. "Canyon of Secrets." *NBC News*, 6 May 2006.
56. "Posey Sentencing Continues with Defense Witnesses." *Albuquerque Journal*, 21 Feb. 2006.
57. "Canyon of Secrets." *NBC News*, 6 May 2006.
58. Ibid.
59. "Teen Convicted of Killing Family Sentenced as Juvenile." *Albuquerque Journal*, 23 Feb. 2006.
60. "New Thompson Suit Blames GTA for 2004 Murder." *Gamasutra*, 26 Sept. 2006.
61. "Teen Who Killed Family on Donaldson Ranch Goes Free." *CNN*, 8 Oct. 2019.

Jasmiyah and Tasmiyah Whitehead

1. Yamagata, Bun, et al. "Female-Specific Intergenerational Transmission Patterns of the Human Corticolimbic Circuitry." *Journal of Neuroscience, Society for Neuroscience* 36, no. 4. (2016): 1254–1260, www.jneurosci.org/content/36/4/1254.
2. Johnston, Joni E. "Matricide by Teen Girls." *Psychology Today*, 16 July 2012, www.psychologytoday.com/ca/blog/the-human-equation/201207/matricide-teen-girls.
3. "Great-Grandmother Hopes Twins Who Killed Their Mother Will One Day Lead Productive Lives." *Rockdale-Newton Citizen*, 18 Dec. 2014.
4. "Mother's Slaying Haunts Loved Ones." *AJC*, 10 Apr. 2016.
5. "Friends Not Surprised Twins Charged in Mom's Death." *AJC*, 26 Sept. 2018
6. "Single Mom Killed by Twin Daughters in Rage Over Strict Home Life." *True Crime Daily*, 27 Oct. 2016.
7. "Twin, 20, Accepts 30-Year Plea Deal for Brutally Murdering Her Mother ... but Her Identical Sister Will Go to Trial and Faces Life After REJECTING a Deal." *The Daily Mail*, 10 Jan. 2014.
8. "Mother's Slaying Haunts Loved Ones." *AJC*, 10 Apr. 2016.
9. Ibid.
10. Ibid.
11. "Great-Grandmother Hopes Twins Who Killed Their Mother Will One Day Lead Productive Lives." *Rockdale-Newton Citizen*, 18 Dec. 2014.
12. "Whitehead Sister Pleads Guilty to Manslaughter." *The Rockdale Citizen*, 9 Jan. 2014.
13. "Twisted Twins: Teen Sisters Confess to Killing Mother." *11 Alive News*, 12 Sept. 2016.
14. "Whitehead Twin Denied Bond." *The Covington News*, 14 June 2010.

15. "Teen Sisters Confess to Killing Mother." *ABC10*, 7 Nov. 2014.

16. "Single Mom Killed by Twin Daughters in Rage Over Strict Home Life." *True Crime Daily*, 27 Oct. 2016.

17. "Teen Sisters Confess to Killing Mother." *ABC10*, 7 Nov. 2014.

18. *Ibid.*

19. "Single Mom Killed by Twin Daughters in Rage Over Strict Home Life." *True Crime Daily*, 27 Oct. 2016.

20. "Jasmiyah and Tasmiyah Whitehead Case Extras: Interrogation Transcripts." *11 Alive News*, 16 May 2014.

21. *Ibid.*

22. *Ibid.*

23. *Ibid.*

24. *Ibid.*

25. *Ibid.*

26. "2nd Whitehead Twin Pleads Guilty to Manslaughter." *The Covington News*, 7 Feb. 2014.

27. *Ibid.*

28. *Ibid.*

29. "Arrendale Prison Hosts First Ever Charter High School Graduation." *Now Habersham*, 23 July 2015.

30. @LoisMDavis, Lois M. Davis. "Education and Vocational Training in Prisons Reduces Recidivism, Improves Job Outlook." *RAND Corporation*, 22 Aug. 2013, www.rand.org/news/press/2013/08/22.html.

31. "Arrendale Prison Hosts First Ever Charter High School Graduation." *Now Habersham*, 23 July 2015.

32. *Ibid.*

Daniel Petric

1. Caniglia, John. "Pastor's Son Charged in Mother's Murder, Father's Shooting." *Cleveland.com*, 23 Oct. 2007, www.cleveland.com/metro/2007/10/loving_child_called_a_killer.html.

2. "Teen Accused of Killing Mother, Shooting Pastor Father." *Cleveland 19 News*, 23 Oct. 2007.

3. "Did Halo Video Game Drive Son to Murder?" *True Crime Daily*, 18 Dec. 2015.

4. Turner, Karl. "17-Year-Old Accused of Killing Mother Over Halo 3 Video Game May Get Verdict Soon." *Cleveland.com*, 16 Dec. 2008, www.cleveland.com/metro/2008/12/trial_of_boy_accused_of_killin.html.

5. "Ohio Teenager Has Surprise for His Parents After They Confiscate His Favorite Game." *Life Daily*, https://www.lifedaily.com/story/ohio-teenager-has-surprise-for-his-parents-after-they-confiscate-his-favorite-game/.

6. Boyer, Brandon. "NPD: 2007 U.S. Game Industry Growth Up 43% to $17.9 Billion." *Gamasutra*, 18 Jan. 2008, www.gamasutra.com/view/news/107957/NPD_2007_U.S._Game_Industry_Growth_Up_43_To_179_Billion.php.

7. Fahey, Mike. "Halo 3 Shooter's Attorney Argues Insanity Due to Video Game Addiction." *Kotaku*, 17 Dec. 2008, kotaku.com/halo-3-shooters-attorney-argues-insanity-due-to-video-g-5112289.

8. "Daniel Petric Killed Mother, Shot Father Because They Took Halo 3 Video Game, Prosecutors Say." *Cleveland.com*, 15 Dec. 2008.

9. *Ibid.*

10. *Ibid.*

11. "Please Pray for the Petrics (My Former Youth Pastors)." *David Covey*, 22 Oct. 2007, davidcovey.typepad.com/david_covey/2007/10/please-pray-for.html.

12. Katie Couric, "How a Video Game Addiction Led Daniel Petric to Murder." Online video clip, YouTube, 1 May 2013.

13. "Did Halo Video Game Drive Son to Murder?" *True Crime Daily*, 18 Dec. 2015.

14. *Ibid.*

15. *Ibid.*

16. "PASTOR'S SON OFFICIALLY CHARGED." *TMCNEWS.NET*, 22 Oct. 2007, tmcnews.blogspot.com/2007/10/pastors-son-officially-charged.html.

17. "Daniel Petric, 16, to Be Charged with Slaying Mother, wounding Father, a Pastor in Wellington." *The Plain Dealer*, 22 Oct. 2007.

18. "Pastor's Son Charged in Mother's Murder, Father's Shooting." *Cleveland.com*, 23 Oct. 2007.

19. "Son Accused of Killing Mother Granted Final Visit." *Cleveland 19 News*, 26 Oct. 2007.

20. The Chronicle Telegram. "Petric Murder Trial. Prosecution Opening." Online clip. YouTube, 15 Dec. 2008.

21. *Ibid.*

22. The Chronicle Telegram. "Petric Trial Defense Opening." Online clip. YouTube, 15 Dec. 2008.

23. *Ibid.*

24. "Daniel Petric Killed Mother, Shot Father Because They Took Halo 3 Video Game, Prosecutors Say." *Cleveland.com*, 15 Dec. 2008.
25. *Ibid.*
26. "Halo 3 Shooter's Attorney Argues Insanity Due to Video Game Addiction." *Kotaku*, 17 Dec. 2008.
27. "Trial Ends for Teen Accused of Killing Parents Over Halo 3 Video Game; Verdict Due Jan. 7." *Cleveland.com*, 17 Dec. 2008.
28. "Defense: Ohio Teen Who Shot Parents 'Just Popped.'" *Cleveland 19 News*, 17 Dec. 2008.
29. x8m8x3k3t. "Judge James Burge: Daniel Petric A.K.A. 'Halo Killer.'" Online clip, YouTube, 15 Jan. 2009.
30. *Ibid.*
31. "Petric Sentenced to 23 Years to Life: Father Says Son Regrets Shooting Mother Over 'Halo 3' Video Game." *The Morning Journal*, 17 June 2009.
32. The Chronicle Telegram. "Daniel Petric Sentencing." Online clip. YouTube, 16 June 2009.
33. *Ibid.*
34. *Ibid.*
35. *Ibid.*
36. "Columbine: Whose Fault Is It?" *Rolling Stone*, 24 June 1999.
37. "Technical Report on the Review of the Violent Video Game Literature." APA Task Force on Violent Media (2015), retrieved from https://www.apa.org/pi/families/review-video-games.pdf.

Cristian Fernandez

1. "A Young Mother Tries to Save Two Sons and Loses Everything." *Tampa Bay Times*, 14 July 2013.
2. "Father, Former Neighbors Stunned by Murder Charge Against Cristian Fernandez." *The Florida Times-Union*, 11 June 2011.
3. "A Young Mother Tries to Save Two Sons and Loses Everything." *Tampa Bay Times*, 14 July 2013.
4. *Ibid.*
5. *Ibid.*
6. Monacelli, Antonia. "Murderous Children: Cristian Fernandez (12) Killed His 2-Year-Old Brother—Owlcation—Education." *Owlcation*, 11 Jan. 2018, owlcation.com/social-sciences/Murderous-Children-Cristian-Fernandez.
7. "New Documents Show 12-Year-Old Killed Kitten, Sexually Abused Brother." *Florida Times-Union*, 25 June 2011.
8. "Father, Former Neighbors Stunned by Murder Charge Against Cristian Fernandez." *Florida Times-Union*, 11 June 2011.
9. "Cristian Fernandez Case: As Someone Surfed Internet, Tot's Life Was Slipping Away." *Florida Times-Union*, 14 Sept. 2011.
10. "12-Year-Old Florida Boy, Cristian Fernandez, Faces First Degree Murder Charge for 2-Year-Old's Death." *Daily News*, 6 June 2011.
11. "A Young Mother Tries to Save Two Sons and Loses Everything." *Tampa Bay Times*, 14 July 2013.
12. News4JAX. "UNCUT: Cristian Fernandez Interrogation." Online clip. YouTube, 17 Apr. 2019.
13. "Biannela Susana Avoids Prison Time." *News4JAX*, 14 Aug. 2013.
14. "Is Angela Corey the Cruelest Prosecutor in America?" *The Nation*, 16 Aug. 2016.
15. "No Prison for Mother of Cristian Fernandez." *Florida Times-Union*, 14 Aug. 2013.
16. "A Young Mother Tries to Save Two Sons and Loses Everything." *Tampa Bay Times*, 14 July 2013.
17. "Baby-Faced Boy's Case Highlights Debate About Trying Juveniles." *Florida-Times Union*, 5 June 2011.
18. "Jacksonville 12-Year-Old Charged with First-Degree Murder of Brother." *Florida-Times Union*, 2 June 2011.
19. *Ibid.*
20. "Baby-Faced Boy's Case Highlights Debate About Trying Juveniles." *The Florida-Times Union*, 5 June 2011.
21. "The 12-Year-Old Who Could Become America's Youngest Ever 'Lifer' for Killing Two-Year-Old Brother." *Daily Mail*, 6 June 2011.
22. "Cristian Fernandez indicted on sexual battery charge." *Florida-Times Union*, 5 Jan. 2012.
23. *Ibid.*
24. "Cristian Fernandez's Mother Pleads Guilty in Death of 2-Year-Old Son." *Florida-Times Union*, 28 Mar. 2012.
25. *Ibid.*

26. "Sexual Assault Charge Dropped Against Cristian Fernandez." *News4JAX*, 8 Nov. 2012.
27. "13-Year-Old Cristian Fernandez Will Face Life Without Parole for Killing Brother, Court Rules." *The Daily Beast*, 21 Nov. 2012.
28. Ibid.
29. Higgins, Melissa. "Sign the Petition." *Change.org*, www.change.org/p/reverse-decision-to-try-12-y-o-cristian-fernandez-as-an-adult?original_footer_petition_id=.
30. "Cristian Fernandez, Now 13, Pleads Guilty, Sentenced to Prison Until He's 19." *Morris News Service*, 8 Feb. 2013.
31. "No Prison for Mother of Cristian Fernandez." *Florida Times-Union*, 14 Aug. 2013.
32. Ibid.
33. "SALVAGING A DAMAGED CHILD'S LIFE." *The Florida Bar*, 15 Jan. 2016.
34. Ibid.
35. "One Day After 19th birthday, Cristian Fernandez Released." *News4JAX*, 15 Jan. 2018.
36. "Mom of Jacksonville's Youngest Killer Charged with DUI." *News4JAX*, 23 Mar. 2019.
37. "Why Children of Teen Mothers Do Worse in Life." *VOX, CEPR Policy Portal*, 22 Dec. 2018, voxeu.org/article/why-children-teen-mothers-do-worse-life.
38. National Research Council (U.S.) Panel on Adolescent Pregnancy and Childbearing. "THE CHILDREN OF TEEN CHILDBEARERS." *Risking the Future: Adolescent Sexuality, Pregnancy, and Childbearing, Volume II: Working Papers and Statistical Appendices*, U.S. National Library of Medicine, 1987. www.ncbi.nlm.nih.gov/books/NBK219236/.
39. "Obama Bans Solitary Confinement of Juveniles in Federal Prisons." *The Guardian*, 26 Jan. 2016.

Melinda Loveless, Laurie Tackett, Hope Rippey and Toni Lawrence

1. "Story of a Murder ... 12-Year-Old's Brutal End Begs the Question, 'Why?'" *The Courier-Journal*, 6 Dec. 1992.
2. "As 4 Teenage Girls Face Trial, an Indiana Town Waits to Learn Who Killed Shanda Renee Sharer—and Why." *Chicago Tribune*, 29 July 1992.
3. "Bizarre Death Shakes Up Town." *The Cincinnati Enquirer*, 12 Jan. 1992.
4. "A TOWN TORN APART Indiana Community Is Shaken by Torture Murder of Young Girl." *The Baltimore Sun*, 21 June 1992.
5. "Story of a Murder ... 12-Year-Old's Brutal End Begs the Question, 'Why?'" *The Courier-Journal*, 6 Dec. 1992.
6. "The Pain of Remembering." *The Courier-Journal*, 14 Jan. 1992.
7. "A Deadly Meeting." *The Indianapolis Star*, 24 Jan. 1993.
8. Jones, Aphrodite. *Cruel Sacrifice* (New York: Kensington, 1994), pp. 61–62.
9. "Teen Killer Endured Life of Horror, Family Testifies." *The Indianapolis Star*, 19 Dec. 1992.
10. "Loveless' Relatives Say That Her Father Was Sexually Abusive." *The Courier-Journal*, 19 Dec. 1992.
11. Jones, *Cruel Sacrifice*, pp. 76–84.
12. "For Dead Girl's Mother, Abuse Still No Excuse." *The South Bend Tribune*, 20 Dec. 1992.
13. Jones, *Cruel Sacrifice*, pp. 110–112.
14. Ibid., pp. 116–117.
15. "Sexual Abuse Surfaces in Torture Death." *The Star Press*, 19 Dec. 1992.
16. "Story of a Murder ... 12-Year-Old's Brutal End Begs the Question, 'Why?'" *The Courier-Journal*, 6 Dec. 1992.
17. "A Deadly Meeting." *The Indianapolis Star*, 24 Jan. 1993.
18. "Story of a Murder ... 12-Year-Old's Brutal End Begs the Question, 'Why?'" *The Courier-Journal*, 6 Dec. 1992.
19. "Shanda's Father Shares His Torment." *The Courier-Journal*, 18 Dec. 1992.
20. "Friend of Loveless Says Tackett Claimed Main Role in Girl's Murder." *The Courier-Journal*, 17 Dec. 1992.
21. "Lawrence's Role in Sharer killing at Issue in Hearing." *The Courier-Journal*, 17 Jan. 1993.
22. "A Deadly Meeting." *The Indianapolis Star*, 24 Jan. 1993.
23. "Girls Describe Torture, Killing of 12-Year-Old." *The Courier-Journal*, 16 Dec. 1992.
24. "Daylight Demystifies 'Castle.'" *The Courier-Journal*, 18 Dec. 1992.

25. Long, Kasy. "The Spooky Tale of Indiana's 'Witches' Castle.'" *History 101*, 30 Dec. 2019, www.history101.com/the-spooky-tale-of-indianas-witches-castle/.
26. "Story of a Murder ... 12-Year-Old's Brutal End Begs the Question, 'Why?'" *The Courier-Journal*, 6 Dec. 1992.
27. "Lawrence's Role in Sharer Killing Disputed." *The Courier-Journal*, 27 Jan. 1993.
28. "Teen Torture Slayer Describes Death of 12-Year-Old Girl." *The Vincennes-Sun Commercial*, 29 Dec. 1992.
29. "Girls Describe Torture, Killing of 12-Year-Old." *The Courier-Journal*, 16 Dec. 1992.
30. "Teen Torture Slayer Describes Death of 12-Year-Old Girl." *The Vincennes-Sun Commercial*, 29 Dec. 1992.
31. "Girl Who Was Tortured Begged Other Teens Not to Hurt Her." *The Indianapolis Star*, 16 Dec. 1992.
32. "Prosecutor Tells Gruesome Story of Girl's Slaying." *The Indianapolis Star*, 15 Dec. 1992.
33. "A Deadly Meeting." *The Indianapolis Star*, 24 Jan. 1993.
34. "In Cold Blood: A Daughter Murdered." *Dr. Phil*, 2011.
35. "Letters Detail Teen's Jealousy, Desire to Kill 12-Year-Old." *The Courier-Journal*, 16 Dec. 1992.
36. "Friend of Loveless Says Tackett Claimed Main Role in Girl's Murder." *The Courier-Journal*, 17 Dec. 1992.
37. "A Deadly Meeting." *The Indianapolis Star*, 24 Jan. 1993.
38. "Lawrence's Role in Sharer Killing at Issue in Hearing." *The Courier-Journal*, 27 Jan. 1993.
39. *Ibid*.
40. "Girls Charged in Torture, Slaying of New Albany Girl." *The Courier-Journal*, 13 Jan. 1992.
41. "300 Attend Funeral Service for Tortured 12-Year-Old Girl." *The Indianapolis News*, 16 Jan. 1992.
42. "Girls Charged in Murder; Town Numb." *The Salt Lake Tribune*, 16 June 1992.
43. *Ibid*.
44. "Teen Charged in Murder Agrees to Plea Bargain." *The Courier-Journal*, 22 Apr. 1992.
45. "Death Penalty Is Sought for 2 Teens in Murder Case." *The Courier-Journal*, 15 July 1992.
46. "Indiana Death Penalty Laws." *Clark Prosecutor*, www.clarkprosecutor.org/html/death/dplaw.htm.
47. "Topics of the Times: A Murderous Child." *New York Times*, 17 July 1989.
48. "Woman's Execution for Murder at 15 Is Barred," *Associated Press*, July 13, 1989.
49. "Defense, Trial Costs for 4 Teens Held in Girl's Death Hard on County Budget." *The Courier-Journal*, 9 Aug. 1992.
50. "Teen Girls Plead Guilty of Torturing 12-Year-Old." *The Montana Standard*, 7 Oct. 1992.
51. "Prosecutor Tells Gruesome Story of Girl's Slaying." *The Indianapolis Star*, 15 Dec. 1992.
52. "Loveless Sentencing Brings to Forefront Brutal Slaying Details." *The Herald*, 15 Dec. 1992.
53. *Ibid*.
54. "Prosecutor Tells Gruesome Story of Girl's Slaying." *The Indianapolis Star*, 15 Dec. 1992.
55. "Sexual Abuse Surfaces in Torture Death." *The Star Press*, 19 Dec. 1992.
56. "Loveless' Relatives Say That Her Father Was Sexually Abusive." *The Courier-Journal*, 19 Dec. 1992.
57. "Friend of Loveless Says Tackett Claimed Main Role in Girl's Murder." *The Courier-Journal*, 17 Dec. 1992.
58. *Ibid*.
59. "Sexual Abuse Surfaces in Torture Death." *The Star Press*, 19 Dec. 1992.
60. "Tackett Says She Suffered Lifetime of Abuse." *The Courier-Journal*, 31 Dec. 1992.
61. *Ibid*.
62. "Tackett Turned Planned Beating into Murder, Loveless Claims." *The Courier-Journal*, 29 Dec. 1992.
63. "Girl's Death in Blaze Is Now a Blur." *The Indianapolis Star*, 30 Dec. 1992.
64. "Tackett Says She Suffered Lifetime of Abuse." *The Courier-Journal*, 31 Dec. 1992.
65. "Two Who Admitted Killing 12-Year-Old Get 60 Years." *The Courier-Journal*, 5 Jan. 1993.
66. "Teen Killers Sentenced." *The Indianapolis Star*, 5 Jan. 1993.
67. *Ibid*.
68. "Two Who Admitted Killing 12-Year-Old Get 60 Years." *The Courier-Journal*, 5 Jan. 1993.

69. "Girls Get 60 Years in Slaying." *The Messenger*, 5 Jan. 1993.
70. "Pair Gets 60 Years for Torure-Slaying of Girl, 12." *The Indianpolis Star*, 6 Jan. 1993.
71. "Two Who Admitted Killing 12-Year-Old Get 60 Years." *The Courier-Journal*, 5 Jan. 1993.
72. "Lawrence's Role in Sharer Killing Disputed." *The Courier-Journal*, 27 Jan. 1993.
73. Ibid.
74. "Lawrence's Role in Sharer Killing at Issue in Hearing." *The Courier-Journal*, 27 Jan. 1993.
75. Ibid.
76. "Teen Apologizes to Parents of Slain Girl, Says Fear for Her Own Life Kept Her Quiet." *The Courier-Journal*, 28 Jan. 1993.
77. Ibid.
78. "3rd Teen Sentenced in Torture." *The Indianapolis Star*, 29 Jan. 1993.
79. "Lawyers Stress Rippey's Role in Girl's Murder." *The Courier-Journal*, 2 June 1993.
80. "Psychologist: Teen Was Led Astray." *Logansport Pharos-Tribune*, 2 June 1993.
81. "Lawyers Stress Rippey's Role in Girl's Murder." *The Courier-Journal*, 2 June 1993.
82. "Teenager Gets 50-Year Sentence." *The Indianapolis Journal*, 3 June 1993.
83. Madison Teen Gets 50-Year Term." *The South Bend Tribune*, 3 June 1993.
84. "Teenager Gets 50-Year Sentence." *The Indianapolis Journal*, 3 June 1993.
85. Ibid.
86. "Crossing the Line ... Mob Mentality Was 1 Factor in Murder's Brutality, Psychologists Say." *The Courier-Journal*, 24 Jan. 1993.
87. Ibid.
88. "Crossing the Line ... Mob Mentality Was 1 Factor in Murder's Brutality, Psychologists Say." *The Courier-Journal*, 24 Jan. 1993.
89. Darley, John M., and Bibb Latané. *The Unresponsive Bystander: Why Doesn't He Help?* (New York, NY: Appleton Century Crofts, 1970).
90. "Loveless' Father Charged with Sex Abuse of 5 Girls." *The Courier-Journal*, 12 Jan. 1993.
91. "Plea Possible." *The Republic*, 4 June 1995.
92. "Shanda Sharer's Story Still Changing Lives." *The Courier-Journal*, 30 Jan. 1995.
93. "A Killer at 15, Indiana Woman Is Getting Out Early Thanks to Prison Volunteer." *The Courier-Journal*, 28 Apr. 2005.
94. "Convict in Girl's 1992 Killing Gets Released." *Journal and Courier*, 12 Jan. 2018.
95. "Shanda Sharer's Mother and Murderer Form Unlikely Alliance." *Wave 3 News*, 21 May 2012.

Bibliography

"Accused Teen Had 'Kill' on To-Do List." *The Charlotte Observer*, 5 Aug. 2004.
"Accused Teen 'Tired of Being Hit.'" *Albuquerque Journal*, 9 July 2004.
A.D.2d 221, *People v. Smith*, 1995.
"After 4-day Hearing, Josh Phillips Returning to Prison." *News4JAX*, 10 Aug. 2017.
"Age Verification for Online Pornography." Home—Parliament of Australia, 4 Mar. 2020, https://www.aph.gov.au/Parliamentary_Business/Committees/House/Social_Policy_and_Legal_Affairs/Onlineageverification/Report/section?id=committees/reportrep/024436/72615#footnote8target.
Aguilar, Claudia. "A Comparative Study of Sons and Daughters Who Commit Parricide: A Pilot Study." Master's Thesis, California State University, Long Beach. ProQuest, 2019, https://search.proquest.com/openview/c11474e59275db4656f994cf2b20e913/1?pq-origsite=gscholar&cbl=18750&diss=y.
"Alleged 15-Year-Old Alyssa Bustamante Confounds Missouri Justice System." *Daily News*, 23 Nov. 2009.
"Alyssa Bustamante, 15, Pleads Not Guilty in 9-Year-Old's Stabbing." *ABC News*, 8 Dec. 2009.
"Alyssa Bustamante Had Troubled Family, History of Depression." *Columbia Missourian*, 20 Feb. 2012.
"Alyssa Bustamante Sentence: Missouri Teen's Diary Says Killing Elizabeth Olten Felt Ahmazing." *Daily Mail*, 6 Feb. 2012.
"Anguish Lingers Over Boy's Slaying One Year Later, Savona Remains Small Town with Big Heartache." *The Buffalo News*, 15 Aug. 1994.
"Answers Not Clear-Cut in King Tragedy." *Pensacola News Journal*, 13 Jan. 2002.
"Arrendale Prison Hosts First Ever Charter High School Graduation." *Now Habersham*, 23 July 2015.
"As 4 Teenage Girls Face Trial, an Indiana Town Waits to Learn Who Killed Shanda Renee Sharer—and Why." *Chicago Tribune*, 29 July 1992.
Associated Press. "Woman's Execution for Murder at 15 Is Barred." 13 July 1989.
asyob. "Alex King Testifies (live on Court-TV)." *YouTube*, 3 Sept. 2009.
"Authorities Searching for Missing Girl." Associated Press, 22 Oct. 2009.
"Baby-Faced Boy's Case Highlights Debate About Trying Juveniles." *Florida-Times Union*, 5 June 2011.
"Behind the Facade." *CBS News*, 12 June 2000.
Bell, Rachael. "Holly Harvey and Sandra Ketchum: 'Kill, Keys, Money and Jewelry.'" *Murderpedia*, www.murderpedia.org/female.H/h/harvey-holly.htm.
"Biannela Susana Avoids Prison Time." *News4JAX*, 14 Aug. 2013.
"Bizarre Death Shakes Up Town." *The Cincinnati Enquirer*, 12 Jan. 1992.
"Blood Brothers: The Derek & Alex King Case." *American Justice*, 2004.
"Boy Denies Killing Family at Ranch." Associated Press, 9 July 2004.
"Boy, 14, Sentenced to 9 Years in Prison for Killing Child." *Los Angeles Times*, 8 Nov. 1994.
"Boy Grows Up in Prison After Killing Young Neighbor." *News4JAX*, 30 Oct. 2008.

Bibliography

Boyer, Brandon. "NPD: 2007 U.S. Game Industry Growth Up 43% to $17.9 Billion." Gamasutra, 18 Jan. 2008, www.gamasutra.com/view/news/107957/NPD_2007_US_Game_Industry_Growth_Up_43_To_179_Billion.php.

"Boy's Death Devastates Town, but Memories of His Life Sustain It." *Los Angeles Times*, 3 Apr. 1994.

"Boy's Death Grieves N.Y. Town; Arrest Is Even More Shocking; Teen's Confession Stuns Neighbors." *The Baltimore Sun*, 23 Aug. 1993.

"Boy's Killer Gets Maximum." *The Free-Lance Star*, 8 Nov. 1994.

"Brain Development During Adolescence." https://courses.lumenlearning.com/wm-lifespandevelopment/chapter/brain-development-during-adolescence/.

"Brothers' Arrests Shock Community." *Pensacola News Journal*, 30 Nov. 2001.

"Brothers Convicted of Killing Father." *The Washington Post*, 7 Sept. 2002.

"Brothers' Murder Case Has Bizarre Twists." *South Florida Sun-Sentinel*, 4 Nov. 2002.

"Bustamante Civil Case Settled." *News Tribune*, 25 July. 2017

Caniglia, John. "Pastor's Son Charged in Mother's Murder, Father's Shooting." *Cleveland.com*, 23 Oct. 2007, www.cleveland.com/metro/2007/10/loving_child_called_a_killer.html.

"Canyon of Secrets." *NBC News*, May 6, 2006.

"Chavis Guilty in King Case." *Pensacola News Journal*, 6 Mar. 2003.

"Children's Exposure to Violence: A Comprehensive National Survey." *U.S. Department of Justice*, 2008, https://www.apa.org/pi/families/review-video-games.pdf.

"The Chilling Case of Joshua Phillips and How the Teen Murderer Was Finally Caught as His Story Airs on Children Who Kill." *Daily Mirror*, 18 Feb. 2018.

The Chronicle Telegram. "Daniel Petric Sentencing." Online clip. Youtube, 16 Jun. 2009.

The Chronicle Telegram. "Petric Murder Trial. Prosecution Opening." Online clip. Youtube, 15 Dec. 2008.

The Chronicle Telegram. "Petric Trial Defense Opening." Online clip. Youtube, 15 Dec. 2008.

"Clifton Family Calls Maddie's Disappearance, Death 'a Nightmare.'" *News4JAX*, 9 Aug. 2017

"Cody Posey." *Academic Dictionaries and Encyclopedias*, enacademic.com/dic.nsf/enwiki/409520.

Colb, Sherry F. "Two Florida Murder Trials for the Killing of Terry King." *Findlaw*, 10 Sept. 2002, supreme.findlaw.com/legal-commentary/two-florida-murder-trials-for-the-killing-of-terry-king.html.

"Cole County Grand Jury Returns Two-Count Indictment Against Alyssa Bustamante in Elizabeth Olten Murder Case." *Office of the Cole County Prosecuting Attorney*, 18 Nov. 2009.

"Columbine: Whose Fault Is It?" *Rolling Stone*, 24 Jun. 1999.

"Confessed Child Killer to Learn Her Fate." *KRCG*, 6 Feb. 2012.

"Convict in Girl's 1992 Killing Gets Released." *Journal and Courier*, 12 Jan. 2018.

"Convicted Killer Gets Behind-Bars GED." *The Atlanta Constitution*, 23 Apr. 2007.

"Conviction, Sentence Upheld for Maddie's Killer." *News4JAX*, 6 Feb. 2002, web.archive.org/web/20110927152000/www.news4jax.com/news/1223416/detail.html.

"Convictions of Boys in Father's Death Overturned." *Los Angeles Times*, 18 Oct. 2002.

Cope, L.M., et al. "Abnormal Brain Structure in Youth Who Commit Homicide." 2014.

"Cristian Fernandez Case: As Someone Surfed Internet, Tot's Life Was Slipping Away." *Florida Times-Union*, 14 Sept. 2011.

"Cristian Fernandez Indicted on Sexual Battery Charge." *Florida-Times Union*, 5 Jan. 2012.

"Cristian Fernandez, Now 13, Pleads Guilty, Sentenced to Prison Until He's 19." *Morris News Service*, 8 Feb. 2013.

"Cristian Fernandez's Mother Pleads Guilty in Death of 2-Year-Old Son." *Florida-Times Union*, 28 Mar. 2012.

"Crossing the Line ... Mob Mentality Was 1 Factor in Murder's Brutality,-Psychologists Say." *The Courier-Journal*, 24 Jan. 1993.

Cruel Sacrifice, by Aphrodite Jones, Kensington Publishing Corp., 1994, pp. 76–84.

D'Amato, Anthony. *Porn Up, Rape Down*. 2006.
"Daniel Petric Killed Mother, Shot Father Because They Took Halo 3 Video Game, Prosecutors Say." *Cleveland.com*, 15 Dec. 2008.
"Daniel Petric, 16, to Be Charged with Slaying Mother, Wounding Father, a Pastor in Wellington." *The Plain Dealer*, 22 Oct. 2007.
Darley, John M., and Bibb Latané. "The Unresponsive Bystander: Why Doesn't He Help?" *New York, NY: Appleton Century Crofts*, 1970.
"Daylight Demystifies 'Castle.'" *The Courier-Journal*, 18 Dec. 1992.
"A Deadly Meeting." *The Indianapolis Star*, 24 Jan. 1993.
"Death Penalty Is Sought for 2 Teens in Murder Case." *The Courier-Journal*, 15 July 1992.
"Deaths Bring Hondo Teen to Court; Lawyer Denies Charges." *Albuquerque Journal*, 9 July, 2004.
De Bellis, Michael D. "The Biological Effects of Childhood Trauma." 2014.
"Defense: Ohio Teen Who Shot Parents 'Just Popped.'" *Cleveland 19 News*, 17 Dec. 2008.
"Defense, Trial Costs for 4 Teens Held in Girl's Death Hard on County Budget." *The Courier-Journal*, 9 Aug. 1992.
DeLong, William. "This 15-Year-Old YouTuber Murdered Her 9-Year-Old Neighbor Just to Feel What It Was Like to Kill." *All That's Interesting*, 11 Mar. 2019, allthatsinteresting.com/alyssa-bustamante.
"Devil Child Slaughters Her Grandparents, Steals Their Car to Pick Up More Pot, Cocaine." *Daily News*, 4 Feb. 2017.
"Diary of a 'Thrill-Kill': Missouri Teen Murders Neighbor Girl." *Crime Watch Daily*, 2018.
"Did Halo Video Game Drive Son to Murder." *True Crime Daily*, 18 Dec. 2015.
DiLulio, J. "The Coming of the Super-Predators." *Washington Examiner*, November 27, 1995.
"Diseased or Evil? Teen Faces Trial in Sadistic Killing of Pre-Schooler." *The Ottawa Citizen*, 25 July 1994.
"Eleven Years After 13-Year-Old Eric Smith Murdered Four-Year-Old Derrick Robie, Smith Explains Why He Killed." *CBS News*, 9 Dec. 2004.
"Elizabeth Kay Olten (1999–2009)—Find a Grave..." Find a Grave, www.findagrave.com/memorial/43450313/elizabeth-kay-olten.
"Elizabeth Olten Murder Suspect, Alyssa Bustamante, Sent to Mental Hospital." *CBS News*, 20 Nov. 2009.
"Emotions Run High During Killer Joshua Phillips' Re-Sentencing Hearing." *Florida Times-Union*, 7 Aug. 2017.
"Envy Drove Smith to Kill, Doctor Says." *Star-Gazette*, 12 Aug. 1994.
"Eric Smith, Who Was 13 When He Killed a 4-Year-Old in 1993, Gets Parole." Democrat & Chronicle, 15 Oct. 2021.
"Evidence in Bustamante Case Detailed." *Columbia Daily Tribune*, 15 Feb. 2012.
Fahey, Mike. "Halo 3 Shooter's Attorney Argues Insanity Due to Video Game Addiction." *Kotaku*, 17 Dec. 2008, kotaku.com/halo-3-shooters-attorney-argues-insanity-due-to-video-g-5112289.
"Family, Friends Grapple with Final Outcome." *Pensacola News Journal*, 15 Nov. 2002.
"Family Life and Delinquency and Crime." *Office of Juvenile Justice and Delinquency Prevention*, 1993.
"Family Returns to Court for Possible Resentencing of Daughter's Killer." *First Coast News*, 8 Aug., 2017.
"Fate of Chavis Rests in Jury's Hands Today." *Pensacola News Journal*, 30 Aug. 2002.
"Fate of Teen Lies in Jury's Hands." *The Post-Star*, 16 Aug. 1994.
"Father, Former Neighbors Stunned by Murder Charge Against Cristian Fernandez." *The Florida Times-Union*, 11 Jun. 2011.
"Father of Alleged Elizabeth Olten Killer Alyssa Bustamante Has Violent Past." *CBC News*, 25 Nov. 2009.
"Father of Teen Who Shot Family Searched for Incest Porn on Computer." *Court TV*, 25 Jan. 2006.
FBI records (used for background).

Ferguson, C.J., and R.D. Hartley. *The Pleasure Is Momentary ... the Expense Damnable? The Influence of Pornography on Rape and Sexual Assault.* 2009.
"Florida Boys Admit They Killed Father; Shorter Term Is Set." *The New York Times*, 15 Nov. 2002.
"Florida Boys Convicted in Father's Death; Family Friend Is Acquitted in Separate Trial." *The New York Times*, 7 Sept. 2002.
"Florida Brothers Blame Father's Murder on Family Friend." *CNN*, 28 Aug. 2002.
"For Dead Girl's Mother, Abuse Still No Excuse." *The South Bend Tribune*, 20 Dec. 1992.
"14-Year-Old Convicted in Murder of Preschooler in Upstate Town." *The New York Times*, 17 Aug. 1994.
"Friend of Loveless Says Tackett Claimed Main Role in Girl's Murder." *The Courier-Journal*, 17 Dec. 1992.
"Friends Not Surprised Twins Charged in Mom's Death." *AJC*, 26 Sept. 2018
Furbish, Lawrence K. Jacksonville Florida Juvenile Justice Program, 10 July 1998, www.cga.ct.gov/PS98/rpt\olr\htm/98-R-0787.htm.
"Georgia Girls Admit to Killing Grandparents." *News4JAX*, 14 Apr. 2005
"Girl Killer's Diary Told of 'Amazing' Murder." *Ottawa Citizen*, 7 Jan. 2012.
"Girl Still Missing: 9-Year-Old's Family Frustrated by Pace of Search." *The News Tribune*, 22 Oct. 2009.
"Girl Who Was Tortured Begged Other Teens Not to Hurt Her." *The Indianapolis Star*, 16 Dec. 1992.
"Girl's Body Found." *News Tribune*, 24 Oct. 2009.
"Girls Charged in Murder; Town Numb." *The Salt Lake Tribune*, 16 Jun. 1992.
"Girls Charged in Torture, Slaying of New Albany girl." *The Courier-Journal*, 13 Jan. 1992.
"Girl's Death in Blaze Is Now a Blur." *The Indianapolis Star*, 30 Dec. 1992.
"Girls Describe Torture, Killing of 12-Year-Old." *The Courier-Journal*, 16 Dec. 1992.
"Girls Get 60 Years in Slaying." *The Messenger*, 5 Jan. 1993.
"Great-Grandmother Hopes Twins Who Killed Their Mother Will One Day Lead Productive Lives." *Rockdale-Newton Citizen*, 18 Dec. 2014.
"Guidance on Criteria for Issuing AMBER Alerts." *Wayback Machine*, Apr. 2004, web.archive.org/web/20041015003050/amberalert.gov/docs/AMBERCriteria.pdf.
"Halo 3 Shooter's Attorney Argues Insanity Due to Video Game Addiction." *Kotaku*, 17 Dec. 2008.
"Harrowing Story of Child Murderer Joshua Phillips Who Killed His Eight-Year-Old Pal Maddie Clifton Aged Just 14 and Left Susanna Reid in Tears on ITV's Children Who Kill." *The Sun*, 14 Feb. 2018.
Heide, K.M. "Juvenile Homicide Offenders Look Back 35 Years Later: Reasons They Were Involved in Murder." 2020.
Helde, K.M. "A Taxonomy of Murder: Motivational Dynamics Behind the Homicidal Acts of Adolescents." *Justice Issues* 1 (1986): 3–19.
"Hell to Pay." *ID Twisted Love*, 2020.
"Her Killer Fights Back Tears When Asked About Maddie and Her Family." *The Times-Union*, 8 Nov. 2008.
Herring, Angela, and Angela Herring. "A Complicated Link Between Aggression and Antidepressant Drugs." *News@Northestern*, 9 Oct. 2012, news.northeastern.edu/2012/10/09/antidepressant/.
Hevner, Stacy. Personal communication. 1 Oct. 2018.
Hibsch, John. Personal communication. 7 Oct. 2018.
Higgins, Melissa. "Sign the Petition." *Change.org*, www.change.org/p/reverse-decision-to-try-12-y-o-cristian-fernandez-as-an-adult?original_footer_petition_id=.
"How Were Amber Alerts Created? The Amber Hagerman Cold Case." *A&E*, Oct. 11, 2019.
"Hundreds Turn Out for Search." *The News Tribune*, 22 Oct. 2009.
"'I Wanted to Kill Him, I Guess,' Smith Told Psychiatrist." *The Ithaca Journal*, 12 Aug. 1994.
"In Cold Blood: A Daughter Murdered." *Dr. Phil*, 2011.
"Incest Sites on Posey Computer." *Albuquerque Journal*, 26 Jan. 2006.

Bibliography

"Indiana Death Penalty Laws." *Clark Prosecutor,* www.clarkprosecutor.org/html/death/dplaw.htm.
"Inside the West Texas Sanctuary for Kids Who Killed Their Parents." *Vice News,* 28 Apr. 2016.
"Is Angela Corey the Cruelest Prosecutor in America?" *The Nation,* 16 Aug. 2016.
"'It's Tragic; It's Unthinkable.'" *Pensacola News Journal,* 30 Nov. 2001.
"Jacksonville 12-Year-Old Charged with First-Degree Murder of Brother." *Florida-Times Union,* 2 Jun. 2011.
"Jasmiyah and Tasmiyah Whitehead Case Extras: Interrogation Transcripts." *11 Alive News,* 16 May, 2014.
Johnston, Joni E. "Matricide by Teen Girls." *Psychology Today,* Sussex Publishers, 16 July 2012, www.psychologytoday.com/ca/blog/the-human-equation/201207/matricide-teen-girls.
"Judge Blocks Missouri Teen's Statement in Her Murder Trial." *St. Louis Post-Dispatch,* 22 June, 2011.
"Judge Decides Life Sentence Is Warranted for Joshua Phillips in Maddie Clifton's Shocking Death." *Florida Times-Union,* 17 Nov. 2017.
"Judge Denies Bond for Girls Accused of Stabbing Grandparents." *The Item,* 20 Aug. 2004.
"Judge Throws Out Brothers' Murder Convictions." *The New York Times,* 18 Oct. 2002.
"Juvenile Arrests." OJJDP Statistical Briefing Book, https://Www.ojjdp.gov/Ojstatbb/Crime/qa05101.Asp?QaDate=2017
"Juvenile Faces Murder Charge." *News Tribune,* 25 Oct. 2009.
Katie Couric, "How a Video Game Addiction Led Daniel Petric to Murder." Online video clip. Youtube, 1 May 2013.
Kevin Collier. Personal communication. 12 Mar. 2020.
"A Killer at 15, Indiana Woman Is Getting Out Early Thanks to Prison Volunteer." *The Courier-Journal,* 28 Apr. 2005.
"Killer Grandkid?" *People,* 20 Sept. 2004.
King, Gary C. *Angels of Death: A True Story of Murder and Innocence Lost,* St. Martin's True Crime, 2003, pp. 5–6.
"King Brothers Confessed, Say Investigators." *Pensacola News Journal,* 29 Dec. 2001.
"King Brothers Sentenced." *Pensacola News Journal,* 15 Nov. 2002.
"Lawrence's Role in Sharer Killing at Issue in Hearing." *The Courier-Journal,* 17 Jan. 1993.
"Lawrence's Role in Sharer Killing Disputed." *The Courier-Journal,* 27 Jan. 1993.
"Lawyers in King Brothers Case Speak Out." *CNN,* 15 Nov. 2002.
"Lawyers Stress Rippey's Role in Girl's Murder." *The Courier-Journal,* 2 Jun. 1993.
"Lesbian Accused of Stabbing Grandparents Had Kill on 'To Do' List." *Advocate,* 6 Aug. 2004.
"Letters Detail Teen's Jealousy, Desire to Kill 12-Year-Old." *The Courier-Journal,* 16 Dec. 1992.
"Life After Murder." *People,* 21 Oct. 2013.
"Life in Prison for Teen Killer." *CBS News,* 20 Aug. 1999.
Lippard, Elizabeth T.C., and Charles B. Nemeroff. "The Devastating Clinical Consequences of Child Abuse and Neglect: Increased Disease Vulnerability and Poor Treatment Response in Mood Disorders." *American Journal of Psychology* 177, no. 1 (2020): 20–36.
Lois M. Davis. "Education and Vocational Training in Prisons Reduces Recidivism, Improves Job Outlook." *RAND Corporation,* 22 Aug. 2013, www.rand.org/news/press/2013/08/22.html.
Long, Kasy. "The Spooky Tale of Indiana's 'Witches' Castle.'" *History 101,* 30 Dec. 2019, www.history101.com/the-spooky-tale-of-indianas-witches-castle/.
"A Look Back: The Disappearance and Murder of Maddie Clifton." *Florida Times-Union,* 3 Nov. 2018.
"Loveless' Father Charged with Sex Abuse of 5 Girls." *The Courier-Journal,* 12 Jan. 1993.
"Loveless' Relatives Say That Her Father Was Sexually Abusive." *The Courier-Journal,* 19 Dec. 1992.
"Loveless Sentencing Brings to Forefront Brutal Slaying Details." *The Herald,* 15 Dec. 1992.

Bibliography

"A 'Mad Switch' Led Teen-Ager to Kill Child, Psychiatrist Testifies." *The New York Times*, 11 Aug. 1994.

Madison Teen Gets 50-Year Term." *The South Bend Tribune*, 3 Jun. 1993.

"Man Serving Life in Maddie Clifton Murder Gets New Sentencing Hearing." *WJCT News*, 8 Aug. 2017.

Mills, Gary. *Sutori*, www.sutori.com/story/the-murder-of-maddie-clifton--8rtVFLKHAxZAhZnVsdWXY3Yh.

"Missing St. Martin Girl Found Dead." *The Spring-field News Leader*, 24 Oct. 2009.

"Mom of Jacksonville's Youngest Killer Charged with DUI." *News4JAX*, 23 Mar. 2019.

Monacelli, Antonia. "Murderous Children: Cristian Fernandez (12) Killed His 2-Year-Old Brother—Owlcation—Education." *Owlcation*, 11 Jan. 2018, owlcation.com/social-sciences/Murderous-Children-Cristian-Fernandez.

Monacelli, Antonia. "Murderous Children: Joshua Phillips (14) Murdered His 8-Year-Old Neighbour." *Soapboxie*, 27 Feb. 2020, soapboxie.com/government/Murderous-Children-Joshua-Phillips.

Montaldo, Charles. "Children Who Kill: Alex and Derek King." *ThoughtCo*, 22 Oct. 2019, www.thoughtco.com/alex-and-derek-king-972684.

"Mother Says Not Responsible for Daughter's Actions." *The Citizen*, 14 Apr. 2005.

"Mother's Slaying Haunts Loved Ones." *AJC*, 10 Apr. 2016.

"Murder File Yields Chilling Details." *The Citizen*, 20 Apr. 2005.

"Murder Trial Begins for Teen-Ager." *The New York Times*, 2 Aug. 1994.

National Research Council (US) Panel on Adolescent Pregnancy and Childbearing. "THE CHILDREN OF TEEN CHILDBEARERS." *Risking the Future: Adolescent Sexuality, Pregnancy, and Childbearing, Volume II: Working Papers and Statistical Appendices.*, U.S. National Library of Medicine, 1987. www.ncbi.nlm.nih.gov/books/NBK219236/.

"Neighbor, 14, Charged in Missing Girl's Murder." *Tampa Bay Times*, 11 Nov. 1998.

"New Documents Show 12-Year-Old Killed Kitten, Sexually Abused Brother." *Florida Times-Union*, 25 Jun. 2011.

"New Thompson Suit Blames GTA for 2004 Murder." *Gamasutra*, 26 Sept. 2006.

"New Trial Sought in 1998 Slaying of Maddie Clifton." *News4JAX*, 16 Dec. 2004, web.archive.org/web/20110927151951/www.news4jax.com/news/4002159/detail.html.

News4JAX. "UNCUT: Cristian Fernandez Interrogation." Online clip. Youtube video, 17 Apr. 2019.

News4JAX. "UNCUT: Josh Phillips Read Letter of Apology for 1998 Murder of Maddie Clifton." Online video clip. Youtube, 5 Apr. 2018."19 Years Later, the Narrative Behind Maddie Clifton's Demise Gets Even Worse." *Florida Times-Union*, 10 Aug. 2017.

"No Prison for Mother of Cristian Fernandez." *Florida Times-Union*, 14 Aug. 2013.

NYS Department of Corrections and Community Supervision. *Parole Board Interview in the Matter of Eric M. Smith*. 5 Oct. 2021.

"Obama Bans Solitary Confinement of Juveniles in Federal Prisons." *The Guardian*, 26 Jan. 2016.

"Odd Behavior Marked Eric." *Democrat and Chronicle*, 3 Aug. 1994.

"Ohio Teenager Has Surprise for His Parents After They Confiscate His Favorite Game." *Life Daily*, https://www.lifedaily.com/story/ohio-teenager-has-surprise-for-his-parents-after-they-confiscate-his-favorite-game/

"One Day Aafter 19th Birthday, Cristian Fernandez Released." *News4JAX*, 15 Jan. 2018.

"The Pain of Remembering." *The Courier-Journal*, 14 Jan. 1992.

"Pair Gets 60 Years for Torture-Slaying of Girl, 12." *The Indianapolis Star*, 6 Jan. 1993.

"Parricide: An Introduction for Clinical and Forensic Mental Health Professionals." *Concordia University, St. Paul Online*, 4 Jun. 2019, online.csp.edu/blog/forensic-scholars-today/introduction-to-parricide.

"Parricides: Characteristics of Offenders and Victims, Legal Factors, and Treatment Issues." *NCJRS Abstract—National Criminal Justice Reference Service*, 1999, www.ncjrs.gov/App/Publications/abstract.aspx?ID=177924.

"Past History May Haunt Accused Molester at Trial." *The Ledger*, 10 Feb. 2003.

"Pastor's Son Charged in Mother's Murder, Father's Shooting." *Cleveland.com*, 23 Oct. 2007.

Bibliography

"PASTOR'S SON OFFICIALLY CHARGED." *TMCNEWS.NET*, 22 Oct. 2007, tmcnews.blogspot.com/2007/10/pastors-son-officially-charged.html.

"Penny Brown." *National Organization of Victims of Juvenile Murderers*, 14 Aug. 2020, www.teenkillers.org/index.php/memorials/york-victims/penny-brown-2/.

People v. Smith, 217 A.D.2d 221 (1995)

"Petric Sentenced to 23 Years to Life: Father Says Son Regrets Shooting Mother Over 'Halo 3' Video Game." *The Morning Journal*, 17 Jun. 2009.

"Phillips Sentenced to Life." *Florida Times-Union*, 21 Aug. 1999.

"Plea Possible." *The Republic*, 4 Jun. 1995.

"Please Pray for the Petrics (My Former Youth Pastors)." *David Covey*, 22 Oct. 2007, davidcovey.typepad.com/david_covey/2007/10/please-pray-for.html.

"Pornography and Missing Underwear: Child Killer Joshua Phillips' Trial Reveals Disturbing Details of 8-Year-Old Maddie Clifton's Murder." *Daily Mirror*, 15 Feb. 2018.

"Posey Says He Was Often Abused." *Albuquerque Journal*, 20 Jan. 2006.

"Posey Scored High on Psychopath Test." *Albuquerque Journal*, 1 Feb. 2006.

"Posey Sentencing Continues with Defense Witnesses." *Albuquerque Journal*, 21 Feb. 2006.

"Posey Trial Begins." *Alamogordo Daily New*, 12 Jan. 2006.

"Posey's Defense Offers Abuse Support." *Albuquerque Journal*, 24 Jan. 2006.

"Processing a Crime Scene." *UniversalClass.com*, www.universalclass.com/articles/law/processing-a-crime-scene.htm.

"Prosecution Calls Posey 'Cold-Blooded Killer.'" *Albuquerque Journal*, 6 Feb. 2006.

"Prosecution Rests in Trial of Teen Accused of Killing Neighbor Girl." *CNN International*, 7 July 1999.

"Prosecutor Chips Away at Defense as Doctor Continues His Testimony." *Star-Gazette*, 10 Aug. 1994.

"Prosecutor Tells Gruesome Story of Girl's Slaying." *The Indianapolis Star*, 15 Dec. 1992.

"Prosecutors Play Boy's Confession; Trial Starts in Triple Slaying." *Albuquerque Journal*, 18 Jan. 2016.

"Prosecutors: Prozac No Defense for Mo. Teen Killer." *St. Louis Post-Dispatch*, 7 Feb. 2012.

"Psychiatrist: Posey Didn't Have PTSD." *Albuquerque Journal*, 31 Jan. 2006.

"Psychologist: Teen Was Led Astray." *Logansport Pharos-Tribune*, 2 Jun. 1993.

"Psychopathic Traits Differ Between Cultures, Experts Claim." *The Independent*, 12 Feb. 2018.

Reif, Andreas, et al. "Nature and Nurture Predispose to Violent Behavior: Serotonergic Genes and Adverse Childhood Environment." 2007.

"Relatives, Friends Testify About Cody Posey's Abusive History." *Albuquerque Journal*, Jan. 24, 2006

"Religion in America: U.S. Religious Data, Demographics and Statistics." Pew Research Center's Religion & Public Life Project, 9 Sept. 2020, www.pewforum.org/religious-landscape-study/state/.

Rettew, David. "Antidepressants and Violence: A Link in Search of a Cause." *Psychology Today*, Sussex Publishers, 30 Sept. 2015, www.psychologytoday.com/ca/blog/abcs-child-psychiatry/201509/antidepressants-and-violence-link-in-search-cause.

Romano, Tricia. "Alyssa Bustamante and the Murder of Elizabeth Olten." *Murderpedia*, murderpedia.org/female.B/b/bustamante-alyssa.htm.

Rovner, Josh, and Henderson Hill. "Juvenile Life Without Parole: An Overview." *The Sentencing Project*, 25 Feb. 2020, www.sentencingproject.org/publications/juvenile-life-without-parole/.

Sabrina, Chiara, et al. "The Nature and Dynamics of Internet Pornography Exposure for Youth." 2008.

"SALVAGING A DAMAGED CHILD'S LIFE." *The Florida Bar*, 15 Jan. 2016.

"The Search for Maddie." *CBS News*, 12 Jun. 2000.

"Search for 9-Year-Old Resumes Today." *The Springfield News-Leader*, 23 Oct. 2009.

"Search Under Way for Missing 9-Year-Old." *The News Tribune*, 22 Oct. 2004.

"Second Chances: Dateline Checks in with Brothers Accused of Killing Their Father in 2001." *Dateline NBC*, 7 Sept. 2009.

Bibliography

"A Second Tragedy Comes in Wake of Savona Trial." *The Buffalo News*, 18 Aug. 1994.
"2nd Whitehead Twin Pleads Guilty to Manslaughter." *The Covington News*, 7 Feb. 2014.
"Self-Injury (Cutting, Self-Harm or Self-Mutilation)." *Mental Health America*, www.mhanational.org/conditions/self-injury-cutting-self-harm-or-self-mutilation.
"Self-Injury (Cutting, Self-Harm or Self-Mutilation)." *NHS Choices*, NHS, www.nhs.uk/conditions/ssri-antidepressants/.
"Sentence Could Vary for Juvenile." *News Tribune*, Oct. 2009.
"Sexual Abuse Surfaces in Torture Death." *The Star Press*, 19 Dec. 1992.
"Sexual Assault Charge Dropped Against Cristian Fernandez." *News4JAX*, 8 Nov. 2012.
"Shanda Sharer's Mother and Murderer Form Unlikely Alliance." *Wave 3 News*, 21 May 2012.
"Shanda Sharer's Story Still Changing Lives." *The Courier-Journal*, 30 Jan. 1995.
"Shanda's Father Shares His Torment." *The Courier-Journal*, 18 Dec. 1992.
Shorstein, Henry. Personal Communication. 17 Dec. 2019.
"Single Mom Killed by Twin Daughters in Rage Over Strict Home Life." *True Crime Daily*, 27 Oct. 2016.
"Slain Father Was Getting Along with Sons, Some Say." *Pensacola News Journal*, 2 Dec. 2001.
"Smith 'Not Be Able to Be in Society,' Doctor Says." *Star-Gazette*, 9 Aug. 1994.
"Smith's Sister Says Life at Home Was 'Hell.'" *Star-Gazette*, 10 Aug. 1994.
Soles, Holly. Personal communication. 14 Apr. 2019.
"Son Accused of Killing Mother Granted Final Visit." *Cleveland 19 News*, 26 Oct. 2007.
"Story of a Murder … 12-Year-Old's Brutal End Begs the Question, 'Why?'" *The Courier-Journal*, 6 Dec. 1992.
Systematic Search for Evidence, flashmedia.glynn.k12.ga.us/webpages/rchunn/index.cfm?subpage=49750.
"Tackett Says She Suffered Lifetime of Abuse." *The Courier-Journal*, 31 Dec. 1992.
"Tackett Turned Planned Beating into Murder, Loveless Claims." *The Courier-Journal*, 29 Dec. 1992.
"Tape Recordings of Confessions from Alex and Derek King Were Played for Jurors." *The Associated Press*, 29 Aug. 2002.
"Technical Report on the Review of the Violent Video Game Literature." APA Task Force on Violent Media, https://www.apa.org/pi/families/review-video-games.pdf
"Teen Accused of Killing Mother, Shooting Pastor Father." *Cleveland 19 News*, 23 Oct. 2007.
"Teen Admits Murdering Neighbor, 9, 'Because She Wanted to Know What It Felt Like to Kill.'" *Daily Mail*, 10 Jan. 2012.
"Teen Apologizes to Parents of Slain Girl, Says Fear for Her Own Life Kept Her Quiet." *The Courier-Journal*, 28 Jan. 1993.
"Teen Brain: Behavior, Problem Solving, and Decision Making." *American Academy of Child & Adolescent Psychiatry*, https://www.aacap.org/AACAP/Families_and_Youth/Facts_for_Families/FFF-Guide/The-Teen-Brain-Behavior-Problem-Solving-and-Decision-Making-095.aspx.
"Teen Charged in Missing Girl's Grisly Slaying." *The Orlando Sentinel*, 11 Nov. 1998.
"Teen Charged in Murder Agrees to Plea Bargain." *The Courier-Journal*, 22 Apr. 1992.
"Teen Cody Posey Convicted of Murder, Manslaughter for Killing His Family." *Court TV*, 8 Feb. 2006.
"Teen Convicted in 2004 Triple Homicide." *Albuquerque Journal*, 8 Feb. 2006.
"Teen Convicted of Killing Family Sentenced as Juvenile." *Albuquerque Journal*, 23 Feb. 2006.
"Teen Girl, Ex Girlfriend Admit Killing Grandparents So They Could Be Together." *The Index-Journal*, 15 Apr. 2005.
"Teen Girls Plead Guilty of Torturing 12-Year-Old." *The Montana Standard*, 7 Oct. 1992.
"Teen Guilty in Ranch Killings." *CBS News*, 8 Feb. 2006.
"Teen Guilty of Killing Girl, Hiding Her in Bed." *Tampa Bay Times*, 9 July 1999.
"Teen Indicted in Slaying of 8-Year-Old Neighbor." *Florida Today*, 20 Nov. 1998.

Bibliography 295

"Teen Killer Endured Life of Horror, Family Testifies." *The Indianapolis Star,* 19 Dec. 1992.
"Teen Killers Confess, Get Life." *The Atlanta Constitution,* 15 Apr. 2005.
"Teen Killers Sentenced." *The Indianapolis Star,* 5 Jan. 1993.
"Teen Says He Had Sex with Chavis 10 Times." *Herald-Tribune,* 12 Feb. 2003.
"Teen Says Sight of Lone Boy Drove Him to Kill." *The Record,* 10 Aug. 1994.
"Teen Sisters Confess to Killing Mother." *ABC10,* 7 Nov. 2014.
"Teen Torture Slayer Describes Death of 12-Year-Old Girl." *The Vincennes-Sun Commercial,* 29 Dec. 1992.
"Teen Who Killed Family on Donaldson Ranch Goes Free." *CNN,* 8 Oct. 2019.
"Teenage Brothers in Florida Plead Guilty to Killing Father." *The Globe and Mail,* 15 Nov. 2002.
"Teenage 'Thrill Killer' Breaks Down in Tears as She Is Jailed for Life for Choking and Stabbing Her 9-Year-Old Neighbor." *Daily Mail,* 8 February, 2012.
"Teenager Gets 50-Year Sentence." *The Indianapolis Journal,* 3 Jun. 1993.
Teicher, Martin H., et al. "Childhood Maltreatment: Altered Network Centrality of Cingulate, Precuneus, Temporal Pole and Insula." 2013.
"3rd Teen Sentenced in Torture." *The Indianapolis Star,* 29 Jan. 1993.
"13-Year-Old Cristian Fernandez Will Face Life Without Parole for Killing Brother, Court Rules." *The Daily Beast,* 21 Nov. 2012.
"300 Attend Funeral Service for Tortured 12-Year-Old Girl." *The Indianapolis News,* 16 Jan. 1992.
"Topics of the Times: A Murderous Child." *New York Times,* 17 July 1989.
"A TOWN TORN APART Indiana Community Is Shaken by Torture Murder of Young Girl." *The Baltimore Sun,* 21 Jun. 1992.
"Town Tries to Make Sense of Murder." *Tampa Bay Times,* 15 Aug. 1993.
"Trial Approaches for Teen Charged with Killing Child." *Pensacola News Journal,* 5 Jul. 1999.
"Trial Ends for Teen Accused of Killing Parents Over Halo 3 Video Game; Verdict Due Jan. 7." *Cleveland.com,* 17 Dec. 2008.
Tunny, John. Personal Communication. 15 Sept. 2018.
Turner, Karl. "17-Year-Old Accused of Killing Mother Over Halo 3 Video Game May Get Verdict Soon." *Cleveland.com,* 16 Dec. 2008, www.cleveland.com/metro/2008/12/trial_of_boy_accused_of_killin.html.
"12-Year-Old Florida Boy, Cristian Fernandez, Faces First Degree Murder Charge for 2-Year-Old's Death." *Daily News,* 6 Jun. 2011.
"The 12-Year-Old Who Could Become America's Youngest Ever 'Lifer' for Killing Two-Year-Old Brother." *Daily Mail,* 6 Jun. 2011.
"Twin, 20, Accepts 30-Year Plea Deal for Brutally Murdering Her Mother ... but Her Identical Sister Will Go to Trial and Faces Life After REJECTING a Deal." *The Daily Mail,* 10 Jan. 2014.
"Twisted Twins: Teen Sisters Confess to Killing Mother." *11 Alive News,* 12 Sept. 2016.
"The 2019 Florida Statutes." *Statutes & Constitution: View Statutes: Online Sunshine,* 2019, www.leg.state.fl.us/Statutes/index.cfm?App_mode=Display_Statute.
"Two Who Admitted Killing 12-Year-Old Get 60 years." *The Courier-Journal,* 5 Jan. 1993.
"Understanding Self-Injury/Self-Harm." *Teen Mental Health,* teenmentalhealth.org/understanding-self-injury-self-harm/.
"Understanding the Teen Brain." Https://Www.urmc.rochester.edu/Encyclopedia/Content.aspx?ContentTypeID=1&ContentID=3051, University of Rochester Medical Center.
Voon, Valerie B., et al. *Neural Correlates of Sexual Cue Reactivity in Individuals with and Without Compulsive Sexual Behaviours.* 2014.
"Whitehead Sister Pleads Guilty to Manslaughter." *The Rockdale Citizen,* 9 Jan. 2014.
"Whitehead Twin Denied Bond." *The Covington News,* 14 June. 2010.
"Why Children of Teen Mothers Do Worse in Life." *VOX, CEPR Policy Portal,* 22 Dec. 2018, voxeu.org/article/why-children-teen-mothers-do-worse-life.
"Why Did Eric Kill?" *48 Hours,* 2004.

x8m8x3k3t. "Judge James Burge: Daniel Petric A.K.A. 'Halo Killer.'" Online clip. Youtube video, 15 Jan. 2009.

Yamagata, Bun, et al. "Female-Specific Intergenerational Transmission Patterns of the Human Corticolimbic Circuitry." *Journal of Neuroscience,* Society for Neuroscience, 27 Jan. 2016, www.jneurosci.org/content/36/4/1254.

Ybarra, Michele L, and Kimberly J Mitchell. *X-Rated Material and Perpetration of Sexually Aggressive Behavior Among Children and Adolescents: Is There a Link?* 2011.

"A Young Mother Tries to Save Two Sons and Loses Everything." *Tampa Bay Times,* 14 July 2013.

"Youth, 14, Draws 9 Years to Life in Prison in Killing of 4-Year Old." *The New York Times, 8* Nov. 1994.

"Youth to Be Tried as Adult in Slaying." *Los Angeles Times,* 17 Nov. 1998.

Index

accessory after the fact 63, 68
ad litem 220, 225
ADHD 29, 65, 67
adolescent brain 3, 102, 105, 107
adolescent homicide 3
aggravated assault 176
aggravated murder 190, 202
alibi 86, 178
aluminum baseball bat 58, 60, 77
Amber alert 116, 117
"America's Most Wanted" 88
amygdala 3
anxiety 44, 88, 95, 126, 128, 172, 248
armed criminal action 125, 132, 138, 140
armed robbery 51
Arrendale State Prison 54, 181
arson 63, 75, 76, 77, 255, 256, 265
asphyxia 8, 9
assault 2, 118, 127, 136, 171, 176, 182, 227
AT&T 112
autopsy 8, 93, 94, 120, 135, 253

Baptist church 41, 50, 55, 67, 236
bath 6, 15, 17
behavioral disorder 25
Bible Belt 42
bilateral frontal lobe lesions 94
bipolar disorder 129, 138
birth certificate 22
blood spatter 40, 57, 60, 172
"The Blooding" 10
blunt force trauma 9, 57, 93, 212
blunt instrument 81, 253
BMX bicycle 12, 16, 23
borderline personality disorder 129, 135, 136, 138, 269
Bradley, Kevin 24, 25, 30, 31
brain function 29
Brookwood Secure Center 34
Brown, Penny 36, 37
bulletproof vests 51
burglary 58, 110
Bustamante, Alyssa 114, 118, 119, 122, 125, 126, 127, 130, 132, 140, 141, 143
bystander effect 270

cadaver dog 114, 115
Cantonment, Florida 56, 67
canvas lunch bag 7, 14
capital punishment 176, 256
Caucasian 93
Chavis, Rick 58, 59, 62, 64, 66, 69, 70, 71, 73, 74, 78, 83
Chidester, Judy 51
child maltreatment 2, 3
child molestation 70, 255
child psychiatrist 25, 27
Cleveland 28, 189
Clifton, Maddie 87, 88, 89, 91, 92, 97, 99, 104
Clinton, Bill 34
co-conspirator 71, 180
codependent behavior 23
Cole County Fire Protection District 113
Cole County Mobile Emergency Operations Center 113
Cole County Sheriff's Department 109, 113
Collier, Carl 40, 41, 42, 46
Collier, Sarah 40, 41, 42, 49, 55
conviction 31, 38, 43, 66, 77, 102, 164, 222
Corey, Angela 98, 217, 218, 220, 223, 226, 227
corporal punishment 20
Court TV 93
crime of passion 172
crime scene 10, 13, 30, 48, 50, 57, 60, 89, 92, 104, 110, 115, 122, 144, 154, 156, 174, 175, 178, 193, 194, 209, 229
criminal confinement 255, 256, 265
criminal investigator 6
cross-examination 28, 73, 135, 157, 197, 264

death penalty 53, 55, 93, 99, 100, 105, 124, 176, 222, 255, 256, 257
death row 55, 256, 257
DeLap, Walt 15
deliberation 31, 36, 76, 95
Delta Air Lines 41
delusional disorder 38
Department of Children and Families 42, 124, 208, 209, 210, 214
depression 23, 28, 50, 95, 101, 125, 126, 128, 129, 136, 138, 139, 141, 142, 155, 157, 237

Index

developmental abnormalities 25, 27, 29
direct examination 72, 154
DNA 10, 175
Dr. Seuss 6
DSM-5 135, 269

Eighth Amendment 100
emergency ping 112
emo subculture 128
envy 29, 258
epilepsy 19
Escambia County 56, 57, 59
Escambia County Sheriff's Department 63
Estrella Vista 83
EZ Serve 63, 77

false imprisonment 78
Fayette County Sheriff's Department 49
Fayetteville, Georgia 40
Fayetteville County 43
FBI Laboratory 93
FBI records 85, 86, 88
felony murder 51, 176, 265
Fernandez, Cristian 204, 206, 219, 221, 223, 225
fingerprints 110, 176
first-degree murder 63, 72, 79, 92, 94, 96, 125, 132, 153, 162, 163, 164, 204, 217, 218, 219, 220, 222
Fischer, Mark 6
Florida Criminal Punishment Code 222
Florida Department of Law Enforcement 93
Florida Supreme Court 98
fluoxetine 135, 136, 141, 142
forced entry 110, 172
forensic pathology 135, 228
forensic psychology 36
foster care 66, 83, 206, 207, 217
foul play 112, 113, 116

Galarraga, David 208, 225
GED 754, 56, 101, 102, 181, 207
genes 3, 4
genetic makeup 4
G.I. Joes 18
Gowanda Correctional Facility 34
Graham v. Florida 100
grand jury 63, 70, 152, 219
Grand Theft Auto 164, 165
Green Eggs and Ham 6
grey matter 3
grid search 110
guilty verdict 31, 32, 76, 79, 162

Hagerman, Amber 116
Halo 184, 185, 186, 188, 194, 195, 196, 197, 198, 200
Harry Potter 66
Harvey, Holly 41, 42, 54
head trauma 212, 219

Heritage Home 66
Herman, Stephen 25, 26, 27, 28, 29, 36
Hibsch, John 9, 10, 11, 12, 13
high school 22, 37, 54, 66, 82, 115, 122, 165, 168, 181, 181, 241
homophobia 43
homosexuality 44, 67, 241
hormones 29
human foot 88
hung jury 161

incarceration 32, 37, 54, 82, 102, 103, 105, 152, 181
infrared radiation 112
inmate 82, 97, 99, 102, 181, 218, 255, 256
intermittent explosive disorder 26, 29, 30, 38
intimidation 20
Italy 5

Jackson v. Hobbs 100
Jacksonville Sheriff's Office 85, 213
jealousy 3, 147, 237, 262
jewelry 47, 48, 49, 240, 266
Johnson, Randall 40
Jordan, Bruce 49
juvenile delinquency 4
juvenile detention 32, 50, 51, 62, 82, 121, 153, 163, 164, 218, 223
Juvenile Justice Program 105

K-9 units 113
Ketchum, Sandra 41, 42, 54
kidnapping 58, 70, 87, 270
King, Alex 58, 78, 80, 82
King, Derek 73
King, Stephen 18, 25
King, Terry 63, 64, 70, 80, 82
knife 47, 48, 49, 52, 53, 89, 122, 125, 126, 131, 138, 177, 178, 179, 236, 243, 245, 246, 247, 253, 266
Kool-Aid 8, 13, 17

Lawrence, Toni 230, 240, 254, 272
Lay, Frank 66, 67, 69
Leatherman knife 89
legal custody 67
leukemia 28
life imprisonment 2, 25, 30, 32, 37, 51, 73, 84, 97, 98, 99, 100, 103, 104, 105, 138, 140, 179, 198, 201, 202
line method 111
Loveless, Melinda 232, 234, 252, 258, 261, 262

malice aforethought 154
malice murder 51, 52, 176
manslaughter 94, 162, 179, 217, 221, 223
matricide 81, 166
maximum sentence 29, 32, 100, 124, 152, 200, 220, 262, 268

Index

McCoy Street 7, 10, 13, 14, 16, 39
mediation 77
mental abuse 61, 62, 68, 76, 259
mental illness 3, 25, 26, 29, 30, 31, 38, 81, 95, 127, 128, 129, 155, 158, 197, 227
military school 67
Miller v. Alabama 100, 222
minor 55, 100, 123, 124, 132, 151, 176, 227, 256
Miranda rights 15, 16, 156, 213, 222
missing person flyers 86, 89, 92
missing persons report 45, 229, 230
Missouri State Highway Patrol 113, 126
Monroe County Children's Center 18
Muscogee Road 56, 57, 58, 77

narcolepsy 65
nature versus nurture 3
neurology 94
New York 5, 6, 15, 18, 35, 36, 37, 241
New York State Police 6, 15
nicotine addiction 28
Nintendo 29
non-suicidal self-injury 128
not guilty 25, 63, 77, 93, 132, 176, 193, 197, 255

Oaklawn Cemetery 92
Obama, Barack 227
Office of Juvenile Justice and Delinquency Prevention 4
Olten, Elizabeth 108, 119, 126, 127, 133
online harassment 2
optometry 22
oral confession 17
overdose 23, 46, 129
Oxytocin 46

paint thinner 73
parole 2, 9, 32, 35, 36, 37, 38, 51, 53, 87, 93, 97, 99, 100, 124, 125, 132, 140, 176, 198, 201, 220, 222
parricide 80, 81, 84, 166
Penny's Law 36
Pensacola News Journal 57
Pentecostal Church 66
perjury 75, 96
person of interest 86
petechial hemorrhages 8
Phillips, Joshua 90, 91, 95, 97, 98, 102, 105, 107
phone records 63
PlayStation 67, 164
plea agreement 51, 52, 77–79, 99, 179, 219, 220, 223, 256, 259, 261, 271
police command post 9
police scanner 58, 77
polygraph 86, 126
pornography 86, 89, 94, 101, 106, 107, 159
Posey, Cody 145, 152, 153, 154, 157, 160, 162, 164, 165

post-traumatic stress disorder 129, 155, 157, 224
prefrontal cortex 1
premeditated murder 62
principal theory 71
prison guard 74
probation 45, 46, 51, 58, 84, 124, 164, 206, 223, 224, 268
Prozac 129, 130, 135, 136, 139, 142
psychiatry 23, 25, 26, 27, 28, 30, 135, 136, 138, 155, 156, 157, 163, 270
psychopathic checklist 155
pubic hair 93
pugilistic stance 228
Purple, Donald 32

Quinn, Kathleen 28, 29

recidivism 164, 181
recreation program 7, 8, 10, 16, 18
"The Redemption Project" 84
Regional West Fire Protection District 113
rehabilitation 79, 99, 102, 104, 126, 163, 181, 217, 220, 223, 225, 227
revenge 3, 19, 241
Rimmer, David 71, 72, 73, 79
Rippey, Hope 230, 240, 257, 267, 268, 272
robbery 2, 51, 150
Robie, Derrick 6, 8, 13, 14, 24, 27, 31, 33, 34, 35, 39
Rochester 5, 18
Roper v. Simmons 99

sadism 27, 28, 266, 269
Savona 5, 6, 7, 8, 18, 21, 24, 33, 36, 39
second-degree murder 29, 31, 37, 76, 79, 99, 132, 140, 162, 218, 220
selective serotonin reuptake inhibitors 141, 142
self-defense 21, 60, 61, 74, 75, 76, 78, 155, 161, 163
self-harm 44, 118, 125, 126, 127, 128, 129, 134, 136, 137
sexual assault 2, 27, 93, 156, 221
sexual battery 219, 220, 221, 222, 271
Sharer, Shanda 231, 252, 257, 262, 263, 272
Shorstein, Harry 93, 94, 95, 96, 98, 99, 102, 104, 222, 227
Silverado (Chevrolet) 40
Smith, Eric 9, 18, 23, 24, 28, 29, 30, 31, 34, 36, 39
solitary confinement 227
spiral method 111
state police 13, 15, 252
state troopers 8
substance abuse 127, 129, 136, 137, 166
suicide watch 51, 126

Tackett, Laurie 239, 242, 252, 258, 259, 260, 261, 262, 266, 272

tampering with evidence 63, 153, 190, 193, 194, 202
temporal lobe 3
theft 2, 58, 164
third-degree murder 77
Trace Evidence Unit 93
trauma 4, 9, 103, 139, 140, 184, 207, 208, 211, 212, 214, 218, 219, 269
trimethadione 27, 29
Tunney, John 28, 24, 30, 31, 38
Tybee Island 49
Tylenol 23, 129

unanimous 76, 96, 138
unconstitutional 99, 100, 132, 222
United States Constitution 100
U.S. Department of Justice 2, 117, 181
U.S. Marshals 49
U.S. Supreme Court 99, 100, 132, 222
University of Florida 105
unusual punishment 98, 100, 225

vandalism 2
verbal abuse 20, 27, 35, 146
verdict 31, 32, 74, 76, 79, 96, 162, 163, 198
video games 4, 68, 72, 185, 186, 187, 194, 196, 197, 198, 199, 201, 202, 203

violence 1, 2, 3, 26, 27, 29, 32, 35, 94, 95, 96, 106, 127, 137, 140, 141, 142, 149, 164, 166, 167, 184, 194, 202, 203, 224, 225, 241, 267
violent pornography 89, 94, 106
voluntary manslaughter 162, 179

Washington 147
weapon of choice 81
White, Greg 112, 117, 122, 123, 125
white matter 3
Whitehead, Jasmiyah 181
Whitehead, Nikki 171, 175, 180, 182
Whitehead, Tasmiyah 179
written evidence 121
Wuornos, Aileen 155
Wyoming 147

Xbox 185, 194, 196

youth violence 3

Zimmerman, George 227
Zoloft 157
zone method 111